D0147222

# JOHN HUS' CONCEPT
# OF THE CHURCH

# John Hus'

## CONCEPT

## OF THE CHURCH

BY MATTHEW SPINKA

PRINCETON, NEW JERSEY

PRINCETON UNIVERSITY PRESS

1966

1415 - 1965

IN COMMEMORATION

OF THE 550TH ANNIVERSARY

OF THE DEATH OF

"THE MOST STEADFAST

CHAMPION OF TRUTH"

# JOHN HUS

# PREFACE

FIVE HUNDRED and fifty years ago a man was burned at the stake, having been condemned by the Council of Constance as a heretic. The man was John Hus. This work was written not only to commemorate the event, but to pay a debt of gratitude to Hus' memory. In my early boyhood, as a member of one of the two Protestant communions in Bohemia, I ardently shared in the loving esteem in which Hus was held. During my sixty years of life in this country, the influence of the life and teaching of this valiant witness to the truth as he saw it has never lost its force among the vast number of other influences which have formed my spiritual self. It is my hope that my personal gratitude may be more widely shared by those who, through these pages, may become better acquainted with this Czech martyr's devotion and courage!

The principal aim of this work is to present Hus' teaching on the Church, which was central to his thinking and was further made crucial for him by having been subjected to the attacks of his enemies. Hus' theological thought has hitherto been generally ignored or has been to a considerable extent misrepresented. I wish to provide the reader with a critical interpretation of Hus' theological thought based on his own writings and on the results of the latest scholarship. I also desire to acknowledge and evaluate critically the recent studies of Hus written by the Belgian Benedictine monk, Dom Paul de Vooght. Furthermore, within the German Roman Catholic Church a demand has arisen that both the trial held, and the verdict pronounced upon Hus, by the Council of Constance be reconsidered and the condemnation be repealed. Although Dom de Vooght does not think that the cardinals and the other leaders of the Church show sufficient concern to repair this ancient wrong, he nevertheless regards the recently adopted decrees of Vatican Council II as going far to validate the demands of reform, including that of Hus, voiced during the fourteenth and the early fifteenth centuries. If, besides the above stated aims, this work of mine should contribute toward this reformist mood within the Roman communion, I should consider myself doubly rewarded.

Perhaps a word needs to be said about my choice of the method of dealing with the extensive writings of Hus included in this work. In order to show the development of Hus' thought, it was necessary to use all pertinent treatises written by him from the very beginning of his career. Only thus was it possible to demonstrate the essential unity and continuity of his thought and to counter the assertion of many writers who claim that he radically changed his opinions after 1412. This developmental method, however, necessarily involved a degree of redundancy, although I endeavored to keep it to a minimum. The repetitions found in this work are, therefore, deliberate, not incidental. Whenever it seemed preferable to combine several treatises in a concurrent analysis, it has been done; but in this method of treatment it is difficult to avoid confusing the reader. I feel confident that the method chosen, even though necessitating a degree of redundancy, is preferable to the alternate choice.

MATTHEW SPINKA

Claremont, California
July 6, 1965

# CONTENTS

Preface     vii

1. Hus Prepares for the Task of Reformer (1390-1402)     3

2. Calm before the Storm (1402-1408)     42

3. The Conflict with Archbishop Zbyněk     79

4. Attacked, Defeated, but Unconquered     107

5. Ecclesiology of Hus' Opponents. I: John of Holešov, the *Tractatus Gloriosus,* and *Contra Octo Doctores*     151

6. Ecclesiology of Hus' Opponents. II: Stanislav of Znojmo     172

7. Ecclesiology of Hus' Opponents. III: Stephen Páleč and the "Anonymous"     209

8. Hus' *De Ecclesia*     252

9. Hus' Czech Treatises     290

10. Hus' Trial at the Council of Constance     329

11. Conclusion     383

Appendix I. Wyclif's Forty-five Articles, Condemned on July 10, 1412     397

Appendix II. The Thirty Final Articles, with Hus' Responses     401

Selected Bibliography     411

Index     419

# JOHN HUS' CONCEPT OF THE CHURCH

## CHAPTER I

# HUS PREPARES FOR THE TASK
# OF REFORMER (1390-1402)

L IKE an alluring mirage on the horizon, there shines throughout the history of the Christian Church the image of the ideal Church. St. Paul dreamed of it when he wrote about the glorious Church "without spot or wrinkle or any such thing, that she might be holy and without blemish."[1] Some of the best sons of the Church devoted their lives to the realization of this ideal, ending their lives as martyrs because of their reforming zeal. When from time to time the fires of love and devotion burned low, some pure souls, catching the vision of the ideal Church, brought the vision, like the phoenix out of his ashes, to renewed splendor.

Such a period occurred in Bohemia in the fourteenth and fifteenth centuries and culminated in the heroic figure of John Hus. He was essentially a reformer. His overwhelming motive was the reformation of the Church; his theology was only a means to this end. It is on the basis of this, his enduring life-aim, that he must be judged. His concept of the Church, like Paul's, was admittedly idealistic, perhaps even unrealistic. From this point of view, his strictures and denunciations of the corrupt papacy of his day, and of the clergy and religious life generally, can be sympathetically understood. Reformers are, as a rule, an irritating and even exasperating lot, particularly to the people whose vices they castigate. Hus, berating the wickedness of the papal system, was indeed sometimes severe or even violent. So

---

[1] Eph. 5:27. The version of the Scriptures quoted (and translated) in this work is the Vulgate, the only version available to the men of the time. It is occasionally modified when the men citing the passages made changes in the wording.

were, however, many others of his day who shared his reformatory zeal. There were many, even among those who finally condemned him to death, who were convinced of the necessity of reform. Could gentler measures have been more appropriate or effective? Was Erasmus' policy of an educational reform from within more successful than Luther's ruthless hammer blows?

Hus' concept of the Church was the principal charge against him both by his antagonists at home and in his trial at the Council of Constance. He was misunderstood then as well as now. His theological views are but little known even in scholarly circles; consequently, opinions about him are not infrequently faulty. What is worse, thanks to the biased and warped judgments of such men as Johann Loserth,[2] Hus has been denied practically all originality and is regarded as a "mere echo" of Wyclif. Unfortunately, the English-speaking scholars, with rare exceptions, have accepted Loserth's thesis. Much truer is the opinion of the Belgian Benedictine, Dom Paul de Vooght, who regards Hus as indeed influenced by Wyclif, but as carefully discriminating between what he regarded as truth and error. "He is a disciple of Wyclif, to be sure, but of Wyclif purged of his dogmatic errors.[3] However, even he largely ignores the fact that Hus derives from the native tradition of reform of some half a century earlier. Milan Machovec, a prominent Czech communist historian and student of the Hussite period, in a recent book surprisingly appreciative of Dom de Vooght, suggests with somewhat unrestrained flight of imagination that the good Benedictine's book is

[2] Johann Loserth, *Hus und Wiclif; zur Genesis der Husitischen Lehre*, 2nd edn. (Munich and Berlin, 1925). The English translation, *Wiclif and Hus*, was published the same year as the first German edition (1884); also his *Joannis Wyclif, Tractatus de Ecclesia* (London, The Wyclif Society, 1886), pp. xxvi ff.

[3] Paul de Vooght, *L'hérésie de Jean Huss* (Louvain, Publications universitaires de Louvain, 1960), p. 181.

*4*

perhaps an attempt to rehabilitate John Hus in an effort, initiated by the late Pope John XXIII, at *rapprochement* with the Protestants.[4]

It is, therefore, of primary importance to reexamine Hus' theological ideas with the view of arriving at a truer perspective and a clearer "image" of the man. To this task, particularly with respect to his concept of the Church, the present work is dedicated. It was this concept which was attacked most vehemently by his foes at the Council. Of the final thirty charges on the basis of which he was condemned to death, twenty-five dealt with the Church; of these twenty-five, twelve concerned the pope. In his concept of the Church, Hus found himself irreconcilably opposed both to the Conciliarists who dominated the Council and considered the Church to be a juridical corporation, comprising the *congregatio fidelium* of which they were the supreme representative; and, at home, to the extreme papalists who regarded the Church as a papal monarchy, of which the pope was the head and the cardinals the body. He viewed the Church as a spiritual fellowship of the redeemed, the mystical body of Christ, of which Christ alone was the head and the predestinate the body.

A word of personal comment is needed here. I recognize and acknowledge the historian's duty and obligation to gather the factual and pertinent information with all the care of which he is capable, as far as possible from primary sources. He then must present it with scrupulous honesty and objectivity. It is quite wrong at this stage of the study to restrict the facts in order to favor the Roman Catholic, Protestant, nationalistic, or any other viewpoint (as is done now, for instance, by the Czech communists). Hus must be faithfully depicted

---

[4] M. Machovec, *Bude katolická církev rehabilitovat Jana Husa?* (Praha, Nakladatelství politické literatury, 1963).

against the background of both the historical circumstances and the theological milieu of his own time.

But I am not so naïve as to believe that the historian's
interpretation of this factual material is anything but
inevitably subjective. In judging other persons and
events, he necessarily reveals his own point of view. Nor
can it be otherwise. Everyone's judgment is the result of
all he has experienced in his intellectual and spiritual
pilgrimage. As Tennyson's Ulysses expressed it, "I am a
part of all I have met." Were the historian not to judge
according to the convictions *he* has formed, he would be
but a mere echo of another man's opinions. I expressed
this principle in an essay on Berdyaev, with whose concept in this instance I am in agreement:

> Thus truth, meaning, are subjective, not objective.
> They exist only in the spirit, not in the thing. Truth
> is within the subject, not empirically in the object. . . .
> A thing, the perceived object, has no meaning in it-
> self; that is supplied by the perceiving subject. . . .
> Knowledge, therefore, even scientific knowledge, is
> never merely objective. . . . It is a composite affair,
> consisting of sensory percepts plus the meaning which
> we as perceiving subjects incorporate into it.[5]

I am aware that this concept conflicts with Ranke's
ideal of complete objectivity, in which I myself was
trained in my university student years. But later experiences and reflections have taught me otherwise. I
realize, for instance, that where I differ in my conclusions from, let us say, Paul de Vooght, although we use
the same factual material as our basis, it is not so much
that one or both of us are wilfully biased, but that we
regard these facts from a different perspective. I anticipate to be severely taken to task for this historical

[5] Carl Michalson, ed., *Christianity and the Existentialists* (New
York, Charles Scribner's Sons, 1956), pp. 61-62.

"heresy." But that will only prove that my "Rankean" critics differ from us by judging from *their* individual perspective, rather than that they are Simon-pure objective, without a trace of personal viewpoint. Such is my understanding of the historian's task. I claim no inerrancy for my own opinions, although I do claim integrity. Nor do I quarrel with another man's convictions, provided he too manifests honest dealings with the facts. We differ because our experiences of life have molded us differently. This is not, however, an excuse for warping or twisting the facts to conform to our preconceived ideas, as Johann Loserth did.

JOHN HUS (1372-73–1415) was born in a small hamlet in southern Bohemia called Husinec (Goosetown)—hence his name. F. M. Bartoš had formerly given the date of Hus' birth as 1370-71. He had based his conclusion on what he supposed to be a dated autograph sermon of Hus'. But in accordance with new evidence, he now tentatively places Hus' birth in 1372-73, probably the latter.[6] Even so, De Vooght had rejected Bartoš' previous dating without specifying any reason.[7] There also exists a controversy as to whether Hus attended the elementary school in the nearby Prachatice or in Prague. Bartoš asserts the former, Novotný and De Vooght the latter.[8]

[6] For the earlier dating, see F. M. Bartoš, *Co vime o Husovi nového* (Praha, Pokrok, 1946), pp. 23-24; his present conclusion is explained in "Kdy se narodil M. J. Hus," *Kostnické Jiskry*, Praha, January 6, 1965.

[7] De Vooght (see n. 3), p. 41, n. 1.

[8] Bartoš (see n. 6), p. 24; V. Novotný, *Jan Hus, Život a dílo*, 2 vols. (Praha, Jan Laichter, 1919-21), I, pp. 5-6; De Vooght (see n. 3), p. 42. (Novotný's two-volume biographical work was published together with V. Kybal's three-volume treatise dealing with Hus' teaching, under the general title, *M. Jan Hus, Život a učení*, 5 vols. (Praha, Jan Laichter, 1919-31). To each author's work was added a subtitle: to Novotný's two volumes, *Život a dílo*; to Kybal's three volumes, *Učení*. Since to list repeatedly both the general title and the subtitle would be awkward and confusing, I have separated

Novotný comments that there is no mention of any school in Prachatice prior to the sixteenth century. That would, of course, settle the matter rather effectively. Although Hus' parents were poor, his mother vowed her son to the priesthood. According to Bartoš, the seventeen-year-old Hus went to Prague in 1390. The other two scholars had of necessity to provide more time for Hus' preparatory schooling in Prague, on the theory that he had had no training previously. They estimate that he arrived there in 1386. His own references to these earliest student years are meagre and without a hint as to where they took place. He tells us that he took part one Christmas in a shockingly coarse and sacrilegious play of "The Feast of the Ass," of which he says specifically that it was performed in Prague.[9] In 1390 he at last entered upon his university studies, graduating three years later with the degree of bachelor of arts, and after an additional three years with the degree of master of arts. Thereupon, in 1398, he became a full member of the faculty. During the winter semester of 1401-02 he even held the office of dean. Later he entered the faculty of theology with a view to securing the highest degree a medieval university could grant—that of the doctor of theology. However, he retained his membership in the faculty of arts. He received the bachelor of divinity degree in 1404 and began lecturing on the Bible. In 1407 he became *baccalarius sententiarius*. As such, he lectured on Peter Lombard's *Sentences* (1407-09). Thereupon, he became *baccalarius formatus*. He would have secured the doctorate within the next year or two but for the controversy over the "crusading bull"

---

the works of the two authors and list them independently: Novotný's as *Jan Hus, Život a dílo*, and Kybal's as *Jan Hus, Učení*.)

[9] "Výklad modlitby Páně," in F. Žilka, ed., *Vybrané spisy Mistra Jana Husi*, 2 vols. (Jilemnice, n.d.), II, pp. 419-420.

of Pope John XXIII and the subsequent conflict over Wyclif, which prevented his completing the course.

Since at that time the members of the faculty of arts received no regular salary but only the student fees and the promotion charges, Hus had to seek some other permanent source of income. This was normally gained in the priestly office. Hus, who had aimed at the clerical career ever since he began his school studies, was ordained in June 1400. On March 14, 1402, he was appointed preacher at the center of the Czech reform movement, the Bethlehem Chapel, founded in 1391. The advowson of this privately established chapel was in the hands of the Czech university masters, the office of the preacher to be held by one of their number. The appointment made Hus the spokesman for the native reform movement which had begun a half century before.

How had Hus, who by his own account had formerly been motivated by the generally prevalent ambition to enter the clerical order in order to secure a position of economic well-being, if not opulence, been converted into a preeminent reformer? He must have experienced a thoroughgoing change, a radical inner transformation, during the period prior to his ordination. Unfortunately, he tells us practically nothing about this basically significant change. As is characteristic of men who have experienced the spiritual upheaval of conversion, he freely laments his former "unregenerate" state. He is exceedingly sensitive even to his smallest faults. He frankly admits, "When I was a young student, I confess to have entertained an evil desire, for I had thought to become a priest quickly in order to secure a good livelihood and dress and to be held in esteem by men."[10]

[10] "Hus on Simony," in Matthew Spinka, transl., *Advocates of Reform*, Library of Christian Classics, xiv (Philadelphia, The Westminster Press, 1953), p. 239.

And no wonder; Hus then had been miserably poor. He speaks of his destitute state with humor: "When I was a hungry young student, I used to make a spoon of bread and ate peas with it until I also ate the spoon."[11] When he received his master's degree, he was as proud of his academic status as he had a right to be. He writes of the delight he felt in his cap and gown with the ornate hood. He writes: "Alas! I too had gowns, robes with wings, and hoods with white fur; for they [the university authorities] had so hemmed in the master's degree with their regulations that no one could obtain the degree unless he possessed such apparel."[12] He also confesses to having liked to play chess—a pastime he bitterly bewailed in his "Last Will" written to his pupil Martin just before his leaving for Constance. "You know that—alas!—before I became priest, I had gladly and often played chess, had wasted time, and by that play had frequently unhappily provoked to anger both myself and others."[13] What, then, caused this unascetic, gay young student and master to abandon this pleasant manner of life and become a zealous reformer, particularly of the life of the clergy? How we wish that he had been more explicit and circumstantial in describing the deep and basic change he had experienced! He touches upon it in another of his "confessions" toward the end of his life when he writes: "When I was young in years and reason, I too belonged to the foolish sect. But when the Lord gave me the knowledge of Scripture, I discharged that kind of stupidity from my foolish mind."[14]

[11] "Výklad desatera," in Žilka (see n. 9), II, p. 386.

[12] "Simony," in Spinka (see n. 10), p. 262.

[13] "Petri de Mladoniowicz relatio de Magistro Johanne Hus," in V. Novotný, ed., *Fontes rerum Bohemicarum*, VIII (Praha, Nadání Františka Palackého, 1932), p. 29; translated by Matthew Spinka in *John Hus at the Council of Constance* (New York, Columbia University Press, 1965), pp. 95-96.

[14] "Výklad desatera," in Žilka (see n. 9), II, p. 420.

Nevertheless, even while teaching at the university, he still feared "to profess and defend" the truth, as he penitently confesses: "I myself—alas!—had been one of them [the timorous masters], for I dared not to preach the truth plainly and openly."[15] Thus it was the study of Scripture which brought about the change. When and how? All he tells us is that it occurred before he became priest. With that we must be content, even though not satisfied.

This leads us to consider the kind of influences which played upon him while he was studying and teaching at the University of Prague. This seat of learning was founded by Emperor Charles IV on April 7, 1348, the first such foundation in central Europe. He expressly declared that he founded it in order "that the loyal inhabitants of our land, incessantly hungering after the fruits of learning, may not be constrained to beg for alms abroad, but may find set out in our realm a table of refreshment."[16] The university had four faculties—those of liberal arts, of theology, of law, and of medicine. Its fame soon attracted thousands of students, for the greater part from the surrounding countries, so that Prague became the most populous city in central Europe. Nevertheless, as time went on, the Czechs increased their numbers, although the foreigners still were in the majority. The masters and students divided themselves into four "nations"—the Czech, Bavarian, Saxon, and Polish. By that time the university numbered several thousand members. Under these conditions, the foreign masters, particularly the Germans, predominated until 1409, when the constitution was changed. Among the most prominent of the foreign masters trained in Prague were the Germans, Henry Totting of Oyta, Conrad Soltau,

15 "Simony," in Spinka (see n. 10), p. 263.
16 O. Odložilík, *The Caroline University, 1348-1948* (Praha, 1948), p. 14.

Albert of Engelschalk, and Matthew of Cracow. The last-named, although born a Pole, cooperated with the Germans. The predominant philosophical tendency was that of late Occamist nominalism,[17] which prevailed at the University of Paris. Since the leaders of the Conciliar movement were mostly nominalists, demands for Church reform were made by the nominalist Prague masters as well. Among them the most radical were Matthew of Cracow and Albert Engelschalk. Matthew, who had been professor of theology at Prague, later went to Cracow. He became bishop of Worms in 1405, and finally joined the faculty of theology at the newly established University of Heidelberg. There he became a strong supporter of Ruprecht of the Palatinate, who had been elected king of the Romans in place of the Bohemian king, Wenceslas. Matthew was appointed by Gregory XII his legate to the Council of Pisa. Matthew's most important reforming treatise is the *De squaloribus curiae Romanae* (1404), completed at Heidelberg.[18] Engelschalk, who became rector of the Prague university in 1391, wrote the *Speculum aureum*, in which he castigated the simony and other money-grubbing practices of the curia as well as of the entire ecclesiastical establishment. Although these denunciations were published long after Hus' student days, yet they indicate the temper of the masters who had dominated the faculty during his student and teaching career.

Thomism, as could be expected, was represented at the Prague university by the Dominicans. When in 1383

[17] For a recent basic reinterpretation of Occamist nominalism, cf. the excellent study of Heiko A. Oberman, *The Harvest of Medieval Theology* (Cambridge, Mass., Harvard University Press, 1963). A survey of the philosophical tendencies at the university of Prague is found in J. Sedlák, "Filosofické spory v době Husově," *Studie a texty k náboženským dějinám českým*, 2 vols. (Olomouc, 1914-15), II, pp. 197-224.

[18] Cf. also his sermon in Paul de Vooght, *Hussiana* (Louvain, Publications universitaires de Louvain, 1960), pp. 360-362.

the University of Paris declared itself in favor of the Avignonese pope, Clement VII, the Dominican masters left Paris for Prague, thus greatly strengthening their influence there. The most eminent among the Thomists was Henry of Bitterfeld, a confidant of Archbishop John of Jenstein, who himself had studied at Paris. A Czech, Nicholas Biceps, also gained considerable fame by his commentary on Lombard's *Sentences*.

Because of its modified philosophical realism and its essential theological Augustinism, Thomism prepared the way for the more fundamental emphasis on these component elements in Wyclifite realism. Among its initiators at Prague was the most scholarly and highly respected Czech master, Vojtěch Rankův of Ježov (Adalbertus Ranconis de Ericinio), a moderate realist, who had studied at Paris and had received there in 1349 degrees in both arts and theology. He became professor at the Sorbonne and later (1335-56) rector of the university. He likewise taught at Oxford, where he became acquainted with Wyclif and corresponded with Archbishop Richard Fitz-Ralph of Armagh. After he returned to Prague, he became a canon and scholastic of St. Vitus' Cathedral (1369). Although he did not teach at the university, his academic preeminence made him influential among its masters and students. He and his onetime pupil at Paris, Archbishop John of Jenstein, are credited with having taken a minor part in the efforts to settle the Schism, although in different ways. Both were indeed partisans of the Roman pope, Urban. But Vojtěch, in his *De schismate*, opposed any violent condemnation of Clement's election. The archbishop, on the other hand, in his treatises *De potestate clavium* and *De veritate Urbani*, took an extremely defensive position in favor of the Roman pope. Bartoš credits Vojtěch with still another treatise dealing with the settling of the papal schism, namely *Tetragonus Aristotelis* (1381-82), in which he utilized the much better known treatises of Henry of Langenstein and Conrad of Gelnhausen. The fairly well-to-do Vojtěch devoted all his property to scholarship endowments at Paris and Oxford. He died in 1388.[19]

Before considering Wyclif and his importance for the Czech religious history we must first cast a glance at the Czech native reform movement. It was initiated in 1363 when Charles IV and Archbishop Ernest of Pardubice called to Prague the celebrated Viennese Augustinian canon, Conrad Waldhauser (d. 1369).[20] In his impassioned preaching he upbraided particularly the monks and the rich German burghers. He aroused the begging friars against himself, and they wrote an *Apology* in their defense. The greatest service he rendered to the reform movement was his winning for it the man who became the Father of the Czech Reform, Milíč of Kroměříž (d. 1374).[21]

Milíč became canon of St. Vitus' Cathedral in 1362, but two years later surrendered his position to devote himself fully to preaching. He preached in Latin, Czech, or German twice or three times on Sundays and holy-days and at least once every day, and spoke eloquently. He lived a life of voluntary poverty and strict asceticism. In his censures he rebuked the vices both of his lay hearers and of the monks, priests, and prelates, demanding of the clergy apostolic poverty. This brought upon

[19] Kamil Krofta, *Francie a české hnutí náboženské* (Praha, n.d.), pp. 24f. For the text of Jenstein's *De veritate Urbani* cf. J. Sedlák, *M. Jan Hus* (Praha, Dědictví sv. Prokopa, 1915), supplement, pp. 2-20. For Vojtěch Rankův's *Tetragonus Aristotelis*, cf. F. M. Bartoš, *Husitství a cizina* (Praha, Čin, 1931), pp. 9ff.

[20] V. Novotný, *Náboženské hnutí české ve 14. a 15. století* (Praha, n.d.), I, pp. 57ff. Also F. Loskot, *Konrad Waldhauser* (Praha, 1909).

[21] Odložilík, *Jan Milíč z Kroměříže* (Kroměříž, 1924); Novotný (see n. 20), pp. 65ff.; Kybal, *Jan Hus, Učení*, I, pp. 119ff.; B. Havránek *et al.*, eds., *Výbor z české literatury doby husitské* (Praha, 1963), pp. 47ff.

him their wrath. Because of the low moral condition of the Church, Milíč fell victim to the common delusion of the time as to the appearance of the Antichrist. He identified him in the end not with a person but with the prevailing spirit of opposition to Christ. In 1367 he went to Rome to induce the pope to undertake a reform of the Church. During his sojourn there he composed a *Libellus de Antichristo*. His real and lasting contribution to the Czech reform was his emphasis on a life befitting the profession of a Christian, and on Scriptural study and preaching as the principal task of the priesthood; he had a burning desire for a Church "without spot or wrinkle." He regarded the Scriptures as the source of "uncreated truth" containing all that is necessary for salvation. All other truths are derivative. Men enter the Church by the leading of the Holy Spirit through the preaching of the Word of God. Nevertheless, only the elect are saved, as he writes in his collection of sermons entitled *Gracie Dei*, for they alone are instructed by the Spirit to understand it aright. Therefore, Milíč demanded that theologians leave the scholastic subtleties based on logic or philosophy and turn back to the "simple gospel," grounded in the eternal truth of Christ. He opposed those "qui ex virtutibus moralibus philosophie naturalis putant se posse salvari, nescientes caritatem expressam in evangelica lege."[22] These men claimed that theology cannot be understood without philosophy and the arts. Toward the end of his life Milíč developed a deep concern for the reformation of fallen women. He founded a refuge for them called Jerusalem. Having been accused of heresy, he was cited to Avignon, where he died before the trial was completed (1374). His clerical enemies succeeded then to secure the closing of the house of refuge. The emperor turned it over to the Cistercian Order.

[22] Kybal, *Jan Hus, Učení*, I, p. 121, n. 1.

Even more outstanding among the leaders of the Czech reform movement was Matthew of Janov (c. 1355-94).[23] He studied at Paris (1373-81), where he received his M.A. degree. He must thus have been a fellow-student of Pierre d'Ailly. Before he had left Prague, he had been deeply influenced by Milíč's preaching. During his theological studies he gave special attention to Scripture and the Fathers. As a determined adherent of Pope Urban, Matthew, on his way back to Prague, visited Rome and received from the pope a reservation for a canonry at Prague. Having arrived there, he actually was received among the canons of St. Vitus' Cathedral. But since Urban had already granted the expectation to the unvacated prebend to five other applicants, Matthew's appointment as a canon was merely a claim to a prebend to be secured later. As a matter of fact, he never received it. Master Vojtěch Rankův, who was then the cathedral scholastic, permitted him to live in his house. Matthew derived meagre support from his appointment as preacher and penitentiary at the cathedral and from a rural benefice, the care of which he had entrusted to a vicar. He preached not only at the cathedral but at another Prague church as well. His denunciation of externalism in worship and of superstitious veneration of images, and his advocacy of frequent, even daily, communion by laymen, brought him into conflict with the archiepiscopal consistory. At first (1388) the Prague synodal meeting ordered that no layman be admitted to communion more than once a month. Then a year later, when the first volume of his chief work, *Regulae veteris et novi testamenti*, was published and contained further urging of the practice, he was cited

23 V. Kybal, *Matěj z Janova, jeho život, spisy a učeni* (Praha, 1905); also Novotný, *Náboženské hnutí* (see n. 20), pp. 146ff.; Augustus Neander, *General History of the Christian Religion and Church* (Boston, Houghton, Mifflin and Co., 1871), v, pp. 194-235.

before the archiepiscopal court and forced to recant that opinion before a synodal meeting. He submitted, but did not change his convictions. He was suspended from preaching for half a year.

Henceforth, disappointed and disillusioned with the hierarchical leadership both of the Prague archdiocese and of the Church generally, he turned to literary activity. He published a number of treatises, among them the no longer extant translation of the Bible into Czech. He also completed his *Regulae*, a five-volume work.[24] Just a year before his death, he was cited before the general vicar of the archdiocese, John of Pomuky (later the notorious St. John of Nepomuky!),[25] on charges of heresy. He was requested to bring with him two of his works, one Czech, the other Latin. Bartoš surmises that the former was a part of the Czech Bible, probably the New Testament.[26] The latter work, the *Regulae*, is a collection of various treatises, some not even written by Matthew: for instance, Milíč's *De Antichristo* and Saint-Armour's anti-monastic *De periculis novissimorum temporum* were included. We shall pay particular attention to the third volume of the *Regulae*, for it contains treatises on subjects of special interest to us: "De unitate et universitate ecclesiae" and "De abhominacione in loco sancto." They deal with Matthew's concept of the Church, which shows particularly clearly the continuity which existed within the Czech reform movement, persisting into the days of Hus. If proof were needed that Hus did not derive all his religious inspiration from

[24] V. Kybal, ed., *Matthew of Janov's Regulae veteris et novi testamenti*, 4 vols. (Innsbruck, 1908-13); O. Odložilík, ed., *ibid.*, v (Praha, 1926).

[25] Cf. De Vooght's excellent studies, "L'Affaire Pomuk" and "Le Mythe de Jean Népomucène," in *Hussiana* (see n. 18), pp. 406-421. For an older work, F. M. Bartoš, *Světec temna, Jan Nepomucký* (Praha, 1921).

[26] F. M. Bartoš, *Čechy v době Husově* (Praha, Jan Laichter, 1947), p. 251.

the views of Wyclif, this connection with his native reforming predecessors would amply furnish it.

In the first place, Matthew derives all truth from God
himself, since in Him exists the primal eternal truth
from which all particular truths originate. Nor has
God left Himself without a witness in the hearts of
men. The supreme revelation of God is Jesus Christ and
is to be found in the holy Scriptures. Matthew's devotion
to the Scriptures was so great that he carried a copy,
written by his own hand, everywhere along with him,
for his defense and consolation. He writes in the preface
to the *Regulae* that he "loved it ever since his youth
and called it his friend and spouse, indeed his mother. . . ." For its interpretation he depended on the early
Fathers, and opposed the later glosses and commentaries.
He declared that the evangelical law is sufficient for the
guidance of every man, layman or cleric. Applying this
basic concept of truth to the Catholic Church, he professes that Scripture is the full embodiment of the divine,
revealed truths. Every Christian receives, first of all, the
baptismal grace [*gratia gratis data*], which enables him,
by living a life of piety and virtue, to acquire the
sanctifying grace [*gratia gratum faciens*]. The baptismal
grace by itself does not make a man Christian. It is but
dead faith, unless it is turned into the saving faith by the
sanctifying grace which culminates in faith formed by
love [*fides caritate formata*]. Matthew thus ignores the
intellectual concept of faith inculcated by the then
current scholasticism. In fact, just like Milíč, he reprobates the neglect of Scriptural study by those who
devote themselves exclusively or predominantly to the
study of the canon law and of "human inventions."

Besides Scripture, Matthew also acknowledges tradition as the source of revelation. He writes in the *Regulae*
that the "law of the Holy Spirit" and of the gospel as
held by the popes, bishops, and priests "is sufficient for

the legitimate direction of all communities of people and every single individual of the community; they are sufficient . . . for the solving of all questions and all discussions in the matters of conscience and judgment. . . ."[27] There are three "laws" for the guidance of men seeking to live reasonably and rightly: those of nature, of society, and of grace. The last of these is written into the hearts of men and is the most important as the rule of life. It consists of the single commandment—that of love. It is constantly taught by the Holy Spirit, the Scriptures, and the saints.

There exist in the Church militant two kinds of members, the predestinate and the foreknown. Only those who have acquired the sanctifying grace are the true Church, the *communio sanctorum*. They are the elect, possessing the spirit of Christ.[28] According to Augustine, they alone belong to the mystical body of Christ. None can be cut off from this body except by committing mortal sin. The most effective means of preserving the unity with Christ is the frequent partaking of the communion. Over against this Church of the saints stands the church of Antichrist. Matthew identifies it with the corrupt church of his day. He enumerates four reasons for its present degradation. The first and chief of these is the corrupt priesthood; the second is the tyranny of secular lords; the third is the tyranny of the prelates; and the fourth is the corruption of the monks. As for the first, he traces the corruption of the priests to the curia. Anyone not blind or spiritually dead must admit that "the son of iniquity" is sitting in the temple, as if he were

[27] *Regulae* (see n. 24), II, p. 263.
[28] *Ibid.*, III, tract. 4: "Dum autem hec loquor, volo caute intelligi, quod signat proprie ecclesia Christi hic accepta, quia congregationem sanctorum dei, qui vivunt et aguntur spiritu et vita Jesu Christi, cuius unitas est pulcherrima et delictabilis." ". . . Ecclesia (Jesu) congregata ex multitudine solum electorum, quos vivificat et agitat spiritus Jesus Christi. . . ." *Ibid.*, III, tract. 5.

earthly god.[29] As the pope lifts himself above the bishops, so the bishops lord it over the clergy. They seek the company of the great canons, the lords, and the rich, and neglect the care of the lower clergy. The latter, in their turn, imitate the bishops in neglecting the care of their parishioners, thus extending the corruption to the common people. Exceeding that of all others is the corruption of the monks who, with but rare exceptions, live parasitically on the whole body of the Church. He advocates the integration of the monks into the corpus of secular priests.

Besides the corruption of the entire hierarchical system, Matthew criticizes the innumerable rites, ceremonies, rescripts, and doctrinal innovations which completely bury under their dead mass the teaching of Christ.[30] As has already been mentioned, he castigates the emphasis on the study of the canon law, which results in the neglect of the study of theology and Scripture. Another aspect is the superstitious veneration of images and statues of the Savior, the Virgin, and the saints. He writes that people, "because they are avaricious, venerate and honor the saints in heaven, build them tombstones, collect their relics and beautify and venerate them excessively."[31] He deplores that the common people put greater trust in prayers to saints than in Jesus Christ. This, he says, leads to idolatry.[32]

[29] "Si igitur in nostra etate nimis manifeste sunt impleta et a tota christianorum ecclesia conspectata, ita quod non nisi cecus prorsus et mortuus in spiritu ea non posset affirmare, quis non dicet, quod iam filius iniquitatis in templo sedeat, ostendens, tamquam ipse sit deus, scilicet in terris, et non deus natura?" *Ibid.*, III, tract. 5. Being a convinced Urbanist, Matthew has Clement VII in mind. He says so explicitly in the same passage, referring to Clement's recognition by the University of Paris.

[30] *Ibid.*, II, tract. 1; III, tract. 1.

[31] Havránek, *Výbor* (see n. 21), p. 66.

[32] ". . . ymmo ab ymaginibus et honoracione eorum omnis *ydolatria* gencium est inchoata."

Matthew further denounces simony and plural benefices. Kybal, quoting Matthew's own words, summarizes
his criticism of the contemporary priesthood as "worldly,
proud, mercenary, pleasure-loving, and hypocritical; they
are the synagogue of sinners, the great Whore, serpents
and young adders, a snare, the apocalyptic locusts,
adulterous women, worse than public prostitutes. They
form spiritually the Great Babylon which is the Great
Whore and the mother of adultery and abomination of
the earth. They do not regard their sins as such, do not
allow themselves to be reproved, and persecute the saintly preachers. There is no doubt that if Jesus lived among
such people, they would be the first to put him to
death."[33]

How, then, is the Church to be reformed? First of all,
by securing its unity. This necessitates that human innovations be reduced to a minimum and that all Christians return to the simplicity of the apostolic Church.
The corruption of the Church had begun, he says, about
the year 1200 when it had grown wealthy and powerful.
This condition reached its culmination in 1378 with
the Great Schism, when the Church divided into three
communions—the Roman, the Avignonese, and the
Greek. Matthew says that reform began about fifty or
seventy years before the time at which he is speaking,
although it is not clear what concrete event he has in
mind.

Hus, then, became the heir of this reform movement.
As will be shown later, most of the ethical demands made
during the days of Milíč and Matthew were emphasized
with undiminished vigor and power by Hus. This does
not, however, in any way deny the impact of John
Wyclif upon the new generation of the leaders of Czech
reform. We must, therefore, consider briefly the thought
of the English scholar who found in the far-off Bohemia

[33] Kybal, *Matěj z Janova* (see n. 23), pp. 141-142.

his most devoted disciples, thus exerting there his most lasting influence.

Of Wyclif's life we have no need to speak. There are available competent and adequate biographies written by recognized authorities.[34] His philosophical realism, which distinguished him sharply from the contemporary nominalists, was basic to his entire system. He thus consciously linked himself with Augustine, Anselm, Grosseteste, and Bradwardine, passing over the *moderni*, Thomas Aquinas and William of Ockham. S. Harrison Thomson defines his realism as comprising "distinct productive archetypes (*ydee, raciones exemplares*) of the divine mind. As such, they exist eternally. They 'communicate their content . . . to God's other and different creatures,' who possess them in varying degrees. Ideas are, therefore, real and indestructible, since they are God's ideas, although embodied in temporal and imperfect forms."[35]

No real thing, therefore, can be annihilated. As the second source of his doctrinal views he names the holy Scriptures. In his *Trialogus* he writes: "Therefore, if there were a hundred popes, and all the friars were turned into cardinals, their opinions in matters of faith should be believed only in so far as they are founded in Scripture." He thus repudiated all dependence on tradition, papal decrees, canon law, or scholastic systems unless they are Scripturally derived and validated. For him as for all other anti-papal reformers the authority

[34] Herbert B. Workman, *John Wyclif*, 2 vols. (Oxford, at the Clarendon Press, 1926); J. C. Carrick, *Wycliffe and the Lollards* (New York, 1908); Gotthard Lechler, *John Wiclif and his English Precursors*, translated by Peter Lorimer, 2 vols. (London, C. Kegan Paul & Co., 1878); Spinka, *Advocates of Reform* (see n. 10), pp, 21-88; Bartoš, *Husitství a cizina* (see n. 19), pp. 20-58; Howard Kaminsky, "Wyclifism as Ideology of Revolution," *Church History* (1963), pp. 57-74.

[35] S. Harrison Thomson, "The Philosophical Basis of Wyclif's Theology," *Journal of Religion* (1931), pp. 86f.

of Scripture had to be absolute in order to overthrow the absolute authority claimed by the pope. Wyclif thus represented a return to the tradition holding that Scripture alone is the sole criterion of faith and practice—the "law of God." In this he had Thomas Bradwardine (c. 1290-1349), whom he called "doctor profundus," as his immediate predecessor at Oxford. Oberman writes that Bradwardine is "one of the first outspoken representatives of Tradition I [as he calls the view that Scripture *alone* is the criterion of doctrine] at the beginning of the fourteenth century."[36] Wyclif also stressed predestination as a foil against Averroist determinism and Pelagian free will, and as a coherent doctrine of justification *sola gratia*.[37] He stated his views most systematically in his *De veritate sacrae Scripturae* (1378). The Scriptures are inspired by the Holy Spirit in every part. They comprise the entire Catholic faith. Every Christian, therefore, is in duty bound to study them. No other source of saving faith is admissible. De Vooght collects Wyclif's references to Scripture from his various writings in the summary statement:

> Scripture is the voice of Christ, the unique word of God, the word of truth, the uniquely perfect word. It is the fountain of wisdom, the nest of the faithful doves, the whole and pure bread without alloy, the clear and pure water, the seamless robe, the mirror and model, the refuge and the rule. It is the law of Christ, the testament of God, the faith of the Church, and the chart guaranteeing to us the reign of God. . . . Its truth is immutable. It is the ground on which all

[36] Oberman (see n. 17), pp. 372; also Paul de Vooght, *Les sources de la doctrine chrétienne* (Paris, Desclée de Brouwer, 1954), pp. 142ff.

[37] Heiko A. Oberman, *Archbishop Bradwardine, a Fourteenth Century Augustinian* (Utrecht, Kernink & Zoon, 1958), pp. 29ff., 179.

judgment rests . . . it is alpha and omega of all Christianity.[38]

All heresy springs from erroneous understanding of Scripture. The opinions of the Fathers may be accepted only as far as they agree with Scripture. Furthermore, "since the Holy Spirit is one with Christ, the truth of the Bible rests entirely upon the centrality of Christ Himself. . . . Wyclif sets forth Augustine's opinion that all law, all philosophy, all logic and all ethics are found in Holy Scripture."[39] Accordingly, it is of unconditional authority and sufficiency, not only for the Church but for the state as well. His insistence on the *lex evangelica* indicates, however, "that he had not yet become fully conscious of the essential difference between Moses and Christ, law and gospel, law and grace."[40]

Concentrating our attention upon Wyclif's doctrine of the Church, we recognize as his chief concept the view that it comprises only the predestinate—it is the *universitas praedestinatorum*. They alone form the mystical body of Christ. Wyclif refuses to identify this concept with the *congregatio fidelium*, as the canonists have done. This is, of course, the Pauline-Augustinian-Bradwardian doctrine. In his *De causa Dei*, Bradwardine asserted that the divine grace alone is the cause of salvation. He summarily repudiated the prevailing scholastic notion that man could deserve grace *de congruo*—by doing good works of his own volition and power, unaided by divine grace. No man can thus acquire saving merit.[41] Wyclif, who held the same view, consciously set himself in opposition to the notion of *meritum de*

[38] De Vooght, *Les sources* (see n. 36), pp. 168-169.

[39] William Mallard, "Wyclif and Biblical Authority," *Church History* (1961), pp. 51-52.

[40] Lechler (see n. 34), II, p. 34.

[41] Henry Savile, ed., *De causa Dei contra Pelagium et de virtute causarum, libri tres* (London, 1618); also Wyclif, *De ecclesia* (see n. 2), p. 138.

*congruo.* Since the Church catholic is composed only of the elect, he likewise refused to identify it with the Roman hierarchy having the pope at its head. None could join that holy Church by his own choice merely by being a member of the Church militant, nor could any power on earth deprive the predestinate of his membership in the *communio sanctorum.* Only he himself could do it by unrepentingly abiding in mortal sin.

As we have seen, Wyclif adopts the current division of the Church into three parts: the militant on earth, the triumphant in heaven, and the dormient in purgatory. The Church triumphant comprises the angels as well as the saints. The Church militant includes the predestinate and the foreknown. It is only in the Day of Judgment that the latter will be separated from the former. Wyclif speaks of them as being *in* the Church without being *of* the Church. There are more tares than wheat in it.[42] He illustrates this concept by the somewhat inelegant allusion to the foreknown as the excrements which are in the body without being of the body.[43] Hus later adopted these tenets verbally. The predestinate have formed one body—the true Church—from the beginning of the world and will continue to do so to the end; but so have the foreknown, who have formed the church of the reprobate. God had foreseen those who, by their free choice of evil and perseverance in sin, are destined to eternal damnation. He writes that "each man that shall be damned shall be damned for his own guilt, and each man that is saved shall be saved by his own merit."[44] He thus asserts man's free will. Accordingly, such a man's punishment is the result of his own choices, although the punishment for sin as such is of God's

[42] *De ecclesia,* pp. 89, 100.   [43] *Ibid.,* p. 75.
[44] T. Arnold, ed., *Select English Works of John Wyclif,* 3 vols. (Oxford, 1869-71), I, p. 42; *De ecclesia,* pp. 60, 63, 281.

eternal ordaining.[45] This view of God's predestination and foreknowledge presents difficulties which Wyclif did not attempt to solve. He satisfied himself with the thought that God's omnipotence is free from all conditioning and limitation.

There exist, therefore, two kinds of societies: the elect, beginning with Adam; and the foreknown [*praesciti*], originating with Cain. In Augustinian terms, these are the *civitas Dei* and the *civitas terrena*. This division applies not only to secular society, but to the Church militant as well. Nevertheless, since no one knows whether or not he is of the predestinate, it is improper to pass judgment as to who does or does not belong to the true Church. The only apparent indication is afforded by the kind of life a member of the visible Church lives. "By their fruits ye shall know them!" Thus the life of piety, of following Christ, is the outward moral sign of election to eternal life. Nevertheless, it is not decisive, for a predestinate may for a time live in sin. Yet, the moral life of the Christian affords the only basis of judgment, no matter how uncertain.

Of the *universitas praedestinatorum* only Christ is the head. So understood, the concept of the Church is an article of faith. Neither the pope nor the hierarchy holds the headship in this *ecclesia sancta catholica*, although some men think they do. Christ's rule is sufficient.[46] Wyclif writes in an English treatise: "When men speak of the holy Church, they understand thereby prelates, priests, and monks, canons and friars, and all men that have crowns (tonsure), though they live ever so cursedly contrary to God's law. . . ."[47] Nevertheless, Wyclif did

[45] G. V. Lechler, ed., *Trialogus cum supplemento Trialogi* (Oxford, 1869), II, 14, p. 122.

[46] ". . . caput Christus cum sua lege est per se sufficient ad regulam sponse sue." A. W. Pollard and C. Sayle, eds., *Tractatus de officio regis* (London, The Wyclif Society, 1887), p. 226.

[47] *Select English Works* (see n. 44), III, p. 447.

not deny for the greater part of his life the rightfulness of the hierarchical jurisdiction in the Church militant. In fact, up to the outbreak of the Schism in 1378 he recognized, within limits, the papal primacy. He did not, however, regard it as absolutely necessary for salvation. The pope may be recognized as the head of the Church *jure humano* but not *jure divino*. He may err and fall into heresy. Wyclif's well-known defense of the English crown against the financial exactions of the papacy, for instance in the negotiations in Bruges in 1374-75, is an example of his conviction that the pope does not possess plenary power in matters temporal. Nevertheless, his recognition of the papal office within these limits is evident in his hearty approval of the election of Pope Urban VI in 1378; he regarded it at first as the beginning of the reformation of the curia. He thanked God that He had removed Gregory XI and installed Urban in his place.[48] It was the election of Clement VII and Wyclif's disillusionment with Urban that caused the radical change in his attitude toward the papacy.[49]

During the next period Wyclif underwent a gradual change, which at first took the form of neutrality vis-à-vis the two popes. This transitional stage is best seen in his *De potestate papae*, completed in 1379. Here he declares that "we English cannot accept either" of the popes, for both act like Antichrists.[50] It were better if both popes were deposed by a general Council (as was done at Pisa in 1409). He asserts further that the qualifications of the pope should be those of Peter: preeminent faith and qualities of character. Only if the pope is truly a follower of Christ and of Peter in humility and service

[48] *De ecclesia*, pp. 38, 358.

[49] Lechler quotes Wyclif's enthusiastic endorsement of Urban (see n. 34), II, p. 134.

[50] J. Loserth, ed., *Tractatus de potestate papae* (London, The Wyclif Society, 1913), pp. 149, 186, 212.

is he worthy of the papal office.[51] Otherwise he is the Antichrist. Since Peter had no jurisdiction over the other apostles, the ruthless usurpation of power over the hierarchy and the Church by the popes is unlawful. The pope is a servant, not the lord, of the Church.

These transitional views finally resolved into his radical repudiation of the entire papal system as having been founded by Constantine, not Christ. No pope before Sylvester claimed to be Christ's vicar and to possess supreme power over both spiritual and temporal realms. Wyclif demanded that the papacy be abolished altogether and that Christ be recognized as the sole head of the Church.[52] For only a return to the primitive order of the Church could bring about an adequate reform.[53]

As for the clergy, Wyclif held that originally there was no difference between presbyter and bishop. He traced the distinction in rank to the corruption of the later ages, particularly to Constantine's endowment of the Church with temporal possessions. Accordingly, a return to apostolic poverty would constitute the chief means of the Church's reform. The clergy should receive a provision sufficient for their necessities, but not for luxuries.[54] Hence, rulers may relieve them of useless wealth, but not in order to despoil the Church.[55]

The elevation of the bishops above the priests and of the Roman bishop above all other bishops in the world

[51] *De ecclesia*, pp. 562-563.

[52] J. Loserth, ed., *Opera minora* (London, The Wyclif Society, 1913), pp. 133, 262; R. Buddensieg, ed., *John Wiclif's Polemical Works in Latin*, 2 vols. (London, The Wyclif Society, 1883), pp. 369, 671, where Wyclif calls the pope "precipuus Anticristus," and p. 664, where he refers to some popes as "dyaboli." The denunciation of the papacy is also summarized in Workman (see n. 34), II, pp. 80-81.

[53] *De ecclesia*, p. 56.      [54] *Ibid.*, pp. 288, 308.

[55] "Sed absit ut aliquis reportet me quod dem occasionem dominis temporalibus ad spoliandum sanctam ecclesiam. . . ." *Ibid.*, p. 281.

was the result of the Constantinian endowment.[56] In the *Trialogus,* Wyclif acknowledges only the orders of priests and deacons on the ground that Christ established no others. The primary duty of the clergy is the preaching of the Word of God. "Preaching the gospel exceeds prayer and administration of the sacraments to an infinite degree."[57] It should be done in the vernacular. In the second place, priests are responsible for the "cure of souls" and the defense of their flock against the "wolves." Once a priest is ordained, he has full power to administer all the sacraments. Even a foreknown priest living in sin ministers validly. If a priest is notoriously negligent in the performance of his duties, the parishioners should withdraw their tithes from him. No one should knowingly attend a mass celebrated by an adulterous priest. Wyclif reprobates the excessive worship of images and relics, the proliferation of ceremonies, superstitious pilgrimages, miracles, and the external observance of rites generally. This is particularly aimed at the veneration of saints, which he finally repudiated altogether. It is remarkable that at first he regarded the Virgin Mary as the mediatrix between the sinner and her Son, without whose help full salvation was impossible.[58] The celibacy of the clergy he pronounces unscriptural. He also repudiates the doctrine of the inexhaustible treasury of merits at the disposal of the pope, who could apply them as indulgences to supplement the insufficient virtues of sinners in purgatory or even in hell. Wyclif argues that were the pope to possess such unlimited powers, he should use them for the benefit of all, rather than restricting them to those who secured his indulgences. For

[56] Wyclif's "Pastoral Office," in Spinka, *Advocates of Reform,* p. 28.
[57] *Ibid.,* p. 49.
[58] J. Loserth, ed., *Sermones,* 4 vols. (London, The Wyclif Society, 1887-90), IV, pp. 388-392; II, pp. 54-55; *Selected English Works,* III, p. 113.

he would otherwise be guilty of the eternal death of those whom he had passed over.[59] He concludes the argument by denying such pretended papal powers as fictitious (cum toti isti materie deficit fundamentum).[60]

Wyclif was likewise a doughty foe of mendicant orders, thus continuing their denunciation by Archbishop Fitz-Ralph of Armagh. He referred to them sarcastically as the Orders of Caim, an acrostic for Carmelites, Augustinians, Iacobites (Dominicans), and Minorites. He charged them with defrauding the parish priests of their rightful duties and emoluments.

Wyclif regarded the priestly office as higher and nobler than civil rule, on the ground that it dealt with matters of eternal import, not merely with mundane concerns. Since Christ refused all civil rule for Himself, it is heresy for the prelates to claim that they inherited it from Him. Christ did not die for worldly gain; therefore, the clergy do not derive temporal rule from Him, but from Caesar. Peter received from the Lord spiritual, not temporal, dominion.[61] It is likewise heresy for the pope to claim that he is above all human judgment and that every Christian and every Church in the world must obey his commands, and that he can bind and loose as he pleases.[62] Wyclif opposed all human traditions then currently preferred to gospel laws: these were papal bulls, decretals, canonizations inspired by avarice or other unworthy motives, and all acts of the Holy See which were regarded as binding as the gospels.

Reformation of the Church was, naturally, the duty of the hierarchy. However, since the prelates, from the pope down to the bishops and abbots, were often the

---

[59] *De ecclesia*, p. 571: "Quam ergo excusationem haberet qui a dampnatione perpetua posset proximum liberare quem debet diligere ut se ipsum, et tamen sine ratione omittit?"

[60] *Ibid.*, pp. 564-566, 570-571.

[61] *Ibid.*, pp. 300-301, 305, 323-324, 365.

[62] *Ibid.*, pp. 357-358, 353.

worst offenders, remedy had to be sought from the secular rulers. He regarded the latter as vicars of Christ's divine nature, while the clergy represented His human nature.[63] Wyclif worked out his theory of dominion in two works: *De dominio divino* (1375) and *De civili dominio* (1376). In the first of these he developed the theory already advocated by Archbishop Fitz-Ralph, that God is the supreme Lord over all. All human possessions and dominion rest upon the divine lordship, and are conditioned upon grace. Man is thus, in a thoroughly feudal fashion, a vassal of God, holding whatever power or property he possesses as a fief from God. In the second treatise this theory is applied to rulers, both civil and ecclesiastical. Their power derives directly from God. If they are in mortal sin and thus not in the state of grace, they deprive themselves of the divinely conditioned right to hold the lordship. It does not mean, as it is often perverted to mean, that they do not or cannot exercise their power any further. They do so, however, *de facto* and not *de jure divino*; not rightfully, "from dignity and merit, but as it were by usurping their powers contrary to the divine suzerainty." They are thus unfaithful vassals, holding their "fiefs" wrongfully, but nevertheless securely. Their right to lordship, based on human constitutions, is not thereby affected or annihilated. Wyclif's theory of divine lordship is a spiritual concept, not a legal theory.[64] Nevertheless, when ecclesiastical rulers grossly abuse their offices, the secular lords have as a last resort the right to deprive them of posses-

[63] A. W. Pollard, ed., *Dialogus sive speculum ecclesie militantis* (London, The Wyclif Society, 1886), pp. 71f.; *De officio regis* (see n. 46), p. 13.

[64] Kaminsky (see n. 34) argues, "It is this aspect of his doctrine which justifies calling it an ideology of revolution" (p. 69); also John Stacey, *John Wyclif and Reform* (Philadelphia, The Westminster Press, 1964), pp. 62-66.

sions of which they are stewards, not masters.[65] For the secular rulers have the duty "to destroy vices and establish virtues in themselves and others."[66] But how to make certain that the secular rulers themselves are righteous or "in grace," Wyclif does not say. Is it not likely that they would despoil the Church to enrich themselves? This view is the sheerest academic theorizing utterly unrelated to the undoubtedly difficult practical situation of Wyclif's or of any other day. The best that can be said is that it had no appreciable effect on the course of events.

The most heinous of Wyclif's heresies, in the estimation of his contemporaries, was his denial of the dogma of transubstantiation. He arrived at this conclusion only gradually. It was definitely formulated in his treatise *De eucharistia* in 1380. He repudiated the dogma adopted by the Fourth Lateran Council in 1215, that the bread and wine were *transubstantiated*, their substance changed into the body and blood of the Lord, although their accidents remained unchanged. It was impossible, in accordance with his realistic philosophy, that the substance of any real object be annihilated while only the accidents continued to exist.[67] As explained earlier, any real thing is but the material objectification of a divine idea; as such, it cannot cease to exist any more than can the divine idea constituting it. This, then, was his doctrine of "remanence." Wyclif did not, however, thereby deny the real

[65] R. L. Poole, ed., *Johannis Wycliffe De civili dominio* (London, The Wyclif Society, 1885), I, chapters 3, 11, 35.

[66] *De potestate papae* (see n. 50), p. 10.

[67] William of Ockham (c. 1300-49) originally held a doctrine concerning the eucharist similar to Wyclif's, and asserted that transubstantiation was not Scriptural. Later, however, he taught that it was "divinely revealed" to the Fathers, and defined authoritatively by the Roman Church. He attacked the notion that after the consecration the accidents inhere in *quantitas*. They are sustained free of substance by the sheer power of God. Cf. his *Quodlibeta septem una cum tractatu de sacramento altaris* (Strassburg, 1491).

presence of the body and blood of Christ in the sacrament; in fact, he asserted it in unequivocal language. Its presence is not material, but *sacramental*. He writes: "Thus we agree that we do not see the body in that sacrament with the bodily eye, but rather with the eye of the mind, that is, in faith, through a mirror darkly. . . . Thus when we see the host, we ought to believe not that it is itself the body of Christ, but that the body of Christ is sacramentally concealed in it."[68] It follows, therefore, that the priest does not "create the body of the Lord" in the mass. "Nothing can be more awful than that any priest can daily make or consecrate the body of the Lord by saying the Mass. For our God is not a God newly made; nor is his body, since it is supremely holy and everlasting, thus sacramentally or freshly created."[69]

Wyclif denies that his doctrine is something new, invented by himself. Indeed, he insists that the official doctrine is the innovation of the *moderni*, and that he has but restored the doctrine of the ancient Church. He particularly appeals to "the triple witness" of such eminent Church fathers as Augustine, Ambrose, and Anselm. It was Pope Innocent III, Thomas Aquinas, and Duns Scotus who had departed from the ancient faith, not he.

Furthermore, this doctrine of the sacramental real presence of the body and blood of the Lord under the form of bread and wine is not "consubstantiation," as it is often called. There are not two "substances" present in the sacrament, but only one—that of the bread and wine. The Lord's body is not present "substantially," but only sacramentally, spiritually. Therefore, it is not the substance of the Lord's body of which the com-

68 Spinka, *Advocates of Reform*, pp. 62, 64. The text was translated by F. L. Battles.
69 *Ibid.*, p. 65.

municant partakes; that can be received only by faith.

Wyclif also denounces indulgences as then practiced, said to be based on the inexhaustible treasury of the supererogatory merits of Christ and the saints at the disposal of the pope. He denies that such a "treasury" exists at all. Forgiveness of sins depend wholly on true contrition of the penitent, and is granted by God.[70]

During the latter years of Wyclif's life, after he had left Oxford and had retired to his pastoral charge at Lutterworth, many of his former friends abandoned him. His opponents, particularly of the mendicant orders, now raised clamorous and insidious demands for his condemnation. Even prior to this time Bishop Courtenay of London had twice cited Wyclif for a trial, but failed to have him convicted, once because of the support of John of Gaunt, Duke of Lancaster, and the second time on account of the outcry of the London populace. In 1382, Courtenay, then already the Archbishop of Canterbury, convened a synod at the Blackfriar Convent which, without citing or mentioning Wyclif by name, condemned twenty-four conclusions presumably drawn from his and his adherents' teachings. Ten of these were declared heretical, while the remaining fourteen were pronounced "erroneous and against the decision of the Church."[71] It is, nevertheless, remarkable that although the archbishop energetically prosecuted Wyclif's close friends at Oxford until all of them recanted, Wyclif himself was not molested. He continued to busy himself with his writings and the training of his "Lollards," the itinerant evangelists who based their preaching on the English Bible translated by Wyclif's collaborators. It was while engaged in such labors that he suffered a

---

[70] *De potestate papae*, p. 208.

[71] The twenty-four theses are cited in full in Workman (see n. 34), II, pp. 416-417. The text is also given in the Appendix of this work.

stroke during the Christmas service and died on the last day of December 1384.

Knowledge of Wyclif's teaching was carried to Bohemia by the Czech students at Oxford. Their numbers increased considerably after Princess Anne, King Wenceslas' sister, married the English king, Richard II (1382). The marriage had been arranged by Cardinal Pileo de Prata, who certainly did not foresee what religious consequences it would have in Bohemia! It must be particularly stressed that prior to 1400 only the philosophical works of Wyclif were known at the University of Prague. Jerome of Prague, who had studied at Oxford and received the master's degree there, brought some of them upon his return home. The English theologian's ideas found enthusiastic reception among the Czech university masters because they powerfully stressed and strengthened the indigenous reform. Thus the two streams—the Czech reform and Wyclif's teaching—coalesced without becoming identical. Some of the Czech masters, such as Nicholas of Litomyšl, John of Mýto, and Stanislav of Znojmo, became thoroughgoing philosophical realists. This adherence of the Czechs to realism set them in opposition to the German masters who, as a rule, were nominalists. Hus' teachers completely won their gifted pupil for Wyclif's philosophical creed, along with many other Czech students, particularly Hus' close friends, Stephen Páleč and Jakoubek of Stříbro. The latter, however, remained basically true to the teachings of Matthew of Janov. Hus became thoroughly acquainted with Wyclif's books, which he read avidly and assimilated substantially. He wrote in 1411 that he "and other members of our university possessed and have read those books for twenty or more years." That points to the year 1391,[72] and in-

---

[72] *Historia et Monumenta Joannis Hus atque Hieronymi Pragensis, confessorum Christi*, 2 vols. (Norimberg, 1715, a reprint of the original edition of 1558), I, p. 135.

dicates that during his student and teaching years he knew only Wyclif's philosophical works. Hus even copied some of the treatises, namely *De individuatione temporis, De ideis, De materia et forma,* and *De universalibus.* In the margins of the last-named book, now preserved at Stockholm, he wrote approving remarks, such as: "Wyclif, Wyclif, you will unsettle many a man's mind"; or "What you have now read is worth a gulden . . ."; and "May God grant Wyclif the kingdom of heaven!"

Let us, therefore, turn our attention to Hus' teachers. The most influential among them were Stanislav of Znojmo and Stephen of Kolín. Stanislav was the acknowledged leader of the realists among the Czech masters. He gained fame for his own writings as well. In fact, one of his treatises, *De universalibus* (c. 1396), was mistaken for Wyclif's and published as such among the writings of the Oxford professor.[73] Stanislav, like Wyclif, argues that ideas are archetypes in God's mind according to which he creates individual things. Thus the universal truths exist prior to men's thinking of them. There are three universals in individual things—genus, species, and distinction—which alone are substantial.[74] He denies that realistic philosophy involves pantheism; indeed, he argues that it is useful in supporting Christian doctrines. Sedlák praises Stanislav's treatise highly, asserting that "no other philosophical work compares with it."[75] Hus always spoke of his teacher with genuine appreciation and high esteem even after Stanislav became his bitter enemy. Páleč bears testimony that Hus

[73] M. H. Dziewicki, ed., Wyclif's *Miscellanea philosophica,* 3 vols. (London, The Wyclif Society, 1902-05), II, pp. 1-151; cf. also Sedlák, *Jan Hus* (see n. 19), supplement VII, "Mgri. Stanislai de Znoyma Tractatus de universalis realibus."

[74] Sedlák, *Studie a texty* (see n. 17), II, p. 201, n. 5: ". . . patet tria et solum tria esse universalia substancialia in individuo, sc. genue, differenciam et speciem."

[75] *Ibid.,* p. 202.

held Stanislav "as if there was no one like him under the sun." When Hus matriculated in the faculty of theology, Stanislav again was his teacher there, having by that time secured his doctorate in theology. Nevertheless, Hus did not follow his beloved teacher in all respects: he refused to accept the doctrine of remanence which Stanislav taught at first. Of that, however, we shall speak later.

Another of Hus' most influential teachers was Master Stephen of Kolín (1360-1407).[76] Of his early life practically nothing is known. The first mention of him occurs in 1383 when he received his master's degree. He became provost of Charles College in 1390 and two years later served as dean of the arts faculty. Since membership in Charles College entailed the duty of the study of theology, Stephen matriculated in that faculty in 1389, although he continued his career in the faculty of arts. The most outstanding theological professors were then Albert Engelschalk and Matthew of Cracow; it is not known, however, what influence they exercised upon Stephen. He was also appointed canon of the College of All Saints, and later became professor of theology. Stephen thus had been Hus' teacher not only during the latter's undergraduate years, but also during his theological studies. Stephen became preacher of the Bethlehem Chapel in 1396 and retained that post until his resignation in 1402, when he was succeeded by Hus.[77] This is another indication of the close relation between the two men, as the nomination to the post was in the hands of the Czech university masters, among whom Stephen undoubtedly had the decisive voice in the choice of his successor. Thus he recognized Hus not only as an elo-

[76] For the fullest treatment, cf. O. Odložilik, *M. Štepán z Kolína* (Praha, 1924); also Havránek, *Výbor* (see n. 21), pp. 80-84.

[77] For an extract from one of his sermons, cf. De Vooght, *Hussiana* (see n. 18), pp. 358ff.

quent and effective preacher, but also as a zealous pro-
moter of the reform movement.

Stephen's views are preserved only in two sermons and
more formally in his *Lectura super Yzaiam prophetam*
and a *Confessional* prepared by him for the use of priests
administering the sacrament of penance. Perhaps we
may be allowed to go beyond the chronological limits of
this chapter in order to present a more complete view
of Stephen's teaching, admitting that some of the influence on Hus implied by it was exerted later. In the first
sermon Stephen exhorts clergy to "walk carefully, not
as unwise men but as wise."[78] The majority of priests,
however, live unworthily in luxury and adultery, and thus
become joined with harlots rather than with Christ. He
denounces their selling of indulgences, excessive beauti-
fication of churches with paintings and gold, while they
let the poor die of hunger. They are not shepherds but
shearers of their sheep. They lack adequate education
for their high office and thus give wrong example to the
lay people. These ideas all correspond to those of Milíč
and Matthew of Janov. The *Confessional* of Stephen is
devoted to the same reform aims. It contains an extensive account of how the priest should conduct the confessional. Confession should be made primarily and as
a rule to a priest, but may also be made to a layman.
Even the latter kind of confession may bring God's forgiveness, although the layman cannot grant the absolution. There then follows an exposition of the Decalogue,
with which Stephen dealt very much as Hus did later.
Finally, in his *Lecture on the Prophet Isaiah*, of which
only a portion is extant, Stephen deals, in the spirit of
Matthew of Janov and Matthew of Cracow, with clerical
degeneracy. He turns to the clergy, rebuking their immorality and avarice:

[78] Eph. 5:15.

The clamor of simony openly rises to heaven because of its obviousness. Some even are accustomed to request unblushingly: "Bring, bring, give the fee, pay down the fee; we will not bury the dead unless you give three, four, or five *grossi!*" Simony, which is the greatest heresy, is publicly committed in the streets and there is no one to rebuke, no one to forbid it![79]

Stephen scathingly rebukes the authorities who often prefer the unworthy and ill-prepared to worthy candidates for benefices. He also complains that lay people not only refuse to listen to a zealous reforming preacher but even denounce him. He advocates a return to deeper and more genuine piety and deplores the excessively ornate and showy ceremonies in church services. The superstitious and inordinate worship of saints also comes in for stern words of scorn. He writes in his *Lecture on Isaiah* that some resort to special prayers against an evil death; some pray that the Virgin may appear to them; some pray to St. Catherine; but they do not correct their lives. He places the greatest emphasis on the study of Scripture. Altogether, he is entirely orthodox in his doctrinal views, as is particularly shown in his rejection of Wyclif's doctrine of remanence. Odložilík summarizes his judgment of Stephen by saying that "Hus' activity is for a considerable time analogous to and continuous with the activity of Stephen of Kolín."[80]

We conclude, then, that Hus, during his student and academic career in the arts faculty, became a thoroughly convinced and even enthusiastic realist in his philosophical views. This conviction he derived not only from his teachers, but also from his independent study of Wyclif. He confessed later that this study of Wyclif "opened his eyes." He was not, however, a "Wyclifite" in

[79] Novotný, *Náboženské hnutí*, p. 243.

[80] Odložilík (see n. 76), p. 44; my whole summary of Stephen's life and views is based on Odložilík's work, pp. 6-23.

the usual sense of sharing the Oxford reformer's doctrinal views indiscriminately and uncritically. Despite his lifelong adherence to and defense of Wyclif's doctrinally acceptable teaching, he passed over, usually without calling attention to the omission, the views of the English master divergent from orthodoxy. We shall have occasion to notice this practice of Hus' on many occasions later. At first Hus' adherence to Wyclif involved only the latter's philosophical views, for no others were available. It was only after Jerome of Prague brought (soon after 1400) the *Trialogus,* the *De eucharistia,* the *Dialogus,* and the *De simonia* to Prague that acquaintance with these theological works was possible. Hus himself expressly declared at the Council of Constance, in answering the question as to why he had spoken well of Wyclif (June 7, 1415), that "twelve years ago, before Wyclif's theological books had been available in Bohemia, and his books dealing with liberal arts he had much approved of, and he had known nothing of his life but what was good . . . ," he had wished that his soul were where Wyclif's soul was.[81] Thus Hus was consciously committed to the indigenous reform ideals, although, along with most of the other Czech masters, he became an ardent adherent of Wyclifite realist philosophy. When he later learned of Wyclif's theological views, he invariably and consistently discriminated between those he judged acceptable from the orthodox point of view and those of which he tacitly disapproved. In view of the indiscriminate and still current assumption that he was a thoroughgoing "Wyclifite" even in the doctrinal sense, implying that any tenet of Wyclif adopted by Hus was necessarily "heretical," Hus' discriminating attitude toward Wyclif cannot be overstressed.

[81] Mladoňovic, *Relatio* (see n. 13), p. 78; translated by Matthew Spinka, *John Hus at the Council of Constance* (New York, Columbia University Press, 1965), p. 174.

Hus' competent acquaintance with Wyclif does not preclude his thorough knowledge of Thomism and Augustinianism. His promotion addresses afford abundant evidence that his students had been competently trained by him in the philosophy of Aristotle as well as in the classical texts then available. A considerable number of these addresses are extant and give an image of Hus very different from that of a stern reformer.[82] Above all, one must never forget that he acquired a surprisingly comprehensive and consummate mastery of Scripture and its patristic commentators. After all, the only reason he gives for the radical change in his early life is that "when the Lord God gave me the knowledge of Scripture, I abandoned that type of life . . ." (i.e., the previous desire of worldly prosperity). Thus the answer to the question posed earlier as to when the "conversion" of Hus occurred which changed an ambitious seeker of comfortable and secure economic well-being into an earnest and devoted reformer, must be answered primarily in terms of his study of the Bible. In this and other respects his experience was identical with those of Milíč and Matthew of Janov.

[82] Evžen Stein, *M. Jan Hus jako universitní rektor a profesor* (Praha, 1948); also Bohumil Ryba, *Nový Hus* (Praha, 1948).

## CHAPTER II

## CALM BEFORE THE STORM

(1402-1408)

WHEN the twenty-nine-year-old Hus was appointed, on March 14, 1402, preacher of the already
famous center of the Czech reform movement,
the Bethlehem Chapel, he entered upon the most important phase of his life. He became the leader of the
Czech populace supporting the reform. The chapel had
been founded in 1391 by two admirers and supporters
of Milíč—John of Milheim, the king's courtier, and the
merchant Kříž, the Old Town councilor. Kříž, being
fairly wealthy, donated for the purpose the garden located behind his house. It was adjacent to the parish
church of Sts. Philip and James. In order to secure a
sufficiently large building lot, a part of the parish cemetery had to be included in it. When the chapel was
erected on the premises, parts of an old building previously standing there were incorporated into the new
structure. They served mainly as the cellar under the
auditorium. An accurate idea of the size of this structure
may be gathered from its reconstruction, completed in
1953; it is capable of accommodating an audience of
3,000 people. During the reconstruction, the remains of
the original chapel, including even the badly damaged
inscription placed on the walls by Hus, were discovered.
After a most exhaustive study of all the available evidence as to the original form, the chapel was faithfully
restored.[1] The central object of the auditorium is the
square wooden pulpit, raised on a stout pillar, placed

[1] The full description of the restored chapel, with a detailed
treatment of its original form, is given in Alois Kubíček, *Betlemská
kaple* (Praha, Statní nakladatelství, 1953); for the inscriptions, cf.
B. Ryba, *Betlemské texty* (Praha, Orbis, 1951).

against the northern wall. It could be entered only from the rear through a door connecting it with the preacher's living quarters. The founders gave the chapel the name of Bethlehem (i.e., the house of bread), for it was intended as a continuation of Milíč' Jerusalem. The preaching was to be exclusively in the vernacular, so that the chapel would provide a center for the Czech reform movement. It quickly fulfilled this purpose: the Czech population of Prague—a city of some 50,000 inhabitants —thronged to its services regularly. Sermons were given twice on Sundays and on all saints' days, although during the advent and fast days only once. Since it is safe to estimate the number of holydays at a hundred annually, Hus had to prepare some two hundred and fifty sermons a year. During his ten-year ministry at Bethlehem, he would have preached more than two thousand five hundred sermons.[2] Besides, Hus introduced daily preaching, although later an assistant assumed some of the burden of this astonishingly ambitious program. Thus it may be confidently asserted that Hus became the leader of the popular reform movement and gained an eminence in this respect that no other preacher could equal. Stanislav of Znojmo and Stephen Páleč, however, continued as leaders of the academic phase of the reform.

Hus had preached for a year prior to his appointment to Bethlehem Chapel. He had been preaching at the Church of St. Michael in the Old Town. His preaching there had attracted large crowds of hearers. The pulpit at Bethlehem, as mentioned previously, had then been occupied by Stephen of Kolín. He resigned the post perhaps as the result of the controversy with Nicholas Zeiselmeister, pastor of the parish church of Sts. Philip and James. Since the chapel was located within this

[2] Flajšhans estimates that Hus, during his entire preaching career of twelve years, wrote about 3,000 sermons. V. Flajšhans, *Mistra Jana Husi Sebrané spisy* (Praha, n.d.), VI, postscript p. iv.

parish, and in fact occupied a corner of its ground, it had been originally agreed between the founders and the then pastor that he be reimbursed by the payment of 90 *grossi* annually. When Zeiselmeister became pastor of the parish, he demanded an increased payment. He secured it by a new contract granting him twice the previous sum.

We are fortunate to possess the sermons Hus preached during most of his ministry at Bethlehem (not counting the *Postil* he wrote in exile). These sermons comprise twelve volumes, and even so some still await publication. The earliest sermons represent his preaching of the first two years at Bethlehem, perhaps including those of 1401.[3] They are limited, however, to the sermons preached on saints' days. They were not written down by Hus himself, but were presumably recorded in shorthand by one of his hearers. There is no doubt of his having preached them except for the last, which was probably copied from some other source, and one other copied from some *Passio*. A number of later interpolations are easily recognizable, for one refers to the communion under both bread and wine, and another to the Council of Constance. The editor, Dr. Šimek, writes of these sermons:

Admitting that the few above-mentioned passages in the Strahov MS. are later interpolations, we shall find in the sermons here comprised nothing which is not dogmatically orthodox, nor a single trace of Wyclif's influence. It is necessary, therefore, to place them within the first period of Hus' preaching activity, i.e., to years 1401-03, when Hus preached either in the Church of St. Michael in the Old Town of Prague (1401) or already in the Bethlehem Chapel. . . . If these presuppositions of mine are correct, then in these

[3] F. Šimek, ed., *Mistr Jan Hus, Česká kázání sváteční* (Praha, Blahoslav, n.d.).

sermons of the Strahov MS. is preserved for us a precious memorial—*Hus' oldest Czech sermons.*[4]

A similar testimony is borne by Jan Sedlák, who usually sees Hus' "Wyclifism" even where there is none. Of these sermons of 1401-03 he testified, albeit with a trace of pejorative undertone:

> . . . these sermons contain mere moralistic exposi-
> tions. . . . Toward the clergy Hus assumes a reform
> stance from the beginning. . . . Nothing harms re-
> ligious life as much [he says] as the sins of the priests.
> His temperament, which does not allow him to remain
> silent about faults, induces him to rebuke them pub-
> licly. . . . As to the doctrinal aspect, Hus appears to
> us in this Postil an entirely orthodox catholic priest.
> He propounds plain catholic doctrine and expounds
> it without anywhere expressing any doubt about it.[5]

Turning now to the sermons themselves, we shall analyze them principally from the point of view of Hus' concern for Church reform and his concept of the Church. They are characterized by earnest exhortations "to follow Christ." He addresses himself primarily to the lay people. Far from being mere moralistic appeals, as Sedlák asserts, they are an urgent demand for genuine spiritual transformation. Hus deals with various aspects of moral conduct, but always stresses motives rather than outward actions. He appeals to Paul's exhortation: ". . . be renewed in the spirit of your minds and put on the new nature."[6] Elsewhere Hus warns that "all other speaking is vain if this uncreated Word [Christ] will not speak within the heart and teach the soul."[7]

Although hortatory appeals predominate, Hus is not

[4] *Ibid.*, pp. xliii-xliv.

[5] Jan Sedlák, "Husův vývoj dle jeho postil," *Studie a texty k náboženským dějinám českým* (Olomouc, 1914-15), II, pp. 397f.

[6] Eph. 4:23-24.　　　　　[7] Šimek (see n. 3), p. 83.

*45*

sparing of denunciations not only of ordinary sinners in his congregation but of kings and nobles as well. He rebukes the latter that in their courts and palaces "much evil and injustice is committed. There is no fear of God among them, but numberless blasphemies against God and various sins are committed by them, as in dancing, lewd behavior, excessive pride, obscene and promiscuous fornication and adultery, drunkenness, and other countless wickednesses."[8]

In dealing with man's lost state, Hus holds the doctrine then current that although the natural virtues, such as reason, were not altogether lost in the Fall, man was bereft of the spiritual virtues of faith, hope, and love. These must then be recovered. The Church provides ample means for their restoration. First of all, baptism cleanses the soul of all sins and guilt, both original and acquired. He traces the healing power of baptism to the pierced side of Jesus' body: "From thence gushed blood and water. This signifies that we are cleansed in our souls by the water of holy baptism, which derives its potency through the shedding of the blood of the Lord."[9] This Hus calls "the spiritual birth." Baptism, which is efficacious for both infants and adults, opens "the gates of the heavenly kingdom to all believers in Christ."

Hus likewise deals extensively with the sacrament of the body and blood of Christ. Even in these early sermons he warns against the view that these sacred elements may be visibly perceived. According to Christ's own declaration, to eat His body sacramentally under the appearance of bread and to drink His blood means to dwell in Him and to have Him dwell in us. For He said: "Whoever eats my body and drinks my blood, abides in me and I in him."[10] There are three kinds of communion: the first is spiritual, of which the saints in

[8] *Ibid.*, p. 127.　　[9] *Ibid.*, p. 115.　　[10] John, 6:56.

heaven and men without mortal sin partake. The second is merely sacramental, partaken of by men in mortal sin. The third is both spiritual and sacramental, in which a man without mortal sin "receives the body of God at first spiritually and then sacramentally. But evil men do not receive it; for they partake of it only sacramentally to their condemnation."[11]

There are ten effects of communion: remembrance of the death of Christ; cleansing from all sins, both venial and mortal; confirmation in virtues; lessening of sinful desires; feeding of the soul; strengthening the soul; affording comfort; reviving the soul; granting grace; and bestowing life eternal.[12]

As for the concept of the Church, there is no specific definition of it in these sermons. Hus nevertheless refers fairly often to "the elect" (never to the congregation of believers) as constituting the membership of the Church. In commenting on the Prologue of John's Gospel, he declares that God sent His Son "in order to win for Him elect sons, desiring to give them His inheritance. . . . Scripture reads: 'Whoever are born of God,' i.e., by His eternal election, 'are born of Him and derive from Him like the rays from the sun. . . .' "[13] In another sermon he speaks of the election as being secret, so that no one can be certain whether or not he is of the chosen number.

Four of the sermons are devoted to the Virgin Mary; one of them deals with her assumption into heaven. Hus refers to her as "the Queen of heaven," "the Mother of the Almighty God," "the Queen of the world and the angels," and by other of her titles current at the time. He asserts that she was ever-Virgin, having no other children save Jesus. He appeals to virgins to emulate her in her virginal state.

[11] Šimek (see n. 3), p. 96.    [12] *Ibid.*, pp. 97-99.
[13] *Ibid.*, p. 89.

As has already been mentioned, the sermons are principally addressed to lay hearers. Nevertheless, priests, prelates, and the university masters are likewise at times included. They are exhorted to be faithful in the discharge of their sacred duties and reprimanded for their frequent failing to live up to their high calling. In a sermon dealing with the call to Andrew to become Christ's disciple, Hus comments on Christ's charge to his disciples: "I command you to be fishers of men . . . to be hunters of human souls, not of benefices, of bodily pleasures, of vainglory, of carnal desires or delights. . . . That hunting is nothing else than the salvation of Christ's sheep. . . . Such is indeed being a fisher of men, a preacher of God's truth; such is being a shepherd."[14] Hus continues by defining the marks of a true priest:

> Thus all who are sent by God may be recognized by the fact whether they seek the glory of God and the salvation of men. It matters little to inquire whether one is sent by a pope or a bishop or whether he has certain papers or confirmations. Instead we should recognize that he is sent of God when he diligently seeks the salvation of men and the praise of God.[15]

He furthermore asserts that priests should live lives of voluntary poverty, citing I Tim. 6:8: "If we have food and clothing, let us be content therewith."

In all this Hus obviously follows the ethical aims of his predecessors. He urges reformation of men's lives, not of doctrine. Nor does he exceed this rôle when he castigates priests for failing to live up to their duties. Priests, who on account of human favor fail to rebuke and chastise men's sins but instead flatter them for their own benefit and gain, are unfaithful to their office. In the sermon dealing with the parable of the wise and foolish virgins, Hus declares as foolish those who "buy

---

[14] *Ibid.*, p. 34.    [15] *Ibid.*, pp. 86-87.

indulgences, masses, and [entrance into] monastic orders, wishing to be pious by the piety of others, to be good by the goodness of others, and to be righteous by the righteousness of others. . . . Therefore, the indulgences, masses, and monkish orders will profit them nothing."[16]

The duties of prelates are described in the sermon on St. Nicholas' day. They are to provide their clergy with four kinds of food: salutary example, proper instruction, material help, and the body and blood of the Lord. Prelates are spiritual rulers over their clergy, "but not their masters, nor should they be so called. . . ."

Of the university masters Hus writes in commenting on the verse in John 1:11: "He came to his own and his own received him not." Applying it to the masters, he remarks: "Thus also the present-day spiritual masters and others who received great divine gifts, yet do not receive Christ in his poor, laborious, and humiliated life, but despise Him and others. They crucify Him in themselves again as far as they are able by their evil deeds."[17]

These sermons show Hus as a true heir of his predecessors in the Czech reform movement. In no way do they betray any outside influences. In fact, in comparison with some of the previous reform leaders, Hus' criticisms are mild and restrained. Doctrinally, there is nothing contrary to the then current orthodoxy.

Along with the intensive preaching at the Bethlehem Chapel, Hus also continued his academic activity, having been chosen dean of the faculty of arts during the winter semester of 1401-02. Furthermore, he had matriculated in the faculty of theology. It is astonishing that he found time to attend to all these duties, every single one of which would have required the full time and assiduous labor of most other men. The course in theology required nine or ten years for its completion. Although

16 *Ibid.*, p. 25.      17 *Ibid.*, p. 88.

we do not know when he began the study, it was in 1404 that he attained the grade of bachelor and began the further stage of *baccalarius cursor* or *biblicus* (1404-06). He lectured on seven chapters of Paul's first letter to the Corinthians, on the seven Pastoral Epistles, and on Psalms 109-118. The lectures occupy 380 folio pages of *Historia et Monumenta* II—a very remarkable accomplishment for a man who preached as often as twice a day besides! He then became *baccalarius sententiarius*, and thereafter attained the next rank of *formatus*. During this period (1407-09), he lectured on all four books of Lombard's *Sentences*.[18] Because of controversies with the members of the theological faculty into which he was afterward plunged, Hus never proceeded any further in his theological course and thus failed to gain the doctor's degree.

The situation at the university changed abruptly when on May 28, 1403, Master John Hübner, a Silesian German, sent to the archiepiscopal office as heretical twenty-four articles of Wyclif, already condemned at the London Blackfriar Synod (1382), to which he added twenty-one additional articles selected by himself.[19] The archiepiscopal officials requested the university to pronounce an opinion on the articles. The meeting at which they were presented to the university masters was an exceedingly stormy one. The Czech masters attended *en masse*, well aware that the attack was directed against them. It was the first time, at least officially, that their philosophical realism had been impugned as a theological deviation from orthodoxy. The German masters, predominantly nominalists, sought to discredit realism by practically

[18] V. Flajšhans, ed., *M. John Hus, Super IV Sententiarum*, 3 vols. (Praha, 1904-06); a Czech translation of this work, by Milan Svoboda, is in M. Svoboda–V. Flajšhans, *Mistra Jana Husi Sebrané spisy* (Praha, n.d.), III.

[19] The text of the forty-five articles is given in Appendix I.

identifying it with heresy. Moreover, the Czech masters regarded all forty-five articles, including those excerpted by Hübner, as falsified. Nicholas of Litomyšl openly charged Hübner with bias. This opinion was shared by the Czech masters generally, including Hus, who retained it to the end of his life.[20] Stanislav of Znojmo and Stephen Páleč were the chief spokesmen for the Czech masters. At the meeting, Páleč threw one of Wyclif's books—perhaps *De universalibus*—on the table and loudly exclaimed: "Let anyone stand up and attack a single word in it, and I will defend it!"[12] Stanislav, the leader of the Czech masters, went even further and declared that the articles were not heretical or erroneous.[22] Nevertheless, since the Germans were in the majority, they easily secured victory. The holding or teaching of the forty-five articles was forbidden. This prohibition, however, was not an official ecclesiastical condemnation, since the university judgment could not be regarded as equivalent to an ecclesiastical verdict of heresy. Moreover, Wyclif's books continued to be read and taught.

Henceforth, the forty-five articles became the test of orthodoxy or heterodoxy. To my knowledge, no one has made a critical study or an extensive comparison between them and the actual teachings of Wyclif to ascertain whether they had been correctly excerpted or interpreted. These articles and Wyclif's actual doctrine were persistently confused throughout this period and have been ever since. Whenever Hus was found to have used any of Wyclif's writings, no matter how acceptable the quotations, it was triumphantly pointed out as a proof of his

[20] F. Palacký, ed., *Documenta Mag. Joannis Hus* (Praha, F. Tempský, 1869), p. 179.

[21] Hus himself reports it in "Contra Paletz," *Historia et monumenta Joannis Hus atque Hieronymi Pragensis, confessorum Christi,* 2 vols. (Norimberg, 1715), I, p. 324.

[22] V. Novotný, *Jan Hus Život a dílo,* 2 vols. (Praha, Jan Laichter, 1919), I, pp. 110-111.

"Wyclifism." No doubt he was an admirer and defender of Wyclif, but not in the sense of the forty-five articles!

By the end of the year Stanislav had written a treatise, *De corpore Christi*, openly defending the doctrine of remanence. This intrepid espousal of Wyclif's theological views made him and Páleč, who likewise shared them, no longer exponents of mere philosophical realism, but full-fledged defenders of the English reformer's theological doctrine. But not all Czech masters followed them in this. Stephen of Kolín, for instance, never accepted remanence and openly declared his faithful adherence to the dogma of transubstantiation. Hus likewise remained sturdily firm in his adherence to that dogma. He would have done better had he also clearly declared his nonadherence to or outright rejection of all the articles with which he disagreed. Instead, he persisted in the method of asserting his own views with clearness and conviction, but passing over in silence the tenets he rejected or modifying them in such a way as to make them entirely innocuous and free of wrong connotation. His unscrupulous opponents took advantage of this and charged him indiscriminately with Wyclifism as a whole. Thus, for instance, his own long-time friend, Stephen Páleč, when he abandoned Wyclifism and became Hus' most formidable foe, audaciously accused him of Wyclif's heresies. On that occasion Hus stoutly declared:

> I indeed confess that I hold the true opinions which Master John Wyclif, professor of sacred theology, declared, not because he declared them, but because Scripture and infallible reason declare them. If, however, he taught any error, I do not in any way imitate him or anyone else in the error.[23]

We shall have occasion to call attention to this critically

[23] "Contra Paletz," in *Historia et monumenta* (see n. 21), I, p. 330.

discriminating attitude of Hus toward Wyclif through-out this work.

Nevertheless, it was probably Hus who shortly after-ward wrote Hübner a letter[24] in which he chided him for having called Wyclif a heretic, because in his writ-ings he had dealt with heresies. By the same reasoning, Hus commented, Augustine, Peter Lombard, and Thom-as Aquinas could also be called heretics. Further, Hüb-ner stated that Wyclif had called "the holy mother Church the synagogue of Satan." Hus replied bluntly that this was not true. "If perhaps you read it in your book, it is an error. You have either not read it correctly or having scanned it, you did not remember it well. For it does not follow that since the Roman curia is the synagogue of Satan, therefore the holy mother Church is the synagogue of Satan. . . ."

Stanislav's treatise advocating remanence promptly called forth an attack on him by a Cistercian, Dr. John Štěkna of Cracow, who had most likely been encouraged by the Prague canons. The young archbishop, Zbyněk, could not ignore the attack. The twenty-five-year-old Zbyněk Zajíc of Hasenburk had secured the designation to the vacant archiepiscopal see in November 1402, al-though he did not assume the full duties of office until May 1403. He had been designated for the ecclesiastical career from childhood. At the age of fourteen he was granted the rich provostship of Mělník coupled with the position of canon in the St. Vitus' Cathedral. However, his training was more military than ecclesiastical. Since he himself was but indifferently versed in the duties of the highest ecclesiastical office in the land, he leaned heavily on the advice of others. Fortunately for the re-

---

[24] V. Novotný, *M. Jana Husi Korespondence a dokumenty* (Praha, 1920), No. 6. He identifies the anonymous writer of the letter with Hus. Jan Sedlák ascribes the letter to Stanislav. Cf. his *M. Jan Hus* (Praha, Dědictví sv. Prokopa, 1915), supplement VIII.

form movement, he was favorably inclined toward it, perhaps because King Wenceslas was, and Zbyněk's sister had married John of Milheim, one of the founders of the Bethlehem Chapel. At any rate, he chose its leaders, particularly Hus, to advise him of anything requiring correction. Hus himself reminded him of this in July 1408, when he wrote: "I very often recall that in the beginning of your administration Your Paternity set up the rule for me that whenever I should observe any defect, I should announce it to you immediately in person or, if absent, by letter."[25] Zbyněk even appointed Hus one of the preachers at the synodical meetings of the clergy.

When the conflict over Wyclifism was precipitated by Štěkna, Zbyněk could not but submit the complaint to a commission, which, of course, declared the charge well founded. Nevertheless, Stanislav was permitted to state whether he had proposed the doctrine of remanence *more scholastico* as a subject of discussion, or as his personal conviction. Stanislav took advantage of the opportunity to affirm the former interpretation. He even "completed" the treatise by adding arguments which negated the assertion of remanence presented and defended in the original version, by confessing his adherence to transubstantiation. Zbyněk declared himself satisfied with Stanislav's obviously insincere evasion. Not so his onetime pupil, Jakoubek of Stříbro. He was so aroused by the unheroic conduct of his teacher that he wrote a treatise of his own, boldly declaring his adherence to remanence. Fortunately, it either did not come to the archbishop's attention or was wisely ignored.

Nevertheless, Zbyněk issued a synodical prohibition against holding or teaching that after the consecration of the elements *anything else* than the body and blood of Christ remained in the sacrament. He even forbade the

[25] Novotný, *Korespondence* (see n. 24), No. 11.

use of the words "bread or wine" in this connection.[26] Anyone who should transgress the order was declared a heretic and was to be punished as such. Although Hus did not share his teacher's views in this matter, yet he felt this pronouncement of the archbishop as a blow at the prestige of the reformist party. Moreover, Zbyněk's definition was doctrinally unsound. Hus therefore wrote a treatise (1406), *De corpore Christi,*[27] intended to present the orthodox catholic position on this dogma. In it he explained that what remained in the sacrament after the consecration was not the body and blood of Christ *alone*, but also the transubstantiated bread. He quoted passages where Christ called himself "the bread come down from heaven," said, "I am the bread of life," and made other similar statements. He also cited Paul: "Whenever ye shall eat this bread. . . ." He further objected to the view of those who regarded the consecrated elements as material and, consequently, as capable of being touched and eaten as if they were the physical body of the Lord. This was implied in the proverbial Czech and German saying, "I have seen the body of God." Hus quoted Augustine's saying that what we visibly perceive is the sacrament, while the body and blood of Christ remain invisible. Dom Paul de Vooght writes most appreciatively of this treatise, testifying that it presents "the two fundamental ideas of the catholic doctrine of eucharist: the real presence and the sacramental character . . . the *substantial* presence of Christ under the *accidents* of bread and wine."[28] He recommends that it be put into the hands of seminarists, for not even their professors could explain the doctrine more clearly.

26 Palacký, *Documenta* (see n. 20), p. 335.

27 *Historia et monumenta* (see n. 21), I, pp. 202-207.

28 Paul de Vooght, *L'hérésie de Jean Huss* (Louvain, Publications universitaires de Louvain, 1960), p. 63.

Nevertheless, the attack on Stanislav's orthodoxy placed the reform party in a vulnerable position. They did not as yet possess all Wyclif's works, a circumstance which rendered his defense difficult. They sent, therefore, two of their young students, Nicholas Faulfiš and George of Kněhnice, to England with a view to securing copies of Wyclif's works not yet known in Bohemia. They probably failed to find such works at Oxford, which had been zealously "purged" of them. Therefore, they went to places where prominent Lollards resided, such as Kemerton near Tewkesbury and Braybroke in Northamptonshire. There they were successful in their search. They returned to Prague bringing not only many treatises hitherto unknown there, but also a letter from the University of Oxford testifying to Wyclif's orthodoxy and his purity of life. They also brought a piece of stone from Wyclif's monument in Lutterworth, which was reverently treasured by his Czech adherents.

In the meantime, Hus continued to preach at the Bethlehem Chapel. We have the sermons he preached between November 30, 1404 and November 22, 1405. They were recently published, critically edited by Dr. Schmidtová.[29] These sermons illustrate the method used by Hus in preparing himself for preaching. He wrote his sermons in Latin, but preached them in Czech. Unlike the earlier sermons (1401-03), they were actually written down by Hus himself. They are in the form of fairly extensive, finished outlines, comprising an astonishing wealth of Scriptural and patristic quotations. The editor suggests that Hus took a great deal of care to write them out in comparatively full detail because they could thus be copied by other preachers for their own use. She further remarks that there is no trace of Wyclif's in-

[29] Anežka Schmidtová, ed., *Magistri Johannis Hus, Sermones de tempori qui Collecta dicuntur* (Praha, Academia scientiarum Bohemoslovanica, 1959).

fluence; Hus either did not have or know or did not use Wyclif's *Opus evangelicum*.[30]

The style of these and all other sermons of Hus is allegorical, anagogic, and tropological. This style had been, of course, in general use throughout the Middle Ages. One may offer as an illustration the story of Christ's feeding of the multitude. Hus converts the five loaves of the Gospel narrative into "the knowledge of sins, sorrow for the loss of good, shame of committing wrong, the efficient keeping of the heart, and the solicitude for salvation; . . . the two fishes are fear and hope."[31]

As we did with the earlier sermons, let us restrict ourselves again to the items relative to Hus' conception of the Church. The sermons are addressed predominantly to lay hearers. Hus exhorts his audience to strive earnestly for spiritual mastery. The highest aim of Christian life is to love God with complete and absolute commitment. This is done by keeping His commandments and by following Christ in His poverty, humility, and virtues. The beginning of this life of true piety is faith, which precedes all other spiritual acquirements. Love is the final endowment. Faith not eventuating in love is inadequate for salvation. This is indeed good medieval theology, but does not approach Luther's basic insight of "the justification by faith," or rather by grace, without any merit of works. We shall see that Hus regularly insisted that "faith without works is dead," and that salvation is attained only when faith is completed in love

---

[30] *Ibid.*, p. 15. Hus makes an obvious reference to himself in the last sermon (pp. 595-596): "Hec ideo tam longe inserui, quia sensi me per illa contra capciosos et veritatis emulos confortari, quatenus intrepide predicem, quamvis multi conveniant, ut me capiant in sermone . . . Hoc exemplum consideret auca, ne, dum avena coram ea ad manducandum proicitur, intus ad capiendum laqueus abscondatur . . . O discipuli dyaboli, si scitis, quia verax est, cur temptatis, cur veritate capere vultis, cur eius discipuli pocius quam phariseorum non estis?"

[31] *Ibid.*, pp. 155, 158.

[*fides caritate formata*].[32] Thus the Christian life is understood as "walking in the meritorious works of the Beatitudes."

Faith is, nevertheless, a free gift of God. "No one exists to whom God's grace is not freely given."[33] "The first grace is given without merit. . . . The second and third graces are with merit. . . . The fourth is given for merit, as has already been said about works. The first grace illumines the mind initially, the second strengthens penitence, the third offers itself as an offering acceptable to God, and the fourth makes the abundance of godliness in the first grace permanent to the end."[34] Among the graces granted by God is free will. God grants men "a soul capable of discerning between good and evil. . . . He also grants them free will so that no one will be compelled to turn from evil and do good, and by that good merit eternal beatitude. . . . For in this dignity of free choice consists the entire dignity of man."[35]

Although Hus does not offer in these sermons a detailed concept of the Church, it is possible to deduce a concrete idea of his thought from the general references to the subject. He distinguishes between the Church of Christ and Antichrist. In preaching on the text dealing with the son of Sarah and the son of Hagar,[36] Hus writes that Paul "calls the holy Church and its sons all the multitude of the elect, while he calls that of the slave [i.e. Hagar] the church of the wicked and its sons the multitude of the reprobate." Thus he clearly teaches that the true Church is composed solely of the predestinate. The foreknown are members of the Church militant along with the predestinate, but will be separated from the latter in the Day of Judgment. The reprobate are in the Church by divine tolerance, not by "spiritual gen-

32 *Ibid.*, p. 189.    33 *Ibid.*, p. 44.    34 *Ibid.*, p. 122.
35 *Ibid.*, p. 123.    36 Gal. 4:30.

eration." Therefore they shall not inherit along with the elect, "who is the son of promise by the grace of predestination, the son of a free mother by the grace of the call, the spiritual son by the grace of justification, and the son of paternal inheritance by the grace of glorification. . . ."[37] This is an explicit statement of the concept of the Church which Hus continued to hold firmly to the end of his life. It was for *this* Church that Christ had shed His blood:

> Christ has indeed shed His blood for the Church triumphant for the sake of its perfection and joy; for the Church militant for the sake of its redemption, of the infusion of grace and cleansing, and its conformity; and for the Church dormient for the sake of its speedy liberation."[38]

Hus mentions the pope and the cardinals only once: he declares that a pope living contrary to God could be dispossessed by the clergy.[39] He also berates the priests-fornicators who dare celebrate the mass, as well as the priests who "worship the devil" by their avarice, who "for the sake of a full moneybag manufacture relics and 'bleeding' hosts."[40] The latter is an allusion to the priests who perpetrated the "miracle" of the consecrated host that allegedly shed blood. Two such "miracles" had been reported to have occurred at Wilsnack in Brandenburg and at Litomyšl in Bohemia. Hus himself had been appointed to investigate the Wilsnack affair and had found it a fraud. Thus he knew whereof he spoke! He further denounces those priests who have hawked "false indul-

---

[37] Schmidtová, *Collecta* (see n. 29), pp. 150-151.

[38] *Ibid.*, p. 161.

[39] ". . . ut dum papa fieret Deo contrarius et mandaret Deus in vindictam peccati talia per clericum operari. Nec est hoc discernendum, cum ministri Dei possunt in dampnacionem perpetuam papa male viventem detrudere." *Ibid.*, p. 92.

[40] *Ibid.*, p. 130.

gences and relics for the deception of the people and those who concocted visions and other miracles."[41] If the blind populace had understood that these claims were false, they would rather have "elevated their minds to the blood of Christ's body reigning in heaven and have directed their faith to the blood in the venerable sacrament. . . ."[42] He further exhorts the preachers to inveigh "against the seeking of miracles in the Lord's blood and in seeing in the host His physical body; for many desire it, regarding themselves to be thus holier than others."[43]

Finally, preaching on the text in I Cor. 15:1, "I would remind you how I preached to you the gospel. . . ," Hus turns to the priests, once more exhorting them "to preach the gospel, not some entertainment, or fables, or plundering lies, so that the people with attentive minds will accept the gospel and both the preacher and the hearer will be grounded by faith in the gospel; . . . that they both, living well in accordance with the gospel, will be saved."[44]

This is wholesome preaching by a man ineluctably bent on reforming the lives of the people and the clergy. Clerical reform is prerequisite to that of the people. It is in this spirit that Hus preached his sermon, "Love the Lord thy God. . . ," before the synod gathered in the archiepiscopal palace (Oct. 19, 1405).[45] In it he exhorts the clergy to seek the upbuilding of the Church which consists "not in appropriation of the transitory temporal goods, as the avaricious and ambitious clerics think, but in the accumulation of virtues in emulation of our Lord Jesus Christ." He then defines the terms used for the Church: the word sometimes refers to the edifice, sometimes to the congregation of the faithful;

[41] *Ibid.*, p. 107.　　　　　　　　[42] *Ibid.*, p. 216.
[43] *Ibid.*, p. 568.　　　　　　　　[44] *Ibid.*, pp. 425-426.
[45] *Historia et monumenta*, ii, pp. 39-47.

at other times it refers to particular churches such as the Roman Church or the Prague Church. "In the third mode the Church is the totality of the predestinate, called the mystical body of Christ, the bride of Christ and the kingdom of heaven."[46] He then distinguishes among the Church triumphant, the Church militant, and the Church dormient; but they all consist of the predestinate, although there also are in the Church militant the fore-known mixed with them. The Church comprises the common people, the nobles, and the clergy (thus con-tradicting the notion that it is restricted to the pope and the cardinals, or the bishops and the clergy). The clergy, he declares, constitute the best part of the Church if they perform their duties rightly. They should, there-fore, relinquish the world and follow Christ most closely. If, however, they are unfaithful to their duties, they be-come the worst part of the Church, the Antichrist him-self. Hus charges that the clergy have, for the greatest part, degenerated and become disobedient to their superiors, particularly the pope.[47] Clerics committing fornication are for the time being sons of the devil. They should be excommunicated, as the canon law demands. He further excoriates the lords, both secular and eccle-siastical, including the pope, for extortionate exactions. Most detestable, however, is the avarice of the monks, "vulgarly called dives and the fat ones of the Lord." He denounces the luxury and simony of the prelates and charges that some priests refuse to bury the dead unless they first receive payment for it. It is the clergy who cause the schisms: "Who causes the schism of the Sara-cens but a cleric? Who causes the Greek schism but a cleric? Who the Latin schism but a cleric? And who now partitions the Roman Empire but a cleric?"[48]

In 1407 Hus again preached before the synodal gather-ing on the text, "Stand, therefore, having girded your

[46] *Ibid.*, p. 40.   [47] *Ibid.*, p. 41.   [48] *Ibid.*, p. 47.

loins with truth. . . ."[49] After praising good priests in the highest terms, he turns then to an equally eloquent denunciation of wicked priests, particularly the fornicators, whose number was apparently very large. He reproves both the secular and ecclesiastical lords, the latter from the pope down to the monastic priors, for permitting the clerical vices out of negligence or fear of the loss of favor. He condemns clerical injustice in the neglect of duties toward the people. Resplendent churches are built, but the relief of the poor is neglected. Instead of preaching the gospel, the clergy seek plurality of benefices, often by simoniacal means. Hus' sermon is replete with quotations, not only Scriptural, but from the canon law and the saints, such as Bernard and Augustine. His language is blunt and unsparingly devastating. He speaks the naked truth at whatever cost. Anyone could anticipate that such a preacher, whom "the zeal of the Lord hath eaten up," just as it had the Psalmist,[50] would sooner or later run into serious trouble with his clerical brethren! In the meantime, however, Archbishop Zbyněk, who was present on the occasion, found no fault with the sentiments expressed by the intrepid preacher. He even issued a decree condemning the priests-fornicators as heretics.

Another series of sermons preached by Hus during this period was published under the title *Sermones de sanctis*.[51] The collection is obviously incomplete. Moreover, it differs from the previous collections insofar as it consists of a running commentary on whole Scripture pas-

[49] The text is from Eph. 6:14. *Historia et monumenta*, II, pp. 47-56. For other sermons preached by Hus before synodical meetings, cf. *ibid.*, pp. 57-84.

[50] Ps. 69:9.

[51] V. Flajšhans, ed., *Sermones de sanctis*, 2 vols. (Praha, 1907-18). The editor places the time of their preaching between 1403 and 1407; but F. M. Bartoš in his *Literární činnost M. J. Husi* (Praha, 1948), dates them 1408.

sages instead of single texts. Nor do we have in it, for the greatest part, Hus' own exposition. He gathers numerous quotations from surprisingly widely scattered sources, such as Chrysostom, Augustine, Gregory, Bernard, and others. One-third of these sermons were preached on Marian holydays and are deeply devout. Hus raises no question about the historicity of Mary's assumption into heaven but merely discusses whether she ascended in body or in spirit.[52] He wisely professes ignorance of the matter. It is surprising, judging from his later cautious opinion about the veneration of saints, that in these sermons he raises no question about this subject. Since what we have here is largely a collection of quotations from the great homiletical works of the past, there is little of Hus' own thought expressed in it. Nevertheless, in the sermon dealing with Peter (No. 22), Hus asserts that the Church is not founded on him but on "the surest foundation, that is, Christ Jesus." In support of his assertion he quotes Paul's passage,[53] " 'No other foundation can be laid than that which is laid, which is Christ Jesus.' The apostles built on that foundation. But I do not know who built more, whether Peter or Paul. It appears, however, that it was Paul, who said: 'I have labored more than they all.' " As for the keys which Christ gave to Peter, Hus comments, as he was to comment many times subsequently, that the first key signifies the power to discern between right and wrong, while the second key is the power to bind and loose. All the apostles possessed these keys in common, not Peter alone. "So it is believed about all true priests." The Church has limited this power, but in case of necessity "all priests have the apostolic power."[54] The pope, who has usurped this power, does not wish to hear that Christ asked Peter three times before

[52] Flajšhans, *Sermones de sanctis*, pp. 17ff.
[53] I Cor. 3:11.
[54] *Sermones de sanctis* (see n. 51), p. 85.

He granted him the keys whether he loved Him. Only after Peter declared his love for Christ did He bid him to "feed His sheep." Now the pope and many priests do not love God and do not feed the sheep; they do, however, snatch the keys in order to possess worldly power.[55] Even worse are those popes and bishops who cause the death of many thousand faithful, for whom Christ died, in order to secure prelacy.[56]

Furthermore, priests faithfully performing their office are "worthy of double honor, especially those that labor in the Word and teaching."[57] Hus values the priestly office above the royal. Since the priest has received his ministry of the Word and of the sacraments freely, he should dispense these gifts freely. Having received adequate material support for his necessities, he should be content therewith. Christ ordered his apostles to possess no gold. This command applies to the priests as well.[58] Hus quotes Wyclif in support of this requirement of voluntary poverty. He asserts further that since riches are the perennial source of corruption and debility, Christ's disciples should not devote themselves to the collection of alms but to the following of Christ in His poverty and sharing with the people their spiritual riches.[59] He reiterates that "preaching is the most useful activity of the Church of Jesus Christ."[60]

In the three volumes of Hus' lectures on Peter Lombard's *Sentences*, given during 1407-09, we have the most complete and systematic exposition of his own theological views.[61] These volumes are thus a priceless source of knowledge of Hus' theology prior to the outbreak of the storm in 1409. Our text does not give us Hus' own composition of the lectures, but only the notes taken down

[55] *Ibid.*, p. 86.   [56] *Ibid.*, p. 137.   [57] I Tim. 5:17.
[58] *Sermones de sanctis*, pp. 196-197, 347.   [59] *Ibid.*, p. 343.
[60] *Ibid.*, p. 245.
[61] Flajšhans, *Super IV Sententiarum* (see n. 18).

by his students. In Kybal's opinion, Hus shows in this
work a remarkable independence of judgment in comparison with other similar works. "His skill in composition and admirable ability to argue clearly and self-reli-
antly make his comments on the *Sentences* the principal
and central parts of Hus' theology."[62] Dom de Vooght
pronounces the lectures entirely orthodox, although "banal."[63] Even Sedlák, who is usually sharply censorious
of Hus, in this instance is quite appreciative. "Hus'
work," he writes, "at least in the Lectures [i.e., *Super IV
Sententiarum*] as well as elsewhere, is more independent
than may appear from a few agreements with Wyclif
[pointed out] by Loserth." Hus bases his comments on
wide reading, quoting Augustine, Gregory, Chrysostom,
Bonaventura, Thomas Aquinas, John of Paris, John Scotus, Thomas and Hugo of Strasbourg, and John Wyclif.
Flajšhans, clearly under the influence of Loserth, declares that Wyclif was Hus' chief source: "the source of
our [Hus'] exposition of Lombard is, of course, in the first
place Wyclif. The agreements with Wyclif are numerous.
. . . Wyclif's seal is indelibly imprinted on our exposition."[64] The "agreements" are based on Loserth's examples. Flajšhans cites them in four instances, most of which
fail to prove the point. Thus in citing Wyclif's *Trialogus*,
the "agreement" is limited to a quotation from Boethius
on *one* verb! Nevertheless, most inconsistently Flajšhans
warns that "we must not over-emphasize the echoes of Wyclif" in Hus' work![65] Sedlák says of these "agreements":
"That is indeed little in such a large work." After citing

[62] V. Kybal, *M. Jan Hus, Učení*, 3 vols. (Praha, Jan Laichter,
1931), III, p. 59.

[63] De Vooght writes of the Commentary on Lombard that it is
"ce temoin majeur de l'orthodoxie et du conformisme de sa pensée."
De Vooght, *L'hérésie* (see n. 28), p. 119; cf. also his *Les sources de
la doctrine chrétienne* (Paris, Desclée de Brouwer, 1954), pp. 224-225.

[64] Flajšhans, *Super IV Sententiarum*, p. xxxviii.

[65] *Ibid.*, p. xxxix.

Hus' actual quotations from Wyclif's *De benedicta incarnatione* and some texts from the *Decalogue* and the *De civili dominio*, he asks: "Is it possible to assert that Wyclif's seal is indelibly imprinted on this exposition?"[66] The independence of Hus' treatment of the *Sentences* is further seen in the fact that he does not always agree with Lombard, but corrects him by Aquinas or by some other authoritative theologian. Even more important is the fact that he carefully discriminates among the articles on which he chooses to comment. As a rule, he omits abstruse speculations and theological conundrums in which medieval theologians delighted, and selects passages which possess concrete ethical significance. His reformist aim is discernible even in these instances.

Moreover, as has already been stated, the work is orthodox despite the use Hus has made of the Oxford doctor's writings. After all, it must not be supposed that everything Wyclif wrote was *ipso facto* "heretical," even though some Prague university masters apparently thought so. Hus bluntly turns upon those who positively affirmed that Wyclif was among the damned in hell:

> I, however, not wishing to pass a temerarious judgment, hope that he is of the number of the saved. If he is in heaven, may the glorious Lord who placed him there be praised; if he is in purgatory, may the merciful Lord free him quickly; if he is in hell, may he, in accordance with God's just judgment, remain there until its eternal fulfillment.[67]

As mentioned before, De Vooght has contemptuously characterized *Super IV Sententiarum* as banal. Whether

[66] J. Sedlák, "K pramenům Husovy lektury na Sentence," *Studie a texty* (see n. 5), II, pp. 130-131. Also *ibid.*, pp. 436ff., where he quotes what he identifies as the actual transcripts by Hus from Wyclif's works. Also cf. Novotný, *Jan Hus, Život a dílo*, I, p. 201, n. 1.

[67] *Super IV Sententiarum*, p. 621.

banal or not, the lectures were well received at the time of delivery and later when they circulated in written form. Yet many of the ideas expressed in them have figured subsequently in the acrimonious controversy that raged between Hus and his erstwhile fellow-reformers. In fact, we shall find these ideas, although in a distorted form, among the final charges preferred against him at the Council of Constance. It was partly on their account that he was then condemned as a heretic.

Since there was no essential difference between the views expressed by Hus *more academico* in these scholastic lectures and in the later heated controversies, they could well be treated as an integral part of the survey of his entire theological *corpus*. Nevertheless, since many writers assume that a radical change, in his views occurred after 1409 and that his essentially orthodox prior views were subverted by "Wyclifism," it seems opportune to set these earlier views apart from the later. In this way the reader will be enabled to compare the two sets of views and may thus arrive at his own conclusion.

Hus begins by dealing with the Scriptures, although what he writes is disappointingly brief and inadequate. He had just completed his very extensive commentary on selected biblical books and felt no need of repeating himself. The sacred Scriptures contain the saving knowledge which Christ revealed to men whereby they might obtain eternal blessedness. Scriptural doctrine is to be firmly held and believed. Following Augustine, he distinguishes between knowledge (*scientia*) and wisdom (*sapientia*). The former is the knowledge of human and natural matters attainable by reason alone; the latter is the wisdom of God revealed in Scripture. This wisdom was granted by grace of the Trinity that men might be saved eternally. Scripture is "the treasure of hidden wisdom and knowledge of God, restoring the soul." Hence, it "should be read, heard, and preached for the sake of eternal life." Theology is but the knowledge of the truths revealed in Scripture. Moreover, Hus advocates the use of Scripture in the vernacular, as an aid to the common people in acquiring saving knowledge.[68] Although indicative of the high regard in which he held Scripture, this treatment of the subject is very meagre in comparison with his later elaborations.

As for the definition of the Church, it is "the congregation of the faithful to be saved, called catholic, i.e., universal, comprising the militant, dormient, and triumphant."[69] Quoting Augustine, Hus calls it "the congregation of the faithful predestinate and justified."[70] These two statements are among the few instances where Hus has used the phrase *congregatio fidelium*, although even here he has coupled it with the concept of predestination. From the beginning of his public ministry Hus usually spoke of the Church as "the totality of the predestinate." The claim of De Vooght that Hus adopted this Wyclifite definition only in 1413 when he wrote the *De ecclesia* is not correct. He admits, however, that prior to that date Hus defined the Church as "Christ's mystical body" of which He alone was the head. That goes a long way toward proving that Hus had in mind only the predestinate. The contrast which De Vooght attempts to draw is that the term *congregatio fidelium* comprises both the predestinate and the foreknown, while "the totality of the predestinate" does not.[71] He concludes that Hus denied the very existence of the Church militant. This kind of invidious reasoning vitiates the charges against Hus to the end. The very first article of the final accusations made by the Council of Constance implies this distorted and wholly erroneous interpretation. Hus con-

[68] *Ibid.*, pp. 14-20, 34.    [69] *Ibid.*, p. 36.

[70] *Ibid.*, p. 616.

[71] Paul de Vooght, *Hussiana* (Louvain, Publications universitaires de Louvain, 1960), pp. 9, 13-14; cf. also his *L'hérésie*, p. 57.

sistently denied it, but to no avail. Even in the very passage quoted here as his definition of the Church he distinguishes between the Church of the predestinate, which
is the mystical body of Christ of which He alone is the
head, and the church of the wicked of which the devil is
the head. He writes:

> It is called "the church of the wicked," which is the
> congregation of all those to be damned, as on the other
> hand the Church of those living holily is the congre-
> gation of all the faithful to be saved. It is called catho-
> lic, i.e., universal, and comprises the militant, dormi-
> ent, and triumphant. . . . The head of the Church of
> the saints is Christ, while the head of the church of
> the wicked is the devil.[72]

Moreover, the Church militant comprises both the predestinate and the foreknown; the dormient comprises the
members in purgatory; and the triumphant consists of
the angels and the saints in heaven. Those in the Church
militant, however, who are to be damned, "do not in reality belong to it, but are as ulcers, phlegm, and excrements which will finally be separated from the body of
Christ, with their foulness and waste, in the Day of
Judgment. The church of the wicked has now infused
the Church of Christ with the foulness of evil example
and the virus of false doctrine, which the Master at present averts sufficiently so that it does not permeate the
members of His Church."[73]

The concept of the Church militant as consisting of
both the predestinate and the foreknown accentuates the
crucial importance of the conditions of salvation. God
indeed wishes all men to be among the saved; but it
does not follow that they all are actually saved. Hus
writes:

[72] *Super IV Sententiarum*, p. 36.       [73] *Ibid.*

> . . . it is one thing to say "God wishes that all men be among the saved" and another to say "God wishes that all men be saved." The first proposition is true about God's antecedent will, but the second is false, because it denotes that all men fulfill His precepts and thus are consequently saved.[74]

Hus thus draws a sharp distinction between predestination, which applies only to the elect and justified, and foreknowledge, which denotes those of whom God knows from all eternity that they will not accept the conditions of salvation. Thus he divides the human race into two categories or, as Augustine calls them, two "cities"—the *civitas Dei* and *civitas terrena*. Predestination involves three stages: the eternal divine purpose concerning the salvation of the predestinate; the means whereby grace is obtained in the present life; and the attainment of glory in the future life. The first does not depend on man's merit but on God's purpose. The other two are the consequence of man's conduct during his life.[75] Divine foreknowledge, on the other hand, does not destroy man's free will or force him to act either well or wickedly. Hus quotes Augustine's dictum: "nor does a man sin because God foreknows that he will sin; for if he were not willing, he would not sin."[76] Accordingly, God's foreknowledge imposes no constraint upon man. When he sins, he does so voluntarily, of his own choice. Hus con-

[74] *Ibid.*, p. 178.          [75] *Ibid.*, p. 168.

[76] Augustine, *The City of God*, John Healy, transl. (London, J. M. Dent and Sons, Ltd. 1942), book v, chap. 1, p. 217. The full quotation is as follows: "Nor does man sin because God foreknew that he would sin: nay, therefore it is doubtless that he sins, when he does sin, because that God, whose knowledge cannot be mistaken, foresaw that neither fate nor fortune nor anything else, but the man himself would sin who, if he had not been willing, he had not sinned." Cf. also "The Spirit and the Letter," in John Burnaby, transl., *Augustine: Later Works*, The Library of Christian Classics, viii (Philadelphia, The Westminster Press, 1955), pp. 238-239, 241, 245.

cludes in his usual nonspeculative, moderate, and sober fashion: "Nor do I wish to be too solicitous about God's foreknowledge, how it does or does not cause necessity; for I am but a worm unable to perceive God's secrets. Rather should I be solicitous to know how to live well now, so as to find the foreknowing God propitious to me."[77]

Although predestination is essentially of eternal divine purpose and cannot be merited by man's good acts, yet there is a possibility of preparing oneself for the reception of the grace. This tenet is based on Jesus' saying to Mary Magdalene[78] that her sins were forgiven because she loved much. Her loving contributed toward her forgiveness. Even more pertinent is the parable of the laborers in the vineyard,[79] some of whom labored the whole day while others only part of the day. Yet, in the evening they all received the same reward—a denarius. When those who had labored the whole day grumbled at the apparent injustice, the householder replied: "Friend, I am doing you no wrong: did you not agree with me for a denarius? Take what belongs to you and go. . . . Or do you begrudge my generosity?" On such examples as this is founded the tenet of *meritum de congruo* and *meritum de condigno*, which Hus held and expounded in his *Sentences*.[80] A man can prepare for the reception of grace by good works, although God is under no obligation to reward him by granting it. If He does, He does it out of His generosity, His good will. It is not a stipulated reward, for prior to the reception of the prevenient grace no human acts are really meritorious. This then is *meritum de congruo*. It is different, however, after the reception of the grace. Thereafter, the good works of man are meritorious, in their own right. God then rewards

[77] *Super IV Sententiarum*, p. 162.
[78] Luke 7:47.          [79] Matt. 20:1-16.
[80] *Super IV Sententiarum*, p. 307.

them out of justice, not merely generosity. It is as if He were paying the stipulated wage for the work done. This is, therefore, the significance of *meritum de condigno*. "It follows that man cannot do good meritoriously without the cooperation of God's grace."[81] Man's voluntary cooperation, however, is likewise essential. The more an act is voluntary, the more it is meritorious.

Thus the real beginning of Christian life occurs when a man, having either prepared for it or without any deserts whatever, receives the prevenient grace. It is infused by God into his soul [*gratia infusa*], and enables him to receive the justifying grace by which he is then capable to proceed on to sanctification. Thereafter, "whether he sleeps or labors, he possesses the Holy Spirit ever united with himself according to God's good pleasure."[82] This is, however, only the beginning of the long process of recovery of the "theological virtues" lost in the Fall—faith, hope, and love. The first of them, faith, is superior to knowledge. God enlightens therewith man's mind in order that he may perceive and lay hold of that which is above intellectual knowledge. Hus bases his definition on Hebrews 11:1, "Now faith is the assurance of things hoped for, the conviction of things not seen." He is fond of making the triple distinction about faith which we shall sporadically meet in his later writings:

> . . . it is one thing to believe in God, another to believe God, and another to believe about God. To believe God is to believe that what He says is true, as even they admit who live wickedly; as we believe a man but not in man. To believe God is to believe that He alone is God. To believe in God by believing to love Him, by faith to be incorporated in Him, by faith to cleave to Him and to join His members. . . . Therefore, faith is the basis of the entire spiritual edi-

[81] *Ibid.*, p. 311.      [82] *Ibid.*, p. 109.

fice, as substance is the basis of accidents which presuppose it; and as it is naturally impossible for the accidents to exist without the subject, so it is impossible without faith to please God. . . .[83]

In this sentence Hus' realist philosophy is plainly evident.

The saving process further requires a life lived in obedience to God's commandments, in doing good works, in partaking of the sacraments, until this development leads to "faith formed by love" [*fides caritate formata*].[84] For "faith without works is dead."[85] It is this life of pious striving which completes the process of salvation. The life eternal is granted only to those who have deserved it by their lifelong virtuous deeds, by the *meritum de condigno*, an earned merit. Thus it may be said that man is saved by works as well as by faith. Should he falter before death, he would fail of salvation. This aspect of medieval thought, wholly shared by Hus, is in sharp contrast with the basic principle of the later Protestant Reformation. Luther asserted with vehemence that the sinner is justified by faith "without the works of law." The requirement to do good works remained, but a man did them because he was saved, not in order to be saved.

Fortunately, God stands ever ready to aid the sinner in his never ending struggle against the forces of evil, the world, the devil, and his own perverted desires. Among many other aids are the sacraments provided by the Church. Hus defines them in the words of Augustine: "The sacrament is an invisible grace in a visible form." There are seven of them, and all were instituted by Christ. Baptism is the indispensable first sacrament; it cleanses from sins, both original and acquired. Confirmation, as the word implies, confirms the recipient in the formation of the good life made possible by baptism. The

[83] *Ibid.*, pp. 452-454.　　　　[84] Gal. 5:6.
[85] James 2:17.

eucharist, which is the partaking of Christ's body and blood, incorporates the believer into the mystical body of Christ. Penance cleanses the sinner of the acquired sins which continually accumulate. Ordination imparts the power to minister the sacraments and the power of the keys. Matrimony preserves from the sin of unlawful sexual intercourse. Thus the New Testament sacraments are remedies against sin, instituted by Christ and granted by divine grace.[86]

Hus then discusses each sacrament in greater detail. He teaches that even a wicked priest baptizes validly, since the baptismal grace is not conferred by him, but is bestowed by God through him. Thus the priest's function is ministerial. Nevertheless, a wicked priest, while in mortal sin, ministers unworthily, to his own condemnation. Moreover, for a layman knowingly to receive the sacramental ministration, particularly the eucharist, from such a priest is a grave sin.[87] Despite Hus' repeated assertions that the acts of such a priest are nevertheless valid, he was to the very end accused of denying that a priest in mortal sin baptizes or consecrates.

The center of controversy was, of course, the dogma concerning the eucharist. Hus taught without the slightest deviation, both in the *Sentences* and on numberless occasions later, the orthodox dogma of transubstantiation. As blood is contained in the human body, so the whole body of Christ is contained in the transubstantiated bread. Christ does not *begin* to exist in the sacrament of the altar, for He has existed from all eternity. The priest, therefore, does not *create* the body of Christ, for in that case he, a creature, would create his own Creator![88] But how can the body of Christ, who sits at the right hand of God, be present in the sacrament in countless places on the earth? Hus answers the question by saying that Christ

[86] *Super IV Sententiarum*, pp. 510-515.
[87] *Ibid.*, p. 585.       [88] *Ibid.*, pp. 572-573.

sits at the right hand of God *extensive, dimensive, et circumscriptive*, while in the sacrament his body does not possess these qualities.

> Hence, although precisely the same body of Christ which was born of the Virgin, which suffered on the cross, ascended into heaven, and is sitting at the right hand of God the Father, is both in heaven and in the sacrament; yet it exists differently in heaven than it did on the cross or in the sepulchre. Similarly, it exists differently in the sacrament than it did on the cross. On the cross it was extended, wounded, bespatted, and crowned. In the sacrament, however, it is not so extended, wounded, bespatted or crowned. . . . Christ, then, is and can be at the same time in various places, because He is personally in heaven *extensive*, but on the altar sacramentally. . . .[89]

Thus He is really and wholly present in the sacrament. Consequently, the believer cannot corporeally see the body of Christ, nor can the priest palpably touch it. Both have before them only the transubstantiated bread.[90]

Hus further discusses the proper way of communing. It is threefold: spiritual, sacramental, and spiritual-sacramental. The spiritual communion is partaken of only by the saints in heaven and those in grace on earth. To partake spiritually of the body of Christ is to believe in Him and unite oneself with Him by love. Hus quotes in this connection Augustine's memorable saying, "Believe and thou hast eaten." Such spiritual communing should always be joined with the sacramental. The latter is defined as "partaking of the sacrament with the intention of receiving the sacrament." If one communes without such an intention, he does not partake of the body of Christ. For instance, a mouse nibbling the host does not

[89] *Ibid.*, pp. 565-566.       [90] *Ibid.*, pp. 569, 579.

commune.[91] He furthermore raises the question whether a layman partaking of the transubstantiated bread alone, without drinking the wine, partakes of the whole body of Christ. Contrary to his later conviction that all communicants should partake of both elements, he answers on this occasion affirmatively. Finally, in replying to the question whether a layman should commune daily, he quotes as his own the opinion of Augustine: "To receive communion daily I neither praise nor blame. . . ."[92]

Another very important sacrament, on which Hus placed the greatest emphasis throughout his ministry, is that of penance. The integral parts of this sacrament consist of contrition of the heart, of oral confession to a priest, and of satisfaction for the sins or wrongs done. Hus is against the fairly general practice of accepting attrition in place of contrition. The difference between attrition and contrition he likens to that between unformed and formed faith. "Therefore, the unformed faith does not remove sins, nor does attrition; but contrition does, as does formed faith."[93]

Hus distinguishes between venial and mortal sins. General penance suffices for the forgiveness of venial sins, for they do not deprive man of grace. "Nevertheless, little sins, if neglected, kill." When repented of, or in purgatory, they are finally expiated. Mortal sins, however, deprive man of grace. If persisted in to the end, they result in final impenitence "which is not remitted either in this or the future life."[94]

The declaration of forgiveness, following upon contrition and confession, is made by the priest *ministerialiter*. It is not he who forgives sins, but God; he merely pronounces the pardon. On God's part there is mercy and justice, while on the penitent's part there must be a firm

[91] *Ibid.*, pp. 560-561.       [92] *Ibid.*, pp. 557, 581.
[93] *Ibid.*, p. 599.           [94] *Ibid.*, pp. 624-625.

intention to sin no more. All sins repented of and confessed are forgiven, except that of final impenitence. This Hus, following Augustine, regards as the sin against the Holy Spirit. It is unforgivable not because God is unwilling to forgive, but because man refuses to repent. "It is clear that the good God never condemns anyone unless he is impenitent to the end and thus blasphemes the Holy Spirit."[95]

As for the satisfaction for the sins committed, it is twofold: material and spiritual. The former consists in visiting the sick, giving drink to the thirsty and food to the hungry, redeeming prisoners, clothing the naked, practicing hospitality, and burying the dead. The spiritual satisfaction (which pertains mainly to the clergy) consists in teaching the ignorant, castigating the delinquent, consoling the sorrowful, declaring remission of sins, sharing the infirmity of others, and praying for all.[96]

The sacrament of orders, with the duties pertaining to the priestly office, is of constant concern to Hus. It confers spiritual power upon the ordinand. He must be under no canonical censure such as being an excommunicate, irregular, under an interdict or a sentence of deposition. The ordination confers on the candidate the power of the keys to open or close the kingdom of heaven. Nevertheless, as in every other instance, this priestly power is only ministerial, declaratory: none but God possesses and exercises it in the absolute form and in His own right.

Relating this power to the pope, Hus declares that he can err both concerning the faith and the use of the keys. This applies to bishops and priests as well. Therefore "it should be believed that the priest rightly binds and loosens only to the degree as he ministers in accordance with the rules of the law of Christ. When he exceeds these rules, he only pretends to bind or loose, but does not do

[95] *Ibid.*, p. 367.　　　　[96] *Ibid.*, p. 596.

so. It is, therefore, catholic to believe that every priest rightly ordained has sufficient power to administer all the sacraments. . . . Nor can the pope absolve otherwise. For as to the power of ordination, St. Jerome teaches that all priests are equal, although the power of the lower clergy is reasonably limited."[97] Thus all priests possess the keys of the Church but not all have their full use. Among the reserved powers of the keys is excommunication. This extreme use of the power should not be applied except for mortal sins, never as a punishment or as a weapon used by ecclesiastical superiors in defense of their prerogatives. Nor does it justly involve deprivation of property or of personal liberty, but consists solely of the exclusion from the membership and ministrations of the Church:[98]

> It is impossible that a man be justly excommunicated unless he first and principally excommunicates himself. . . . From that follows first that no one should cease from praising Christ [i.e., worshipping] on account of fulminated [i.e., unjust] excommunication.[99]

The unjustly excommunicated should bear the infliction humbly, rejoicing that he is deemed worthy of suffering for Christ's name.

Such, then, were Hus' theological views at the time he lectured on Lombard's *Sentences*. They do not exceed the limits of the then current orthodoxy, although they interpret such current doctrines "liberally." De Vooght declares them to be "ce temois majeur de l'orthodoxie et du conformisme de sa pensée."[100] Whatever influence Wyclif had on his thought at the time did not involve him in any error or heresy.

[97] *Ibid.*, p. 607.

[98] It was only in John Locke's *Letter concerning Toleration* that such sentiments were advocated again!

[99] *Super IV Sententiarum*, p. 610.

[100] De Vooght, *L'hérésie*, p. 119.

## CHAPTER III

# THE CONFLICT

## WITH ARCHBISHOP ZBYNĚK

THE storm broke in the Fall of 1408 when some Prague pastors submitted to Archbishop Zbyněk a complaint against Hus. The relation of Zbyněk to Hus, hitherto so friendly, gradually deteriorated. In the Fall of the previous year, as we have seen, Hus had been invited to preach at the synodical meeting, and delivered the already mentioned sermon, "Stand, therefore. . . ."[1] This was the last time he was so honored. The great prelates, who felt personally attacked by his uncompromising condemnation of their profligate living and exorbitant exactions, now determined to muzzle the irritating criticisms of Hus and of his reforming party. At the synodical meeting held on June 16, 1408, they passed a resolution forbidding the denunciations of prelates in Czech sermons. Moreover, they renewed their attack on the whole reformist party by charging it with Wyclifite heresy. That the party had among its members some who were indeed professed adherents of Wyclif was quite true. At their head stood the most celebrated of the Czech masters, Stanislav of Znojmo, with whom was associated his younger colleague and pupil, Stephen Páleč. Of the same persuasion was the ardent and eloquent Jerome of Prague, who had returned in 1406 from his extensive studies abroad with master's degrees from the universities of Paris, Oxford, and Heidelberg. He was said to have brought with him a portrait of Wyclif with a halo round his head. His vibrant lectures at the university resounded with Wyclif's praises.

---

1 In *Historia et monumenta Joannis Hus atque Hieronymi Pragensis, confessorum Christi*, 2 vols. (Norimberg, 1715), II, pp. 44-56.

Jakoubek of Stříbro was likewise an intrepid and sturdy defender of the Oxford doctor. When Stanislav had so ignominiously emasculated his treatise professing remanence, Jakoubek hastened to write his own profession of the dreaded doctrine.[2] The youngest of the group was Matthew of Knín. It was he who was chosen by the higher clergy of Prague as the target for the attack. He was accused of holding the doctrine of remanence and of having called Wyclif "the evangelical doctor."

Matthew was arrested and placed on trial (May 15, 1408); Zbyněk himself presided. The general vicar of the archdiocese, John Kbel, then demanded that the accused master recant his adherence to remanence. Matthew refused, since he had not been convicted of any heresy. The vicar, however, insisted that he recant even if he had never held any heresy.[3] The archbishop also peremptorily commanded Matthew to answer the charge. This the accused refused to do. Turning to Zbyněk, he appealed to him to spare him and the Czech nation the shame of being branded heretical in the presence of the German masters without having been convicted of the charge. He was indeed not forced to recant while the German masters were present, but did submit after they had left. Nevertheless, his recantation soon became known generally. The archbishop thereupon demanded that the Czech masters renew their declaration concerning their non-adherence to the forty-five articles. He felt that his prohibition of them made in 1403 had not been observed.

This obvious defeat of the Czech reformist party was a severe blow to its members. About sixty masters and 150 bachelors met at their quarters at the "Black Rose" to consider what course to take. They refused to accept

2 Jakoubek of Stříbro, "Tractatus de remanencia panis," in F. M. Bartoš, *Literární činnost Jakoubka ze Stříbra* (Praha, 1925), p. 23.

3 V. Novotný, *Jan Hus, Život a dílo*, 2 vols. (Praha, Jan Laichter, 1919), I, pp. 219-220.

the blank condemnation of the forty-five articles; instead, they adopted a resolution declaring that they should not be taught in their "heretical, erroneous, and offensive" sense. This obviously implied that they could be held in their correct sense. The bachelors were also forbidden to lecture on Wyclif's *Trialogus, Dialogus,* and *De eucharistia.*

Furthermore, Zbyněk ordered that all Wyclif's books be delivered to the archiepiscopal palace by July 4 "for examination." Hus obeyed and himself delivered his copies of Wyclif to the archbishop. He spoke with Zbyněk, hoping to moderate his future acts. In this effort he failed.

Perhaps the most serious action of the anti-reformists was the bringing of charges against Stanislav and Páleč at the papal court. They employed for this purpose Ludolf Meisterman, one of the German masters at the university. Before he left for the curia, he had secured from the Heidelberg university an approval of his project. With this recommendation and the financial support of the Prague higher clergy he arrived at the papal court. He laid charges against Stanislav and the other Czech "Wyclifites," particularly mentioning Stanislav's remanentist tract without stating that it had been rendered innocuous. He demanded that the matter be investigated and those found guilty be subjected to the severest penalties. His request was complied with, and on April 20, 1408, the cardinal in charge of the case issued his decree strictly forbidding all teaching or holding of Wyclifism. He also cited Stanislav to appear before him within two months. Stanislav obeyed and, accompanied by Páleč, proceeded toward Pope Gregory's court. When they reached Bologna, however, the two Czech masters were seized and imprisoned by Cardinal Baldassare Cossa. He had interpreted their journey as an act of submission to Gregory, whom the cardinals had abandoned in June. The Czech masters were robbed of their money and horses and thrown into prison. When the circumstances were cleared up, they were released and returned to Prague. They had, however, been so shaken by their experiences that they ceased to head the reformists for fear of further consequences. This was a most serious defection from the ranks of that party. For during the previous year two of its most prominent members, Stephen of Kolín and Peter of Stoupno, had died. These circumstances brought Hus to the leadership of the party at a time when such prominence became dangerous.

The charges of Wyclifite heresy so freely bandied about could not but sooner or later involve Hus as well. Nevertheless, when sometime between August and September he was accused by the anti-reformist Prague clergy at the archiepiscopal court, he was *not* charged with heresy. The charges themselves are not extant, but can be plainly reconstructed from Hus' reply.[4] He was not accused of Wyclifism, but with excessive denunciation of the extortionist practices of the clergy. The first accusation charged that in July 1407, he had preached that priests who demanded payment for confessions, sacraments, funerals, and other priestly functions, were heretics. In the second place he was charged that in the same sermon he had said about the recently deceased Master Peter of Všeruby, a notorious pluralist, that "he would not take the whole world to die with so many benefices." Another charge, not actually specified in Hus' summary but included in his reply, stated that he had declared that he wished his soul to be where the soul of Wyclif was. Finally, it was charged that in a sermon preached in 1408 he had denounced the clergy so unsparingly as

[4] V. Novotný, ed., *M. Jana Husi, Korespondence a dokumenty* (Praha, 1920), No. 12; F. Palacký, ed., *Documenta Mag. Joannis Hus* (Praha, F. Tempský, 1869), pp. 155-163.

to bring them into disrepute and contempt before the people.

Hus introduced his defense by an affirmation of his sincere intention to abide by the faith of the Church:

> First in general I confess that whatever Jesus Christ and His universal Church wish to be believed, that I firmly believe. Furthermore, whatever in particular I shall be instructed to believe, that I will firmly believe and hold. I am ready, according to the admonition of St. Paul, to give reason for my belief not only to Your Reverence, but to anyone who should ask for it, so that those who slander me as a malefactor may be ashamed.[5]

Thereupon he analyzed and answered at great length the accusations. As for the first point, he asserted that exactions of payment for priestly ministrations were contrary to canonical rules. He quoted the decree of the Council of Tribur forbidding the practice as heresy. Furthermore, he called attention to the fact that the censure applied only to those pastors who were guilty of the practice. In regard to the second charge, he declared that he had exhorted his congregation concerning the late Peter of Všeruby so that they might pray for his soul, and had not condemned him as if he had not been a good Christian. He admitted that as for himself, "he would not take the whole world to die with such and so many benefices," but that he had said it as a warning against avarice to the priests present at the service.[6] Then Hus dealt with the charge that he had declared his wish that his soul were where Wyclif's soul was. He admitted that he had said it, but added: "Since I do not know from Scripture or revelation about any man whether he is damned, I consider him incomparably better than myself. . . . For I dare not condemn anyone whom

[5] *Ibid.*, p. 31.     [6] *Ibid.*, p. 37.

Scripture or the Church informed by revelation does not condemn."[7] This charge was to appear among the "testimonies of witnesses" at the trial before the Council of Constance, and the judges made a great deal over it! Finally, the charge concluded with the statement that "remanence is held by many in this city." It did not charge Hus personally with the grave and dreaded accusation; apparently, even his foes knew well that he did not hold it. Hus requested the archbishop to demand that they name the men they had thus charged. As we shall see, Zbyněk, under pressure from the king, had just published an edict stating that he had found no one holding that error. In reply to the last article, that he had denounced the clergy excessively, contrary to the recent synodical prohibition, Hus declared that to preach the truth does not come under the prohibition. Only by lying would he "exceed" the truth, and thus be guilty of disobeying the edict. He castigated the sins of the clergy as Jesus had denounced the scribes and Pharisees. "From the above it is evident, Most reverend Father, that the first charge is false, the second is defective, and the third I deny."[8]

Hus later expanded these arguments into a treatise, *De arguendo clero pro concione*,[9] where the whole question of the public critique of clerical delinquencies is treated *more scholastico*. Another set of charges, preferred against Hus by the priest Protiva (1409), at one time preacher at Bethlehem, was referred to the Inquisitor, Maurice Rvačka, before whom Hus was cited. The charges were all found false; nevertheless, they were incorporated later into the "testimonies of witnesses" at the trial of Hus before the Council of Constance. We

[7] *Ibid.*, p. 38.

[8] *Ibid.*, p. 41. Cf. also the treatment of this affair by Paul de Vooght, *L'hérésie de Jean Huss* (Louvain, Publications universitaires de Louvain, 1960), pp. 98-103.

[9] *Historia et monumenta*, I, pp. 185ff.

shall cite here only one of them,[10] namely, that Hus had declared that the Antichrist had placed his foot in the Roman Church which could hardly be moved. Hus declared in response, that he had never rejected the Roman Church, since he spoke of it, along with Jerome and Augustine, as consisting of "all Christians who hold the faith of Christ which was taught in Rome by the holy apostles Peter and Paul."

If Hus' adversaries exerted themselves to damage his reputation with the archbishop, his friends concerned themselves with defending it. One such sincere well-wisher was a monk, John of Rakovník, formerly a university master. He knew Hus well, admired him, and was sympathetic with his aims. He was, however, disturbed by the reply Hus had made to the accusations of the Prague clergy. It did not satisfy him. He suspected that Hus' foes might use it to accuse him of Wyclifism—as they actually did later. The monk John, who apparently knew Wyclif only from the forty-five articles, wrote Hus a letter urging him to repudiate Wyclif outright.[11] He did not accuse Hus of holding Wyclif's errors or of defending them. But any favorable word in Wyclif's behalf, no matter how justified and how solidly supported by Scriptural proofs, was damaging and dangerous. Consequently, it would be best if Hus would resolutely and explicitly repudiate Wyclif. That would secure peace and concord the soonest. For by denouncing the avarice of the clergy, Hus was causing schism within the Church. This the good monk deplored.

Novotný regards John of Rakovník as "one of the noblest spirits, whom circumstances transformed from admirers of Hus into his future foes."[12] He thinks that

10 Palacký, *Documenta*, p. 166.
11 Novotný, *Jan Hus, Život a dílo*, I, pp. 264ff.; De Vooght, *L'hérésie* (see n. 7), pp. 102-103.
12 Novotný, *Jan Hus, Život a dílo*, I, p. 267.

perhaps an unequivocal repudiation of Wyclif's errors on the part of Hus would have satisfied John. Hus, on the other hand, invariably avoided denunciation of Wyclif's deviations from orthodoxy, of which he knew and which he personally regretted. He professed only such of Wyclif's tenets as were unexceptionally dogmatically acceptable. Was this sheer obstinacy on his part? There is no doubt that his enemies utilized it to cause irreparable damage to his reputation. In his behalf it may be urged that, in the first place, he was never convinced of the accuracy of the forty-five articles; and secondly, that he now felt responsible for the reform program of his party, which would undoubtedly suffer certain defeat were he to repudiate Wyclif outright.

The monk John's fears that Hus himself would be charged with Wyclifite heresy were soon realized. Nothing else could have been expected. One particularly tawdry case was the charge of heresy leveled at Hus by Záviš of Zapy, pastor at Prachatice. Hus knew the place well, since it was close to his birthplace. In this instance he wrote Záviš a stiff letter of rebuke.[13] He stated that he had heard that Záviš had called him a heretic, and requested that he write him directly, so that he could prove to him his orthodoxy. In his turn, Hus mounted an attack upon the Prachatice pastor who had "sheared his sheep" for the last thirty years without ever residing there:

> You ought to take your own conduct to heart rather than to call your neighbor a heretic. Or if you know him to be a heretic, you should admonish him once or twice according to the apostolic rule. . . .

All these reckless charges of Wyclifite heresy greatly perturbed King Wenceslas. He feared that the reputation

[13] Novotný, *Korespondence* (see n. 4), No. 20. Although this letter is dated August 1410, I have inserted it here as a prime sample of the calumny Hus had to suffer throughout this period.

of Bohemia would gravely suffer. He therefore demanded that Zbyněk declare that after an examination throughout his archdiocese he had found no heresy or heretics. The king wanted to use such a pronouncement to counter the unfavorable impression created abroad by the affair of Stanislav. Moreover, he intended to send it to the curia in order that the charges pending there be annulled. The archbishop understandably hesitated, since he himself had taken part in sending the charges to Rome. His officials, particularly the general vicar, John Kbel, fearing the king's wrath, took refuge at Roudnice, to which place Zbyněk had preceded them (July 13, 1408). They took along with them the cathedral treasures, thus greatly increasing the king's anger. Thereupon, to quiet the storm, the archbishop returned to Prague. At an extraordinary meeting of the synod a few days later, the desired decree was issued. It declared, in the archbishop's name, that "after diligent and assiduous inquiry, he had found no heresy in his diocese, particularly as regards the venerable sacrament."[14] So much for the archiepiscopal veracity!

Meanwhile, an even graver occasion of strife occurred in the conflict between the rival popes, Gregory XII and Benedict XIII. Gregory, on his election to the papacy, had promised to secure the end of the Schism by resigning, on condition that Benedict should do likewise. When his evasion of the promise proved to the cardinals that he was unwilling to redeem his pledge, they abandoned obedience to him. The French cardinals joined them in this action by renouncing allegiance to Benedict (May 1408). Toward the end of November the cardinals, now

---

[14] Novotný, *Jan Hus, Život a dílo,* I, p. 250; F. M. Bartoš, *Čechy v době Husově* (Praha, Jan Laichter, 1947), pp. 292-293; Palacký, *Documenta,* particularly n. 2, p. 392: ". . . in civitate, diocesi ac provincia sua Pragensi, facta et habita diligenti etiam et exacta inquisitione, neminem errorum ver haereticum reperit, nec potuit reperire."

forming one body, called a general Council to meet at Pisa the next year. A French embassy was sent to King Wenceslas to win him for the program of terminating the Schism by deposing both popes and electing a new one acknowledged by all. The embassy was accompanied by Master Jacques de Nouvion, who represented the Paris university. At a banquet held in his honor by the Czech university masters, the discussion veered in the direction of "apostolic poverty," advocated particularly by Jakoubek of Stříbro, the disciple of Matthew of Janov. The French scholar, on his part, stoutly defended the propriety of clerical possessions, if rightly used. He was, however, driven to the extreme position of claiming that it was not altogether necessary to observe all Christ's counsels.[15] For the Church, directed by the Holy Spirit, cannot err in matter of faith and morals, nor can general Councils. Doctrinal tenets do not depend for their authority on Scripture, but on the Church. Christ did not declare the four Gospels to be authoritative; the Church did.

The French delegation succeeded in gaining Wenceslas for the conciliar plan. He had been deposed by the electors from his position as the Roman king (1400) and replaced by Ruprecht of the Palatinate; he now acceded to the French delegation's pleading on condition that he be reinstated in his former dignity. He did not, however, as yet renounce his obedience to Gregory. The delegation also demanded that the university declare itself for the plan. The university had thus to make the difficult decision whether or not to abandon Gregory XII, whom it had hitherto obeyed. The archbishop and

[15] Jan Sedlák, ed., "Jacobi de Noviano, magistri Parisiensis, Disputatio cum Hussitis," *Tractatus causam Mg. Joannis Hus e parte catholica illustrantes* (Brno, 1914), quoted in Novotný, *Jan Hus, Život a dílo*, I, pp. 244ff. Cf. also De Vooght, *L'hérésie*, pp. 89-92, and *Hussiana* (Louvain, Publications universitaires de Louvain, 1960), pp. 111-115.

many prelates, particularly the influential and pugnacious Bishop John of Litomyšl, opposed such a step. So did the German university masters, who feared the loss of benefices bestowed on them by Gregory. At the meeting of the university on December 7, 1408, the Czech masters declared themselves for "neutrality" between Gregory and the cardinals, which in practice amounted to a virtual repudiation of obedience to him. Hus was among them, and was promptly denounced by his foes as "a disobedient son of the mother Church." Zbyněk thereupon suspended him from preaching. Hus wrote him a rather interesting letter,[16] in which he professes his obedience to the Church and explains his "neutrality."

> Therefore, Your Paternity may know that it has never been, nor ever will be, my intention—as I trust in the Lord—to abandon the obedience of the mother Church. For in accordance with the precept of the blessed apostle Peter, it is my intention to obey not only the Roman pontiff and Your Paternity, but "to be subject for the sake of God to every human creature," whether it be the king as the highest or the secular lords as sent by him. . . . Whatever, therefore, the Roman pope Gregory XII, or the holy mother Church, or even Your Paternity shall rightfully command, I wish humbly to obey. But I cannot render aid in the contentions about the priority of honor [between the popes], for the Saviour forbade it to His disciples in Luke 12. Nor can I side with the apostolic lord [Gregory] in the fact that he does not keep his pledged oath, as is evident to almost all Christendom. For I would thus be opposed to Christ who said in Matt. 5: "Let your speech be Yea, yea, Nay, nay. . . . "

[16] Novotný, *Korespondence*, No. 13; V. Kybal, *Jan Hus, Učení*, 3 vols. (Praha, Jan Laichter, 1923-31), I, pp. 370f. De Vooght, *L'hérésie*, pp. 126-127, mistakenly asserts that Hus was ready to obey *both* popes.

> Therefore, on account of these two things [i.e., the conflict between the pope and the antipope and the non-fulfillment of his oath] I am neutral.

He therefore begged Zbyněk to rescind the suspension of preaching imposed on him. The archbishop seems to have done so.

Another event which complicated the already involved situation was the decision of the Czech university masters to hold a *Quodlibet* on January 3, 1409. The subjects chosen and the men selected to discuss them were unmistakably Wyclifite. The orators were Matthew of Knín, but recently released from the archiepiscopal prison, and Jerome of Prague, the firebrand of the reformist party. The latter concluded his speech, after most of the audience had left, by denying that Wyclif had been condemned in England and by producing a letter from Oxford University which declared that Wyclif had been a man of irreproachable morals and "an evangelical doctor." The *Quodlibet* was plainly held in defiance of the archbishop and the king: for the former had forbidden all "Wyclifism," while the latter was deeply concerned about the good name of the country, which any defense of Wyclif jeopardized. Zbyněk, therefore, again ordered Wyclif's books to be surrendered "for examination." Hus obeyed this order and himself brought the books. Not all, however, followed his example. Five students refused to give up their copies and appealed against Zbyněk's command to the cardinals gathered at the Council of Pisa. The archbishop thereupon excommunicated them along with their advocate, Mark of Hradec. His order for the surrender of the books was repeated at the June synodical meeting. Hus now protested against it in a sermon which resulted in a popular demonstration before the archiepiscopal palace. Zbyněk, thereupon, cited him before the inquisitor,

Maurice Rvačka. This represented the final rift between the two men. The inquisitor zealously collected charges against Hus and presented them to him for sworn replies. We do not know what answers Hus gave to the accusations; he refused, however, to take an oath. Thus began legal proceedings which continued from the archiepiscopal to the papal court until ultimately they ended in Hus' condemnation and death at the stake in Constance.

Meanwhile, the negotiations of King Wenceslas with the French delegation continued. They demanded that he secure a definite commitment from the university as to its renunciation of obedience to Gregory, and that he make a public declaration of his own decision. The king, who was then residing at his magnificent palace at Kutná Hora, called delegations from both the Czech and the foreign "nations" to his court. It was then that he learned that the Czechs favored the action, while the foreigners, predominantly German, did not. Prior to this occasion, because he had not known of the recalcitrance of the German masters, and because he had been provoked by the *Quodlibet* held by the Czechs a few days before, he had broken into a choleric reprimand of Hus and Jerome.[17] When the king now learned of the stubborn opposition of the Germans to his decision, which incidentally included their resistance to the transfer of the title of the Roman king from Ruprecht to Wenceslas, he decided to favor the Czechs. On January 18, 1409, he issued the famous decree of Kutná Hora, whereby he radically altered the constitution of the university. Henceforth, the Czechs were to wield three votes to every one vote of the Germans. A few days later he informed the

17 "Petri de Mladoniowicz, Relatio de Magistro Johanne Hus," in V. Novotný, ed., *Fontes rerum Bohemicarum,* VIII (Praha, Nadání Františka Palackého, 1932), p. 106. Cf. my translation in *John Hus at the Council of Constance* (New York and London, Columbia University Press, 1965), p. 177.

French delegates of the university's adherence to the conciliar plan and of his own repudiation of obedience to Gregory XII.[18]

When on March 25, 1409, the Council opened its sessions at Pisa, both Gregory XII and Benedict XIII were in due course deposed and excommunicated as heretics. Thereupon in June, against the advice of Jean Gerson, who had urged that the Council first make sure of a general unanimity on the part of all nations, they elected Alexander V as the new pope. They agreed on him largely because he was a Greek and thus belonged neither to the Italian nor to the French factions. Unfortunately, the two deposed pontiffs retained the obedience of some nations, so that the longed-for unification of the Church was not secured. In fact, the Schism was made worse; for instead of two, there were now three popes.

It was this situation, over which Hus had no control, which further aggravated the tension between him and Archbishop Zbyněk, who refused to acknowledge the new pope. Since Hus did accept the conciliar policy of Wenceslas, his relation to the archbishop gravely deteriorated, although it had already been almost irretrievably damaged. Moreover, in October of 1409 he was elected rector of the reorganized university; he thus assumed the burden of the inevitable conflict with the German masters, who had violently repudiated the new order. After exhausting every effort to secure from the king an annulment of the decree of Kutná Hora, about 1,500 Germans left Prague *en masse* and established their own university at Leipzig. Their hatred of Hus, however, continued henceforth and pursued him even to the Council of Constance. They fastened on Hus the aspersion of heresy and spread it abroad far and wide. This circumstance had virtually decided his case even before

[18] Bartoš (see n. 14), pp. 304-306.

the trial at Constance began. He was regarded as "grave-ly suspect of heresy," which according to the contempo-rary juristic notions differed but little from actual proof.

The defiant attitude of the archbishop went so far that he sent two representatives to the Council of Civi-dale, called by Pope Gregory to counter the Council at Pisa. Bishop John of Litomyšl likewise sent two mem-bers of his clergy there. Zbyněk was appointed Gregory's legate for his archdiocese.

Meanwhile, the cardinals at Pisa received the appeal of the five students of the Prague university. They uti-lized this otherwise trivial occasion to put pressure on Archbishop Zbyněk, and initiated legal proceedings against him. The archbishop, actually fearful of the out-come, sent two canonists to Pisa to announce his sub-mission to Alexander V and to sue for the stopping of the process. He, moreover, complained of the spread of Wyclifism both in Bohemia and Moravia, claiming that it had infected the hearts of many, and requested author-ity to proceed against it. Alexander was, of course, over-joyed with this turn of events. In order to bind Zbyněk firmly to himself, he gladly complied with his request. On December 20, 1409,[19] he issued a bull (Hus always claimed that it was bought) authorizing Zbyněk to ap-point a six-member commission to examine Wyclif's books, which he was then "to remove from the eyes of the faithful" [ut a fidelium oculis amoveri]. He was further to uproot Wyclifism from the country and punish all who should be found professing "these damnable heresies," particularly the doctrine of remanence. Final-ly, he was to prohibit preaching anywhere but in the cathedral and parochial and monastic churches. No ap-peal from this decree was permitted. The bull reached Zbyněk on March 12, 1410, but he did not make it

---

[19] Palacký, *Documenta*, pp. 374-376. Zbyněk's recognition of Alex-ander, dated September 2, *ibid.*, pp. 372-373.

public until the usual June synodical meeting. He de-
layed, perhaps expecting Hus' submission. He did, however, appoint the commission to examine Wyclif's books,
composed of four members of the theological faculty,
Hus' enemies, and two canonists. When Hus made no
gesture of submission, Zbyněk at last announced the
terms of the bull on June 16, 1410, declaring also the
verdict of the commission. As could be expected, that
body found Wyclif's works heretical and condemned fifteen of them, among them some purely philosophical
and even some mathematical and physical ones.[20] The
archbishop then forbade holding or promulgating any
of Wyclif's tenets, and once more demanded the surrender of his books, particularly on the part of the five
students who had appealed Zbyněk's previous order.
Most important of all, Zbyněk prohibited preaching anywhere but in the cathedral and parochial or monastic
churches, as specified in the papal bull. Hus obeyed the
order about surrendering the books, but not about the
preaching. He personally brought his copies of Wyclif's
works to the archbishop, ironically requesting him to
mark any places he found erroneous so that he could
warn his congregation against them.

The indiscriminate condemnation of Wyclif's books
was protested by the whole university. The masters, meeting on June 21, signified their refusal of Zbyněk's decree,
particularly the condemnation of the non-theological
books, by appealing to the newly-elected Pope John
XXIII, who had succeeded Alexander about a month
earlier. Hus regarded the whole affair as sheer abuse of
papal and archiepiscopal power. It was, moreover, strictly
speaking, illegal, since after Alexander's death in May
his bull had, in Hus' opinion, lost its validity. A few

[20] Kybal, *Jan Hus, Učení*, i, p. 54, speaks of eighteen books so
condemned.

days after the synodal meeting Hus preached a sermon[21] in which he charged the prelates with being more audacious than Christ Himself who said that "He judges no one," while they dared to condemn Wyclif's works and forbade under pain of excommunication preaching in chapels. He asked sarcastically whether God had declared to them that Christ and the holy doctors had erred in commanding preaching to all nations. Christ said to his disciples, "Whatever I do, do ye also." Since God cannot err, all the prelates must be in error.

Then on the nearest Sunday (June 22) Hus preached on the text prescribed for the day: "While the people pressed upon him to hear the word of God. . . ." He pointed out, first of all, that Jesus preached standing by the lake Gennesaret, thus demonstrating that preaching could take place anywhere, even though the Pharisees and the scribes opposed it.

> Because our scribes desire the same, commanding that there be no preaching in chapels, even such as had been approved by the apostolic authority; therefore I, wishing to obey God rather than men, and, to conform to the acts of Christ rather than to theirs, appeal from this wrongful command first of all to God, to whom belongs the principal authority to grant the power to preach, and further to the apostolic see, which should radiate greater authority than that of the prelates.[22]

He insisted that he did not thereby disobey God. For if the superiors ordered something illicit, they should not be obeyed. "One should not obey except the precepts and counsels of the Gospel." Should preaching be for-

---

[21] A fragment of it is published by Jan Sedlák, *M. Jan Hus* (Praha, Dědictví sv. Prokopa, 1915), supplement, pp. 168-170. Cf. also Novotný, *Jan Hus, Život a dílo*, I, pp. 406ff.

[22] Sedlák, *Jan Hus* (see n. 21), supplement, pp. 159-160. This text was Luke 5:1.

bidden in Christ's name? Indeed not! Such command was made rather in the Antichrist's name!

Finally, on June 25, at a sensational service, when the chapel was thronged to its utmost capacity, Hus read his appeal to Pope John XXIII from Zbyněk's order. It was made not only in his name, but in the name of a number of others, among whom were three of the five students who had appealed previously. It had been prepared by John of Jesenice to ensure its having correct legal form. Hus thus explicitly acknowledged papal authority and professed obedience to it (quam, sc. sedem apostolicam semper corde, ore et opere profitemur).[23] Hus preached at the time a particularly eloquent and deeply stirring sermon,[24] in which he exclaimed:

> Behold, the recently deceased pope [Alexander V], having been incited by the Prague prelates, writes in his letter to the Prague archbishop about the extermination of the errors sown by Wyclif's books in Bohemia and Moravia; that there are many people who hold Wyclif's articles contrary to the faith, and that the hearts of many are infected by heresy. . . . But I say, and thank God, that I have hitherto seen no Czech being a heretic.

He also added that the prophecy of James of Tharamo had been fulfilled: he had prophesied that in 1409 would arise the man who would persecute the gospel and the faith of Christ. When Hus dramatically concluded by asking the overflowing congregation whether they would support him in his appeal, they shouted thunderously their assent. This was a moving demonstration of the love and devotion in which the beloved preacher of the Bethlehem Chapel was held.

[23] Palacký, *Documenta*, pp. 387-396.
[24] This sermon has not been preserved except for the quotations sent by Zbyněk to Rome. Cf. Novotný, *Jan Hus, Život a dílo*, I, p. 408. Palacký, *Documenta*, p. 405.

It is no wonder that Hus was immensely aroused by the prohibition of preaching in "private" chapels, a provision obviously directed against him, although no names had been named in the bull. Had he obeyed this order, Hus would have been completely and permanently silenced; for he would certainly have been excluded from every other pulpit as well. This is what his foes had long desired to accomplish. Now they seemed to have done it. It was impossible for him to submit. He therefore resolutely refused to obey.

Hus not only appealed from the archbishop's order and continued to preach, he also published a treatise, *De libris haereticorum legendis*,[25] in which he cited Paul's statement, "oportet haereses esse,"[26] and quoted copiously from the Fathers. He argued that it was necessary to know heresies in order to combat and refute them successfully. He repeated Augustine's definition that "heresy is an erroneous doctrine, contrary to the Holy Scriptures, stubbornly defended."[27]

Thereupon the archbishop, extremely angered by these acts of defiance, ordered the surrendered books of Wyclif to be burned immediately (July 16) in the courtyard of his palace. The papal bull did not explicitly authorize him to burn the books, but merely to "remove them from the eyes of the faithful." The burning of the books was accompanied by the ringing of all the bells of Prague and the solemn chanting of the *Te Deum*. Zbyněk thus destroyed some 200 copies of Wyclif's works, although many others remained extant. Furthermore, the archbishop excommunicated Hus and his fellow-protestors as rebels, disobedient, and impugning the catholic faith. Thereupon, feeling unsafe in Prague, he took refuge on his estate at Roudnice. The excommunication was, how-

[25] *Historia et monumenta* (see n. 9), I, pp. 127-131.

[26] I Cor. 11:19.

[27] Augustine, "De utilitate credendi" (J.-P. Migne, *Patrologia latina*, XLII, p. 64ff.).

ever, ignored for the greatest part, so that Hus continued his work both at the chapel and at the university. Prague, in the meantime, rose up in riots. The university also took action by organizing a disputation about Wyclif; but since the members of the commission which had condemned Wyclif's books refused to take part in it, it was exclusively in the hands of Hus' adherents. Hus chose for his part the defense of Wyclif's *De Trinitate*, which was entirely orthodox.[28] Five other masters defended other books, all but one philosophical in character. Jakoubek alone, having chosen Wyclif's *Decalogue*, was the exception. Zbyněk, thereupon, imposed the major excommunication on Hus and his fellow-disputants.

Furthermore, the archbishop sent to the curia new charges against Hus, and requested that his own burning of Wyclif's books be approved. John XXIII appointed four cardinals to deal with the request. They in turn asked the opinion of the University of Bologna. There could, of course, be no doubt of that university's opinion: its masters could not condemn books on logic and philosophy which they, as well as the University of Paris, freely used. They, therefore, declared the action of Zbyněk unjustifiable.

The charges against Hus were turned over for adjudication to Cardinal Odo de Colonna (later Pope Martin V). Despite the letters in defense of Hus written by King Wenceslas and Queen Sophie, the cardinal, notorious for his rigid opposition to anything having a heretical tinge, quickly confirmed the excommunication of Hus. Furthermore, he ordered Zbyněk to continue his action against Hus, calling to his aid, if necessary, the secular arm. He also cited Hus to appear before him in Bologna, where the curia then resided. When this verdict became

[28] Cf. the new edition of this work by Allen duPont Breck, *Johannis Wyclif Tractatus de Trinitate* (Boulder, Colo., University of Colorado Press, 1962); Novotný, *Korespondence*, No. 19.

known in Prague, the king was highly indignant. He insisted that the cardinal annul the excommunication, since Zbyněk had but recently officially testified that there was no heresy in the land. He even suggested that the cardinal or another papal legate come to Prague to investigate the case on the spot.

The struggle between Hus and Zbyněk attracted the attention of the English Lollards. Sir John Oldcastle, Lord Cobham, wrote to Wenceslas' favorite, Voksa of Valdštejn, and perhaps to another noble, praising him for his zeal in the faith and exhorting him to continue his support of the reforming group.[29] Moreover, Richard Wyche, a prominent disciple of Wyclif, wrote to Hus directly, and sent him some of Wyclif's books in lieu of those burned by Zbyněk. Wyche wrote:

> Therefore, you, Hus, beloved brother in Christ, although unknown to me in person, but not in faith and love; for the distance between our countries cannot separate us, since the love of Christ binds us, be strengthened in the grace which was granted you. Labor like a good soldier of Jesus Christ; preach, stand firmly in word and example, and call to the way of truth whomever you can.[30]

Hus read the letter to his congregations consisting "of well-nigh ten thousand." He also replied to both Lord Cobham and Wyche.[31] To the latter he wrote that in Bohemia the people would not hear anything but the holy Scriptures; that "our king with his whole court, the queen, the nobles, and the common people are for the word of Jesus Christ. The Church of Christ in Bohemia sends greetings to the Church of Christ in England, desiring to participate in the confession of the holy faith in the grace of the Lord Jesus Christ." Even more curious

[29] Novotný, *Korespondence*, No. 21.
[30] *Ibid.*, No. 22, p. 78.      [31] *Ibid.*, No. 24.

is the fairly extensive missive sent to Bohemia by a zealous Scots knight, Quintin Folkhyrde.[32] It consists of four "epistles," in which the Scots Lollard assails the hierarchy and clergy of Scotland for their profligacy and immorality.

In 1411, when John Stokes, a member of an English embassy to King Sigismund of Hungary, stopped at Prague, he provoked a violent dispute. He declared that Wyclif was a heretic and that whoever had read his books would necessarily fall into heresy. Furthermore, he made the curious remark that Wyclif was German, not English. Hus challenged him to a debate, which Stokes declined unless it were held on some neutral ground, such as Paris or Rome. Hus nevertheless wrote a refutation of the charges.[33] He declared that Wyclif was not a heretic, or at least that he hoped he was not. He chose to think the better of his neighbor unless he knew for certain the worse about him. Therefore, "he hopes that Master John Wyclif is of the saved." Hus professes to be inclined to that opinion on account of the charity with which one should regard one's neighbor: Wyclif's writings, which castigate all wickedness and which advise all men to resort to Scripture, and his love for Christ's law, prove him to be a righteous man. Let anyone show that Wyclif is heretical in accordance with Augustine's definition of heresy as an opinion contrary to Scripture held obstinately! He further cites the letter of the Oxford university testifying to Wyclif's orthodoxy. Moreover, Hus argues that if everyone who has read Wyclif's books must necessarily fall into heresy, the works of Aristotle should be prohibited as well. Since some men like Sabellius and

[32] J. H. Baxter, ed., *Copiale prioratus Sanctiandree* (Oxford University Press, 1930), pp. 230-236; also Sedlák, *Jan Hus*, supplement, pp. 182-188; cf. my article, "Paul Kravař and the Lollard-Hussite Relations," *Church History*, 1956, pp. 16-26, where it is briefly summarized.

[33] *Historia et monumenta*, I, pp. 135-138.

Arius fell into heresy reading Scripture, it too should not be read. Augustine, Jerome, and Chrysostom read books of heretics and did not fall into heresy. Hus concludes that the arguments of Master Stokes are fallacious.

We fortunately possess Hus' own sermons at Bethlehem Chapel during the years 1410-11, and are thus able to judge of his development under the increasing pressure of the gathering storm.[34] These sermons were delivered in spite of the papal and archiepiscopal prohibition against preaching in chapels. Naturally, they show the effect of such defiance. They are already noticeably influenced by Hus' study of Wyclif, particularly by the latter's *Opus evangelicum*. Nevertheless, as usual, Hus follows the Oxford doctor only in doctrinally sound teaching. He draws besides on a large number of Church Fathers, and uses extensively his own commentary on Lombard's *Sentences*, on several occasions literally. The sermons were recorded by some of his hearers from his spoken word. Consequently, we cannot expect to find in them the degree of accuracy manifested in the sermons written by himself. In these sermons, Hus defends not only the freedom of preaching he claims for all priests, but also the duty to preach laid on them by God Himself. Thus in the sermon on Hebrews 13:17 preached on April 23, 1411, he asserts:

> I have a proof from Scripture that God has ordered the preaching of the Word of God in all the world, everywhere, even in the streets. . . . And because the late Pope Alexander and our prelates forbid preaching in chapels, although they cannot support it from Scripture and are opposed to Scripture, we ought not obey them, for they are false witnesses. Because God has ordered us to preach everywhere, and I as a faithful

[34] V. Flajšhans, ed., *Mag. Io. Hus Sermones in Bethlehem, 1410-11*, 5 vols. (Praha, Královská česká společnost nauk, 1938-42).

Christian should obey Him, I will not stop preaching until death. . . .

In a sermon dealing with obedience preached on December 20, 1410, Hus exclaims rhetorically:

Someone will say, "But you, Hus, do not wish to be subject to your prelates, do not obey the elders, not even the archbishop. . . . I reply that I desire to be as Balaam's ass. Because the prelates sit on me, wishing to force me to go against the command of God to stop preaching, I will press the feet of their desire and will not obey them, for the angel of the Lord stands before me in the way.[35]

He makes a plain reference to himself in the sermon on Acts 6:12: "And they stirred up the people, the elders and the scribes. . . ." He comments: "Thus they now shout throughout the whole world that the Czechs are heretics. . . . And above all they call Hus a heretic, asking, 'Is that heretic still alive?' "

As for the doctrinal teaching contained in these sermons, it seems best to analyze it later. We shall then integrate it into the summary treatment of Hus' theological views.

Returning now to the consideration of the process against Hus at the curia, it was furthered by the emissary of Zbyněk and of the St. Vitus' canons, Michael de Causis. This notorious priest, who had fled the country because he had swindled the king himself in a project having to do with the restoration of some gold mines, established himself at the papal court as a procurator *in causa fidei* (hence his name). He now charged Hus with the heresy of remanence, and with preaching that a priest in mortal sin does not consecrate or absolve. These absurd and wholly unfounded charges were hence-

[35] A. Císařořá-Kolářová, transl., *M. Jan Hus, Betlemské poselství* (Praha, 1947), ii, p. 65.

forth to be fastened upon Hus despite all his denials. The king also sent his diplomatic officials, Dr. John Náz and Master John of Rejnštejn, surnamed "the Cardinal," to inform the pope of the real situation. Hus likewise sent to the curia his procurators, the chief among them being John of Jesenice. The pope, in the meantime, had transferred the case from the hands of Cardinal Colonna to the auditor of the sacred palace, John of Thomariis. In spite of the fact that Colonna was no longer in charge of the case, he issued, in February 1411, a ban on Hus for non-compliance with his citation for personal appearance before him. He did not, however, decree that Hus was a heretic. Nevertheless, it was a victory for Zbyněk, who promptly published the pronouncement in Prague. There, however, with the exception of two churches, the decree was not proclaimed, and Hus continued to preach at Bethlehem. He now frequently asserted that it was the duty of Christians to obey their superiors, both civil and ecclesiastical, in all things lawful, stressing the all-important adjective, "lawful." They must, however, discriminate whether or not such orders are indeed in accordance with Scripture. When the pope or prelates forbid preaching, they must refuse to obey. "It is meet to obey God rather than men." If one is excommunicated for such refusal, the excommunication is of no effect before God, even though it may have validity in the ecclesiastical courts.

The attitude at the curia may be judged by the advice given the pope by one of the prominent officials of his court, Dietrich of Niem.[36] He counseled the pontiff to waste no time investigating the case, but to proceed instantly with the extermination of the Wyclifite heresy in Bohemia. There is no evidence that he himself took

36 Jan Sedlák, *Studie a texty k náboženským dějinám českým*, 2 vols. (Olomouc, 1913-19), I, pp. 45-55; Bartoš (see n. 14), p. 351, asserts that Michael de Causis induced Dietrich to give the fanatical advice to the pope.

the trouble to read Hus' writings. To him a mere suspicion of heresy was enough. He therefore urged the pope: "incarcerare, degradare, tradere brachio seculari." Yet, this high papal official was one of the most resolute advocates of Church reform, urging its necessity from top to bottom including "the head and members . . ."!

King Wenceslas, always jealous of the good name of his kingdom, felt provoked with the perennial charges of heresy leveled at his land by his own archbishop. Since Zbyněk had not fulfilled the requests of the royal commission imposed on him the year before, the king now ordered the sequestration of the properties of the canons and priests adhering to the archbishop. From his retreat at Roudnice, Zbyněk replied by hurling the sentence of excommunication at the executors of the royal command. In exasperation, Wenceslas seized the cathedral treasures and had them transported to his castle of Karlstein. He further ordered the visitation of the ecclesiastical properties in the whole kingdom. In June, Zbyněk struck back by placing Prague and its environs under an interdict. The king forbade all clergy to obey the order and it was ignored even by the archbishop's own party. Once more Zbyněk was faced with an inevitable defeat. He thereupon decided to negotiate for terms of peace. The king was willing to grant such negotiation and decided to submit the conflict to arbitration. He appointed a most distinguished commission composed of both high secular and ecclesiastical dignitaries. This body proposed to the archbishop that he submit to the king, annul the interdict, and write the pope that he knew of no heresy in the land. He was further to request that all who were under papal excommunication be released and the curial processes against them be stopped. If these conditions were fulfilled, the confiscated benefices and properties would be restored to their possessors.[37] Hus, was likewise

[37] Palacký, *Documenta*, pp. 437-440.

requested to write a humble letter of submission to the pope, enclosing along with it a statement of his orthodoxy. Hus promptly complied with the request, and after enumerating the false charges leveled against him, he added his plea:

> Wherefore, Supreme Vicar of Christ, I humbly implore Your Holiness' clemency, that You may deign, for the sake of the mercy of the Almighty God, graciously to absolve me from appearing personally and from the other consequences therefrom; . . . for I am now in complete accord with the aforesaid most reverend father in Christ, Lord Zbyněk.[38]

His most respectful letter of submission was supported by a testimonial of the university, witnessing to his unimpeachable character, faith, and conduct. Hus wrote a similarly humble letter to the cardinals,[39] supplicating them "on his knees" for the same merciful consideration he had implored from the pope. He reminded them that during the time of the Pisan Council he had exerted himself in his preaching to sway his hearers to support the cardinals, while Zbyněk still had firmly opposed them. It was on this account that the archbishop had excommunicated him.

That these submissive letters of Hus were not forcibly imposed on him, or expressed insincere sentiments on his part, may be seen from the sermon he preached on August 28, 1410, on the text "Ye are the salt of the earth."[40] He exhorted his audience to pray for the "vicars of the apostles": the late Alexander V, that God might receive him into His glory, and John XXIII, that

---

[38] Novotný, *Korespondence*, No. 31; also Mladoňovic, *Relatio* (see n. 17), p. 62; my translation in *Hus at the Council*, pp. 147-149.

[39] Novotný, *Korespondence*, No. 32.

[40] *Historia et monumenta*, II, p. 70. The scriptural quotation, Matt. 5:13.

the Lord might preserve him from evil and graciously grant him to be the "salt of the earth." He concluded the sermon by appealing for prayers for "the prelates of the Church, the patriarchs, cardinals, archbishops, bishops, and even the priests of the lowest order." There certainly is nothing rebellious in Hus' attitude toward his superiors in these appeals!

The demand proved too much for Zbyněk's pride. He consulted his close friend, Bishop John of Litomyšl, as to what he should do. The latter counseled him to refuse. Zbyněk thereupon wrote the king a letter from Litomyšl, in which, after enumerating his own unredressed grievances, and complaining of the opposition to his administration, he declared that it would be "against his soul and honor" to write the pope as directed. He, therefore, announced to the king his intention to take refuge with King Sigismund in Hungary.[41] Most unexpectedly, however, he died at Bratislava on September 28, 1411. Thus closed a fateful chapter in the struggle between Hus and Archbishop Zbyněk.

[41] Palacký, *Documenta*, pp. 443-446.

## CHAPTER IV

## ATTACKED, DEFEATED,

## BUT UNCONQUERED

THE death of the thirty-six-year-old Archbishop Zbyněk did not put an end to, or even cause a respite in, the struggle in which he and Hus were engaged. Dr. Albík of Uničov, the king's personal physician—an excellent physician, but quite unfitted for the highest ecclesiastical office in the country—obtained the vacant see and was indeed quite willing not to reopen the controversy. The curia, however, was otherwise minded. The pope had entrusted the case to four cardinals (June 1411), headed by Francesco Zabarella, the famous Florentine jurist. In January 1412, Zabarella ruled that the action of Cardinal Colonna in refusing to hear Hus' procurators and declaring him excommunicate was precipitous and unjustified. He therefore appointed a hearing at which they were to be given an opportunity to state their case.

In one of his minor Czech treatises, Hus himself describes the Roman process with details that cannot be found elsewhere.[1]

The pope [John XXIII] did not allow a hearing [to the procurators], which they demanded at his court exclaiming: "Grant us a hearing, as you should do to a pagan, a Jew, or a heretic, or even to the devil if he came to you and demanded a hearing!" He, however, always turned away his head and transferred the whole case to cardinals. They, then, accepting from my foes beautiful horses, silver goblets, and precious rings, refused to pass judgment. The pope then turned the

[1] "Knížky proti kuchmistrovi," in K. J. Erben, ed., *Mistra Jana Husi Sebrané spisy české* (Praha, 1866), III, pp. 241-254.

case over to others, but the same thing happened: some of [these cardinals] are already dead, while others are being jailed by the king of Naples. After that the pope once again assumed charge of that trial, saying that he himself wished to be its judge and that "Everyone else has already profited by that trial except I." Once again an appeal was made to him to grant a hearing to the procurators, but he refused it; for he was looking for the golden knights [i.e., presents of gulden], but the goose [Hus] did not have them nor wish to send them to him. But he, wishing to receive those knights, seized my procurators and thrust them into prison. When God helped them to escape—one of them having been in prison a year and a half and another the same length of time—they returned home as did also the third. When again after the priest Zbyněk's death, by the plotting of my foes other enemies secured from Cardinal Peter my excommunication, and I realized that God's truth has no place with the pope, I appealed my case to the Lord God: for to appeal means to ask help from a higher judge. . . . Consequently, I did not appear before the pope because he had refused to hear the truth, had jailed the procurators, and had robbed Master Stanislav and Master Stephen, having despoiled them of two hundred and seven gulden and their horses. Also I did not appear because I am engaged in God's trial against the pope and know that he would not condemn himself. . . .

This is Hus' own account of the proceedings of his trial before the curia. It must be conceded that it is more of a general summary than a strictly accurate account. Moreover, it goes considerably beyond the stage of development we have so far reached. Let us, therefore, return to the story as depicted in the official documents. When by Zabarella's ruling Hus' case assumed a more favorable aspect, Zbyněk's agent, Michael de Causis, was not caught napping. He utilized all his important connections to induce the pope to transfer the case once more. This time it was placed in the hands of Cardinal Rainald de Brancacci, who for over a year simply did nothing about it. He refused to give an audience to Hus' representatives and forbade them any further pleading. Consequently, Colonna's excommunication and personal citation of Hus remained in force. In fact, Michael accused John of Jesenice, Hus' chief procurator, of Wyclifite heresy. The latter was imprisoned, but succeeded in escaping from Rome. Nevertheless, the curia did not proceed against Hus with the most terrible of its weapons—imposition of the interdict. That measure was reserved for an even more violent crisis involving Hus in a fatal conflict with the papacy, the conflict over the "crusading bull" of Pope John XXIII.

King Ladislas of Naples was a supporter of Gregory XII. Pope John naturally resented the aid given his deposed and excommunicated Roman rival. On September 9, 1411, the very month in which Zbyněk died, John issued a bull[2] declaring a crusade against Ladislas and Gregory. It ordered all patriarchs, archbishops, bishops, and prelates, under pain of excommunication, to declare Ladislas an excommunicate, perjurer, schismatic, blasphemer, heretic and relapsed heretic, conspiring criminally against the pope and the Church. He was damned unto the third generation. Should he die in this state, he must be refused the funeral rites in perpetuity. John called upon all rulers, secular and ecclesiastical, to destroy Ladislas. All who participated in the crusade were granted remission of sins, provided they were heartily

2 "Bulla indulgentiarum Pape Joannis XXIII," in *Historia et monumenta Joannis Hus atque Hieronymi Pragensis, confessorum Christi,* 2 vols. (Norimberg, 1715), I, pp. 212-213; "Responsio scripti octo doctorum theologiae," *ibid.,* I, p. 394.

contrite and confessed them. Likewise those who would equip and support a soldier for a month would partake of the indulgences.

A second bull was published on December 2, 1411,[3] in which John appointed two commissioners of indulgences, and condemned Gregory anew as a heretic and schismatic. Wenceslas Tiem, dean of Passau, and Pax de Fantuciis of Bologna were appointed commissioners for the lands of the Bohemian crown. They arrived in Prague on May 22, 1412, and proceeded to organize the campaign. The king did not oppose the execution of the bull, nor did the majority of the university masters. That dangerous task remained to be undertaken by Hus and his most devoted friends. In two treatises[4] he denounced the indulgences; he denounced not the principle but only the manner in which they were offered for sale. Hus himself, as a youth, had spent his last *grossus* in buying indulgences during the Jubilee of 1393, and never afterward expressly denied their propriety, if properly administered.

In the first treatise, *Adversus indulgentias papales*, Hus asserts that the powers of the pope are limited, not absolute. He can sin and err, as history shows. In the present instance he errs in the terms of the bull; to oppose it is not to oppose God. To declare that the pope cannot err or sin, is blasphemy: Peter sinned; Pope Leo was a heretic; Gregory XII and his rival were condemned as heretics by the Council of Pisa. Scripture bears witness to no saint who ever said to anyone: "I forgive you your sins, I absolve you." Nor has any saint granted indulgences. Hus furthermore denies that it is lawful for the pope to fight with the sword, for Christ ordered Peter to sheathe his sword. Christ reproved his disciples

[3] "Alia bulla commissariis," *ibid.*, pp. 213-215.
[4] "Disputatio Joannis Hus adversus indulgentias papales," and "Contra bullam Papae Joannis XXIII," *ibid.*, pp. 215-237.

when they wished to call down fire upon Samaria. Contrary to Christ's example, the pope has ordered Christians to exterminate other Christians. The Church possesses only the spiritual sword to be used against the Antichrist. The bull, on the contrary, is a veritable appeal to violence and murder. It permits simony in allowing the subletting of whole archdeaconries and parishes, thus granting them a share in the profits of the sale of indulgences. The pope should conquer his foes by prayer, for Christ declared, "My kingdom is not of this world."[5] Hus asserts that some obey the bull out of ignorance, others from opportunism, and others out of fear. In the last category are the theologians, "who say one thing about the bull in private and another in public . . . for they fear the loss of their benefices, of men's worldly honor, and of their earthly life." He quotes Chrysostom, "Whoever does not defend the known truth is a betrayer of truth." He objects to the prescribed form of absolution offered by the sellers of indulgences. It contains, he says, an agreement to pay for the forgiveness of sins, and blasphemously pretends that the seller forgives sins. It contains the words, "I give and concede to you the fullest remission of your sins, both as to punishment and guilt." No man can grant forgiveness of sins, only God. The gifts of God are not for sale. There is no forgiveness of sins without penitence, and nothing beyond penitence can be required. The pope cannot know whether the purchaser has truly repented and therefore whether God has forgiven his sins; hence, he cannot declare them forgiven. In pretending to do so, he usurps God's prerogative. The bull does indeed stipulate that the granting of indulgences is conditional on contrition and confession, but it is obvious that its real purpose is to induce Christians either to fight a war or to support it. If the pope has the power

[5] John 18:36.

to forgive sins absolutely, why does he limit it to those who buy indulgences? He should then forgive the sins of all men. Moreover, since the forgiveness extends to those in *articulo mortis*, such practice, if persisted in, would empty purgatory. Finally, the indulgences are superfluous, since forgiveness of sins is granted without any money payment to all who are truly penitent and confess their sins. The real aim of the bull obviously is to collect money.

The second treatise, much shorter than the first, adds but little to what Hus has already written. He comments, however, that in the absence of the requirement of full penance in the bull, "even if the devil came and repented and gave money, he would immediately go to heaven."

De Vooght deals at great length with Johann Loserth's charge that Hus copied in this treatise Wyclif's *De ecclesia* (chap. 23) word for word. After the initial definition and to the end of the conclusions which follow, all, Loserth said, is the intellectual property of Wyclif.[6] De Vooght,[7] although admitting that Hus did copy Wyclif, since "les théologiens recopiaient sans scrupule," as Wyclif himself had done, examines this charge minutely. He concludes that the claim is greatly exaggerated. Hus followed Wyclif in the items doctrinally unexceptionable and neatly avoided the latter's reprehensible expressions. He in no way denied the sacrament of penance. On the contrary, he defended it against the abuses of the "crusading bull." This De Vooght approves as just, emphasizing particularly that Hus did not follow

[6] Johann Loserth, *Hus und Wiclif, zur Genesis der Husitischen Lehre*, 2nd edn. (München and Berlin, 1925), p. 148; and in his *Joannis Wyclif, Tractatus de ecclesia* (London, The Wyclif Society, 1886), p. xxvi.

[7] Paul de Vooght, "Les indulgences dans la théologie de Wiclif et de Huss," in *Hussiana* (Louvain, Publications universitaires de Louvain, 1960), pp. 303-334.

Wyclif in denying "the treasury of merits." He concludes:[8]

Ni matériellement ni formellement, il [Loserth] n'est conforme à la vérité de prétendre que Huss tient *tout* de Wiclif. Au seul point de vue matériel, sa part à lui est quatre fois plus considérable que celle de l'Anglais. Formellement non plus, il n'est pas qu'un disciple ou qu'un plagiaire. Dans les textes de Wiclif, Huss a opéré des tris et des choix d'après ses convictions et ses opinions propres.

Hus returned to the theme of indulgences and forgiveness of sins again and again, since he was repeatedly attacked for his denial of the "crusading bull." A few examples of this sort must suffice. We may note the references to it he made in his *Sermones in Bethlehem*, for they are among the earliest of his polemics against the bull. In the sermon on Balaam's ass, Hus touched upon it: "They say, 'Give us nothing but money and you will have remission of sins from punishment and guilt!' And the blinded people give and sin even more by deserting the gospel of Christ." The sellers extend their palms and say: "Whoever places money here, his sins will be forgiven."[9] In the sermon on St. Wenceslas' Day,[10] Hus uses an illustration of a wicked master who bought from the pope indulgences, and a good layman who did not. They both died on the same day:

Then according to the pope's bull the master would immediately go to heaven, but not the layman, be-

[8] *Ibid.*, p. 332.

[9] V. Flajšhans, ed., *Sermones in Bethlehem 1410-11*, 5 vols. (Praha, Královská česká společnost nauk, 1938-42), v, p. 101.

[10] *Ibid.*, v, p. 82; the same subject is discussed in *Mistr Jan Hus, Postilla* (Praha, Komenského ev. faculta bohoslovecká, 1952), p. 173; also "Výklad modlitby," p. 475, where Hus asserts that "the bull does not demand from the penitent the third requirement of penance—the satisfaction for his sins."

cause he had venial sins. Would such a judgment of the Lord God be just? Surely not! . . . Therefore, consider this matter, dear brethren, so that you will not suffer yourselves to be seduced by empty words and will not believe that blessedness can be bought by money alone. . . .

Finally, on the Feast of St. Lawrence,[11] speaking about Paul, Hus exclaimed:

Did Paul grant indulgences? Certainly not! Nor did he beg from the churches in order to cast large bells or build enormous churches, but he begged for the sake of priests who preached the Lord's word. He did not grant indulgences such as now the mendicants sell, but declared, according to Scripture, what God wished to grant. . . .

In Hus' *Exposition of the Decalogue*, written in Czech while he was in hiding, he says of people who buy indulgences that "it were well for them to demand to be assured from Holy Scripture or by God's revelation, or by a physically perceptible proof [that the indulgences are valid]. When no such proof is shown them, then people should demand guarantees so that they would be certain they had not paid their money for nothing. . . ."[12]

A particularly devastating passage about the "crusading bull" is found in *Postilla*, also written in exile. Hus declares there:

. . . they erect the cross and call for holy war and for holy battle, granting remission of sins and punishments to those who aid the war. A strange thing! They cannot rid themselves of fleas and flies and yet want

[11] *Ibid.*, IV, p. 330.
[12] "Výklad desatera," in F. Žilka, ed., *Mistra Jana Husi Vybrané spisy* (Jilemnice, n.d.), p. 309.

to rid others of infernal tortures by means of money payment, without their praying for it or otherwise living well! And if some faithful Christian preaches against their wickedness, they hate him and by devised plots they stop God's services, if they cannot otherwise stop preaching which reveals their wickedness to the people. [About the interdict he writes:] For what can cause Christians greater deprivation than to refuse them funeral, baptism, confession, and the Lord's body?[13]

Although De Vooght pronounces Hus' objections to the papal bull "perfectly catholic" and John's remission of sins for money "a vast project of simoniacal swindle,"[14] it was this brave declaration which deprived Hus of the support of the king and of his former close friends and supporters, Stanislav and Páleč. They now became his bitter and inveterate enemies. Hus himself declared:

[It was] the sale of indulgences and the raising of the cross against Christians that had first separated me from that doctor [Páleč]. If he would confess the truth, he would admit that he had declared the formula of absolution, which he had first shown me with his own hand, as containing palpable errors. . . . To him I said at last and have never conversed with him since: "Páleč is a friend; truth is a friend; and both being friends, it is holy to prefer the truth."[15]

Hus' statement that Páleč had first shown him the bull and declared that it contains palpable errors was acknowledged by Páleč himself. He even added that he did not allow the articles to be read in his church. Nevertheless, he tried to justify his conduct by saying that he

[13] *Postilla* (see n. 10), pp. 22-23.
[14] Paul de Vooght, *L'hérésie de Jean Huss* (Louvain, Publications universitaires de Louvain, 1960), pp. 194, 196.
[15] *Historia et monumenta* (see n. 2), I, p. 330.

did not on that account "blaspheme" the supreme pontiff as did Hus and his "fellow-apostles."[16] Hus had thus burned his bridges behind him. There was no going back, no retreat for him. Henceforth, his face was set toward the final tragedy in Constance. To be sure, protests against the bull had been raised in England, France, and Vienna, as even Dietrich of Niem testified.[17] But they made no difference as far as Hus' fate was concerned.

Not satisfied with his personal protests, Hus wished to induce the university to make a similar pronouncement. Rector Mark of Hradec, a devoted disciple of Hus, allowed a disputation. Hus chose to discourse on the theme, whether the faithful should approve the bull.[18] In this he was supported by Jerome of Prague. Both received enthusiastic applause from the students. Thereupon, the theological faculty sent two of its representatives to Archbishop Albík, the chancellor of the university, to request that any further protests against the bull be forbidden. Hus was cited before the archbishop and confronted with the papal legates, who demanded whether he were willing to obey the apostolic mandates. In his own description of this interesting scene, which is not without its humorous aspect, Hus writes:

> I responded that I heartily aspire to fulfill the apostolic mandates. The legates, however, considering the apostolic mandates and those of the Roman pontiff as interchangeable terms, thought that I was willing to submit and to preach to the people in behalf of the

[16] Stephen Páleč, "De ecclesia," in Jan Sedlák, *Jan Hus* (Praha Dědictví sv. Prokopa, 1915), supplement, pp. 280-281.

[17] H. van der Hardt, *Magni et universalis Constantiensis concilii tomi VI* (Berlin and Leipzig, 1697-1700), II, part xv, cols. 371-372: "Unde contra ipsum una voce valde multi dicebant quod sanam conscientiam non haberet."

[18] "De indulgentiis sive de cruciata Papae Joannis XXIII," in *Historia et monumenta*, I, pp. 215-235.

raising of the cross against Ladislas, king of Naples, as well as against all his people and against Gregory XII. Thereupon the legates said: "Behold, Lord Archbishop, he is ready to obey the mandates of our lord." To whom I said: "Lords, understand me. I said that I heartily aspire to fulfill the apostolic mandates and to obey them in everything; but I call apostolic mandates the teaching of Christ's apostles. In as far as the mandates of the Roman pontiff are in harmony with the apostolic mandates and teaching, according to the rule of Christ's law, to that degree I am most willing to obey them. But should I find any of them as opposed, those I will not obey, even if the fire to burn my body were placed before my eyes!"[19]

Thereupon, the theological faculty prepared a complaint to be presented to the king. They protested against Hus' disputation denouncing the bull, declaring this action to be a great rebellion against the king, the archbishop, and the pope. They complained that Hus had publicly defamed the papal bull as well as themselves. In the complaint they say, "we believe simply as our fathers believed and as Christendom for hundreds of years have held and believed, that the pope can grant full remission of all sins . . . ; we also believe that the pope can, in case of necessity, call upon Christ's faithful and demand from them temporal aid in defense of the Roman city and the church. . . ."[20]

Moreover, popular riots broke out in Prague against the sellers of indulgences. Their money boxes were smeared with filth and the sellers themselves abused and maltreated. Jerome, always fiery in his eloquent denun-

[19] "Contra octo doctores," *Historia et monumenta*, I, p. 367; V. Novotný, *Jan Hus, Život a dílo*, 2 vols. (Praha, Jan Laichter, 1919-21), II, p. 92.

[20] F. Palacký, ed., *Documenta Mag. Joannis Hus* (Praha, F. Tempský, 1869), p. 450.

ciations, declared publicly that the indulgences were worthless. He actually boxed the ears of a Minorite friar who reviled him.[21] The king's favorite, Voksa of Valdštejn, organized a public procession in which a student decked in a prostitute's finery rode in a wagon amid a jeering crowd. When the procession reached the New Town Square, the bulls, which the student had hung around his neck, were burned in a bonfire.[22]

These events infuriated the king, whose temper was never far from the boiling point. Regarding the riots as a flagrant defiance of his will, he ordered the theological faculty and Hus to come to terms. When this effort failed, he convoked the theologians at the castle of Žebrák, where he was then staying. Páleč, then dean of the theological faculty, demanded of Hus and Jakoubek that they submit to him in writing their recent academic disputes about the indulgences. Hus refused on the ground that he had taught nothing in secret. He was willing to surrender the written copy of his disputation, if the king ordered it, but on condition that the doctors undertake, under pain of death, to render an account of their faith.[23] Jakoubek complied with the faculty's request. Páleč furthermore prepared, prior to the meeting, his *Tractatus gloriosus*, with which we shall deal in Chapter V.[24] The royal Council, which was in charge of the meeting, held it at the Žebrák house of Bishop Conrad Vechta of Olomouc. The members of the Council consisted of Bishop Vechta, of Olomouc; John of Chocenice, captain of the dukedom of Wratislaw and of Svídnice; Master Zdeněk of Labouň, prior of the

[21] Novotný, *Jan Hus, Život a dílo*, ii, p. 104.

[22] *Ibid.*, ii, p. 105.

[23] Hus, "Contra octo doctores," in *Historia et monumenta*, i, p. 366.

[24] J. Loserth, ed., "Tractatus gloriosus," in "Beiträge zur Geschichte der Husitischen Bewegung," iv, *Archiv für Oesterreichische Geschichte*, Vol. 75 (Wien, 1889), pp. 333-399.

College of All Saints; James of Dubá, prior of Vyšehrad; and other officials of the king. Páleč, in the name of the eight members of the theological faculty, first of all denounced Hus for not surrendering the text of his disputation and called it an act of disobedience. Then he presented a defense of the indulgences and the above-named *Tractatus gloriosus*. In the end the faculty recommended that the forty-five articles of Wyclif, already condemned three times since 1403, be condemned anew. The faculty designated which among these articles were heretical, erroneous, false, seditious, scandalous, contrary to good morals or the Church, or a combination of several of these designations.[25] Only seven were declared out and out heretical, although later no such distinction was recognized. The faculty was not, however, satisfied with these oft-condemned articles alone, but added seven of their own.[26] The first of these asserts that "whoever thinks of the sacraments and the keys of the Church otherwise than the holy Roman Church does, shall be reputed a heretic." The third states that anyone who asserts that the customs of the Church not specifically contained in Scripture are not to be held, is in error. The sixth states it is an error to say that "whoever denies that the pope cannot, when there is necessity, call upon the persons of Christ's faithful, requesting from them temporal aid in defense of the Apostolic See and of the status of the holy Roman Church and the city, [demanding of them] to restrain and repel foes and enemies of the Christian Church by supporting liberally and faithfully Christ's faithful, and granting full remission of sins to the truly penitent who confess and are

[25] Palacký, *Documenta* (see n. 20), pp. 451-455; the Latin text of the forty-five articles is given in Appendix I; also in a slightly different wording in Jan Sedlák, *Studie a texty, k náboženským dějinám českým*, 2 vols. (Olomouc, 1912-19), I, pp. 58-62.

[26] Palacký, *Documenta*, pp. 455-456. Later these articles are referred to as being six in number.

contrite." Finally it affirms "that the mandate of our lord king and civil lords that no one clamor against the preachers of indulgences nor against the papal bulls, is and has been just, reasonable and holy."

The royal Council approved these recommendations of the faculty and ordered them proclaimed in the king's name. The very next day, however, an event occurred which caused a most serious popular uprising against the sale of indulgences. At three of the principal churches of Prague—St. Vitus' Cathedral, the Týn, and St. James—three young men, Martin, John, and Stašek, protested against the preaching of indulgences. They were seized and imprisoned in the Old Town Hall. Hearing of this, Hus immediately went to intercede for them, offering himself in their stead, since they had acted on impulses derived from his preaching. The councilmen promised to inflict no serious punishment on the prisoners. After Hus left, however, they at once proceeded, in accordance with the king's order, to have the young men beheaded.[27] The execution created an immense commotion. A great crowd gathered in front of the Town Hall. The bodies of the men were reverently lifted and carried to Bethlehem in a procession headed by Master John of Jíčín and singing "Ita sunt martyres." They were then interred in the chapel after Hus had celebrated the martyrs' mass for them. The excited and refractory crowds then besieged the Town Hall, remonstrating against the councilmen. Unable to control the dangerously disturbed masses, the councilmen appealed to the king for help. This infuriated Wenceslas still more, so that he shouted, "Even if there were thousand

[27] Dr. John Náz, the king's emissary at the Council of Constance, testified there that such was the king's order. Cf. "Petri de Mladoniowicz relatio de Magistro Johanne Hus," in V. Novotný, ed., *Fontes rerum Bohemicarum*, VIII (Praha, 1932), pp. 106-107; my translation in *John Hus at the Council of Constance* (New York and London, Columbia University Press, 1965), pp. 219-220.

such, let them suffer the same fate as the others! And if there are not enough justices and officers here in the kingdom, I will have them brought from other areas."[28]

Furthermore, being in this extremely irritated mood, the king yielded to the request of the theological faculty that the Žebrák decisions be announced to the clergy and the university. He called a meeting at the Old Town Hall (July 16, 1412), to which both the clergy and the university masters were summoned by the royal Council. Hus, however, was absent, having left the day before; he returned three weeks later.[29] The meeting was presided over by Patriarch Wenceslas Králík and Bishop Conrad of Vechta, and attended by the burgo-master and the councilors of the Old Town. The inquistor, Bishop Nicholas of Nezero, delivered a speech describing the evil repute in which Bohemia was held on account of the rumors of heresy. He then read the Žebrák decrees of July 10. Anyone daring to defend any of the forty-five articles of Wyclif and to deny or attack the indulgences, was to be exiled from the country. All university disputations about Wyclif's theses were likewise proscribed. Not even the notarial record here cited is complete. In his polemics with Páleč, Hus adds other details about the meeting that he must have learned from others, since he himself was not present. He writes that it was said that "He who shall not obey the pontifical decree shall die!" To that Páleč later replied that he was referring to the Lord's command to the Levites in Deut. 17:2-7, that the man or woman who has gone to serve other gods shall die on the evidence of two or three witnesses. Since the place of the Levites has been taken by the pope and the

28 *Ibid.*

29 F. M. Bartoš, *Čechy v době Husově* (Praha, Jan Laichter, 1947), p. 358. Others do not mention this long absence of Hus' from Prague, and therefore date his defense of Wyclif toward the end of July. Cf. also Sedlák, *Studie a texty,* I, pp. 36ff.

cardinals, the command now is transferred to them and they have the right to execute it.[30] Bishop Nicholas then requested all those present to give their consent to all he had read. First of all, he demanded that Rector Mark of Hradec announce the decisions to the entire university. Then he asked whether he personally regarded the forty-five articles as heretical. The rector demurred on the ground that not all were heretical (even the theological faculty had not so described them), but that some could be understood in a good sense. He did not, however, hold them in the sense ascribed to them by the theologians. With the exception of several masters, Procopius of Plzeň, Friedrich Epinge, and others,[31] all the rest of the university masters gave the required assent. Despite this seeming unanimity on the part of the university (with the exceptions noted), the next day Rector Mark called the masters to a meeting in Charles College where, in the absence of the theologians—who pretended to fear that they would be mishandled—they passed a resolution to the effect that certain articles of Wyclif could be defended "in their acceptable sense."

This enabled Hus upon his return to undertake, in three sessions, a public defense of six of the forty-five articles. He chose for this purpose articles 13, 14, 16, 18, 15, and 4.[32] Jakoubek of Stříbro defended article 32, on apostolic poverty. Friedrich Epinge chose article 11, on prelatical excommunication. Of the articles dealing with the pope or papacy, not a single one was included, although there were thirteen of them. Kybal remarks, although without being able to cite any specific statement of Hus' to that effect, that Hus left them out of the

---

[30] Stephen Páleč's "Antihus," edited by J. Sedlák in *Hlidka* (Brno, 1911), pp. 10, 12.

[31] "Contra Stanislaum," in *Historia et monumenta*, I, p. 332.

[32] The text of all six disputations is found in "Defensio quarundam articulorum Joannis Wicleff," in *Historia et monumenta*, I, pp. 139-167.

disputation, "thus admitting their faultiness and mani-festing even then tact and a sense of fitness, mildness and restraint. This shows clearly that Hus was concerned with factual and positive reform, not with sterile clamor and provocative heckling."[33] Hus prefaces his disputa-tion by saying that although he does not regard the chosen theses as necessarily orthodox, they have an ac-ceptable sense which he wishes to expound. It verges on great danger to one's salvation, he declares, to condemn truth without a reasonable inquiry into the grounds on which it is predicated. Christ said: "Do not judge and you will not be judged."[34] The doctors have ignored this warning. Hus asserts further that the university re-fused to accept the Town Hall decrees and accepted the forty-five articles as far as they are just and true, until those who condemned them prove from Scripture that they are false. He then proceeds to defend the thesis, not condemned as heretical either at the Blackfriar synod of 1382 or at Žebrák, that those who cease preach-ing or hearing the Word of God on account of an unjust excommunication, are themselves excommunicated by God. Furthermore, they shall be regarded as traitors to Christ at the Day of Judgment. He argues that the com-mand to preach the gospel is divine. Jesus sent His disciples principally to preach.[35] Thus preaching is ob-ligatory, not optional. The command to hear the law of Christ is likewise prescribed. Those who cease to hear the gospel preached on account of an unjust excommu-nication, are likewise themselves excommunicated. For they neglect the God-appointed means to salvation. Bish-ops holding the catholic faith should not obey a pope

[33] V. Kybal, *Jan Hus, Učení,* 3 vols. (Praha, Jan Laichter, 1923-31), II, p. 24. The speeches of Jakoubek and Epinge are included in *Mag. Johannis Hus, Tractatus responsivus,* edited by S. Harrison Thomson (Boulder, Colo., University of Colorado Press, 1956).

[34] Luke 6:37.

[35] Matt. 10:5-23 and elsewhere.

heretically ordering them anything contrary to Scripture. Nor should a priest cease from preaching on account of such an order. Since Hus regarded Pope John XXIII as a heretic, to disobey his command forbidding preaching, as he had done for the last two years, was not only permissible but obligatory.

Hus then passes on in his disputation to the next article, that it is lawful for a deacon or a priest to preach the Word of God without the authority of the Apostolic See or of the bishops. He argues in behalf of this article's validity and truth: "Being instigated by the spirit of Jesus Christ, a deacon or priest can, without any special licence of the pope or bishops, preach the Word of God."[36] The spirit of Christ has greater authority than any human-invented papal or episcopal licence. Once ordained, priests need not seek official permission every time they preach, since that is their duty. As no bishop can forbid the faithful to give alms to the poor, so no bishop can forbid a priest to share his spiritual gifts with the needy. The gift of preaching is God-given, and to impede it is to impede the Word of God. Hus is well aware that the canon law prohibits preaching without episcopal permission. He counters by pointing out that the gloss pertaining to the law explains that this means "without a general licence which is obtained and granted when the bishop appoints a priest to rule the people."[37]

Hus then goes on to argue about the next article, "the temporal lords may at will withdraw temporal goods from habitually delinquent ecclesiastics." This is an excellent illustration of Hus' usual treatment of the teachings of Wyclif with which he disagrees. In this instance he omits the second clause of the article, "the commonalty may at will correct delinquent lords."[38] Furthermore,

[36] "Defensio . . ." (see n. 32), I, p. 142.
[37] *Historia et monumenta,* I, p. 143.
[38] In the Žebrák text this is No. 17.

most significantly he prefaces his discussion with a statement, "It is not my or the university's intention to
counsel princes and secular lords to withdraw goods
from the clergy whenever they want or however they
want and divert them to whatever they want. Our intention is to scrutinize if the article concerning the with-
drawal of temporalities from the clergy can have a true
sense in which it must be sustained without condemnation."[39] Hus thereupon offers no less than forty-four reasons in proof of the proposition. He quotes Old and New
Testament examples of such practices on the part of
kings and adds illustrations from history. Even Christ
paid tribute to Caesar and thus acknowledged his rule.
Paul appealed to Caesar. It is lawful for secular lords to
punish clerics for civil offenses, although Hus would have
them do it in a brotherly spirit. He argues convincingly
against the claim that all the endowments granted by the
king of Bohemia to the Church belong to the pope
absolutely, for then "our king would not be the king of
the whole of Bohemia. For more than a quarter [of the
land] would fall to the clerics, i.e., in dead hand. Since
every day the clerical possessions are increasing while
those of the barons, the military, and of the other seculars
are decreasing, it could easily happen that all property
would devolve to the clerics of the kingdom of Bohemia,
as has happened in the Empire."[40]

In this radical statement concerning the relation of
Church and state, Hus subjects all clerical possessions,
without any limitation whatever, to secular rulers. The
Church does not own its properties "in fee simple," but
only as usufruct. Accordingly, the king and secular lords
have the right to deprive the "habitually delinquent"
clerics even of the use of these possessions. This is an
act of moral discipline which the state is in duty bound

[39] *Historia et monumenta*, I, p. 147.
[40] *Ibid.*, p. 153.

to exercise over all its subjects, civil as well as ecclesiastical. Hus thus repudiates the current opinion that the Church is superior to the state.

It cannot be denied that Hus' proposal was a remedy as inequitable as the undoubted disease it was supposed to cure. It was an invitation to the civil rulers to despoil the Church unscrupulously, despite the safeguards he wished to impose on them. Hus succumbed in this instance too largely to Wyclif's unrealistic and purely theoretical notion of "dominion," advocated in his *De dominio divino* and *De civili dominio*. The evils Hus sought to correct were real enough; but to insist on an enforced "apostolic poverty" of the whole Church by inviting the equally rapacious and unscrupulous civil rulers and nobles to impose it on the clergy was as morally questionable as it was potentially dangerous. Unless the Church were to reform itself voluntarily— of which admittedly there was but a meagre chance— it would be extremely difficult to find an equitable remedy.

In an earlier tract written against the inquisitor Maurice Rvačka,[41] who used to spy upon Hus by attending his preaching with his hood drawn over his forehead to prevent being recognized, Hus argues that when Christ drove the money-changers and other traders out of the temple, he thereby authorized the secular rulers to discipline wicked priests. The rights of the seculars to uphold and defend justice and to punish transgressors of the law are specifically asserted by Paul in Romans 13. In this sense the rulers are, as Augustine teaches, vicars of Christ the King exercising in His divine capacity authority over the wicked and providing protection for the good. He thus conceives of civil rule as ethical, not merely juridically coercive or punitive in respect of public morals.

[41] "Contra occultam adversarium," *Historia et monumenta*, I, pp. 168-179.

Again tacit omission of Wyclif's full text is to be noted in Hus' dealing with article 18.[42] He limits it to the first clause, "Tithes are mere alms," omitting without mention the second clause, "and parishioners may withhold them at will on account of the sins of their prelates." Hus cites the definitions of Augustine, Chrysostom, and Aquinas, finally quoting Christ himself as saying, "Give alms and, behold, all things are clean to you."[43] The gifts of food and clothing given to the apostles were not a duty but a voluntary offering. Tithes were likewise originally given voluntarily for the sake of God. Later these free-will offerings became customary. Finally the custom became obligatory, a legal requirement. Nevertheless, to make tithes a duty is contrary to the original character of alms. Clerics, furthermore, are not rightful owners, but merely custodians of alms intended not only for their support, but for the relief of the poor. To squander such *Christi patrimonium* on their own luxurious and profligate living is a great offense, a kind of robbery.

Hus then undertakes to argue in defense of the article which was later to be cited against him in a particularly damaging way: "No one is civil lord, no one is prelate, no one is bishop, while he exists in mortal sin."[44] It is to be noted that in discussing this article Hus draws on two of Wyclif's books, the *De civili dominio* and the *De dominio divino*. As to property, Wyclif and Hus distinguish three forms: private [*naturalis*] possessions, justly or unjustly acquired or held; public property held by secular powers; and property held in the evangelical manner, relevant to those who are in grace. This third mode Hus calls the most excellent. Wyclif

42 "De decimis," in *Historia et monumenta*, I, pp. 156-159.

43 Luke 11:41; cf. Kybal's treatment of this thesis in his *Jan Hus, Učení*, II, pp. 369ff.

44 *Historia et monumenta*, I, pp. 159-167.

followed in this view Augustine, who did not accept
the identification of private or public property rights
with the divine precept about them. Augustine insists
that the improper use of property destroys one's title to
it. In other words, property is not an absolute possession
but is held as a stewardship.[45] Wyclif makes this distinction of Augustine's even sharper: he regards the "evangelical" form as the only divinely appointed one. He
does not deny, however, that property held in the other
two forms as based on human laws is valid *de facto* but
not *de jure divino*. Thus his is a theological not a legal
concept. Nevertheless, those who are not in grace usurp
their property, since they are unfaithful to their suzerain,
God, from whom all good gifts come. Hus' view must be
understood in the light of these considerations, although
even here subtle differences between him and Wyclif
may be discerned. Without denying the other two forms
of property rights, Hus regards the "evangelical" as the
only perfect one. He specifically refers to the other two
forms as valid, for they are divinely instituted for the
special conditions under which those not possessing grace
live. For the true Christian, however, only the third,
the stewardship of property entrusted to him by God,
is normative. With this explanation in mind, we turn
now to Hus' treatment of Wyclif's article. After a long
and elaborate argument garnished by many quotations
ranging from Aristotle to the Church Fathers, Hus
finally arrives at his own interpretation of what he calls
its true sense: "None is worthily and justly civil lord
while he is in mortal sin."[46] The tremendously important modifiers, "worthily and justly," entirely change
Wyclif's thesis from one which might be interpreted

[45] R. L. Poole's Introduction to Wyclif's *De civili dominio* (London, The Wyclif Society, 1885), I, pp. xxi f.; also Kybal, *Jan Hus,
Učení*, II, pp. 381-387.

[46] *Historia et monumenta*, I, p. 162.

as socially subversive, into a wholly acceptable one. On the same principle, a prelate or a bishop while he exists in mortal sin, does not worthily and justly hold his office. If a man existing in mortal sin does not merit to be called Christian, equally and even more does he not merit to be called a bishop or a priest.[47] Mortal sin destroys Christian character by depriving man of divine grace. "Thus as not all who are of Israel are Israelites; so also not all who are called Christians are Christian. . . ." Such prelates do not hold their office worthily, "for they are not truly, justly, and by grace such, but only nominally and putatively, for, as stated above, God does not approve such rule, dignity, or office."[48] Nevertheless, this does not mean that God, "through such unworthy and unclean ministry does not perform fully worthy and clean ministerial acts: for instance, baptism, absolution, and preaching of the Word of God."

The last article defended by Hus reads: "If a bishop or priest exists in mortal sin, he does not ordain, transubstantiate, consecrate, or baptize."[49] This would indeed be a highly incriminating admission, contrary to Hus' own interpretation of the article previously dealt with, were it accepted at its face value. Here again, however, Hus changes the sense into a wholly acceptable one by introducing the saving modifier "worthily." In his version the sentence then reads: "It is clear . . . that such a man is not a bishop or a priest worthily and therefore does not worthily ordain, transubstantiate, consecrate, or baptize."[50]

Was Hus right in defending what he regarded as the true sense of Wyclif's articles, even though he had to transform them substantially in order to avoid what he himself considered objectionable? This action, which resulted in the final rupture with his former friends,

47 *Ibid.*, I, p. 165.      48 *Ibid.*, I, p. 166.
49 *Ibid.*, I, p. 167.      50 *Ibid.*

Stanislav and Páleč, as well as with the king, shows the intrepidity—not to say foolhardiness—of Hus in defending at all costs what he believed to be right. He never ceased to regard the forty-five articles as biased and distorted; therefore, they had to be reinterpreted to get at the real thought of Wyclif. Even so, he never defended more than six of them. Despite all these considerations, it is obvious that he played directly into the hands of his enemies. They gleefully seized upon this defense as a proof of Hus' Wyclifism, ignoring without the slightest scruple or a modicum of concern for the truth the carefully delimited scope of his choice of articles and his treatment of them in their "correct sense." It is, therefore, not a question of whether it was right, but of whether it was prudent for Hus to lay himself open to such attacks. The latter it certainly was not. Prudential considerations, however, never impeded or deterred Hus from doing what he believed to be right.

As to Hus' judgment in his defense of the six articles, De Vooght agrees with him about four of them.[51] He declares that Hus "corrected [Wyclif] in the catholic sense." He concurs in Hus' defense of the right of the secular lords to withhold temporal goods from delinquent clergy and, with reservations, also in his defense of the thesis "Nullus dominus. . . ." But he sharply criticizes Hus' defense of the lawfulness of preaching without the permission of ecclesiastical authorities, calling it "anarchistic." He declares Hus' opinion about tithes as alms "a dialectical hodge-podge of incredible sophistry." Why? Does he not admit that alms have been given for the specific purposes enumerated by Hus?

De Vooght quite rightly defends the principle of jurisdiction of bishops and the higher prelates, including the pope, over their subordinates. Nevertheless, as he himself says, such jurisdiction must be exercised not

[51] De Vooght, *L'hérésie*, pp. 207-215.

arbitrarily, but according to the due process of law. Nor should the refraction be punished by death, as he himself asserts in dealing with Gerson's comment on this statement.[52] Hus would have fully agreed with him. He never denied the authority of his superiors, but preached obedience to both the ecclesiastical and civil rulers in all things lawful. When forbidden to preach at Bethlehem, he appealed to Pope Alexander as "from the pope ill-informed to the pope better informed," and later he repeated this appeal to John XXIII. What he protested against was not the pope's authority—which he acknowledged by the very appeals he had made—but its arbitrary use or abuse. Later, when cited to the papal curia, he did not repudiate the papal jurisdiction, but protested against the personal citation, which certainly would have been as dangerous to him as it had proved to be to his legal representatives. This is no mere surmise since we know what happened to him at Constance. He continued to preach *under appeal* which was never answered. He was not, therefore, acting "anarchistically," as De Vooght charges. Indeed, it was he who demanded that the authorities cease exercising their rightful jurisdiction arbitrarily, "anarchistically." It was he, therefore, who insisted that "all things be done decently and in order."[53] The defense of Wyclif's articles was merely a welcome occasion to strengthen the protest Hus had made and continued to make on his own behalf.

Hus' defense of the right of preaching contrary to ecclesiastical orders and even in spite of excommunication calls for even more far-reaching consideration. Hus himself did not realize the full extent of the right and duty of individual conscience to declare the truth of

[52] *Ibid.*, p. 298, he remarks: "Sur quoi se fondaient-ils? Mystère." Cf. Novotný, *Jan Hus, Život a dílo*, II, pp. 392-393, where Gerson advises that the Czech heretics be judicially condemned rather than argued with.

[53] I Cor. 14:40.

which one is convinced. Hus' age was not ready for this. Nor was society ready to concede freedom of conscience for several centuries thereafter. Even in the evangelical states during the Reformation the principle of *cujus regio ejus religio* held sway. The Anabaptist pioneers in Zurich were ordered drowned by the City Council in 1525, and were savagely hunted throughout many lands thereafter. Queen Elizabeth ordered the separatist pioneers, Greenwood and Barrow, to be put to death. The "Pilgrim Fathers" and the Puritans were compelled to seek refuge in the New World. The Scottish Covenanters fought for decades for their faith. Not until 1689 was the principle of individual liberty of conscience granted by the Act of Toleration, and even then not completely. John Locke, who had inspired it, asserted the further principle of what amounted to separation of Church and state, and declared that excommunication does not extend to a person's life or property. Hus thus really foreshadowed the right of individual conscience; he himself could not envisage the consequences of his stand.

The king naturally regarded Hus' daring to argue in defense of Wyclif as a new defiance of his express orders. This completely alienated him from the reform party and its now almost isolated leader, Hus. An opportunity was thus offered to Hus' foes to beat the iron while it was hot. Both Stanislav and Páleč hastened to seize it. Stanislav preached at the Týn church (August 28) against five of Wyclif's articles, three of which had been defended by Hus. Although the sermon was aimed at Hus, Stanislav actually dealt with Wyclif's theses in their condemned version, completely ignoring Hus' modifications and explanations. He declared that it is both heresy and insanity to say that no one in mortal sin is lord, prelate, or bishop. He passed over in silence Hus' restatement of the article using the words "worthily and justly." Stanislav argued vehemently that if the article were true, pagans would have no right to any rule or property since they are all in mortal sin. Even among Christians a rigorous application of the principle would result in anarchy. For no man could then assert of another or of himself that he was lord, prelate, or king. No one would be certain of his authority or property rights. No judge could decide who or what was right. Stanislav condemned as well the article about the right of secular lords to alienate ecclesiastical property, declaring that all the Church possesses is sacred and inviolable. He argued: "The consecrated possessions, called ecclesiastical, are specifically God's possessions. . . ."[54] He further completely ignored Hus' warning of the danger to the king's rule over the country if the already enormous properties of the Church were to increase unchecked. Stanislav declared that the property of the Church is exempt from all secular jurisdiction by reason of its consecration to the uses of the Church. This lifts Church possessions above the category of unconsecrated secular possessions. They thus become *bona Dei*. To alienate such goods is sacrilegious, since it is paramount to robbing God. The secular rulers have the duty of protecting the goods of the Church, but under no circumstances can they seize them. Nor have they the right to judge the spirituals, although the latter can judge the seculars by reason of the power of the keys. Finally, Stanislav declared that tithes are of divine ordinance and are not voluntary alms. They belong to the clergy by divine and human right. To refuse them is to sin against God's command.[55]

Páleč preached on September 4,[56] indiscriminately

[54] J. Sedlák, ed., "Mgri. Stanislai de Znoyma Sermo contra 5 articulos Wiklef," *Hlídka* (Brno, 1911), p. 54. Cf. also Kybal, *Jan Hus, Učení*, II, p. 29.

[55] Kybal, *Jan Hus, Učení*, II, pp. 371ff.

[56] J. Sedlák, ed., "Mgri. Stephani de Páleč Sermo contra aliquos articulos Wiklef," *Hlídka* (Brno, 1911), pp. 63-81. This treatise

charging all his opponents with "Wyclifism." He like-wise completely ignores Hus' carefully chosen and de-limited selection of Wyclif's articles and their exposition in an acceptable sense. He declares that Hus' party falsifies Scripture by its dishonest and distorted interpre-tation of it. As to the sacraments, the error of Hus' adherents "is exceedingly perverse and insane [when they say] that when a bishop, prelate, or priest is in mortal sin he neither baptizes, consecrates, nor administers other sacraments. This is the worst error. Another is when they say that priests do not forgive sins but only declare their forgiveness. . . ."[57] Further, the recalcitrants repudi-ate the power of the keys by teaching that prelates in mortal sin lose the authority to use them. They falsify ec-clesiastical traditions which Páleč defines as the system of Church government based on Scripture, papal constitu-tions (called "major universal traditions"), and episcopal constitutions. It is unlawful, he declares, to transgress such traditions and constitutions. He then somewhat immod-estly assails the forty-five articles of Wyclif on the ground that they have been "prohibited and condemned by three famous communities, i.e., the University of Prague, the Bohemian nation, and the theological faculty. According to the truth of the matter and the decision of the theo-logical faculty, none of them is catholic, but they all are either heretical, erroneous, or scandalous. . . ."[58] When one remembers that Páleč was dean of the theological faculty, one of the "famous communities" he mentions, it is obvious that he did not depreciate himself. After all, an opinion of his theological faculty was not equiv-alent to a papal decision! Finally, Páleč denounces as erroneous the two articles defended by Hus, namely,

has a notation at the end that it was preached against Hus and his sectaries who hold the articles of Wyclif.

[57] *Ibid.*, p. 67.

[58] *Ibid.*, p. 73; cf. also Kybal, *Jan Hus, Učení*, ii, pp. 27-29.

that preachers who cease preaching on account of an unjust excommunication are traitors to Christ and that
priests can preach without prelatical permission. What is
truly amazing is that after condemning Hus for the first-
mentioned "error," he proceeds to give an example which
affirms the same position! He states that when a pope is
a heretic and orders a bishop not to preach against the
heresy under pain of excommunication, such an order
and excommunication are invalid![59] Could Páleč discern
some essential difference between the case he presents
and the thesis of Hus which he condemns? Yet he declares concerning the latter that such practices would
"disturb and distort the entire ecclesiastical and political order in the world."[60] Nor is there, he says, any
need of repudiating "the perfect and full establishment
of the ecclesiastical order."

Páleč later preached a Czech sermon on the same
theme at St. Gall's church. He censured Wyclif as the
most seductive heretic who had ever lived. For Wyclif
the pope was a nonentity, the priests had no power to
forgive sins, and the monastic vows were mere human
inventions. Wyclif, he says, repudiates auricular confession, veneration of relics and images, and insists on
priestly apostolic poverty.[61]

In the meantime the process at the curia, indefatigably
pressed by Michael de Causis, proceeded inexorably and
irresistibly toward its tragic conclusion. Pope John
XXIII convened a rather undistinguished and poorly attended Council at Rome, which began its sessions on
April 14, 1412. The temper of the meeting toward the

---

[59] *Ibid.*, p. 76: "Quodsi tamen ponatur casus, quod papa teneat
heresim et sit hereticus et mandet alicui episcopo, quod contra
talem heresim non predicet sub pena excommunicacionis; re-
spondetur quod in tali casu mandatum illius, qui ponitur esse papa,
nullum est et sentencia excommunicacionis nulla. . . ."

[60] *Ibid.*, p. 77.

[61] De Vooght, *L'hérésie*, p. 219.

Czechs may be judged from the letter written to King Wenceslas by someone attending it. This correspondent remarks that the Czechs "are disrespectfully received by all and are generally called heretics."[62] He recommends that Wyclifism be exterminated and the splendor of the university be restored by recalling the Germans. The Council appointed a commission to examine Wyclif's works. This body reported in August that his teaching was heretical. It also declared that among his books, both philosophical and theological, not one could be regarded as free from errors, heresies, and sedition. The commission then referred to the examination of the books made by the University of Oxford, which resulted in their condemnation as "heretical, erroneous, offensive to pious ears, seditious," and in their being burned as such. Further, the commission called attention to the citation of Wyclif to the curia by Pope Gregory XI and to the fact that since he had appealed to the king, and the pope had died in the meantime, the trial had come to nothing. The teaching of Wyclif has spread not only throughout England, but to Bohemia and Portugal. The commission recommended that Wyclif's "memory, doctrine, books, and treatises" be condemned by both the Council and the pope. This recommendation was carried out to the letter.[63] Wyclif's books were burned on February 10, 1413, in front of the basilica of St. Peter. This was the first time that Wyclif was condemned by conciliar and papal authority. The previous condemnations at London and Prague were regional, not binding on the Church as a whole.

Hus' legal adviser, John of Jesenice, wrote an extended comment on the papal bull which condemned Wyclif.[64]

[62] Sedlák, *Studie a texty*, i, pp. 66-67.

[63] Palacký, *Documenta*, pp. 467-469, where the text of the papal bull is found.

[64] "Glossa contra bullam papae," in Palacký, *Documenta*, pp. 470-471.

He lashes out with biting sarcasm at the text, declaring that not a single condemnation is supported by Scriptural proof. He comments on the phrase "certain of the venerable brethren" who composed the commission examining Wyclif's books, by suggesting that perhaps they consisted of the pope's nephews, raised to the cardinalate, who could hardly read Latin and knew nothing of Wyclif's books. The pope forbids the condemned books to be "read, commented on, and taught . . . or even cited publicly or secretly," although the canon lawyers must willy-nilly read heretical books in order to pass judgment on them. He ridicules "those cardinals, bishops, monks and others, professors of law, who in four days have read through, examined, and drawn up a judgment on all the books of John Wyclif . . . which even a hundred of the smartest devils schooled in all wickedness" could not do.

Under these circumstances it is no wonder that Hus' case, begun two years before, was now revived. It was transferred once more (July 1412), this time to the jurisdiction of Peter degli Stephaneschi, Cardinal of Sant' Angelo. He took the extreme measure of placing Hus under major excommunication for non-obedience, although not for heresy.[65] This implied that no one was to speak with him, give him shelter, food, or drink, sell him anything, or in any way aid him. Furthermore, the cardinal demanded that Hus appear before him within twenty days. In case he should ignore the summons, after another twelve days an interdict would be imposed on Prague or any other place where he should reside. Should he die, ecclesiastical interment would be refused him.[66]

[65] Gratian's *Decretum* states that the minor excommunication removes from the participation of the sacraments, while the major excommunication separates from the communion of the faithful: E. Friedberg, ed., *Corpus juris canonici*, 2 vols. (Leipzig, Tauchnitz, 1879), 1, p. 912.

[66] Palacký, *Documenta*, pp. 461-464.

The sentence was publicly announced at the synod of the Prague clergy held as usual on October 18.

Feeling quite rightfully that any further appeal to the curia was useless, Hus now took a step which was to be used against him in the final verdict by the Council of Constance—an appeal to God and Christ.[67] This was something wholly outside the canon law. Deeply moved by the blow dealt him by this gravest of ecclesiastical weapons short of death, Hus declares the sentence unjust. He explicitly states that he did not personally go to Rome when cited not because of disobedience or *ex contemptu*, but from reasonable and proper causes which his procurators were ready to explain. Despairing of any human aid, he writes:

> I appeal to God from this grave wrong. . . . To Him I commit my cause, following in the footsteps of the Savior Jesus Christ. . . . I, John Hus of Husinec, master of arts and *formatus* bachelor of sacred theology of the University of Prague, and an appointed priest and preacher of the chapel called Bethlehem, make this appeal to Jesus Christ, the most just judge, who knows, protects, judges, declares, and rewards without fail the just cause of every man.[68]

Nevertheless, he continued to preach. This infuriated his German opponents who, led by Bernard Chotek, "clad in armor, with crossbows, halberts and swords, attacked Bethlehem while I was preaching," as Hus himself reported. But nothing came of it. "Later the Germans, after consulting together, wished to pull down Bethlehem, having conspired among themselves at the Town Hall." The Czechs, however, refused to cooperate and the whole thing also proved futile.

[67] *Ibid.*, pp. 464-466; also Novotný, *Korespondence*, No. 46. My translation of the document is found in *Hus at the Council* (see n. 27), Part II, No. 1.

[68] Cf. the text of my translation in *Hus at the Council*, pp. 238, 240.

Hus having refused to answer in person the cardinal's citation, Peter degli Stephaneschi issued reaggravated excommunication, and placed Prague under the interdict. Hus was now confronted with the extremely difficult decision of whether or not to defy the awesome and utterly ruthless measure. He was uncertain whether he would not act contrary to God's command if he abandoned his flock. After all, just recently he had argued in the university disputation that a priest unjustly excommunicated, if he ceases to preach, betrays Christ. Of course, Hus did not intend to cease preaching, but it would not be to his Bethlehem congregation. In this dilemma he consulted the two or three of his fellow-ministers of the chapel.[69] On their advice, and in order to spare the beloved city the horrors of this most terrible measure, the interdict, which would have deprived the citizens of all ministerial acts, Hus left Prague. He took refuge with friendly nobles in southern Bohemia. The crowning irony of the tragic situation was that the immediate cause of it all, the "crusading bull" of Pope John, had been withdrawn. Pope John had concluded peace with King Ladislas on June 17, hardly a month after the sale of indulgences had begun in Prague. This was officially announced on October 16, the very month Hus went into exile.

Hus' friend, the lawyer John of Jesenice, came to Hus' aid on December 18 in a university disputation proving the invalidity of Cardinal Peter's condemnation.[70] He argues that no one should be excommunicated

[69] Novotný, *Korespondence*, No. 47.

[70] "Repetitio Mag. Joannis Jessenitz pro defensione causae M. Joannis Hus," in *Historia et monumenta*, I, pp. 408-419; De Vooght, *L'hérésie*, pp. 243f. De Vooght agrees with Jesenic that "le motif invoqué par Stephaneschi est faux." Cf. F. M. Bartoš, "Husův advokát" in *Bojovníci a mučedníci* (Praha, Kalich, 1939), pp. 10-13; and the recently published extensive study by Jiří Kejř, *Husitský právník, M. Jan z Jesenice* (Praha, Československá akademie věd,

except for "a reasonable cause," while Hus was condemned on a false charge, i.e., that he did not trouble himself to answer the cardinal's citation [*non curavit excirpere*]. Jesenic bluntly calls this a lie. Not only Hus' legal representatives, but the king and queen, and the Czech and Moravian nobles, had repeatedly written the pope and the cardinal-judges, fully explaining the reasons for his personal non-appearance. Furthermore, Cardinal Peter possessed only delegated authority to try Hus. Such authority is strictly limited in law to the matters referred to the judge and cannot be extended by him. If the judge transgresses these limits, his whole judicial decision is rendered invalid. Stephaneschi acted illegally in excommunicating persons not named in the process against Hus. Thus his judgment is invalid. Furthermore, Hus' rights had been violated insofar as his legal representatives had not been allowed to present his case before the cardinal—a right neither the emperor nor pope had the authority to nullify.

Hus in exile did not cease to show concern for his university friends and his Bethlehem flock. He wrote to the masters, encouraging them to remain constant. He also explained to them what it meant to recant.[71] To his Prague congregation he wrote several times, exhorting them to remain firm in the faith.[72] In his letter, written perhaps in November, he refers to the order, without saying who issued it, to destroy the Bethlehem Chapel. Nor did Hus cease fighting. He encouraged some of his friends to continue preaching despite the interdict. Sometime early in December he sent, from an unknown hiding place, a letter to the lords attending the supreme court of the land.[73] He writes:

---

1965), pp. 68-71. He asserts that the *Repetitio* belongs to the best legal works ever delivered at the Prague university.

[71] Novotný, *Korespondence*, No. 48.

[72] *Ibid.*, Nos. 49, 50, 53, 55.     [73] *Ibid.*, No. 54.

I am grieved that I cannot preach the Word of God, since I have no wish to have the divine services stopped and the people distressed. Consider, dear lords, even if I were fully guilty, whether they should restrain the people of God from the praise of the Lord God and grieve them by such excommunications and cessations of the divine services. . . . Therefore, dear lords and heirs of the kingdom of Bohemia, strive to stop such grievances in order that the Word of God may be preached freely among the people of God. . . . I hope that Your Graces, along with the king's and the queen's graces, will do all that the Almighty God has taught you to do for the benefit of the land.

The nobles indeed intervened in Hus' behalf and secured the king's cooperation. Wenceslas ordered the new arch-bishop of Prague, Conrad of Vechta, and Bishop John of Litomyšl to call a synodical meeting of the clergy for January 3, 1413, in order "to make peace and con-cord between the clergy and the people."[74] It was per-haps some time later that he also requested the university to present its opinion as to the best means of settling the dispute. This appears to have been an afterthought, possibly suggested by the king's counselors favorable to Hus. The meeting was held at the archiepiscopal palace on February 6; the synod was no longer a body bound by a common determination to put the papal decisions into effect, but an arbitrating assembly. Perhaps for that rea-son Bishop John "the Iron" did not attend. Archbishop Conrad presided alone.

Arbitration between the two parties proved as impos-sible on this as it had been on the previous occasion when a similar meeting had been held at the Old Town Hall (July 16, 1412). If the king desired peace, the papal party aimed at war to exterminate their oppo-nents. The theological faculty, comprising eight members,

[74] Palacký, *Documenta*, pp. 472-474.

drew up, on February 6, 1413, a *Consilium*,[75] in which it analyzed the causes of the controversy and demanded a radical remedy. Since this document was to prove the source of the subsequent tremendous and acrimonious literary battle between Hus' foes and himself, it well deserves, even demands, to be presented in fairly full detail.

First of all, the document states that the root of the matter lies in the fact that the reformist party refuses to accept what the rest of the Czech clergy hold as the manifest truth.

[That clergy] has ever held and faithfully believed concerning the seven sacraments, the power of the keys, the offices and censures of the Church, the customs, rites, ceremonies, rights, freedoms, sacred things, the veneration of relics, indulgences, ordinances of the Church, and the religious, not only with the whole clerical community in the world, but with the entire Christendom as well, as the Roman Church does and not otherwise. Of that Roman Church the pope is the head and the cardinals the body. They are the manifest and true successors of the prince of the apostles, Peter, and of the other apostles of Christ. In their ecclesiastical office they discern and define the universal catholic and ecclesiastical matters and correct and purge errors in them. They also possess priority in these matters over the faithful of Christ in all other churches. . . . Nor can there be found or given on earth other successors [of Peter] than the pope as the head and the college of cardinals as the body of the above-named Roman Church. . . .

Certain of the clergy in the kingdom of Bohemia, however, declaring that the condemnation and prohibition of the forty-five articles is iniquitous and un-

[75] *Ibid.*, pp. 475-480.

just, have been and are opposed to the above statements, refusing to believe that the tenets of Wyclif and others are false. . . .

[The second cause of the dissension is the readiness of the Czech clergy to accept] in all matters catholic and ecclesiastical the faith, definition and determination of the Apostolic See and the Roman Church. For the pope being the head and the cardinals the body of the Roman Church, in their ecclesiastical office they discern and define ecclesiastical causes, as the true successors of the prince of the apostles Peter and the college of the other apostles of Christ. . . .

Certain of the clergy of the kingdom of Bohemia, however, little considering the pope and the cardinals, and refusing to consent [that the pope is the head and the cardinals the body of the Church], desire to have the holy Scriptures as the judge in such matters; which Scriptures they interpret and are wont to interpret according to their own understanding—an interpretation not current among the learned of the Church. . . .

The third cause: The clerical community in the kingdom of Bohemia, along with the whole community of the clergy in the world and of the entire Christendom, has held and faithfully believed as the Roman Church does and not otherwise, that according to the evangelical and apostolic doctrine as well as that of the holy doctors, the inferiors must be obedient to the Apostolic See, the Roman Church, and the prelates in all things whatsoever, where they do not prohibit anything purely good or prescribe anything purely evil, but the intermediate. . . .

But certain of the clergy of the kingdom of Bohemia, refusing to consent to it, strive as much as they are able to induce the faithful to disobedience toward the prelates and irreverence toward the papal, episcopal, and priestly dignity. . . .

Then the document, reiterating that none of the forty-five articles is catholic and that anyone holding any of them would be exiled from the country as a heretic, concludes with the hypocritical assertion:

It is not for the Prague clergy to judge whether the excommunication of Master John Hus and its aggravation by the Roman curia is just or unjust.

Even Dom de Vooght disagrees with this analysis of the causes of dissension. He writes that the Prague theologians did not defend the legitimate authority of the papacy, but rather justified Pope John XXIII and his "pseudo-croisade et son similacre d'indulgences."[76] He rejects the claim that the pope and the cardinals form the head and body of the Church, or that Rome alone is the place chosen by God as the seat of supreme authority. He likewise makes short shrift of the claim that obedience is due to all papal commands whatsoever. Finally, the accusation that Hus and his party recognize Scripture alone as the doctrinal authority and interpret it according to their own understanding [*secundum capita sua*] is false. Hus' appeal to the interpretation of the Church Fathers "is to be found on every page of his writings."

No wonder that the position taken at the meeting proved irreconcilable with the views of the reformist party. One of Hus' closest friends among the university masters, Jakoubek of Stříbro, came to Hus' defense in a public declaration, which was followed by the declaration of all university masters.[77] Nor did Hus himself re-

[76] De Vooght, *L'hérésie*, pp. 249-251.

[77] Palacký, *Documenta*, pp. 403-499. The masters' declaration is entitled "Replicatio magistrorum Pragensium contra conditiones concordiae a faculta theologica latas."

main silent. Having learned some time after Easter of the terms of the *Consilium*, he wrote a sharp reply to it.[78] He points out that the theological faculty itself refused to obey the command of Pope Innocent VII ordering them (in 1406) to receive Master Maurice Rvačka as a member of their body. They also disobeyed the king when he had requested the clergy to contribute a half-year's income toward the intended delegation to Rome for the settling of the present controversy. Likewise he reminded them of the fact that Stanislav and Páleč had defended some of the forty-five articles "before they had fallen into mundane fear." In another document incorporated into the *Replicatio magistrorum Pragensium*,[79] the second part of which was written by Hus, he taunts the doctors by ironically asking whether they mean Stanislav when they speak of the "pestiferous clergy." For had he not defended remanence? In commenting on the definition of the Roman Church as consisting of the pope as its head and the cardinals as its body, he inquires how a foreknown pope could be the head of the Church or the manifest successor of Peter, when he is not even a member of the body of Christ, which consists of the predestinate alone. The same applies to the cardinals. Scripture teaches no such tenet as that asserted in the *Consilium* about the pope and the cardinals. Furthermore, since Pope Boniface IX had approved of the deposition of Wenceslas from the Roman kingship and deprived Sigismund of the Hungarian crown, why did not the theologians obey his order? Or which of the articles of Wyclif have they proved from Scripture not to be catholic?

Since the February attempt at conciliation proved utterly unsuccessful, the Crown Council appointed a

[78] Novotný, *Korespondence*, No. 57; Palacký, *Documenta*, pp. 52-53.

[79] Palacký, *Documenta*, pp. 499-501.

new, four-member commission, composed of the former archbishop, Dr. Albík; provost Zdeněk of Labouň, of the College of All Saints; protonotary of the chancery, James of Dubá; and the rector of the university, Christian of Prachatice. The last-named had for a long time been Hus' benefactor and supporter. The commission as a whole was not unpropitious toward Hus.[80] The members met at Christian's parsonage, of St. Michael's Church, some time before Easter, which fell that year on April 23. They had cited the representatives of both parties to present their case to them. The theological faculty was represented by Stanislav and Peter of Znojmo, John Eliášův, and Stephen Páleč. Hus' party consisted of his legal adviser, John of Jesenice, Jakoubek of Stříbro, Simon of Tišnov, and another unnamed person. The royal commission, as was customary in such procedures, demanded that both parties declare in advance their submission to its final decision. In case of refusal, the recalcitrant party was to pay one thousand *grossi* and be exiled from the land. The theologians were at first unwilling to accept these stringent terms but they submitted at last, hoping to gain victory as they had done at Žebrák. They then offered their proposals, the *Conditiones concordiae,* which were not essentially different from the February *Consilium,* although they were couched in milder terms.[81] The papal party demanded that their opponents solemnly disown by an oath the forty-five articles and accept the exclusively Roman doctrine as *they* had formulated it. The non-conformists were further to submit in all things to the Roman curia and the prelates. Furthermore, they demanded that Hus stop preaching until he secured absolution from the

[80] Bartoš (see n. 29), p. 365; De Vooght adds to the four members, Conrad of Vechta.

[81] Palacký, *Documenta*, pp. 486-488, 507-510. The latter is Páleč's description of the meeting. Cf. also De Vooght, *L'hérésie*, pp. 260-261; Kybal, *Jan Hus, Učení,* ii, pp. 86-91.

curia and not remain in Prague either openly or secretly. These conditions were just as unacceptable to the party of Hus as the previous ones had been. As counterproposal, they suggested that both parties submit to the decisions and definitions of the Roman Church "as every good and faithful Christian should," without defining what was implied by the phrase. The theologians were at first fearful that if they accepted this formula the royal commission would regard the negotiations as terminated; they also distrusted the limiting clause, specifying submission in the manner in which a good Christian should obey, rather than as the Roman Church had defined it. In the end both parties accepted this ambiguous and double-meaning formula, each holding to its own interpretation of it. The theologians were then requested by the commission to write to the curia "that they know of no error in Bohemia and that none has been found." Thus a hollow, insincere "peace" was presumably secured, and the colloquy was terminated. The four theologians, however, refused to write the required letter to the curia. According to the conditions agreed upon, all four were deprived of their benefices and exiled. John Eliášův and Peter of Znojmo found refuge in Moravia; Páleč at Litomyšl.[82] From other sources we learn that Stanislav also went to Moravia.

The royal commission was thereupon ordered to continue its efforts at conciliation. That required, however, that other members of the theological faculty be induced to serve. Understandably, many were reluctant to risk the loss of benefices and university positions that had befallen their colleagues. Although there is no documentary evidence for it, it is probable that the doctors willing to undertake the dangerous venture demanded that the basis of negotiations be the February *Consilium*.

---

[82] C. J. Hefele–H. Laclercq, *Histoire des conciles*, 10 vols. (Paris, Latouzey et Ané, 1907-38), vii/i, p. 153.

When this proposal was submitted to Hus (perhaps in July), he decisively and summarily rejected it.

It was Christian of Prachatice who corresponded with Hus about the course of the trial. He had written to Hus even prior to the pre-Easter meeting. Hus answered him declaring that no conciliation was possible between the two parties on the basis proposed by the faculty.[83] In another letter[84] he answers Christian's inquiry as to whether he would be willing to accept the definition of the Roman Church formulated by the theologians. He declares that the proposals of the doctors are as dangerous "as a snake in the grass." If the Roman Church consists of the pope as head and cardinals as the body, it could happen, he writes, that the see of Peter would be occupied by Satan himself and twelve of his proud devils. All then that they would decree would have to be held as of the faith. He declares that he acknowledges the pope as Christ's vicar, but does not hold it as an article of faith [*sed non est mihi fides*]. If the pope is of the predestinate, he is the head of that part of the Church militant which he rules under the supreme headship of Christ. If he lives contrary to Christ, he is a thief and a robber, a rapacious wolf and a hypocrite. Men should heed the words of Christ Who warned them that false Christs (i.e., popes pretending to come in Christ's name) would appear. He professes to accept whatever the pope or the cardinals should command, provided it agrees with the law of Christ. Otherwise, they are not to be obeyed. He quotes with approval the statement[85] of Henry of Segusia (Hostiensis) that the Roman curia may err and often has erred both in faith and morals.

Finally, Hus wrote to Christian the so-called *Responsio finalis*.[86] In it he declares in a truly heroic mood:

[83] Novotný, *Korespondence*, No. 58.
[84] *Ibid.*, No. 60; Kybal, *Jan Hus, Učení*, ii, pp. 106-108.
[85] Gratian's "Decretum," in Friedberg (see n. 65), i, p. 970.
[86] Novotný, *Korespondence*, No. 63. He is of the opinion that this

With the help of the Lord Christ, I will not accept the consilium of the theological faculty even if I should stand before the fire prepared for me. I hope that death will sooner remove me or those two turncoats from the truth [i.e., Stanislav and Páleč] either to heaven or hell than that I agree with their opinions. I have indeed known both of them formerly as rightly confessing the truth according to Christ's law; but out of fear they succumbed and turned to lies and flattery of the pope. Páleč calls us Wyclifites, as if we had deviated from Christianity. Stanislav calls us infidels, perfidious, insane, and slanderers of the clergy. . . . I hope, however, with God's grace to oppose them until I am consumed by fire. And if I cannot liberate the truth for all, at least I will not be an enemy of the truth and will by my death disapprove of the conspiracy. . . . It is better to die well than to live wickedly. One should not sin in order to avoid the punishment of death. . . . He who speaks the truth, breaks his head; whoever fears death, loses the joy of life. Truth conquers all things.

This brave and noble declaration, to which Hus adhered throughout the ensuing controversies lasting for a year, made further attempts at conciliation useless. Nevertheless, at some unspecified date Hus issued his counterproposals to the faculty's *Conditiones concordiae*.[87] They did not, however, lead to a renewal of the negotiations. He prefaces his nine conditions by declaring that "For the honor of God and the free preaching of His gospel, the salvation of the people, and the

---

letter was written to John of Rejnštejn. Bartoš (see n. 24), however, still holds that the addressee was Christian of Prachatice (p. 368). I accept Bartoš' judgment because of the statement: "Vos scilis, quomodo Palecz loquebatur prius in domo vestra." This points to Christian.

[87] Palacký, *Documenta*, pp. 491-492.

purging of the sinister and mendacious defamation of the kingdom of Bohemia, margravate of Moravia, the city of Prague and its university, and the restoration of peace and unity between the clergy and the seculars," he demands, first of all, that the conciliation concluded between him and Archbishop Zbyněk in 1411 be recognized as the basis for negotiation. He also insists that "the Bohemian kingdom be left with the rights, freedoms, and customs enjoyed by other kingdoms. . . ." He aims thereby at preventing the papal judgments from being promulgated in the land without the king's consent. In other words, he appeals to the king to protect him from the papal condemnation. He demands that whoever wishes to accuse him of error or heresy, declare himself openly on condition that if he fails to prove his charge, he will undergo equal punishment. This should be announced throughout the land, and such as desire to enter the lists should register their names at the archiepiscopal chancery. If no one does so, the theologians, canon lawyers, and the cathedral canons who reported to the curia that there exist heresies in the land should be required to name the heretic. If they cannot do so, they should be required to record the statement under their seal before a notary public. No one then should be allowed to call another man erroneous or heretical. If he does, he should be punished. Hus then suggests that the king require a subsidy from the clergy for the purpose of sending an embassy to Rome to purge the good name of Bohemia from the calumny of heresy. Finally, while all these measures are pending, he requests that he be allowed to preach freely.

The battle was now decisively joined. There was no possibility of retreat for either party. Henceforth, they engaged in a long-drawn-out, spirited, often acrimonious and ruthless literary duel which terminated only with Hus' departure for the Council of Constance.

## CHAPTER V

# ECCLESIOLOGY OF HUS' OPPONENTS, I: JOHN OF HOLEŠOV, *TRACTATUS GLORIOSUS*, AND *CONTRA OCTO DOCTORES*

**B**EFORE we take up our main task of examining Hus' concept of the Church, it seems necessary to consider in some detail his opponents' concepts. In fact, we shall learn much of Hus' thought from just such a confrontation. Furthermore, it is thus alone that it will be possible to place in correct perspective his own views and understand his reactions against the tenets he so energetically combatted. Only if we are aware of the extreme and adamant papalism with which he had to contend can we understand why he resorted to such spirited arguments to counter it. Indeed it may be asserted that it was this very struggle which made his concept of the Church so prominent a feature of his thought. Had he not been challenged on this doctrine, he might have remained but a zealous reformer of the lives of the clergy and the lay people without venturing too far into the dogmatic structure of the contemporary Church. Hence, we shall consider in this and the two following chapters the ecclesiological views of some of the outstanding contemporaries of Hus: John of Holešov, Stanislav of Znojmo, Stephen Páleč, and the rest of the theological faculty of the university, as well as the unknown author usually referred to as the Anonymous.

John of Holešov was a monk of the Benedictine monastery of Břevnov on the outskirts of Prague. In 1412 he wrote a concise polemical treatise, patently directed against the reform movement of the day. He entitled it

*An credi possit in papam.*[1] It is one of the most unin-
hibited statements of the supreme importance of the
papal office written in his day.

John begins his treatise by arguing that one should
believe in the Church as well as in God. This contention
is obviously directed against Hus' assertion that one
should believe *in* God alone, because such faith by
definition necessarily also presupposes the supreme love
of God. Holešov actually quotes from Augustine and
Peter Lombard the very passages upon which Hus bases
his own assertion; yet he argues to the contrary. He is
compelled to do so in order to be able to say that "he
who believes in God must necessarily also believe in the
means to that final goal."[2] The Church is the means to
the end of eternal salvation. To recite in the creed "I
believe in God the Almighty" necessarily includes believing *in* Jesus Christ, the Holy Spirit, the communion
of saints, remission of sins, resurrection of the flesh, and
the life everlasting.[3] Moreover, since Christ *is* the Church,
being its supreme head, "If we believe *in* Christ and *in*
the Holy Spirit, we can and should also believe *in* the
above-mentioned corollaries, because all these things
are most truly Christ and the Holy Spirit."[4]

Furthermore, since according to Augustine the Church
is the *congregatio fidelium*, this *congregatio* is composed
"principally of the ecclesiastics: first the lord pope, then
the cardinals, patriarchs, primates, archbishops, bishops,
and other lower ecclesiastics, the presbyters and priests;
for they comprise the Church principally. . . ."[5] The
pope is the *sanctissimus* among the *sancti*, "if not by life,
at least by the dignity of power and office." He is also
*sanctissimus* because he is the immediate vicar of Christ,

[1] Jan Sedlák, ed., "An credi possit in papam," *Hlídka* (Brno, 1911),
pp. 1-24; Paul de Vooght, *Hussiana* (Louvain, Publications universitaires de Louvain, 1960), pp. 116-122.

[2] *An credi* . . . , p. 5.  [3] *Ibid.*, p. 7.
[4] *Ibid.*, p. 9.  [5] *Ibid.*, p. 9.

the intermediary between men and God. Holešov bases his argument on the crucial passage in Matt. 16:18, "Thou art Peter, and on this rock I shall build my Church. . . ." But he differs from others in interpreting this passage by holding that the Church is not founded on Peter personally, but on his confession made at Caesarea Philippi: "Thou art the Christ, the son of the living God."[6] Christ then called Peter, Cephas,[7] which Holešov interprets to mean "head," although, of course, it is the Aramaic for "rock." This interpretation is needed for Holešov's argument that it was Christ himself who had appointed Peter the head of the Church. Nevertheless, Christ is the principal head, while Peter and his successors are only secondary heads. Although Holešov interprets the name "Peter" as he "who is firm in the faith of Christ beyond all others," he vehemently berates those "who assert that Christ alone is the foundation [of the Church], not Peter as well. For although Christ is the principal foundation . . . Peter is the secondary foundation because he was firmer [than others] in the faith of Christ." Thus the pope as the immediate vicar of Christ and successor of Peter, along with the cardinals and bishops, should be held in the highest honor. We should "look up to them, to obey their precepts, to adhere to them and be incorporated into their body . . . i.e., by the love of faith to enter with them and all the faithful into one perfect spiritual body."[8] He even goes so far as to interpret the term *amare* as equivalent to *colere* and thus to *adorare*, and does not scruple to apply it to the pope. He exclaims:

Quomodo inpium vel indignum est nos papam colere et nostros superiores? Nam utique sanctissimus est, si ipsi superiores nostri non colunt salubriter procurando, et nos colere debemus eos aspiciendo, obedi-

[6] Matt. 16:16; *An credi . . .* (see n. 1), p. 23.
[7] John 1:42.  [8] *An credi . . .* , p. 9.

*153*

endo, amando, desiderando et debite honorando et adorando.[9]

This blasphemous confusion of the worship of God with the worship of the pope, Holešov professes to deduce from the teachings of Christ, Augustine, and others. He asserts that "they teach that the pope with his vicars are secondary dispensators of the kingdom of God and of our salvation."[10] It is a lie to declare that anyone can obtain salvation without the pope as the means. This shocking deduction is allegedly based on Jesus' saying, "On the seat of Moses are seated the scribes and Pharisees; all things therefore whatsoever they command you, do."[11] Holešov concludes that the pope is infallible because whatever he teaches as the doctrine of the "seat of Moses"—and how closely this approaches the modern *ex cathedra* infallible papal pronouncements!—is of divine revelation and not the pope's own personal opinion: ". . . all things they teach are true and cannot be false. . . ."[12] Moreover, they are true even if the pope and his cardinals are not of particularly exemplary morals. For Christ concluded the above-quoted saying, "but do not follow them in what they do." The pope's moral qualifications or the lack of them are thus neatly ignored as if they did not matter. The pope cannot err "because the Holy Spirit ever assists him on account of the faithful in the world and because he acts and rules according to the sacred canons of the Church infallibly dictated by the Holy Spirit."[13] Holešov admits that the pope can err as a man, but not in the exercise of his duties established by divine Providence, being guarded by the Holy Spirit.

In propounding his arguments, John of Holešov has committed some gross blunders. Thus he refers to "Pope"

[9] *Ibid.*, pp. 12-13.     [10] *Ibid.*, p. 13.     [11] Matt. 23:2-3.
[12] *An credi* . . . , p. 13.                    [13] *Ibid.*, p. 22.

Cyprian, apparently intending Bishop Cyprian of Carthage (c. 200-258), for there was no pope by that name. He refers to Cyprian as teaching that after Christ's resurrection all the apostles derived their authority from Peter alone.[14] This is, of course, a capital blunder. Cyprian in his treatise on the *Unity of the Church* argued just the contrary; namely, that all bishops exercise equal authority. On that ground he refused to submit to the Roman pope. It is fairly clear that Holešov never read Cyprian's treatise.

He also quotes Pope Nicholas as having ruled that whoever does not accept the dogmas and other pronouncements of the Apostolic See, incurs anathema.[15] He then goes on to oppose some objectors who assert that Pope Leo erred in subscribing to the Arian heresy and therefore that the popes can and do err.[16] Holešov's "explanation" is a most curious and lame attempt at a rebuttal. He writes:

> Pope Leo along with others erred not as pope and bishops ordained by God, but as mere men. Furthermore, their error did not persist long. Leo was soon convicted of it by Bishop Hilary, and by a divine miracle was expelled from the Church, so that he could not infect it. Then going aside to ease himself, Pope Leo at that same time suddenly fell dead.

This convenient miraculous intervention, a veritable *deus ex machina*, took the form of the pope's death! Holešov thus admits that after all a pope *can* err, but not for long, or "damnably or dangerously" for the Church.

[14] *Ibid.*, p. 11.

[15] *Ibid.*, p. 17. Holešov misquotes his source. The statement is not in Gratian's *Decretum* (E. Friedberg, ed., *Corpus juris canonici*, 2 vols., Leipzig, Tauchnitz, 1879, I), dist. 79, but in dist. 18.

[16] *Ibid.*, p. 22. This is another mistake. It was Pope Liberius (352-366) who approved the Arian Creed of Sirmium (358) and thus became guilty of heresy.

Holešov then takes up another objection of his adversaries, namely, that the Church according to Augustine being the *congregatio fidelium* (he never mentions Augustine's phrase *congregatio praedestinatorum*) does not consist of the pope alone. He answers that the Church is composed not only of the pope, but of the cardinals, bishops, and the clergy as well.

> For they are the most powerful and principal members of the *congregatio fidelium*. Moreover, it could happen that the pope alone would hold the right faith. For example, at the time of Jesus' crucifixion, only Christ and His mother Mary constituted the Church, for they alone persisted in the catholic and orthodox faith.[17]

Thus in an extreme case it may happen that the pope alone would retain the faith of Christ and thus constitute the Church. For infallibility inheres in him alone.

Lastly, Holešov protests against those who declare that anyone in mortal sin is not a member of the Church. Yet, he insists that those in mortal sin are *in* the Church, but as "rotten members" who will ultimately be cut off. Some of them may yet repent and receive the saving divine grace. Moreover, some wicked men are in the Church by reason of their high ecclesiastical dignity, as are wicked popes and bishops. The Lord indeed commanded that the tares be allowed to remain among the wheat until the harvest. The mixed character of the Church is willed by God so that the mystical body of Christ be united essentially by the profession of faith. Here Holešov confuses the mixed membership of the Church militant with "the mystical body of Christ"— an *idée fixe* of the papalist theologians which Hus combatted vigorously. Nor does the ministration of wicked priests render the sacraments invalid. For their efficacy

[17] *Ibid.*, p. 19.

does not depend on the character of the ministrant, but on divine grace.[18] De Vooght remarks that Holešov defended the sort of papalism which finally triumphed at the Vatican Council.[19] His sturdy papalism is characteristic of the entire anti-reformist party of which he was a member, although not the most prominent one.

Páleč, preparing for the Žebrák meeting, wrote a treatise which he bombastically called *Tractatus gloriosus*.[20] It presumably represented the opinions of the eight members of the theological faculty. The meeting was held on July 10, 1412, and the treatise was presumably written shortly before that date. Hus did not reply to it until in the middle of the next year, in his *Contra octo doctores*.[21] For easier comprehension of the arguments of the two adversaries, we shall deal with these treatises *seriatim*—interweaving Páleč's charges and Hus' answers. The principal subjects dealt with are the "crusading bull" and the sale of indulgences, as well as their less prominent corollaries.

The first charge against Hus in *Tractatus gloriosus* is that he incurred punishment for disobedience, having refused to submit his declaration about the bull of indulgences to the dean of the faculty. The royal Council likewise ordered, at the king's command, that the statement be submitted to the faculty. Furthermore, Hus became suspect as to his doctrinal position, and by his presumably erroneous doctrine deceived the simple believers.[22]

[18] *Ibid.*, p. 22.

[19] Paul de Vooght, *L'hérésie de Jean Huss* (Louvain, Publications universitaires de Louvain, 1960), p. 169.

[20] "Tractatus gloriosus," in J. Loserth, ed., "Beiträge zur Geschichte der Husitischen Bewegung," IV, *Archiv für Oesterreichische Geschichte*, Vol. 75 (Wien, 1889), pp. 47-53 (in reprint).

[21] "Contra octo doctores," in *Historia et monumenta Joannis Hus atque Hieronymus Pragensis, confessorum Christi*, 2 vols. (Norimberg, 1715), I, pp. 366-407.

[22] *Tractatus* (see n. 20), p. 47.

To this Hus answers in the *Contra octo doctores*, that although the charges were presented in the name of the eight doctors of the theological faculty, they had in reality originated "in the heads of Stanislav and Páleč." He bluntly calls them "broth" [*brodium*]. He declares that he was willing to offer his statement about the bull before the royal Council at Žebrák, provided that "whichever side was declared in the wrong, should be ready to suffer the punishment of burning." The faculty members, frightened at this challenge, thereupon withdrew for a private consultation. When they returned, they offered that only one of their number be so obligated. Hus, however, replied that since all of them had brought the accusations, all must accept the challenge. The royal Council then bade them to come to an equitable accord with one another.[23] One would like to know how the matter was settled, but Hus does not enlighten us on the subject. To the second and third charges he answered as Jesus had answered the Jews: "I have spoken openly to the world. . . ."[24] So also Hus said: "I have openly spoken and taught in schools and at the Bethlehem Chapel, where masters, bachelors, pupils, and the common folk gathered, and in secret have I said nothing wherewith I would seduce the people from the truth."[25] The doctors, on the other hand, dared not to open their mouths against the bull either in their school or in public sermons. They are, therefore, seducers of the people by not telling them the truth.

A further accusation of the doctors is that Hus refused to obey the papal bulls against preaching in chapels, and even angrily censured them, thus holding the Apostolic See in grave contempt.[26] Hus replies that he did not hold the papacy in contempt, but opposed the order to cease preaching in Bethlehem because it would

---

[23] *Contra octo doctores*, p. 366.
[25] *Contra octo doctores*, p. 366.
[24] John 18:20.
[26] *Tractatus*, p. 48.

have deprived the people of the Word of God. He therefore appealed from that command. Furthermore, he refused to accept and believe the crusading bull as if it were the gospel until he had first searched the Scriptures to see whether he were bound "to believe it under pain of damnation and of God's, Saint Peter's and Paul's anathema, as the bull stated."[27] He further denies that he denounced the bull in anger; he warned against it in order that people would not be misled into believing that they could receive remission of sins without repentance and in order to protect them against being despoiled. The crusading bull was not universally promulgated as the doctors affirmed, for it was rejected by the French, the English, and the Neapolitans. He had asked the doctors whether the bull was in accordance with Christ's law and for the salvation of the people, but received no answer.

The doctors further charge that by refusing to obey the pope's command he committed as grave a transgression as if he had refused to obey apostolic commands.[28] To this Hus replies that the doctors esteem the papal bulls as being "of the same authority, benefit, and power as the apostolic commands, and consequently as the commands of the Lord Jesus Christ. For the apostolic commands are nothing else than the commands of the Lord Jesus Christ."[29] He most energetically and positively rejects such an identification. It is false, he declares, to assert that papal bulls are to be believed in the same way as the apostolic letters or the gospels of Christ. Papal bulls are often revoked when it is found that the pope was ill-informed or when he dies. Hus further recounts the scene which took place at the archiepiscopal palace previously described to which he was summoned by Archbishop Albík. Just because the pope claims to speak with

27 *Contra octo doctores*, p. 367.          28 *Tractatus*, p. 48.
29 *Contra octo doctores*, p. 367.

apostolic authority is no proof that his command agrees with the apostolic teaching. To assume that it does would be tantamount to regarding him as incapable of sinning [*impeccabilem*].

In the *Tractatus* the doctors declare that Hus demanded that they prove their case from Scripture. Disclaiming the possibility of doing so, they accuse him of being one of "the Armenian sect," who refuse to accept any other authority, such as that of the Church, of the saints, or of the doctors, save the Scriptural authority alone. The doctors further censure him for interpreting the Scriptures arbitrarily, according to his own understanding, in the manner of the Waldensian heretics. Moreover, he teaches that the letters of popes, emperors, kings, and princes should not be credited by the subjects unless their truth and reason be first clearly shown them from Scripture. Who can estimate how much confusion such an error would cause in the world?[30]

Hus admits that he really asked the doctors to prove their case "ex lege Dei et ex ratione efficaci." But he decidedly denies that this makes him one of "the Armenian sect." For in that case Augustine and Jerome must have belonged to it as well, for they likewise regarded Scripture as supremely authoritative in matters doctrinal. He quotes many other Fathers to prove that conformity with Scripture is essential in all cases dealing with faith. Since the raising of the cross against King Ladislas and the sale of indulgences for that purpose cannot be proved from Scripture and the Fathers, in what way can it be said to be an apostolic mandate? He then solemnly declares:

> I confess that I desire nothing but simply to believe, hold, preach and assert as faith that which is necessary to salvation, unless I have the following theolog-

30 *Tractatus*, pp. 48-49.

ical demonstration: Thus the sacred Scriptures have declared explicitly or implicitly, therefore we should thus believe, hold, and assert it as faith. Accordingly, I humbly accord faith, i.e., trust, to the holy Scriptures, desiring to hold, believe, and assert whatever is contained in them as long as I have breath in me.[31]

The Apostolic See cannot exceed what is taught in the law of God. In this stand against the excesses of papal or prelatical commands Hus was dogmatically correct. He further expresses the hope that "our eight doctors will not deflect me from the truth of Christ by their lies and threats of secular powers."[32] For such are the weapons of Antichrist, not of the sons of God. The faithful have the duty of vigilantly seeking to ascertain "whether the papal or princely letters contain anything contrary to the law of Christ." If they find that they do, they should resist them to death and under no circumstances obey them. Here is a valiant assertion not only of the right but of the duty of exercising private judgment! Hus further argues that since the doctors deny such a right to a critical examination of the papal commands and profess to obey the papal or royal orders without a demur or scrutiny, they would have to obey even if they were ordered to kill all the Jews in Prague, as they accepted the command to exterminate the Christian Neapolitans. They would be ready to murder Hus and his party as well, if the pope ordered it in a crusading bull (as the Council and Pope Martin V actually did later)! Thus there could ensue a terrible persecution of Christians. Nor would there follow an indescribable confusion in the world, as the doctors alleged, if the papal letters were scrutinized to see whether they accorded with Scripture. Rather truth and justice, peace and concord, would follow. Otherwise all papal com-

---

[31] *Contra octo doctores*, p. 369.
[32] *Ibid.*

mands would have to be obeyed indiscriminately, whether they were good or bad.

The theologians further accuse Hus that since he refuses to acknowledge anything but Scripture, he rejects tradition. This imputation is as false as the others. Hus accepts tradition, but subordinates it to Scripture. It must in no way contradict Scriptural doctrine. He accepts, in the first place, the apostolic tradition, as has already been mentioned several times. Christ appointed the apostles not only as His witnesses, but also as messengers of His gospel. They were the authors of the Apostles' Creed, which is an authoritative summary of the Christian faith, the *regula fidei*. He likewise acknowledges the other creeds, the Nicene and the Athanasian, as authoritative. He accepts and copiously quotes on all occasions the teachings of the Church Fathers, particularly those of the first five centuries—Ambrose, Jerome, Chrysostom, Basil, Gregory of Nazianzen, Augustine, and Gregory the Great. His dependence on Augustine is evident in nearly everything he wrote. Augustine is for him "the great Doctor." After Augustine he quotes Chrysostom most often. Later saints and theologians, such as Bernard, Anselm, Aquinas, Bonaventura, and others including Wyclif, are also frequently mentioned in his pages. Bernard is frequently mentioned because of his devastating verbal skill in denouncing papal and prelatical luxury and immorality and his advocacy of apostolic poverty. Hus accepts the decisions of the ecumenical Councils, particularly the first four—the Councils of Nicaea, Constantinople, Ephesus, and Chalcedon. As to the decrees of the popes, he is critical of them principally when they are regarded as binding on all Christians in every case whatsoever. He summarizes with blighting effect on his foes' charges his attitude to tradition as follows:

I believe in the authority of the holy doctors of the Church, but not in the authority of the eight doctors, except in so far as they spoke the truth. . . . I do not rely on my own head [*innitor capiti proprio*] but on the head of the Lord Jesus Christ. I do not rely on the heads of a few heretics, but on those of the holy apostles and the doctors whom I have previously mentioned. . . . I do not rely on the Waldensian heresy, but on the truth of the Lord Jesus Christ. Nor do I follow the Armenian sect, but the sect of the holy apostles, who did not pride themselves on the power granted them by the Lord, as did those eight doctors, or dared to assert that anything was of the faith except what the Lord Jesus Christ taught through them. Therefore Paul, the chosen vessel, by means of whom Christ has passed on [*tradidit*] to the faithful the greater part of His law, said in Romans 15: "I dare not say anything about those things which Christ has not wrought through me."[33]

The doctors, as has already been noted, utterly repudiate the demand that "they should give from Scripture more effective and clear reasons that the papal bull contains in all and every word clear and manifest truth and reason."[34] In fact they declare that they cannot. They call on the king and the royal Council to declare as inadmissible any criticism of the bull. It should be accepted unconditionally in accordance with the requirement of the *Decretum*, dist. 94.[35] Hus' claim of the necessity of Scriptural basis for all papal and princely pronouncements will not be valid "to all eternity." Moreover, the notion that it is uncertain whether the pope can grant indulgences and full remission of all

[33] *Contra octo doctores*, p. 379. The Scriptural quotation is from Romans 15:18.
[34] *Tractatus*, p. 49.
[35] Gratian's *Decretum* (see n. 15), dist. 94, chap. 2.

sins derives from Hus' confused understanding or from that of the Waldensian heretics, not "from the faith preserved for centuries until our times by the Roman Church and Christianity."[36]

Contrary to their disclaimer, however, the doctors themselves immediately appeal to Scriptural proof to bolster their argument. They argue incongruously and irrelevantly that as Paul wrote to the Corinthians: "In Christ Jesus through the gospel I have begotten you,"[37] to grant indulgences by apostolic authority is no less than to beget sons to Christ.

To this Hus scornfully replies that every schoolboy would know that the doctors' argument contains a contradiction. They "do not show themselves ready to give reason for the faith that is in them," as Peter requested.[38] Their chicanery is but a subterfuge. As to the statement that Scriptural conformity will not be valid in all eternity, Hus asks: if God in the Day of Judgment will not recognize any truth in the bull, is the faith of the doctors valid to all eternity? As for the argument that the tenet concerning indulgences has been held by Christians for centuries, he replies by defining indulgences as a free forgiveness of the penalty the penitent owes for his guilt. Forgiveness of sins is threefold: authentic, subauthentic, and ministerial. The first belongs only to God. The second had been exercised by Christ because he possessed the hypostatic union of the human and divine natures. Only the third, the ministerial, pertains to priests.

> This is my faith about the remission of sins, not uncertain but certain: that full remission from punishment and guilt is possessed by every saint who had been a sinner but after his death has gone to the joy of heaven. It shall be enjoyed by all members of Christ's Church who lived in sin, when after the gen-

[36] *Tractatus*, p. 49.  [37] I Cor. 4:15.  [38] I Peter 3:15.

eral resurrection Christ the Bridegroom shall present it to Himself glorious, having neither spot nor wrinkle nor any such thing.[39]

Accordingly, neither the pope nor any other man has the power to grant remission of all sins. Only Christ the Lamb "takes away the sins of the world." No priest should arrogate to himself such a function. He is but a dispenser of the sacraments, not their creator. "No one can bind or loose a man unless God had first 'causaliter, temporaliter, vel instanter ipsum liget. . . .' "[40] Furthermore, the pope, a mere man, cannot grant indulgences and remission of *all* sins. He cannot grant them to damned men or devils, nor to the unrepentant. Thus the statement of the doctors to the contrary is heretical, for it is opposed to the gospel. On the other hand, both the pope and every other priest can grant indulgences and full remission of sins to anyone who is truly penitent.

Moreover, Hus points out that the Apostle Paul in spiritually begetting the Corinthians did not of his own power make them sons of God. He was but God's instrument. Paul himself testifies that God alone can adopt men as His sons by means of predestination, "having chosen us in Christ before the foundation of the world."[41] The conclusion the doctors draw from the verse in Corinthians is fallacious in both "materia et forma." Paul could not grant remission of sins by his own power, but merely ministerially; neither can the pope. Moreover, many popes lack the power to beget spiritual sons to Christ through the gospel, although they do not lack the power to beget sons carnally.[42]

As for the second assertion, that since Christ forgave sins, the pope, His vicar, can do so also, Hus repeats

[39] *Contra octo doctores*, pp. 377-378.
[40] *Ibid.*          [41] Eph. 1:4.
[42] *Contra octo doctores*, p. 381.

his previous definition that the latter's power is not to be understood in the same sense. The doctors dare not assert that bishops possess all powers whatever. Christ granted the apostles the power to heal the sick and to raise the dead. If the present-day bishops had the same power, how splendidly and profitably they could use it for making money! God did grant them, however, the power to benefit the Church, not themselves. Modern bishops abuse this power by negligence; thus they received it in vain. The apostles exercised their power by preaching the gospel in all the world. Our popes, cardinals, and bishops, Hus says, refuse to "go into all the world to preach the gospel to every creature." They abhor humility and labor. They lack the knowledge necessary rightly to perform their office of "binding and loosing." "The pope, bishops, and other prelates do not absolve sinners by baptizing, preaching, or praying, but bind and loose people for money in their chancelleries." They declare anyone heretical who objects to this practice by quoting the word of Christ: "Freely ye have received, freely give." The present-day pope is but a shadow of the "most holy Father." He rides on a high breastplated horse, while he is clad in imperial robes and adorned by a golden crown. Although this "shadow" seems to be greater than St. Peter and although men adore him, so riding, on bended knees, he does not heal many of their diseases. Christ forbade His disciples to adore Him and they forbade others to adore them. The pope, however, not only allows it but demands it. Hus accuses Stanislav of such abject adulation of the pope. According to Stanislav, the pope is "the head of the entire Church militant, its heart, its river-bed, the unfailing source, and the most sufficient refuge *capitaliter, fontaliter, et alveariter*."[43] Hus quotes Paul writing to the Corinthians that "neither is he who plants [Paul

[43] *Contra octo doctores*, p. 385.

himself] nor he who waters [Apollos] anything; but God who gives the growth."[44] What then of the pope who neither plants nor waters? All he does is to move his tongue to dictate the word *Fiat* to his scribe in ordering the bull of indulgences.

Páleč goes on to state in the *Tractatus gloriosus* that Paul said to the Corinthians, "To whom you forgive anything [that is, sins, offenses, and due punishments], I forgive."[45] Since thus Paul granted indulgences and forgiveness of sins, the bishops can do the same regionally in their dioceses, while the pope can do so universally and totally.[46] In his reply, Hus denies this in accordance with his already mentioned distinction among the authentic, subauthentic, and ministerial grants of forgiveness. He asks tartly whether the pope was crucified for us, or Paul was beheaded and Peter crucified for us or for the law of the supreme pontiff, Jesus Christ. He calls attention to the prohibition of the proud title of the supreme pontiff as applied to the pope, which was declared by the African Council as well as by Pope Gregory.[47] The pope can, for his part, forgive injuries and pray for his enemies, as Paul did, but he cannot grant indulgences for money for *all* sins.

Páleč further cites Christ's words to Peter: "I will give you the keys of the kingdom of heaven . . ."; and to all the apostles: "Whatever you bind on earth . . ."; and finally to all of them, "Receive the Holy Spirit; whosesoever sins you forgive, they are forgiven; and whose soever you retain, they are retained."[48] He argues that these words would lose their meaning "if the pope did not have, on the one hand, the authority and the fullest ecclesiastical power to judge justly, to vindicate and punish excesses and negligences, sins and crimes, inju-

[44] I Cor. 3:7.    [45] II Cor. 2:10.    [46] *Tractatus*, p. 50.
[47] *Contra octo doctores*, p. 386.
[48] John 20:22-23; Matt. 16:19 and 18:18.

ries and offences, against the kingdom of heaven; and, on the other hand, mercifully and graciously to forgive and remit injuries, offences, and due punishments on earth, by granting indulgences and remission of sins." In the secular kingdom the royal vicars are granted such power and authority by their kings and potentates. How could then the truth of the above-mentioned texts be established if the pope did not possess similar authority? What kind of judge would he then be?[49]

Hus' answer is the already familiar assertion that Christ's vicar cannot bind or loose anyone unless God and Christ have first done so. As for the keys, Peter received two: namely, of discernment and of authority. The pope then and every other priest should have both these keys in order to discern the transgression of the penitent and apply the right remedy. If, however, the pope, bishop, or priest does not know the Decalogue or the articles of faith, he lacks the key of discernment. Hus then quotes Lombard's *Sentences* to the effect that many do not have the key of knowledge, and therefore cannot properly use the key of authority. Peter did not use the keys for granting absolution for money, but said to Simon: "Thy money perish with thee!"[50] Hus exclaims, "O, that all Peter's vicars would do likewise!" To avoid all misunderstanding, Hus reiterates his former assertion that the true successor of Peter has the ecclesiastical power to judge justly, to seek out and punish excesses and negligences, and all other items referred to by Páleč. In fact, he admits that this power is possessed by the pope in a wider form [*plus laxata*] than by the rest of the hierarchy. He remarks that it is both spiritual and secular, and both may be exercised by him rightly or wrongly. Therefore, since Paul writes, "The spiritual man judges all things,"[51] the lay people have the duty to judge the deeds of their superiors to find

[49] *Tractatus*, p. 51.    [50] Acts 8:20.    [51] I Cor. 2:15.

whether they are right, as Paul judged the conduct of Peter at Antioch. However, the superiors have the same duty toward the inferiors, provided both have tested themselves whether they themselves are "spiritually minded." Such duty also devolves on the pope that he judge spiritually matters both ecclesiastical and secular without usurping secular rule. He as well as other prelates can rightfully excommunicate princes and kings, if their deeds are worthy of such punishment, but he cannot interfere with their secular rights and duties, if they perform them rightly.[52]

In the next place the doctors assert that the pope has authority to demand subsidy of the faithful for the defense of the Church, of the Apostolic See, the city of Rome and the adjacent territories. He also has authority to punish corporeally and even to exterminate the incorrigible. They justify this position by citing the example of Moses who ordered, in the Lord's name, that the children of Israel who rallied to him against the idolatrous worshippers of the golden calf "slay every man his brother, his companion, and his neighbor."[53] After quoting other similar examples from the Old Testament, the doctors conclude that the pope out of the plenitude of his power can not only call upon the people to fight against those oppressing him and his land, but also demand subsidy for such an undertaking. Since the crusading bull is founded on such sure grounds, who can justly protest against it? It is a great temerity to impugn the truth or reason of that bull.[54]

In his reply, Hus first of all makes several distinctions in regard to killing.

It is one thing to fight and another to counsel fighting; one thing for the clerics to fight and another for layman; one thing for the Levite and priest of the Old

[52] *Contra octo doctores*, p. 391.
[53] Ex. 32:27.    [54] *Tractatus*, pp. 51-53.

Testament to fight and kill men, and another in the New; one thing to fight by the express command of God and another in one's own cause and by one's own authority. . . .[55]

He then defines a "just war" as depending on three conditions: a just claim, lawful authorization, and the right intention. It must aim at divine justice, not territorial possessions, ambition, vainglory, or one's own revenge. No one should expose himself to the mortal danger incident to war except for such divine justice. As for the lawful authorization, war must be resorted to only in a case of necessity and as a means to peace. War is not good in itself. As for the third condition, war must aim at vindicating an injury of the divine order, and must not be based on love of domination and of plunder, or on any other criminal act. Thus it is one thing to say, as the doctors did, that the pope has the authority to call men to fight and to demand subsidy from them, and another to say that he exercises this authority lawfully. In Hus' opinion, the pope in issuing the crusading bull committed three wrongs: first, ascribing to men heretical pravity and thus adjudging them worthy of burning; second, declaring Ladislas and his associates as excommunicate, perjured, schismatics, blasphemers and relapsed heretics, abettors of heretics, enemies of the Church, guilty of *lèse-majesté*, and as such to be punished; thirdly, declaring men as enemies of the Church, who, in reality, obstruct his own cupidity and petulance.[56]

Hus denies that the pope has the right to judge about the first condition, for by invoking war he sins against love. He has no divine authorization for such a war. Nor does he have the right intention when he orders all ecclesiastics to denounce Ladislas. Furthermore, the pope commands the priests and the religious to take part in the extermination of his enemies. They have

[55] *Contra octo doctores*, p. 393.   [56] *Ibid.*, pp. 393-394.

no right to engage in war. Christ did not fight but suffered injustice and injury. Nor did the apostles fight. Hus appeals to the words of Bernard that "it is unlawful for a priest, and particularly the pope, to fight." He cannot absolve men to engage in the extermination of other Christians, even though they be his enemies. Christ indeed taught in his parable of the Great Supper that men should be compelled to enter the banqueting chamber, but "to compel" is different from "to exterminate."[57] He sums up his argument by declaring that "neither from any verse of sacred Scripture nor from the canon law cited does it clearly appear that the pope, out of the plenitude of the power he possesses, can lawfully raise the cross [i.e., declare war] against Christians and approve their extermination under the guise of granting the remission from punishment and guilt of all sins."[58] The bishops should indeed defend the Church, but with spiritual not material weapons, as St. Paul teaches.[59] The contemporary bishops, unfortunately, are not defenders of the Church, but of their own possessions and privileges, on account of which they incite wars. As for the conclusion of the doctors' argument, that the pope has the right to demand subsidy from the faithful, for it is done for their good, Hus declares it entirely fallacious. Penance consists of contrition for sins committed and a firm determination to sin no more. The priest cannot induce genuine contrition in the faithful; only God can do that. To offer indulgences as if they were means toward the real contrition is a sheer pretense; for the real aim is collecting money.

This initial conflict was only an opening salvo in the acrimonious struggle in which Hus now engaged with his foes. One of the greatest of these was his former teacher and friend, Stanislav of Znojmo. We shall now plunge into a review of that memorable struggle.

[57] *Ibid.*, p. 395.     [58] *Ibid.*, p. 405.     [59] Eph. 6:13-18.

## CHAPTER VI

ECCLESIOLOGY OF HUS' OPPONENTS, II:

STANISLAV OF ZNOJMO

STANISLAV, as we saw earlier, had been the honored and generally acknowledged leader and the foremost representative of the extreme wing of the reformist movement. It was he who had introduced the realist philosophy into the university. In his Wyclifism he had gone so far as to acknowledge publicly his adherence to the doctrine of remanence, although he shortly afterward cravenly withdrew the statement. He and Páleč had stood in the forefront of the party until their imprisonment in Bologna, when they both returned to Prague changed men. They gradually withdrew from their former friends. When the "crusading bull" of John XXIII produced the crisis in which Hus proved the dauntless opponent of the sale of indulgences, the old companions in arms parted company permanently.

Stanislav's *Tractatus de Romana ecclesia*[1] is a surprisingly concise polemical treatise. This is a remarkable fact in itself, because his style of writing is usually excessively prolix, ponderously abstruse and convoluted, and endlessly repetitious. He is a virtuoso of abstract phrase, the meaning of which is lost in congestion of words. This short treatise, by contrast, comprises the kernel of his ecclesiological position. It was written in 1412 and devoted exclusively to the proposition that the Roman Church is the mystical-ecclesiastical *compositum* of the pope as its head and the college of cardinals as its body. Christ is presented exclusively as "the light of

[1] J. Sedlák, ed., "Stanislav of Znojmo, Tractatus de Romana ecclesia," *Hlídka* (Brno, 1911), pp. 85-95; cf. V. Kybal, *Jan Hus, Učení*, 3 vols. (Praha, Jan Laichter, 1923-31), II, pp. 112-117.

the world, actively and objectively enlightening the whole world toward believing rightly," i.e., the catholic and ecclesiastical doctrines. Before His return from the world to the Father, Christ constituted the mystico-ecclesiastical *compositum* as the "official source of light of faith" [*officiariam fontalem lucem fidei*] of the world by appointing Peter as its head and the apostles as its body. He said to them: "You are the light of the world."[2] This source of light, in order that it remain in the world even after the death of Peter and the apostles, was then passed on to their successors, the pope and the cardinals. The Roman Church then consists of the mystico-ecclesiastical."[4] He is forever speaking of the *compositum* and the cardinals as the body. No other such body, possessing the authority and the power to illumine the world with the light of the right faith, can be found or given anywhere else in the world. Moreover, as to the form (i.e., essence), the Roman Church is ever the same as it was in the days of Peter and the rest of the apostles. It is called Roman because Peter and Paul through their martyrdom consecrated Rome as the seat of the Church. The fact that the popes sometimes reside elsewhere does not invalidate the claim.[3]

Aside from its doctrinal function as the light of the right faith, the Church also has jurisdictional authority over the world. This is the primary burden of Stanislav's concept of the Church. The papacy is for him above all a juridical corporation. For that purpose Christ, before leaving this world, poured upon it "plenitude of power and of ecclesiastical office for the ruling and directing of all particular churches and the totality of Christ's faithful in all matters catholic and ecclesi-

2 Matt. 5:14.
3 *De Romana ecclesia* (see n. 1), pp. 85-86.
4 *Ibid.*, pp. 86-87.

its doctrinal-jurisdictional function. In his usage it denotes a composite entity, an amalgam or condominium
of the pope and the cardinals, the principal task of
which is to act as a juridical corporation in judging all
doctrinal and ecclesiastical causes.

Stanislav then changes the figure of speech from light
to the human body. As in the body the mind constitutes
the common center of perception and discernment of all
things, while the particular senses deal with particular
percepts; so the Church exercises its overall universal
authority in doctrinal and ecclesiastical matters through
the pope who possesses general centralized authority
over the universal Church and all Christ's faithful, while
the cardinals deal with particular functions. Thus the
Roman Church alone is universal, all others being only
particular. All cases of serious disputes, either doctrinal
or jurisdictional, on the part of the particular churches
or believers, must be presented to the Roman Church
for adjudication. The pope and the cardinals alone
have supreme authority to judge of the merits of such
disputes and to render valid decisions. Stanislav claims
that this supreme authority of the Roman Church has
been acknowledged not only by the saints, such as
Jerome, Augustine, Ambrose, Gregory, and Bernard,
"but by the learned community of doctors both ecclesiastical and scholastic for more than a thousand years,
and similarly by the community of all clerics in the
world and by the entire Christendom."[5] He does not
scruple to call this *compositum* of the pope and the
cardinals "the kingdom of heaven."[6]

Stanislav further explains that the "material" or objective parts of this mystical-ecclesiastical entity consists
*per accidens* of the persons of the popes and the cardinals
following upon each other in uninterrupted succession.
These parts are of course impermanent and, sporadically,

[5] *Ibid.*, p. 88.  [6] *Ibid.*, p. 89.

the Church may remain, by reason of the pope's death or of a papal interregnum, "acephalous" for a time. Moreover, the popes and cardinals in their private capacity as men "may gravely err in morals and fall away from the right faith. But the Roman Church ever remaining the same as to its formal essence . . . and incapable of being infected by errors either in morals or in faith, remains . . . ever holy and free from all pernicious errors in morals and faith."[7]

Our author then turns upon those who would make the Church a communion of "the just and elect" alone. He argues that since no one knows whether or not he is of the elect, there could be no certainty in cases needing adjudication and determination as to whether the judges were of the elect. He pronounces this notion *valde erroneum*. To say that the Church consists of the whole body of Christians which alone can determine the serious problems arising in matters of doctrine or jurisdiction is likewise foolish; for no such body can ever be gathered.[8] This is obviously directed against the Conciliarists, although Stanislav does not expressly say so. And lastly, he writes, some assert that Scripture alone should be held as decisive on such occasions. But since these men interpret it according to their own understanding, such individual interpretation results in "infinite errors and causes infinite division in the rule of the Church."[9] For some interpret it in one way, others in another. In such a manner the kingdom of heaven on earth would be infinitely more confused than the temporal kingdoms. Therefore, the notion must be rejected.

So far all is perfectly clear, although hardly acceptable to anyone but an already convinced extreme papalist. The Roman Church consists at its core only of the

[7] ". . . persone paparum et cardinalium potuerunt et possunt graviter in moribus errare et in errores circa fidem a recta fide cadere." *Ibid.*, pp. 88-89.

[8] *Ibid.*, p. 90.      [9] *Ibid.*, p. 91.

pope and the cardinals. Nothing is said about the bishops, clergy, or the laity. Christians of all the world, resorting to the pope and the cardinals, do not come "principally to such human persons, representing humanity, but rather through them to the essential and formal being [*forma et formale esse*] of the Roman Church itself, which essential form in them and through them directs Christ's faithful in all matters catholic and ecclesiastical. Moreover, Christ as the mystical soul of His mystical body of the entire Church on earth, residing mystically in the essential form as the principal source of virtue of the official power of His mystical body on earth . . . directs and rules through them His ecclesiastical body in all doctrinal and ecclesiastical matters."[10] There is the rub! Stanislav distinguishes between two Roman churches: one which is composed of the pope and the cardinals, and another of which Christ is the "mystical soul of His mystical body." The former is affirmed as the substance of the Roman Church so many times and in such unmistakable terms that there can be no doubt about it. The latter is somewhat vaguely mentioned sporadically. No explanation is offered as to how Christ exercises His rule over the Church in a fashion really independent of the pope and the cardinals. On the contrary, it is explicitly asserted that He does so "by and through them." Since the pope and the cardinals are fallible both in morals and doctrine, it is incomprehensible how the "Roman Church" ever remains holy and immune from all pernicious errors in morals and concerning the faith! All Stanislav does is to conclude his argument by reiterating that "the holy catholic and apostolic Roman Church is holily and justly ordained by Christ and the Holy Spirit, ever permanent as to its substantial form, of which the pope is the head, the college of cardinals the body, being the manifest and true successors in the

[10] *Ibid.*, p. 89.

ecclesiastical office of the prince of the apostles Peter
and of the other apostles of Christ, authoritatively and
universally illuminating the totality of Christians dis-
persed over the circumference of the earth; illuminating
them . . . to know and believe rightly in all matters of
faith. . . ."[11]

Stanislav's other treatise, *Alma et venerabilis . . .* ,[12]
was written by him as a rebuttal to Jesenic's and Hus' *Replicatio magistrorum Pragensium*,[13] their replies to the
*Conditiones concordiae* of the theological faculty. These
*Conditiones*, consisting of twelve short paragraphs, were
adopted some time after the meeting held on February
6, by "all the doctors and masters of the University of
Prague assembled at the court of the lord archbishop
and in the presence of the lord archbishop." In general
they repeat the terms of the *Consilium*, although in a
milder form. Jesenic's treatise is concise and incisive.
In order to obviate the repetition of his charges when
presenting Stanislav's reply, we shall integrate the two
documents. Stanislav, like Jesenic, wrote in the name of
his colleagues, the "alma et venerabilis facultas theologica
studii Pragensis. . . . " That faculty consisted at the
time of Stephen Páleč as dean, Stanislav himself, Peter
of Znojmo, John Eliášův, John Hildesen, Andrew of
Brod, Hermann the Eremite, and Matthew of Zbraslav.
Stanislav boasted that the faculty was entirely free from
all erroneous opinions. He knew that the response of
the university masters was written by John of Jesenice
and that to it was appended Hus' response; therefore,
he addresses himself throughout to the one or the other

11 *Ibid.*, pp. 91-92.
12 "Alma et venerabilis . . . ," in J. Loserth, ed., "Beiträge zur
Geschichte der Husitischen Bewegung," iv, *Archiv für Oesterreichische Geschichte*, Vol. 75 (Wien, 1889), pp. 75-127 (in reprint);
also cf. Kybal, *Jan Hus, Učení*, ii, pp. 117-128.
13 F. Palacký, ed., *Documenta Mag. Joannis Hus* (Praha, F.
Tempský, 1869), pp. 486-488, 495-501.

"scriptor." Before he undertakes to answer Jesenic, Stanislav prefaces his treatise by reiterating for a hundreth time that the refractory masters erroneously defend Wyclif's forty-five articles. He posits against them three "truths": (1) Not a single one of the articles is catholic, but every one is either heretical, erroneous, or scandalous. He remarks concerning the masters that "some indeed have gone insane, having been made drunk by the honeyed poison of Wyclif and others. . . ." (2) All must believe about the sacraments and all other doctrines as the Roman Church believes, of which Church the pope is the head and the cardinals the body. (3) In everything in which they or other superiors order nothing which is purely evil or oppose nothing which is purely good, but is medial or neutral, they must be obeyed. "For all decisions of the holy Roman Church . . . are true and catholic."[14]

Stanislav then accuses the opposing party that they refuse to submit to the decisions of the Roman Church "or to any other competent ecclesiastical judges on earth." They indeed profess to acknowledge the Roman Church as the *congregatio fidelium* and accept its decisions, but they qualify that clause by adding, "as every faithful and devout Christian is bound to hold" that faith. Since they assume that their party comprises the greater part of the Czech nation which holds such a faith, their whole profession of submission is a subterfuge.[15]

After this preliminary statement, Stanislav plunges at great length into an analysis of the university masters' document. First of all, he deals with what Jesenic regards as a false cause of the controversy, namely, that "certain clergy in the kingdom of Bohemia are pestiferous and erroneous, believing wrongly about the sacra-

[14] *Alma et venerabilis* . . . (see n. 12), pp. 75-76.
[15] *Ibid.*, pp. 77-79.

ments." And with Jesenic's further declaration that this accusation will not stop the dissensions and that peace will not be reestablished and the kingdom will be further defamed, unless the doctors prove the "pestiferous errors" of the evangelical clergy, binding themselves to suffer the same penalty as the latter if they fail to do so.[16] Stanislav reaffirms the charge that the kingdom of Bohemia bears ill fame because the adherents of Hus dare not declare Wyclif's articles heretical. This is indeed the cause of the dissension among the clergy of Bohemia. Moreover, the "evangelical" clergy declares publicly that the raising of the cross against the "obstinate excommunicates" is ridiculous, thus spurning and dishonoring the papal bull.[17]

Jesenic brands as false Stanislav's fulcral tenet that the pope and the cardinals are true and manifest successors of Peter and the other apostles, and that the pope is the head and the cardinals the body of the Church. For all bishops and priests are successors of the apostles. Moreover, no one knows whether or not he is of the predestinate. If the pope and the cardinals are not, they certainly cannot be regarded as the true successors of the apostles. The Roman Church does not comprise all Christendom, for there are other churches as well, such as those of France, England, and Bohemia. They all adore the same Christ and observe the same rule of truth. Why, then, do the doctors elevate the customs of the Roman Church as if they were ecclesiastical laws in an exclusive manner? Moreover, Christ alone, not the pope, is the head of the Church, and all faithful Christians, not the cardinals alone, are the body of the catholic and Roman churches. This is affirmed by sacred Scripture and the doctrine of the holy Fathers. Paul wrote to the Thessalonians and the Colossians that Christ is

---

[16] Palacký, *Documenta* (see n. 13), p. 495.
[17] *Alma et venerabilis* . . . , pp. 80-82.

the head of all the churches.[18] Therefore, the doctors' assertion, that the Church is composed of the pope and the cardinals, is false. Such a church is not "catholic." In fact, at present there exist three "papal" churches besides one that is neutral (the Eastern). None of these partial churches can be called catholic, i.e., universal.[19]

Stanislav in reply contents himself with repeating the relevant passage in the *Conditiones*.[20] He counters the objection that all the churches—in France, England, and Bohemia—and not Rome alone "adore Christ and observe the same rule of truth" by saying that Rome alone possesses the universal rule, while the others are merely particular churches. The further objection that only Christ and His faithful constitute the Church, Stanislav rebuts by his ever-recurrent formula of the synthesis of the pope and the cardinals, who have authority over all Christendom. From the pope's plenitude of power flow subordinate powers to the college of the cardinals and to all individual churches. Nevertheless, Christ is the head of the Church in His own right, while the pope is His vicar *officiale et ministeriale*. The grant of the vicarial authority is of grace, not of merit. Therefore, it can "exist along with mortal sin even in a foreknown pope, as the apostolate and episcopate existed in the apostle Judas."[21]

To the charge that there are three popes and therefore three "faiths," and the fourth part is neutral,[22] Stanislav answers by dubbing it as absolutely false. The antipopes do not possess the plenitude of power. There is only one Church, the Roman, which wields such power, "for that Church ever remains one and indivisible." Some parts of Christendom may err in this regard, but

[18] The first scriptural reference should be to Eph. 5:23; the second is Col. 1:18.
[19] Palacký, *Documenta*, pp. 495-496.
[20] *Alma et venerabilis . . .* , pp. 82-85.
[21] *Ibid.*, p. 85.          [22] *Ibid.*, pp. 86ff.

not the Roman Church in its essential being [*quoad formam*]. He illustrates the concept by referring to the river Vltava, which is ever the same although its water ever changes. So is the Roman Church which remains ever the same although the popes and the cardinals come and go. Stanislav then repeats word for word the statement he made in the previous treatise that Christians do not resort to the persons of the pope and the cardinals, but to the "essential formal being of the Roman Church itself. . . ."[23] Christ then as the mystical soul of that body directs and rules the entire Church through these mediating and occasionally sinful persons.

Jesenic further declares[24] that the evangelical clergy rightly rejected as "iniquitous, unjust, and temerarious" the condemnation of the forty-five articles. According to the decrees of the Fathers and church canons, neither doctors nor bishops, nor archbishops have the authority to decide major controversies, particularly those dealing with the faith. Moreover, since the doctors themselves referred the matter to the pope, nothing new should have been attempted by them while the decision was pending. But no decision of the pope or the cardinals is valid and is to be obeyed unless it conforms to Scripture. The doctors foolishly reprimanded the evangelical clergy for demanding that all things be judged according to Scripture, it being the "lex Dei et via, veritas et vita." Their claim that the recalcitrant clergy interpret Scripture "according to their own heads" and repudiate the injunction in Deuteronomy 17, is false. (This Deuteronomic passage, which both Stanislav and Jesenic mistakenly assumed to deal with leprosy, they actually derived from Leviticus 13:9-17, where the command is given that a man suspected of leprosy come for an examination to a priest. They conflated the two passages and ascribed the whole to Deuteronomy.) The doctors

23 *Ibid.*, p. 88.     24 Palacký, *Documenta*, pp. 496-497.

interpret it as if the passage commanded that all causes be submitted for decision to the pope and the cardinals. Jesenic denies this fanciful interpretation which would mean that all Christians were obliged to resort to the pope in all matters catholic. The doctors themselves ignored this alleged necessity and without waiting for the pope's decision passed judgment on the forty-five articles. They further cited, for confirmation of their position, Jerome, who had written to Augustine asking him for elucidation of some doctrinal matter, and had addressed him as "the most blessed pope." This was supposed to prove that Jerome had resorted to the pope with his doctrinal problem. Jesenic makes short shrift of this by branding it an irrelevant argument. In the first place, Augustine was no pope, and by referring to him, Jerome proved just the opposite of the doctors' assertion, namely, that other men besides the pope could decide doctrinal matters. It also follows, since Augustine as supposedly a pope did not live in Rome, that Rome is not divinely designated as the seat of the Church: for Christ lived in Jerusalem, Peter at first in Antioch, and only later in Rome. Several popes lived in Bologna, Perugia, and Avignon, and could now reside, if they chose, in Prague. For the place of papal residence is wholly a voluntary matter.

To the charge that papal pronouncements are valid only if they are consonant with Scripture, Stanislav replies[25] that Christ Himself declared, "Many things I have yet to say which you are not able to bear."[26] Therefore, Christ and the Holy Spirit through the Roman Church can pass on [*tradere*] to the faithful truths that are not contained in Scripture, either in the Old or New Testaments. Where, for instance, is it stated that the vigils of Sts. Peter and Paul should be celebrated? If, however, the objection is to be understood in the

[25] *Alma et venerabilis* . . . , pp. 88-99.  [26] John 16:12.

sense that the Roman Church should decree nothing contrary to Scripture, then it is true. But no one can doubt that all decrees [*sentencia*] of the Roman Church which it has passed on to the faithful are "consonant with the sacred Scripture. . . ." Such a statement is, of course, an obvious begging of the question; there were many who doubted this and on very good grounds! Stanislav even declares that to doubt the decrees of the mother Church is infidelity!

> For in truth it is not possible that the whole visible government of the Roman Church consisting of the pope as the head and the cardinals as the body could be at any time infected by any heresy. . . . The omnipotent Christ knows and is entirely able to prevent this and ever to preserve the holy Roman Church, so that no part of its visible rule in whole or in part become unfit and disordered by heresy, and thus preclude that noble and radiant essence from illuminating the world as to the correct faith and all matters catholic. For to radiate in such a manner is its principal task.[27]

Stanislav admits that in juridical matters the Church can err and has erred, having been misled by the testimony of false witnesses. Yet even so it is in agreement with Scripture, which decrees that "at the mouth of two or three witnesses shall the matter be established."[28]

Stanislav further asserts, in contradicting Jesenic's contention that the doctors had no authority to condemn the forty-five articles, that bishops have the right to punish errors in their dioceses. Therefore, they had the right to condemn the articles even before the pope condemned them. He does not mention, however, that such decision is regional, having no authority throughout the Church. He likewise ignores the objection that the doctors themselves insisted that all major controver-

---

[27] *Alma et venerabilis . . .* , p. 93.  [28] Deut. 19:15.

sies, particularly concerning the faith, must be sub-mitted to the pope for adjudication.

Stanislav then preceeds to deal with the objection that the doctors deride the evangelical clergy because they regard the holy Scriptures as God's law, way, truth, and life, accepting them as their rule in all matters.[29] He protests, first of all, their assumption of the name of the "evangelical clergy." He charges some of them with dis-honoring the kingdom by calling the pope Antichrist. They dishonor the supreme spiritual mother on earth—the Church. They incite the lay people against the clergy. They oppose the ecclesiastical censures, offices, rites, morals, and the power of the keys generally. "Therefore, it is the most foolish pride and consummate foolishness to call themselves the evangelical clergy."[30] The doctors justly excoriated these men who regard Scripture alone as a competent judge and refuse to recognize or submit to the judgment of any ecclesiastical judge. He reproves the evangelical clergy for denying that Christians should resort to the pope in all matters catholic and ecclesias-tical, or that Rome is the seat of supreme authority.

Jesenic charges that the third and fourth causes of dis-sensions specified by the doctors are also false. They ac-cuse the evangelical clergy of falsifying the Scriptures and the canons and insist that the popes must be obeyed in all things. But many popes were heretics, and one was a woman, whom it is prohibited to obey or even to com-municate with. Nor is the pope to be obeyed in all things "neutral." The Greeks do not, nor did the French, who for the last thirty years did not obey the Roman pope; yet, they were not condemned on that account at the Council of Pisa. Moreover, the popes often retract their bulls and err. Thus they themselves are not obeying their bulls. The evangelical clergy therefore correctly

[29] *Alma et venerabilis* . . . , p. 94.
[30] *Alma et venerabilis* . . . , p. 95.

places the teachings of our Lord Jesus Christ above all papal and prelatical decrees.[31]

Stanislav retaliates,[32] as he did in his *De Romana ecclesia*, that not the doctors but the writer (i.e., Jesenic) is guilty of falsifying the Scriptures which command: "On the seat of Moses sit the scribes and Pharisees; whatever they say to you, observe and do. . . ."[33] Indeed, the pope sits on the seat of Peter and even of Christ, who said: "He who hears you hears me. . . ."[34] Turning then to the mention of the woman-pope, he resorts to the strangest argument: he charges the masters with falsifying Scripture which commands that women keep still in church gatherings.[35] Since then the Apostle prohibits women to speak and teach in the church, how can the writer maintain that a woman was a pope? This statement allows of no other understanding but that Stanislav denies there ever was a woman-pope, although he does not say so explicitly. The belief in the woman Agnes, who ruled as Pope John, had been at the time universal. As for the charge that many popes were heretics, Stanislav replies that the doctors did not say that such popes should be obeyed, but asserted the contrary, namely, that the faithful must obey their superiors in all things "intermediate" between the purely evil and prohibitions of the purely good. How the faithful are to discern what is neutral or intermediate and disobey the other commands Stanislav does not say. He, however, actually admits the necessity of discriminating among the orders of the superiors, thus affirming the freedom of judgment. But that is what Hus and his party have demanded right along! Stanislav immediately thereafter modifies his concession by affirming that if the pope's heresy is

[31] Palacký, *Documenta*, p. 497.
[32] *Alma et venerabilis . . .* , pp. 99-103.
[33] Matt. 23:2-3.  [34] Luke 10:16.
[35] I Cor. 14:34 and I Tim. 2:11-12.

not plainly evident, the faithful must obey him. To refuse obedience is tantamount to a denial of Scripture
as well as of moral life. For whatever those who sit in
Moses' seat command, God commands by and through
them. Whatever evil they do, however, they do contrary
to God and His commands. The ordinary Church members must not rely on their own judgment, but on the
decision of their superiors. They should not judge
whether these commands are in agreement with God's
law and interpret them according to their own understanding, but must observe whether the prelate commands something neither purely evil nor prohibits something purely good. How they can do it without "relying
on their own judgment" Stanislav does not discuss. What
could he say to free himself from such a dilemma of self-
contradictions?[36]

Stanislav further rebuts the charge that the French
and other nations who had been disobedient of the
Roman pope were approved by the Council of Pisa. He
replies that on that occasion it was not opportune to
revive the controversy about the Schism; therefore, the
pope in the plenitude of his power brought it to a close.
He seems to forget that both popes had been deposed
by the Council of Pisa, and thus took no part in the
proceedings of the Council. Moreover, would Gregory
XII have so easily given the French his approval? When
the new pope, Alexander V, was elected, the French had
already been very active in the proceedings of the Council and had helped to elect him.

Jesenic declares that items six through eleven are all
based upon the false presuppositions described above,
and thus are not conducive to peace but rather to further
dissensions. The real causes of quarrels among the clergy
of Bohemia are the three vices—simony, luxury, and

[36] *Alma et venerabilis* . . . , pp. 99-103.

avarice. If they were eliminated, peace and unity would be restored.[37]

In answering this charge, Stanislav repeats the assertion of the doctors that it is the adherence of the recalcitrant clergy to the forty-five articles rather than to the faith of the Roman Church which causes the dissension. He specifies that the differences consist of the contrary opinions about the seven sacraments, the keys, the censures, and other matters. He reiterates the well-worn phrase that the orthodox clergy hold "in all things the definitions and determinations of the Apostolic See and the Roman Church . . . ," and its corollary, that they believe "in obeying the pope and the prelates in all things whatsoever, as the gospel declares. . . ."[38] The disagreement is caused by the vituperative denunciations of the pope and his cardinals, whose admirable synthesis was founded by Christ Himself. He even accuses the dissenters of the same vices they charge against the clergy faithful to the Roman see.

Finally, Jesenic maintains that the last argument of the doctors lacks even a modicum of juridical basis. For the doctors argue that the process against Master John Hus is to be received as just because the Prague clergy receive it as such. As if we were to obey the devil because our parents Adam and Eve obeyed him, or as if Pilate rightly condemned Christ because the Jerusalem Jews condemned him! They say that the Prague clergy cannot judge whether Hus' excommunication is just or unjust, for that would be extolling one's judgment above that of the authorities. Above all, it is against the Church's constitution which requires that its decrees be accepted without scrutiny as to whether they be "unjust, mendacious, or suspect of falsity." The truth is, however, Jesenic categorically declares, that canonically

[37] Palacký, *Documenta*, pp. 497-498.
[38] *Alma et venerabilis . . .* , pp. 104f.

the process against Master John Hus is null and void, because the canons require that innocent men be not condemned without their cause being diligently heard and examined by the bishops. This was not done in Hus' case. He further charges that those who defend or consent to the process against Hus as just blaspheme and commit sacrilege and are themselves subject to excommunication.[39]

To this, Jesenic's final censure, Stanislav replies that the writer distorts the doctors' statement. They asserted that the condemnation of Hus was received by the Prague clergy because it "did not prohibit anything purely good or command anything purely evil. . . ."[40] Further, regarding the accusation that the doctors falsely assumed that the clergy had no right to judge whether the sentence was just or unjust, he retorts that for the Prague clergy to pronounce adversely on the pope's or the cardinal's judgment would be tantamount to disobedience. In a remarkable passage Stanislav asserts that the clergy, being inferior to Cardinal Peter, who, by the authority granted him by the pope, excommunicated Hus, "do not have the power to judge the sentence whether it be just or unjust, for then they would have authority to confirm or retract such sentence. That would completely disrupt the order of ecclesiastical judgment . . . , since it is said in the gospel, 'Do not judge and you will not be judged.'" The writer erroneously demands that the Prague clergy declare their father, the above-named lord cardinal, to be an unjust judge, imposing an unjust sentence of excommunication and its aggravation.[41] But in that case, what becomes of Stanislav's laboriously reasoned necessity for discerning whether a judgment is not commanding the purely evil or forbidding the purely good, but is "intermediate"? It

[39] Palacký, *Documenta*, pp. 498-499.
[40] *Alma et venerabilis* . . . , p. 107.  [41] *Ibid.*, p. 108.

is obvious that Stanislav's real purpose is to assert the duty of submitting to the decrees or the pope or cardinals without any discrimination whatever!

Stanislav responds to the charge that the process was juridically null and void by haughtily declaring that the word of the cardinal-judge is to be credited in preference to that of the writer and his accomplices. He bluntly and gratuitously calls them liars and deceivers of the people and falsifiers of the canons. As to the objection that Cardinal Peter did not observe canonical rules in pronouncing the excommunication, Stanislav justifies that action again by simply declaring, without any attempt at a proof, that the judge did observe all the rules relevant to obstinate contumacy and that such procedure is "a just and reasonable ecclesiastical censure." The writer himself is heretical, erroneous, and a scandalous deceiver of the people, in impugning the process as null and void.[42]

In the second part of his treatise Stanislav deals with Hus' comments on the *Conditiones* which follow after those of Jesenic.[43] In these comments, Hus first of all, calls the doctors to account for their derogatory reference to the "pestiferous clergy." He turns the charge against them and retaliates by asserting that it is the simoniacs, of whom there are many, who defame the kingdom. They also include the clergy living in concubinage, who in their avarice sell absolutions, indulgences, and relics of the saints. He inquires sarcastically whether these were meant by the designation of "pestiferous clergy," or perhaps Stanislav himself, who had contemned the venerable sacrament "in teaching concerning which perhaps no one has erred more gravely."

Stanislav reacts violently to this most vulnerable chink in his armor.[44] He defends himself by stating

[42] *Alma et venerabilis* . . . , pp. 111-112.
[43] Palacký, *Documenta*, pp. 499-501.
[44] *Alma et venerabilis* . . . , pp. 112-116.

that although he did write the *De corpore Christi* (1403) avowing remanence, his public repudiation of it cleared him as being truly catholic and as believing what the Roman Church believes. He claims that he propounded the remanentist thesis *more scholastico*, and thereafter asserted his true belief. It is those who still defend Wyclif's position who belong to the "pestiferous clergy," not he. Stanislav does not berate Hus as holding the tenets of Wyclif, but merely as knowing well that Wyclif taught them. That is, of course, true; but it does not incriminate Hus anymore than it incriminates Stanislav himself, who also knew them well. The important thing is that he did not hold those which were contrary to the faith.

Hus further attacks Stanislav's most cherished and fulcral definition of the Church as consisting of the pope as the head and the cardinals as the body. For if the pope is of the foreknown, how can he be the head of the Church? Moreover, if he lives contrary to Christ, how can he be regarded as the manifest successor of Peter? Similarly about the cardinals. All these charges and countercharges, of course, everlastingly recur; nevertheless, it is not possible to omit them in analyzing these polemical works.[45]

Stanislav retaliates curtly by saying that the proofs given previously both from Scripture and the canons are sufficient to prove his position. He further remarks that if Judas could have held the apostolic office, although he was a thief and a robber, so can the popes and the cardinals, even though their morals be contrary to the spiritual requirements. Hus fails to make the correct and relevant distinction between the person and the office of the pope. For the office does not depend on the occupant's moral qualities.[46]

[45] Palacký, *Documenta*, p. 449.
[46] *Alma et venerabilis* . . . , pp. 116-117.

Hus next proceeds to show, after quoting Augustine's saying that if anyone accepts anything beyond the Scriptures received by the Church catholic, let him be anathema, that no Scripture teaches that the pope is the head and the cardinals the body of the Church universal. Hence, the doctors exceed Scripture by teaching this doctrine and thus bring upon themselves the anathema. Despite that, they threaten anyone refusing to accept their conjectured thesis with heresy and death.[47]

Stanislav replies that by this argument the writer himself would be condemned, since his party declared that the works of Wyclif burned by Archbishop Zbyněk were "the gospel of Jesus Christ." Furthermore, it is false to assert that no Scripture teaches the sole headship of the pope and the cardinals. "For the scripture of the canon law, received by the universal Church, teaches it (". . . nam scriptura iuris canonici, quam recepit universalis ecclesia, docet. . . .").[48] It is hardly necessary to point out that this statement is patently evasive and non-responsive to Hus' objection, since Stanislav applies the term "scripture" to the canon law. Stanislav further asserts that it is Scripture, the canon law, and the faith of Christendom, not the doctors, which impose the death penalty for denial of the above teaching. Finally, he reiterates that the Roman Church has never erred and that its decisions are always true and consistent with the sacred Scriptures.[49] If, however, the pope should be misinformed and for that reason fail to render correct judgment, the faithful should humbly and reverently inform him of the truth. They should never criticize him disrespectfully. Furthermore, arguments about papal decisions by private persons are not sane, and to contradict papal decisions is contrary to divine precepts. In other words, Stanislav again plainly declares that mem-

[47] Palacký, *Documenta*, pp. 499-500.
[48] *Alma et venerabilis* . . . , p. 118.      [49] *Ibid.*, p. 119.

bers of the Church must accept papal pronouncements unconditionally and without demur.

We may omit the passage about obedience, since this question has already been treated adequately and more than once. Let us therefore pass on to the incident about the deposition, by Pope Boniface IX, of Wenceslas and Sigismund from the imperial and royal dignities and offices. Hus asks tauntingly: "Why do not the fabricators of the *consilii* hold those degradations as of faith?" For these were acts of a pope, whose commands, according to Stanislav and the doctors, should be unconditionally received.

Stanislav's rebuttal is decidedly weak considering his many affirmations that papal orders must be obeyed. He remarks that popes are sometimes misinformed, in which case the faithful are not in duty bound to obey them. He then adds the surprising sentence: ". . . the writer inveighs against them [popes and cardinals] foolishly . . . that the subjects must hold as of faith whatever they decree."[50] Was it not rather Stanislav who held that? Nor does he explain in what way Pope Boniface had been misinformed so that his act of deposition was not binding on them, or why else they disobeyed. Nor does he explain their disobedience to the order of Pope Innocent VII regarding Maurice Rvačka. At any rate, in both cases they passed judgment on the validity of papal orders—the very thing they condemned in Hus' case.

Finally, Hus remarks with a cutting verbal quip that the process against him was received and obeyed by the Prague clergy and therefore should be received and obeyed! The doctors should be ashamed of such logic! Stanislav replies that enough has already been said on that subject. What else could he say in reply to Hus? The doctors' reasoning in this case exposed them to the

---

[50] *Alma et venerabilis* . . . , p. 124.

devastating remark of Hus, and nothing Stanislav could say would remedy the situation.[51]

The treatise concludes with a gloss, written either by Stanislav or someone else, stating that this is "an explicit catholic reply of the professors of sacred theology to certain heretical and erroneous writings of the heresiarch Hus and his accomplices. . . ."[52] Although the greater part of the document that Stanislav was answering was written by Jesenic, yet the answer was aimed at Hus, who is already summarily declared to be a heresiarch!

This extensive reply of Stanislav to Jesenic and Hus bears witness that he took his task seriously and dealt with it with a considerable measure of skill. It is certainly not free from sophistry, subterfuge, and even rancorous untruth. He must have known Hus sufficiently well not to impute to him out of ignorance a disregard for truth. Presumably, he himself was a man of probity. At least such was the reputation he enjoyed. How could a man of his standing and character descend to such misrepresentations of his former friend's position? Was it wholly *rabies theologicum*? After all, this was no mere academic squabble; a charge of heresy was a matter of death at the stake, and Stanislav knew it. Yet he continued to press it adamantly, as far as he was able, to its tragic end.

Stanislav's treatise was too important to be left without an adequate answer on Hus' part. He therefore replied to it with a formidable array of counterarguments in a work usually referred to as *Contra Stanislaum*.[53] It was written after the completion of his *De ecclesia*, on which he had worked from the end of 1412 to June 8, 1413. He did not then have the complete text of Stanislav's treatise; what he possessed at the time of writing con-

[51] *Ibid.*, pp. 123-125.      [52] *Ibid.*, p. 127.
[53] "Responsio Joannis Hus ad scripta M. Stanislai," in *Historia et monumenta Joannis Hus atque Hieronymi Pragensis, confessorum Christi*, I, pp. 331-365. Hereafter cited as *Contra Stanislaum*.

cluded with chapter 5; it thus lacked the part given in the last seven pages of Loserth's edition (pp. 120-127). Nor did he choose to deal with all of Stanislav's criticisms of the *Replicatio*, but only with such arguments as he considered controversial. Moreover, he had answered some charges in his *De ecclesia* and did not wish to repeat himself—for which we may be sincerely grateful!

Hus begins with a sincere expression of appreciation of his former teacher, "from whose lectures and academic activity I had learned many good things."[54] Then he takes the offensive, first of all dealing with Stanislav's prefatory comments that none of Wyclif's forty-five articles is catholic, but every one is either heretical, erroneous, or scandalous. Once upon a time, Hus reminds Stanislav, he defended these articles as catholic and vehemently denied that any one of them was heretical. Nor does he now prove his reverse position from Scripture, reason, or divine revelation; indeed, he cannot prove it, "particularly since Christ's life and the opinions of the saints obviously approve the opposite."[55] The articles declaring that "to endow the clergy is contrary to Christian rule" (art. 32) and that "Pope Sylvester and Emperor Constantine erred in endowing the Church" (art. 33) may perhaps be offensive to many clerics and prelates, but cannot be shown by a Scriptural proof to be erroneous. The opinions of the doctors lack even a modicum of reason. Hence, Hus does not consent to their conclusions. He further rebuffs Stanislav's charge that the dissident party brings infamy upon itself by refusing to accept the decisions and decrees either of the Roman Church or of any other competent ecclesiastical court of justice. Hus repudiates the charge as a scurrilous aspersion. Our party, he says, defamed itself no more than Nicodemus had defamed himself by refusing to join the Jewish "pontiffs" in condemning

[54] *Ibid.*, p. 331.                    [55] *Ibid.*

Christ. What kind of infamy did Rector Mark of Hradec, Friedrich Epinge, and Procopius of Plzeň incur by repudiating the doctors' pronouncement adopted at the Town Hall? Concerning the statement that some members of Hus' party have become insane by partaking of the honeyed poison of Wyclif's teaching, Hus again recalls to Stanislav's memory that he had formerly praised the English reformer as "the eminent theologian and philosopher,"[56] while now he has changed his praises to vituperation. When Stanislav charged Hus with willingness to accept the faith only to the degree that "every faithful and devout Christian is bound to," he retorted with devastating verbal force that "even if Master Stanislav were the pope, and all the doctors, pontiffs [sic], canons, and monks who along with him have pontificated at the Town Hall their conclusions they called catholic, were turned into cardinals, the faithful are not bound to believe that these conclusions are the catholic faith unless they are grounded in Scripture."[57]

Hus then undertakes to deal with the principal argument of Stanislav, his definition that the Roman Church consists of the pope as its head and the cardinals as its body. He analyzes and disproves this rhetorically ponderous and abstruse argument point by point. First he shows that the *compositum* likened by Stanislav to the natural human body, directing by its mind all its actions, differs radically from the concept of the mystical body. The

[56] The full statement quoted from Stanislav's commentary on Lombard's *Sentences* reads as follows: "A certain doctor, Master John Wyclif, an eminent theologian and philosopher above others, asserts the above-stated tenet [about the sacrament of the body and blood of Christ]; he has publicly and frequently testified, as it stands in his writings, that as a faithful son of the Church he is ready to believe the contrary, if he be so instructed, and is even ready to be punished by death. Many less perspicuous declare him to be a heretic in this and other matters and besmirch the fame of those who read his writings, ignoring the fact that among the thorns we gather the most beautiful roses." *Ibid.*, p. 334.

[57] *Ibid.*

latter is not merely natural psycho-physical organism, but possesses as its additional distinctive element the supernatural grace of predestination.[58]

> Thus the mystical body of the universal Church is truly constituted of Christ and the body of the predestinate, having a certain similarity to the human body in accordance with the words of the Apostle in I Cor. 12:12, As the body is one and has many members, and all the members of the body, though many, are one body; so it is with Christ. . . . Therefore, not in the pope aside from Christ, but in Christ do the predestinate form one mystical body. . . . It follows that no foreknown in mortal sin is a member of Christ and participates in the mystical body of Christ. For he lacks the enduring bond of predestination.[59]

Hus then demands that Stanislav prove that the pope and the cardinals are the *corpus mysticum*, having in addition to the natural human endowments the super-added grace of predestination. In order to do so, he would have to prove that "Pope John or his successor is the head of the mystical body, in whom are hidden the treasures of wisdom and knowledge of God for the ruling of the Church and the endowment of its every member with the life and sensitivity without which none could live or move spiritually. If, therefore, Stanislav can prove these three things, then his assumption is valid. . . . But because he will never prove nor can prove without divine revelation that Pope John XXIII with his twelve cardinals constitute Christ's mystical body, anymore than he can prove that the pope and his cardinals are bound by the bond of predestination, it is clear that his entire position in regard to this matter lacks firm foundation."[60]

Furthermore, Hus deprecates the pride of the popes

[58] *Ibid.*, p. 335.      [59] *Ibid.*      [60] *Ibid.*, p. 336.

who publicly demand that they be acknowledged as heads of the Church. Christ in his humility did not publicly claim that title for Himself, nor did the apostles call themselves popes, the most holy fathers, supreme rulers of churches, or the source of the plenitude of power, but servants of Christ. Paul, "the prince of the apostles," as Hus calls him, confessed himself the least of the apostles, unworthy to be an apostle.[61] The doctors, on the contrary, "expecting temporal remuneration from the pope, or fearing him servilely,"[62] render him abject adulation and teach men that he wields power to do all things; nor can anyone say to him, "What doest thou?" These extravagant honors are the cause of the pope's pride. It would suffice if Stanislav were to call the pope the Roman pontiff, the vicar of the Apostle Peter, and the cardinals the vicars of the other apostles. They would truly be such if they served the Church as well as the apostles had done. On the contrary, the popes have shown themselves to be vicars of Caesars rather than of Christ. Our Lord taught His disciples not to rule or to seek to lord it over others, but to serve. The catholic faith does not require us to believe that John XXIII, Alexander V, or Gregory XII, "are or have been true successors and manifest vicars of Peter, the apostle of Christ." To believe it is "credulitas sive opinio praeter fidem."[63] Every member of the body of Christ, however, is in duty bound to believe that the twelve apostles after Christ's ascension were His vicars, but not that the twelve cardinals, "praeter scripturam Christi introducti," are their manifest successors. There is perhaps an adequate presumption to believe that the pope is Peter's vicar; but there exists much obscurity as to whether the cardinals are to be regarded as the vicars of the other apostles.[64] Not all of them are even in priestly orders, nor

[61] I Cor. 15:9.
[62] *Contra Stanislaum*, p. 337.
[63] *Ibid.*, p. 338.
[64] *Ibid.*

do they preach and baptize as the apostles did. Nor does even a wholly legitimate election make the pope a true successor of Peter unless the pontiff thus elected justifies it by his conduct in office and his service to the Church. Thus moral character and devout life are the necessary qualifications for holding the papal office worthily. This was always the bone of contention between Hus and his papalist foes. Nevertheless, from Hus' spiritual concept of the Church and his reformist point of view it is for him the absolutely essential condition for all ecclesiastical offices from the highest to the lowest. On this point he is adamant. It is Stanislav, Hus claims, not he, who errs by declaring that the office makes the pope and in arguing that since Judas was an apostle, even wicked popes may worthily hold their office. At that Hus exclaims: "Behold the astounding condescension of the doctor in comparing Judas with the successor of Peter!"[65] Such popes are, therefore, Judas' rather than Peter's successors! Hus comes near to asserting here that a wicked pope is not a pope at all, rather than that he is an unworthy *de facto* occupant of Peter's seat.

In chapter 3 of his *Contra Stanislaum* Hus crystallizes even more definitely his concept of the Church in contrast to Stanislav's legalistic formulation. That the mystical body of the Church consists of Christ and the predestinate is again placed in sharp contrast with the concept of the juridical corporation of the pope and his cardinals. Hus quotes Paul in support of his view. Paul enumerates nine gifts with which the Spirit endows the different ministries of the Church.[66] These ministries comprise the apostles, prophets, teachers, workers of miracles, healers, administrators, and speakers in tongues. "Nor did he place in this order of election first the pope, then the cardinals, as Doctor Stanislav did, but he first

[65] *Ibid.*, p. 341.
[66] I Cor. 12:8-11, 28.

placed the apostles. Nor did he rank Peter first as pope."[67] In fact, the popes and cardinals as "administrators" occupy almost the lowest position in this list. Stanislav's argument that the pope's authority extends over the whole Church in the world Hus rebuts by declaring that such an assumption cannot be validated except by divine revelation; and such revelation does not exist. Stanislav's characterization of the pope as "the mystical heart, head, foundation, and the river-bed," from whom all offices and powers, both ecclesiastical and civil, are derived, is fantastically exaggerated. Hus challenges him to apply these adulatory terms to Pope John XXIII. "Prove then first that John XXIII is the person in whom resides that most general and fullest plenitude of power and in no other person on earth, humanly speaking."[68] Christ granted no man power except for the edification, not the destruction, of the Church. Thus it is not enough to assert that John XXIII was legitimately elected. Such elections may have been prompted by men's favor, fear, or cupidity. He must prove his worthiness by moral life and saintly works, not by the fulmination of terrible censures against his opponents. Were it not so, heretics, such as the Arian pope Liberius, or even women, and the papess Agnes, or even the Antichrist himself would and could have been as legitimate holders of the see as the

[67] *Contra Stanislaum*, p. 341.

[68] *Ibid.*, p. 342. To *prove* that John XXIII is of the predestinate (for that is what Hus' demand amounts to) is as impossible as it is concerning any other pope or any person whatsoever. The only criterion Hus sets up is that of good life: "By their fruits ye shall know them!" This is actually not a proof, but a reasonable presumption. It is obvious, however, that from Stanislav's point of view, or of any other hyper-papalist, or even of one who regards the Church as a legal corporation, Hus' concept is as impossibly utopian and unrealistic as Stanislav's. For the latter, no moral qualifications are required for the papal office, but his legitimate election; for the former, they are the *sine qua non* for the *worthy* holding of the office, although he recognizes an unworthy occupant as *de facto* pope.

best among the popes. Moreover, since many emperors created popes and prelates, it is absurd to say that they endowed them with the supreme power on earth. They did not themselves have it, and if they did they would not have parted with it.

Stanislav is also in error, Hus further argues, in asserting that the plenitude of power is limited to one person—the pope. Cyprian taught that Christ after His resurrection granted equal power to all His apostles. Furthermore, He sent them to various regions to preach and baptize. They did not consult Peter about their individual tasks. Paul significantly says that when he went to the Jerusalem Council, those who were regarded as the pillars of the Church added nothing to him.[69] He even rebuked Peter at Antioch for refusing table-fellowship with the converts from paganism. Since "God is no respector of persons," it follows that Peter did not possess superior powers above the other apostles by reason of being the Roman pope. He excelled others by his firmness of faith, not by official authority. Peter did not *appoint* Matthias an apostle in place of Judas, but Matthias was *elected* by all the eleven apostles.[70] Also at the Jerusalem Council it was James and the other members, not Peter alone, who approved Paul's ministry among the gentiles and freed his converts from some Jewish cultic requirements.[71]

In chapter 5 Hus disputes Stanislav's argument that if a foreknown pope is not the head of the Roman Church, neither can it be said that the king is the head of the kingdom of Bohemia, since it is not known whether or not he is of the predestinate. Hus asserts that the argument is *non sequitur*, for the two situations are disparate. Because Christ rules His Church, *in spiritualibus,* the pope's vicarial rule is not so essential or necessary as the king's rule *in temporalibus.* He summarily

[69] Gal. 2:6.    [70] Acts 1:23-26.    [71] Acts 15:6-29.

declares that "there is not a spark of apparent necessity that a [vicarial] head *in spiritualibus* be ever ruling the Church and permanently abide with the Church militant, unless infidels would heretically assert that the Church militant should form an abiding society on earth and not seek the future one."[72]

Repudiating Stanislav's basic definition that the pope is the head of the entire Christendom, Hus asserts that in the days of the papess Agnes and during interregnums no pope exists as the head of the Church. Stanislav himself admitted that at such times the Church is acephalous, although even so it retains its mystical essence. Hus taunts him by saying that Stanislav contradicts his fellow-member Páleč, who taught that when Christ ascended into heaven, he did not leave the Church acephalous, but appointed the pope as the head. The two doctors should arrive at a common understanding of this important doctrine! "The doctor will not be able to prove till the Judgment Day that the Church has another head than Jesus Christ. He cannot give a reason how in the days of Agnes the Church militant could have been acephalous for two years and five months while nevertheless many of its members lived in Christ's grace. For Christ could better rule his Church without such monstrous heads through his faithful disciples scattered over the circumference of the earth."[73] Nor can he prove how, when the pope, who is said to be the heart, the head, the fount, and the river-bed of the total plenitude of power, dies, these life-giving powers can be restored to the dead body of the Church.

Hus also assails the assertion that the pope is "the perfect refuge" for all true Christians. Christ alone is such a refuge. It is false to claim, as Stanislav does, that the apostles had recourse to Peter in carrying on their evangelistic tours. Christ abides with the Church for-

[72] *Contra Stanislaum,* p. 346.    [73] *Ibid.,* p. 347.

ever, as he promised to do in Matt. 28:20. He sent his apostles to preach and to baptize all nations. The papal "apostles," however, do not leave the papal palace to teach as Christ commanded but as the pope commands. They "extol his commands above those of the Lord Jesus Christ." Furthermore, Christ did not appoint Peter over all the world, but each apostle went to evangelize a certain specific region. Nor did He say to Peter exclusively to go and evangelize the whole world, subjecting the other apostles to himself. All the apostles shared in the mission in an equal capacity. The popes today send their "apostles" not to evangelize, but to collect money.[74]

In the sixth chapter Hus continues his attack upon the contemporary papacy by asserting that the greatest errors and Schisms have arisen, having been incited by the papacy, and are continuing hitherto. Not only are the Saracens, Greeks, and Jews scandalized thereby, but the Christians are torn into three parties by the quarrels of the popes as well. Stanislav asserts that to denounce such evils is to show disrespect to the holy mother Church. Hus, on the other hand, replies that to criticize the evils of the papacy is not detracting from the Roman Church or opposing Christ. Apostle Paul reproved Peter, and saints such as Augustine, Jerome, Gregory, Chrysostom, Bernard, and Ambrose wrote and spoke against unworthy bishops and priests, thereby edifying the Church.

In countering Stanislav's assertion that Christ gave Peter the power of the keys, Hus, following Augustine, argues that the power was given to the Church in general, Peter on that occasion representing it. Nor do the keys confer upon the Church any coercive secular power, but are purely spiritual in character, consisting of the knowledge of the gospel and the power of discerning and forgiving or retaining sins. By means of

[74] *Ibid.*, p. 348.

these keys, the kingdom of heaven is opened to the penitent and closed to the unrepentant. The conditions of salvation apply to the laity as well as to the clergy. Christ said, "Woe to you, scribes and Pharisees, hypocrites, who shut the kingdom of heaven against men; for you neither enter yourselves nor allow those who would enter to go in."[75] Furthermore, the words of Christ, "Receive ye the Holy Spirit . . ."[76] are obviously spoken to all His disciples, not to Peter alone. Therefore, all priests have the power to forgive sins, although not of their own personal authority, but only *ministerialiter*.

The last proof that Stanislav offers in behalf of the exclusive and supreme authority granted to Peter and, therefore, to his successors, is presumably found in Christ's words to Peter, "Feed my sheep."[77] Hus explains these words, upon which the exclusive authority of the papacy has been founded throughout its history, by asserting that Peter received the prerogative because of his preeminent love of Christ. He pastured the sheep of Christ, not his own, with the words of the gospel and the example of holy life. He did not, however, pasture all Christ's sheep, for his ministry did not extend to all. Hus denies that the words "Feed my sheep" prove the pope's right to rule the Church universal; for Peter worked among the Jews, at first in Antioch and later in Rome. Other apostles evangelized other regions. Accordingly, Christ's words apply to all faithful bishops, not only to the pope. In fact, the Roman pontiff should ponder the conditions under which Peter was appointed the shepherd of Christ's sheep; it was only after Christ asked him three times, "Do you love me?" If the pope "does not love the God Christ, or feed the sheep with the word of the gospel and with the example of a humble, poor, and patient life, he is not their shepherd. . . ."[78]

[75] Matt. 23:13.    [76] John 20:22-23.    [77] John 21:17.
[78] *Contra Stanislaum*, p. 353.

In the next chapter Hus rebuts Stanislav's charge that it is a manifest infidelity on the part of the recalcitrant party to suspect the holy mother Church of perverse opinions. Hus retorts that Stanislav ascribes to them many lies: for Christ, when He left the earth, sent His Spirit to "teach us all the truth." Thus it is the Holy Spirit who is "the doctor of the Church," and He needs no Jerusalem or Rome to take His place; for He is ever present in the Church. Consequently, Christ and the Paraclete teach the Church, not Peter or his alleged successors. Moreover, "the apostles and faithful priests of Christ had firmly ruled the Church in things necessary for salvation before the papal office was instituted. They could do so if there were no pope—which is highly possible—till the Day of Judgment."[79] Thus the papal office is not absolutely necessary to the Church, although Hus does not demand its abolition, as Wyclif had done. When properly administered for the benefit of the Church, the papacy is actually useful.

Stanislav further argues that as it would be most monstrous for a thing to have two causes, so likewise it would be monstrous for the Church to have two vicarial heads, both of which would be the source of the plenitude of power. He thus attempts to prove, at the time when there were three popes, that the pope is the sole head of the Church militant! Hus concedes the obvious truism of Stanislav's argument, but denies that aside from Jesus Christ there can exist any other head of the Church universal. He thus does not repudiate the rule of a *worthy* pope as vicar of Christ, provided he does not attempt to usurp the position occupied by Christ alone. All the twelve apostles, including Paul, were such worthy vicars of Christ, possessing equal powers. The Savior "did not wish to burden His spouse, the holy Church catholic, with heavy labor. Therefore, He

[79] *Ibid.*, p. 354.

did not designate Rome or another city the sole refuge to which it would be necessary to recur. Consequently, He sent into all the world His apostles, each of whom, with the Lord Christ's assistance, could teach, strengthen, and direct Christ's sheep in the way of eternal salvation, and constitute bishops and priests without recourse to Peter. . . . Thus the humble priests of Christ, having Christ as their Great Pontiff, resort to Him for aid in times of need."[80]

It may be pointed out that this federal concept of several vicarial heads of particular churches, together comprising all Christendom, is of very great importance for the understanding of Hus' view of the Church. The Roman Church is only one of the particular churches comprising Christendom. Hus was really not saying anything new, for such was and still is the actual existing situation. Nevertheless, it was an exceedingly daring and revolutionary thing to say on the part of a priest of the Roman Church! For Christendom at the time, as it had been before and was to be even to a greater extent afterward, was divided into separate ecclesiastical communions. There existed the four historic Eastern patriarchates (soon to be joined by the autocephalous Russian metropolitanate), and the Roman patriarchate (then torn into three parts), and the multitude of various heterogeneous communions, as the Nestorian, Monophysite, and others. These non-Roman bodies could not, by the widest stretch of the imagination, be said to recognize papal supremacy over them.

In the tenth chapter Hus deals with Stanislav's statement that although the popes and cardinals can individually gravely err and fall away from the right faith, it is impossible for the whole Roman Church in all its members to be infected by any heresy.[81] He quite reasonably asks how it is possible, if the Church consists of

[80] *Ibid.,* p. 356.     [81] *Contra Stanislaum,* p. 357.

the pope and the cardinals who can err, that the Church cannot err. The pope with his cardinals fall into error by reason of ignorance, avarice, deceit, unlawful decrees, and many other causes. The feeble excuse of Stanislav's that even so they are justified by the Scriptural dictum that "In the mouth of two or three witnesses shall every word be established,"[82] is but an evasive chicanery trumped up by him to justify the errors of the papacy. Hus says that not even a hundred thousand false witnesses would suffice to condemn a just man. Scripture alone contains inerrant truth, and the Church, itself infected by sinful pride and misled by false testimony, judges contrary to Scripture. Hus, confident of his own integrity, declares:

> I will confess the evangelical truth as long as God permits, for I trust in that Witness whom no multitude of witnesses can divert from the truth, nor the Roman curia can terrify, nor any gift can suborn, nor any power can conquer![83]

In the eleventh chapter Hus defends the evangelical clergy against Stanislav's charges of disobedience, of spreading errors, and of slandering the Church. Hus rebuffs the charge that he vilifies the Church by revealing the wickedness of the popes, cardinals, and other prelates by citing the examples of the evangelist Mark who recorded Peter's denial of Christ, the apostles who abandoned Christ to His fate, and Paul who rebuked Peter. He retaliates by charging Stanislav with an attempt to cover up the misdeeds of the entire clerical establishment and with bridling at any criticism of the pope or of his decrees. The sole exception Stanislav makes is that of a pope's notorious and generally admitted heresy. Hus then concludes by praising the moral courage of those lay and clerical faithful members of the Church

[82] Deut. 19:15.      [83] *Contra Stanislaum*, p. 359.

who opposed Pope John's crusading bull, the selling of indulgences, and the closing of chapels.

In the final chapter Hus deals with Stanislav's assertion that whatever the pope or the cardinals decree to be held and believed by the faithful is *ipso facto* consonant with Scripture.[84] He again declares that Stanislav cannot prove it. In fact, he assails the whole Cardinal College as an arbitrary creation of the popes without any Scriptural justification. He points out that it was not created by Christ's appointment, but in imitation of the pagan governmental system. It is of comparatively late development, comprising originally the *presbyteri cardinales* of the twenty-five Roman local churches, which number was later reduced to the four major ones. To the cardinal-presbyters were later added cardinal deacons, and finally cardinal bishops. The College attained its high juridically administrative functions only in the eleventh and twelfth centuries, when it received the exclusive right to elect the popes. Stanislav endowed this purely juridical corporate body with membership in the mystical-ecclesiastical *condominium* along with the pope—an illusory pretense—and declared it to be of divine origin and appointment. With which Scripture does this claim agree? Hus therefore refuses to acknowledge the Cardinal College as divinely instituted or as forming, along with the pope, the supreme and essential body of the Church, whether Roman or universal. He bases this repudiation on his favorite ground of predestination: no one can know whether or not he is of the predestinate, and therefore even a member of the mystical body of Christ. Without divine revelation Hus refuses to judge of the status of the Cardinal College.

Finally, he rebukes Stanislav for his servile adulation of the Roman curia. As for himself, Hus declares, "I

[84] *Ibid.*, pp. 362-363.

regard it better to suffer humiliation for the truth than by adulation to seek a benefice. . . ."[85]

St. Ambrose wrote that by preaching the truth without flattery one would receive no thanks of men. Hus then continues:

> Nor do I marvel or am grieved that the Doctor gathers such great reproaches against me as to endanger me, now saying that I faithlessly, stupidly, insanely and perfidiously dishonor the pope and the cardinals by my clamor . . . and then again that I am in the habit of smiting the spiritual father and mother, the pope and the Roman Church, with intemperate language. . . . For I know that the Corrector of pontiffs, scribes and Pharisees forewarned his disciples saying: "You will be delivered up even by parents, kinsmen and friends, and some of you will be put to death; and you will be hated by all for my name's sake." What marvel that the Doctor, at one time my instructor, in his reply heaps reproaches and dishonor on me and my brethren as much as he can! For he is less believed because he had been one of us, and the party which he now flatters by bowing his head and bending his knees, used to assert for a long time that he had been the most eminent [among us].[86]

No wonder that there existed a fixed gulf between Hus (and his fellow-reformers) and Stanislav (and the rest of the theological faculty)! The gulf was unbridgeable unless one or the other party changed its position radically. Such a surrender on the part of either was unthinkable.

[85] *Ibid.*, p. 365.
[86] *Ibid.*; the scriptural quotation is from Luke 21:16.

## CHAPTER VII

# ECCLESIOLOGY OF HUS' OPPONENTS, III:
## STEPHEN PÁLEČ AND THE "ANONYMOUS"

THE other most formidable opponent of Hus was his former intimate friend, Stephen Páleč. He took a most resolute and effectively harassing part in the controversy by writing several treatises against Hus. First of all, it appears that Páleč himself regarded Stanislav's definition of the Roman Church as too narrow, and he therefore undertook to broaden it in his *De aequivocatione nominis ecclesia*. This was answered by Hus in his *De ecclesia*, which included his reply to the *Consilium*. Páleč then hastened to counter Hus' *De ecclesia* in his own treatise of the same name. Even prior to this, Páleč answered the *Replicatio magistrorum Pragensium* (also dealt with by Stanislav, as we have just seen) with his *Replicatio contra Quidamistas*, to which Hus replied in his *Contra Paletz*. On his part, Páleč retaliated in his *Antihus*. Finally the controversy was concluded by Hus' treatise *Contra octo doctores*, which we have already considered.

We may, therefore, first turn our attention to Páleč's short treatise, *De aequivocatione nominis ecclesia*, written in 1412.[1] While Stanislav could find no more than one definition of the Roman Church, Páleč supplied no less than six! In the first place he applies the word "Church" somewhat inaptly to the church building, because God is worshipped therein. In the second place, the Church is "the congregation of the wicked and iniquitous men, as heretics and schismatics," although this usage has no merit. In the third place, the Church stands

---

[1] J. Sedlák, ed., "De aequivocatione nominis ecclesia," *Hlídka* (Brno, 1911), pp. 99-106 (in reprint). Also V. Kybal, *Jan Hus, Učení*, 3 vols. (Praha, Jan Laichter, 1923-31), II, pp. 166-168.

for the general Council gathered to consider matters of faith or other ecclesiastical concerns. Its decrees, whether Scriptural or traditional, are to be obeyed, as Augustine teaches.[2] The fourth significance of the word refers to the prelates and other officials heading the Church, such as the pope and his cardinals, patriarchs, archbishops, and bishops. In this sense are to be understood Christ's words, "If your brother sins against you . . . tell it to the Church,"[3] that is, to the prelates of the Church. Obviously, Christ meant no such thing; Páleč's gratuitous addition to Christ's words subverts their meaning. He further contradicts the plain meaning of Christ's words by insisting that it *does not* mean the whole body of believers or of laymen, "but solely the authoritative correction of the prelates in ecclesiastical matters, although fraternal in respect of all." Further, the word "Church" includes metropolitan and episcopal churches, such as those of Prague, Litomyšl, Olomouc, as well as the local churches of these metropolitanates, as those of Žatec, Brod, or Beroun. Nevertheless, "The mother of all the churches, their head and mistress, is the Roman Church." He quotes a number of patristic proofs for this thesis. "Of this Roman Church the pope is the head, the true and manifest successor of the prince of the apostles, Peter, and the college of cardinals the body of the said Roman Church, the true and manifest successors of the other apostles of Christ." Later he adds that "others" are successors of the seventy disciples.[4] Although here Páleč repeats Stanislav's formula, he does not say that the pope and the cardinals form a mystico-ecclesiastical synthesis! This succession was by the appointment of the Holy Spirit. Páleč then cites Augustine's warning against ignoring the bishops, who

---

[2] Augustine, "De doctrina christiana," in J.-P. Migne, *Patrologia latina*, 221 vols. (Paris, Garnier Frères, 1887), XXXIV, chap. 8, p. 40.
[3] Matt. 18:15-17.
[4] *De aequivocatione* (see n. 1), pp. 102-103.

held their offices by divine appointment. The Roman Church, Páleč says, "has the authority and the ecclesiastical office to discern and define catholic and ecclesiastical causes and to correct, purge, and care for errors concerning them in the said causes of other churches and all Christians. It can judge all concerning all things but no one is permitted to judge it, because the lower have no authority to judge the higher, but the higher the lower."[5] Moreover, whatever the Roman Church ordains in matters catholic or ecclesiastical must be obeyed by all. Whoever does not obey is a heretic. To it all must have recourse in controversial matters. We are here on familiar ground, since these are the perennial theses of the papalist party.

In the fifth sense the word "Church" signifies the universal and total congregation of all the predestinate or believing who are in grace and are vivified by the spirit of Christ. This is the Church universal which, however, does not possess the privileged functions of the Roman Church:

> This Church catholic does not possess the office of discerning and defining the catholic and ecclesiastical causes, for it has never been gathered as such nor is it known about anyone whether he is of the predestinate. . . . Therefore, the rule of that Church for such a purpose requires the manifest and true successors of the prince of the apostles Peter and the college of the other apostles of Christ. Nor can such successors be given or found on earth except in the pope and the college of cardinals.[6]

The sixth significance of the term "Church" refers to the community of all those who are baptized and believe the twelve articles of faith (i.e., the Apostles' Creed). The Savior compares the kingdom of heaven or the

[5] *De aequivocatione*, p. 103.    [6] *Ibid.*, p. 105.

Church militant to the wise and foolish virgins,[7] or to the field yielding both wheat and tares.[8] Such then are Páleč's definitions of the Church, which include Stanislav's, but extend to other concepts as well.

Although Páleč does not speak in his definition of the "mystico-ecclesiastical synthesis," the favorite phrase of Stanislav's, he in no way departs from the substance of that definition. The Roman Church consists of the pope and the cardinals as the ruling authority of the Church universal. This is his principal definition of the Church, with which he consistently operates. Only in one place does he include bishops as successors of the outer circle of the disciples; but they do not belong to the ruling body. He explicitly excludes from the concept the whole body of believers and the lay members (definition four), although he seems to include them in the next definition where he speaks of "the universal and total congregation of all the predestinate and believing." This body, however, does not rule the Church, but is subject to the rule of the pope and the cardinals. Páleč thus takes a position diametrically opposed to that of the Conciliarists who regarded themselves as representing all the faithful. Too bad this was not known to the fathers of the Council of Constance! Moreover, how could Páleč acknowledge John XXIII as the rightful pope, since he had been elected in succession to the Pisan Alexander V? And how nimbly Páleč changed his tune when he came to Constance, where he was accepted as the representative of the orthodox Czech clergy!

In the meantime, Hus produced his chief work, *De ecclesia*, in which he attempted to summarize his thought on the subject of the Church in a consistent and systematic way. We shall deal with this work more fully in the next chapter, even though this arrangement will unavoidably cause inconvenience in comparing Páleč's

[7] Matt. 25:1-13.　　　　[8] Matt. 13:24-30.

answer with it. Nevertheless, to incorporate it in this chapter would not permit us to do justice to it and would make the exposition of matters more directly relevant to this chapter cumbersome. Hus began working on the *De ecclesia* perhaps late in 1412 or early in 1413 and completed it in May 1413. It was read at the Bethlehem Chapel, as one of its colophons expressly states, on June 8.[9] Páleč could not leave such a challenging pronouncement unanswered. He replied in a treatise bearing the same name, *De ecclesia*.[10] Strangely enough, this important work of Páleč's was not recognized for what it was until 1912, when Dr. Sedlák found its complete text in Cracow. The version previously current in Prague was incomplete and was ascribed to Stanislav. The first twenty-six chapters comprise a point-by-point answer to Hus' first ten chapters. The remaining chapters, 27-45, are directed against Hus' reply to the *Consilium* of the theological faculty (February 6, 1413). Unfortunately, since the entire text has not been published by Sedlák, a complete comparison of the two works is not possible. Thus the treatment of this controversy must of necessity be inadequate.[11]

First of all, in dealing with Hus' concept of the Church as the totality of the predestinate Páleč reduces his own six definitions, previously described, to two; namely, the

[9] S. Harrison Thomson, ed., *Magistri Johannis Hus Tractatus de ecclesia* (Boulder, Colo., University of Colorado Press, 1956), p. xvi; F. M. Bartoš, *Literární činnost M. J. Husi* (Praha, Česká akademie věd a umění, 1948), p. 86. A Czech translation, based on Thomson and other sources, was published by F. M. Dobiáš and Amedeo Molnár, *Mistr Jan Hus, O církvi* (Praha, Československá akademie věd, 1965).

[10] J. Sedlák, *M. Jan Hus* (Praha, Dědictví sv. Prokopa, 1915), excerpts from *De ecclesia* in the Supplement, pp. 202-304 (*partes selectae*); also the same author's summary account of the contents in "Pálčův spis proti Husovu traktátu 'de ecclesia,'" *Hlídka* (Brno, 1912).

[11] The subject is treated as fully as possible under the circumstances by Kybal, *Jan Hus, Učení*, II, pp. 256-274.

Church of the believing and the church of the wicked. Thus in reference to the former he differs from Hus in speaking of the *congregatio fidelium* rather than of the *congregatio praedestinatorum*. They agree that the Church militant consists of both the elect and the reprobate. Páleč further distinguishes between the material part, consisting of the building and its services, and the spiritual. The material church, of course, reminds one of the first definition of his *De aequivocatione*, although it is unknown to catholic theology. The Church is not a building! The spiritual church Páleč identifies with the *congregatio fidelium*, characterized by right faith but not right life. Furthermore, while in his previous definition (the fifth) he confusedly includes in the Church universal the predestinate *or* believing, in the present work he distinguishes between the two concepts. In agreement with Hus he recognizes that the Church of the predestinate, comprising all the elect from the beginning of the race to the end of time, is one and unchanging [*una et invariata*]. Along with it, however, he acknowledges also the Church militant and the Roman Church.[12] Thus he distinguishes three "churches" within "the Church," and all are "holy." He denounces Hus for declaring only one Church, that of the predestinate, as holy, while the foreknown in the Church militant, although being *in* the Church are not *of* it.[13] His criticism of Hus centers, therefore, upon the latter's concept of the Church militant, not on that of the predestinate. Kybal graphically illustrates the difference between the two antagonists by diagramming Hus' concept as consisting of three concentric circles, the innermost being the communion of the predestinate, the next of the dormient, and the outer of the militant. The last-named comprises both the predestined and the foreknown, although only the

[12] *Ibid.*, II, pp. 256-260.
[13] Thomson, Hus' *De ecclesia* (see n. 9), chaps. 2 and 3 passim.

former are really *of* the Church. Páleč's idea, on the other hand, is illustrated by three separate circles representing the predestinate, militant, and Roman churches, comprised in the "spiritual" or holy Church. For him the Church militant consists of all believers holding the Apostles' Creed and partaking of the sacraments. Accordingly, for Páleč there appears to exist no real difference between the churches of the predestinate and the militant, or, for that matter, between the Church militant and the Roman Church. They are all "holy." His assertion that in Hus' concept not even the Church of the predestinate should be called "holy," because some of its potential members are as yet not actually such, not only misses the point but militates against his own concept. More important is his stubborn insistence that Hus' concept annuls the reality of the Church militant as well as of the Roman Church.[14] He succeeded in convincing the Council of Constance of the validity of his erroneous interpretation; it was always placed first among the charges on the basis of which Hus was condemned as heretic.

Similarly, there exists a fundamental difference between the two men as to the bond whereby the members of the Church are bound to Christ. Hus considers predestination to be the bond; for Páleč it is sanctifying grace. If Hus is right, then a foreknown pope is not even a member of the Church, not to say its head. This Páleč declares to be "an insane error."[15] He concludes that Wyclifites, who refuse to obey Christ's vicar, refuse to obey Christ Himself, who said: "He who hears you hears me; and he who spurns you spurns me."[16] To be sure, this was said to the outer circle of the seventy disciples whose successors, according to Páleč, were the bishops, not the pope or the cardinals. But he was apparently of

---

[14] Sedlák, Páleč's *De ecclesia* (see n. 10), pp. 203, 241.
[15] *Ibid.*, p. 204.     [16] Luke 10:16.

the opinion that consistency is the vice of small men. He was not one of them.

In chapters 9 to 14 Páleč deals with the Roman primacy. He asserts, as we have already noted, that "the power and authority of the Apostolic See is universal, having, as has often been declared, not partial and particular but general and total rule, in order to discern and define not only ecclesiastical but also civil causes...."[17] Christ had indeed been the *caput supremum* of the Church, but upon his leaving the earth he appointed Peter as his vicarial head. Páleč supports this thesis by the rhetorical "proof" alleging that when Paul went to Jerusalem three years after his conversion, he did not go to see Peter *corporaliter* (in fact, he did not go to see Peter at all, but "the pillars of the church, of whom James was the head"). He went because he "knew that there was one universal Church of God on earth.... He also knew that that Church on earth had one head, namely, Peter, ... in which head existed the plenitude of power on earth of discerning and defining every cause on earth in respect of the salvation or of the danger to souls according to the forementioned two keys of the kingdom of heaven...."[18]

Without pointing out that Paul did no such thing and believed no such thing, but the very opposite, let us continue Páleč's argument. This plenitude of power cannot exist in two persons at the same time. It could not exist in both Peter and Paul, but in Peter alone. The pope, therefore, as Peter's vicar and Paul's superior, can dispense men of any or all of Paul's precepts, declarations, or ordinances.[19] This plenitude of power of the pope as the head of the College of Cardinals had been acknowledged and professed for more than a thousand years by the doctors and learned men of the Church and

[17] Páleč's *De ecclesia*, p. 217.
[18] *Ibid.*                    [19] *Ibid.*, p. 219.

school. It had also been confessed by the community of all the clergy of entire Christendom. They have ever professed that the ecclesiastical and mystical synthesis of the pope as the head and the cardinals as the body (here appears Stanislav's phrase again!) constitutes the Roman Church. Páleč quotes many patristic proofs in support of this position. He particularly relies on Jerome, who, however, does not use Stanislav's familiar definition.[20] The important thing is that despite the effort Páleč has expended in his previous treatise to broaden Stanislav's definition, in this instance he arrives at the same conclusion: the basic concept, a kind of *Ding an sich* of the Church, is the mystico-ecclesiastical synthesis of the pope and cardinals, whose chief functions are administrative and juridical. The Church is therefore essentially a juridical corporation. Páleč quotes approvingly of Pope Boniface VIII who in his bull *Unam sanctam* declared that subjection to the Roman pontiff is necessary to salvation. Innumerable canons (which Páleč calls *scriptura*) testify to the same doctrine. Therefore, it is false to assert, as the Wyclifites do, that Christians should resort to the Church of the predestinate in dubious doctrinal matters. To turn away from the doctrine of the Roman Church is foolish and altogether insane. Such an act is contrary to sacred Scripture, the holy doctors, sacred canons, and reason.[21] From this supreme body, power flows to the bishops and the clergy, who do not participate in the ruling function. The laity is utterly dependent upon this Church order without constituting a meaningful part of it. Páleč's concept thus completely negates the conciliar principle. Kybal remarks that it was "a bloody irony" that the Council did not know the views of Hus' accuser on whose charges it condemned Hus.[22]

20 Kybal, *Jan Hus, Učení*, II, p. 260.
21 Páleč's *De ecclesia*, p. 222.
22 Kybal, *Jan Hus, Učení*, II, p. 260.

Nevertheless, Páleč speaks of general Councils in terms surprisingly conciliatory. A Council, to be sure, cannot be called without the pope's authority, and its decisions must be approved by him. Only in this way can it be regarded as representing the Roman Church. In case the pope should be a manifest heretic (how can that be determined when no one can judge him?) and the cardinals should refuse to act, a general Council may be called without the pope's consent (by whom?).[23] Even so its decisions must be approved by the new pope. In some cases the Council is above the pope and the cardinals (did Páleč have Pisa in mind?). Yet despite this apparent concession to the concilar theory, this statement clearly contradicts Páleč's basic definition which he shared with Stanislav. Thus it must be regarded as an aberration or an opportunistic evasion to meet the objection to his recognition of Pope John XXIII.

Páleč then plunges into a condemnation of Wyclif and his disciples for refusing to accept the above-described "truths." He calls Wyclif the most pernicious heresiarch. No other heretic had disseminated so much false doctrine as he.

> He wrote erroneously in his books about the sacraments of the Church, of the offices and censures of the Church, of morals, rites, ceremonies, laws, liberties, and *sacramentalia* of the Church, of the veneration of relics, of indulgences, of the orders and the religious in the Church.[24]

Other heretics erred in one or a few points, but Wyclif aimed in all his points at a total annulment of the teaching of the Church.

Páleč then goes on to consider faith as the basis of the Church. He argues that "the Roman Church, the pope and the cardinals, have never erred in judgments and

[23] *Ibid.*, p. 262.    [24] Páleč's *De ecclesia*, p. 227.

decisions which they have passed on [*tradit*] to the faithful in all matters whatsoever. . . ."[25] Whoever denies the pope's authority even in a single article is a heretic. Hus demands that the papal bulls should be believed only insofar as they conform to Scripture. Páleč, on the contrary, asserts that in both legal and doctrinal matters they are to be accepted even though they are "not infrequently" unscriptural. Since "no one is permitted to judge the pope's judgment," the same applies to his decrees.[26] But in the very next sentence he admits that the pope may be misinformed. If such an error is proved, his decrees may not be received, and the pope should be respectfully informed about the correct facts. In the meantime, before the error is proved (by whom?), the pope's decisions must be accepted. For if all men were allowed freely to impugn them, great confusion would result. As for the pope's pronouncements concerning matters of faith, however, they must be received at all times, even though they be unscriptural. For "Christ and the Holy Spirit have passed on to Christ's faithful through the Roman Church many decisions to be universally held, thought, and believed which are not contained in the text of the Old and New Testaments."[27] These decisions are preserved in traditions, pronouncements of Councils and of the Roman Church, as well as in provincial statutes. Although they are not literally contained in Scripture, if they are not contrary to it they should be believed. For the Roman Church has never erred concerning the faith. Hus, however, with his Wyclifites howling like wolves, contradicts and deviates from the canonical definition that "the first demand of salvation is to keep the rule of faith and to deviate in no way from what the Fathers have established."[28]

Thereupon, Páleč engages in a controversy about Peter

[25] *Ibid.*, p. 228.      [26] *Ibid.*, p. 229.
[27] *Ibid.*, pp. 230-231.      [28] *Ibid.*, p. 231.

as the head of the Church. He asserts that it is insanity to deny that Peter and his successors are the ministerial and vicarial heads of the Church. This is what Hus does when he claims that the Church universal was founded on Christ, not on Peter. In expounding the ever-controversial Matt. 16:18, "Thou art Peter . . . ," Hus, following Augustine, explains it to mean that Peter was not the rock [*petra*], but was the confessor of the true Rock, Christ.[29] Although Páleč acknowledges Augustine's interpretation, he holds that Christ, is the *principal* foundation while Peter, as Ambrose taught, is the secondary—ministerial and vicarial—foundation. These two statements, Páleč maintains, do not contradict each other, but are complementary. He writes that Christ did not say that He would build the Church *super me, petram*; or *super hanc petram, quam confessus es*; or *super te, petram*; but *super hanc petram*. Páleč thus accepts all three senses as catholic. Nevertheless, the concept he chooses preeminently is that both Christ and Peter are the "rock" upon which the Church is built, but in different senses: "Christ on account of his authority, because He carries all and is carried by none; Peter on account of his administrative function as His supreme vicar, because he carries others by his authority and is carried by Christ."[30] Peter was appointed to this function because of the firmness of his faith. His function was altogether institutional, that of ruling and judging. Hus never admitted the double foundation of the Church, nor did he conceive of Peter's function as being so exclusively jurisdictional as Páleč does. Furthermore, Páleč criticizes Hus for "closing his right eye to the fact that in the pope, Christ's vicar, and in the other prelates, is to be seen ecclesiastical authority, while he opens his left eye solely to look at the life of the pope and the

[29] Hus' *De ecclesia* (see n. 9), chap. 9.
[30] Páleč's *De ecclesia*, pp. 238-240.

*220*

prelates. . . . For not on account of his life, but on account of ecclesiastical authority is Christ's vicar to be principally assessed."[31] He exercises his authority not because of his life, but because he has been endowed with it by Christ in Peter. It is, therefore, false to assert, as Hus does, that unless the pope follows Christ in morals and life, he is not a true vicar of Christ, but of the Antichrist. The Savior chose Judas an apostle although He new of his avarice. He said: "Have I not chosen you twelve, and one of you is a devil?"[32] The papal office is, therefore, freely given, not depending on the character of the one chosen for it. "To deny it is an insane and stupid error."[33] For were it not so, the faithful would be extremely confused about their soul's salvation. They would not know whether their pastors and prelates were true vicars of Christ or hypocrites and secret heretics. The same doubt would apply to the sacraments. This is particularly true of the sacrament of Christ's body, of which the Wyclifites declare that "the material bread remains in the sacrament after consecration. . . . They allege publicly in sermons that it was the belief of the ancient Church that the material bread remains, while the modern Church asserts it does not remain. . . ."[34] Thus the Wyclifites create doubts and suspense in the minds of men about this matter, although the Church has already defined its correct interpretation.

Páleč then turns to chapter 10 of Hus' *De ecclesia*, which is devoted mainly to the discussion of the power of the keys. Hus has a high regard for this doctrine. It derives from Christ for the purposes of dispensing discipline in the Church, of preserving the purity of faith, and of administering all the sacraments. It was granted not only to Peter in Christ's words, "I will give thee the keys of the kingdom of heaven," but to the whole Church

[31] *Ibid.*, p. 242.
[32] John 6:70.
[33] Páleč's *De ecclesia*, p. 245.
[34] *Ibid.*, p. 244.

militant represented in the person of Peter. This power consists in discerning and judging of sin and in declaring God's forgiveness upon the sinner's contrition, confession, and satisfaction. Hus complains that priests act as if they could forgive sins on their own authority whenever and to whomever they pleased. But no priest, not even the pope, can forgive sins unless God has first forgiven them. For He alone knows whether the penitent is truly contrite.

Páleč radically repudiates these views. The validity of the sacraments does not depend on the character of the ministrant, but on the sanctity of the sacraments, which are valid whenever the proper formula of their consecration is used. The spiritual power of the keys (*clavis ordinis* and *clavis iurisdictionis*) is conferred on every priest at ordination. The first key cannot be taken away, since the ordination is indelible; but the second can be limited or taken away altogether. The spiritual power is not the same for all priests. Only the pope has jurisdiction over the entire Church, while the bishops are limited to their dioceses and the priests to their parishes. Furthermore, in absolving the penitent from sin the priest acts in God's stead, ministerially. Here again a basic difference between Hus and Páleč comes to view. Hus ascribes forgiveness of sins directly to God, Páleč to the Church, i.e., its priests, even though they act only ministerially. It may be remarked that Hus follows Augustine, Peter Lombard, William of Paris, and others in this matter. Páleč's view, on the other hand, possessed no official authority until the Council of Trent adopted it in order to brand the Reformation doctrine false.

Beginning with chapter 11, Hus deals directly with the text of the *Consilium* profferred by the eight doctors of the theological faculty on February 6, 1413.[35] He

[35] F. Palacký, ed., *Documenta Mag. Joannis Hus* (Praha, F. Tempsky, 1869), pp. 475-480.

appears not to have had the text of this document prior to that time. In that chapter he defends the "evangelical clergy" against the charge that their denunciations of the clerical wickedness have caused the dissension in the country. Hus has, ever since he began preaching, denounced simony and other abuses of clerical power. In his acrimonious rebuttal, Páleč produces five arguments, wresting the sense of Hus' charges from their rightful meaning. For instance, he writes that when Hus mentions "the beast" of the Revelation, he tries to suggest to the people that this refers to the pope, while in reality it is spoken regarding the Antichrist.[36] He refers to "a certain of Hus' fellow-apostles" who publicly called John XXIII Antichrist. That is true of Jakoubek of Stříbro who made the statement in the *Quodlibet* of 1412; but Hus neither joined him nor could restrain him. He was not personally responsible for all the members of his party. Páleč furthermore charges Hus with blasphemy for "sanctifying" the three young men who had protested against the bull of indulgences and on that account had been beheaded. Hus, of course, did not and could not do any such thing. Páleč admits that the simoniacs act nefariously; but he declares that the "pestiferous" clergy who do not observe the decisions of the Roman Church act even worse. The statement of Hus' that the preaching against the wickedness of the clergy is the cause of the dissension is false, Páleč claims, because it is not the preaching as such but the insinuation of Wyclif's errors into it which is the cause of the dissension.

Páleč further brands as erroneous Hus' assertion that the papal dignity derives from emperors Constantine, Phocas, and others. He concedes that the title of the popes had originally been shared by other heads of churches before Constantine's conversion. When, how-

---

[36] Páleč's *De ecclesia*, p. 256.

ever, the preeminence of the Roman see was recognized in the days of Constantine and of Pope Sylvester, the title was restricted to the Roman bishop alone. Constantine furthermore allowed the calling of Councils, particularly that of Nicaea, at which—according to Páleč—Arius died by vomiting his entrails! The emperor also built churches, he himself ordering the erection of the Church of St. Peter and of the Lateran palace, and assigned to the successors of Peter the city of Rome, all Italy, and the Western regions. Above all, he declared the pope to be the head of all the churches. Seeing that all these acts were for the benefit of the Church, Sylvester accepted them, for "he could not resist such an exaltation of the status of the Church."[37] The fable of "the Donation of Constantine" was thus accepted by both Hus and Páleč, along with the whole medieval Church. Hus, however, regarded the Donation as destructive of the spiritual character of the Church, while Páleč deemed it beneficial.

In chapter 13 Hus, rejecting the thesis that the pope and the cardinals constitute the Roman Church, contends that no pope is the head of the Church catholic, but only Christ Himself. As for the Roman Church, the pope is its head if he is one of the predestinate; and since no one can know that except by revelation, although holy life is a proof presumptive of it, we should not assert that every pope whatsoever "is the head of any particular holy church. . . . It is not of the substance of the catholic faith to believe explicitly that Liberius, John [i.e., Agnes], Boniface, Clement, or Urban were predestinate or members of the holy mother Church."[38] This was indeed the very crux of the controversy. Unfortunately, Sedlák did not see fit to publish the text of Páleč's reply, but only its summary couched in his own words. Páleč calls it an error to say that no pope is the

[37] *Ibid.*, pp. 268-269.      [38] Hus' *De ecclesia*, p. 108.

head of the Church along with Christ (Hus of course specified the Church catholic, not the Roman Church), or that no pope is the head of any particular church unless he is of the predestinate. He likewise denies that the doctors have not adequately proved that the pope is the head of the holy Church. The ambiguity of this statement consists in Páleč's calling all three concepts of the Church—the catholic, the militant, and the Roman—"holy." Hus, of course, restricts the term to the Church catholic. Thus they are not discussing the same thing. It is this kind of ambiguity which characterizes the whole controversy.

Páleč's answer to chapter 14, which deals with the cardinals, is again available only in Sedlák's summary. In replying to chapter 15, which deals with the proposition that the Church does not absolutely need the pope and the cardinals for its rule, Páleč insists that a "visible" head vicarially ruling the Church is essential [*oportet*]. To say that the primacy of the pope both temporal and spiritual is derived from Caesars is a crude error. Hus, however, did not deny that the spiritual power of the pope is derived from Christ through Peter; it is only the secular power which was bestowed on him by Constantine and other emperors.

In the next three sections of his polemic (chapters 34-36) Páleč contends against Hus' assertion that Scripture is the criterion of all ecclesiastical judgments. The doctors, in the *Consilium*, accused Hus and his party that they would have none but Scripture to judge them and that they interpreted it "according to their own understanding [heads]."[39] Hus bluntly calls both these statements lies. He dubs as the "biggest lie" the doctors' imputation that the recalcitrant party does not observe the Scriptural command in Deut. 17:8-12, directing Israelites to submit certain cases requiring decision to the

[39] Palacký, *Documenta*, p. 476.

Levitical priests. "The man who acts presumptuously, by not obeying the priest who stands to minister there before the Lord your God, or the judge, that man shall die." Hus cites in his defense the generally acknowledged Scriptural commentator, Nicholas of Lyra, who remarks concerning the passage that no man's judgment is valid if it contains a manifest falsity or error.[40] Páleč, whom Hus takes to be the author of this section of the *Consilium*, replies that Lyra's comment on the passage is indeed correct, but that Hus uses it as a mere excuse for his disobedience of the pope. Hus, on the other hand, who certainly considered the pope's judgment to contain a manifest falsity, felt justified in his disobedience. This is another example of the contrary assumptions from which the two men judged. Páleč also calls false Hus' assertion that the doctors refuse to have Scripture as judge, for what they really hold is that they do not want it *alone* as judge. Neither did Hus. For he acknowledged as proper judges *principally* God and Christ, but also the Councils, the holy doctors, and even papal pronouncements if they agreed with Scripture. Páleč further argues against Hus' charge that the imposition of the death penalty on those who refuse to obey the pope's judgment is cruel. He exculpates the doctors on the ground that they merely obeyed the king's decree that those who refuse to accept the papal "crusading bull" be put to death.

Thereupon, Páleč plunges into a rebuttal of Hus' declaration (chapter 17) about obedience due to papal commands. But since Sedlák again chose to leave out Páleč's own reply and because this particular subject has already been discussed *ad nauseum*, we may pass on to Páleč's partial answer to chapter 18. He replies there to Hus' statement of the reasons for refusing to obey Pope Alexander's and Archbishop Zbyněk's prohibition

[40] Hus' *De ecclesia*, pp. 164-166.

of preaching in the Bethlehem Chapel and Pope John's bull of indulgences. Páleč pronounces both actions as damnable disobedience and Hus' reasons no excuse at all. He defends the pope's right to forbid preaching in certain places as Christ forbade his disciples to go among the gentiles and the Samaritans.[41] Hus' own urging of Christ's command to preach to every creature Páleč counters by asserting that not all Christ's actions are to be followed, but must be interpreted according to the cause, place, and time.[42] The pope was not acting contrary to Christ when he reasonably suspended preaching, particularly in the Bethlehem Chapel, where he perceived that errors were being disseminated. He did not intend to obstruct the Word of God or the salvation of the people, but to close "the conventicles and the satanic school of that impious Wyclif."[43] The pope not only has the right but the duty to suspend from preaching anyone suspected of heresy, lest the venom of his error or heresy infect those redeemed by Christ's blood.[44] By this means the Word of God is not "bound," as Hus alleged. Páleč even claims that Hus was free to preach in other churches in Prague or elsewhere. This is not true, for the authorities and the clergy of Prague agreed among themselves not to afford him a place of preaching. Páleč could not have been unaware of this; thus his statement is patently hypocritical. He further charges that Hus has engineered the exile of the "catholic preachers" and the "spoliation" of the clergy. This too is absolutely untrue. Finally Páleč, derisively calling Hus "little Hus" [Husko], taunts him that his disobedience of Alexander V has brought him ruin, and the exile has lost him his place and office among the clergy. He reiterates the declaration of the *Consilium* that disobedience is mortal sin.

[41] Matt. 10:5.

[42] Páleč's *De ecclesia*, p. 287.

[43] *Ibid.*, p. 288.

[44] *Ibid.*

The stubborn conflict carried on by the two former friends continued in Hus' defense of himself in his *Contra Paletz*.[45] In it, Hus dealt not only with Páleč's *De ecclesia*, but also with another of his opponent's treatises, *Replicatio contra Quidamistas*.[46] This was Páleč's violent comment on the university masters' reply to the *Consilium*. *Quidamistae* was a jeering term applied to Hus' party as being "pestiferous" and heretical clergy. It refers to the repeated mention in the *Consilium* of "certain" [*quidam*] Czech clergy who refuse obedience to papal commands. We may, at the same time, consider Páleč's *Antihus*,[47] his rebuttal of the *Contra Paletz*. This will unfortunately complicate the argument but will facilitate dispatch.

First of all, Hus recalls to Páleč's memory the so-called German mass, asserting that Stanislav of Znojmo begat Peter of Znojmo, who in turn begat Páleč, who then begat Hus. He suggests that they better make their recantation known abroad. Páleč, after abusing Hus and his "fellow-apostles" for regarding themselves as "the only learned masters in Israel," replies by repudiating any aspersion on his or his colleagues' purity of faith. They have not erred in *materia fidei*. "If, however, as I propound but do not concede, we have erred in anything, it is no wonder, since even the holy doctors and apostles have erred. It is human to err, but diabolical to remain in error. I am ready to correct such an error. . . ."[48] He then paraphrases Hus' own statement about Páleč, declaring: "Thus Hus is a friend, truth is

[45] "Responsio Mag. Joannis Hus ad scripta M. Stephani Paletz, theologiae doctoris," in *Historia et monumenta Joannis Hus atque Hieronymi Pragensis, confessorum Christi*, 2 vols. (Norimberg, 1715), I, pp. 318-331. Hereafter cited as *Contra Paletz*.

[46] "Replicatio contra Quidamistas," in J. Loserth, ed., "Beiträge zur Geschichte der Husitischen Bewegung," IV, *Archiv für Oesterreichische Geschichte*, Vol. 75 (Wien, 1889), pp. 344-361.

[47] J. Sedlák, ed., "Antihus," *Hlídka* (Brno, 1913).

[48] *Antihus* (see n. 47), p. 8.

a friend; but because Hus and the truth are wholly in disagreement, the truth should be preferred to Hus."[49] He exculpates Stanislav as well as himself of any guilt in having held remanence, and professes to be ready to suffer death rather than to hold any error contrary to the teaching of the Roman Church. Despite all the admonition to the contrary, he continues, Hus has contemptuously repudiated obedience to the Roman Church and for many years has preached and administered the sacraments contrary to the pope's prohibition. He has even dared to call the pope Antichrist. (In reality Hus never did this, although the same cannot be said of Jakoubek.) Hus did not suffer for the sake of Christ, but because of his own rebellion and errors. The cause of dissension is the rejection, on the part of Hus' party, of the "three catholic truths," which consist of (1) the acceptance of the faith held by the Roman Church; (2) obedience to the judgments of the Roman curia in every ecclesiastical matter; (3) obedience to the Roman Church and its prelates in all "intermediate" matters (i.e., where they command nothing purely evil or oppose nothing purely good). This is not even correct catholic doctrine, but extreme papalism. Strangely enough, Hus passes over the occasion to point out the baselessness of the "three truths." He replies only to Páleč's declaration, made in the Old Town Hall meeting, that "he who does not obey the papal decree should be put to death." To the taunt why he did not obey the citation to Rome he replies with the oft-repeated reasons. "Rome does not take sheep without wool." He also demands that such trials should be held in Prague, not Rome.

To this Páleč retorts that it would be impossible to secure a fair trial in the kingdom of Bohemia. No matter how guilty a man might be, he could always find

[49] *Ibid.*, p. 9.

some protectors and defenders in these perverse times! As to the threat of death for non-obedience of the papal commands, Páleč justifies himself by saying that it was not he but the king who forbade all demonstrations against the crusading bull on pain of death. As to the citation to Rome, he brushes aside Hus' reasons for non-appearance and insists that since Hus was condemned in Rome, to Rome he should go.[50]

In the second place, Páleč, in *Antihus*, brands as "a most insane error" Hus' statement that a pope, bishop, or prelate in mortal sin is not a true pope, bishop, or prelate, because his life is not consonant with his profession. He objects that Hus, in quoting the authorities supporting this interpretation, omits those doctors who contradict it. Páleč argues that being a Christian is not the same thing as being a pope, bishop, or prelate.[51] The latter is a designation of office, the former characterizes a life. There is, therefore, no contradiction, for the manner of life of the holders of the office does not affect the validity of the sacraments, "for not life but office and authority validate and consecrate the sacraments." It follows therefore, that the pope and the cardinals are manifest successors of the apostles *ex officio* not because of their morals or life. Furthermore, in answering the objection that the saints declared no mortal sinner to be a Christian, Páleč maintains that anyone holding even by unformed faith all that should be believed by a catholic is worthy of the name of Christian. Therefore, "all Christians, even the wicked, having an unformed faith, are faithful and consequently true Christians by reason of the truth of faith, although not of life."[52]

This was indeed a radical negation of the most fundamental ideas of Hus, for whom no one but a predestinate striving by a life of pious works to attain ultimately to a faith formed by love, was a true Christian. He retorted

[50] *Ibid.*, pp. 10-15.     [51] *Ibid.*, p. 23.     [52] *Ibid.*, p. 24.

that saints Augustine, Jerome, Chrysostom, and Bernard taught that no one in mortal sin is a true Christian. According to John 10, they are in fact thieves and robbers.

> We concede, indeed, that a wicked pope, bishop, prelate or priest is an unworthy minister of the sacraments, through whom God nevertheless baptizes, consecrates, or otherwise acts for the perfection of his Church. . . . Thus a wicked and pestiferous minister does not indeed baptize, transubstantiate, and consecrate worthily, but exercises his ministry of Jesus Christ unworthily to his damnation.[53]

Hus then refers to Gratian's *Decretum*, where Jerome is quoted as saying: "Not all bishops are bishops . . . for the ecclesiastical office does not make a Christian."[54]

Páleč in his turn berates Hus as a great heretic for not distinguishing between the office and the life. Were the validity of the sacramental acts to depend on the character of the ministers of the Church, the faithful would be thrown into utmost confusion and perplexity about them, since no one without a private revelation could know whether the officiating priest was of the predestinate. Moreover, since Hus admits that God acts even through wicked priests, they are therefore true priests. This was, of course, an evasion of Hus' critique that such ministration is exercised unworthily. Páleč ignores this point, the only point at issue. Hus had stated it innumerable times; Páleč could not have been ignorant of it.

In the next place, Páleč asserts that Hus errs grossly in teaching that a sinner who is sincerely contrite and confesses his sins to God need not confess them orally to a priest, even though he has an opportunity to do so. When Hus averred that God alone forgives sins, and had

---

[53] *Contra Paletz*, p. 319.
[54] Gratian, *Decretum*, in E. Friedberg, ed., *Corpus juris canonici*, 2 vols. (Leipzig, Tauchnitz, 1879), I, 2, quest. 7.

it so inscribed on the walls of the Bethlehem Chapel, he contemned the authority of the Church. Páleč declares that all who give occasion to or follow false opinions, or understand the holy Scriptures otherwise than the Holy Spirit demands or the Roman Church teaches, or who defend heretics, are heresiarchs.[55] He then expostulates with Hus, urging him to consider whether all these marks of heresy are not present in him, for no sin is graver than heresy. Hypocritically calling Hus "his dear brother in Christ," he exhorts him to repentance in order to save his soul.

Even at the risk of wearying the reader to exasperation, we dare to emphasize why this topic formed a constant subject of controversy. In one sense, there was little difference between the disputants. Hus did not deny that the sacramental ministration of wicked priests is valid; he only insisted that it was unworthy. Without conceding this term, Páleč admitted that some priests and prelates were wicked although their acts were valid. Thus the real difference went deeper. It consisted of the intransigent demand of Hus in respect of the character qualifications of the clergy from the pope all the way to the humblest deacon. Páleč, on the other hand, doggedly and with equal vehemence emphasized that the validity of the pope's office depends on legal election and not on his life. His authority was *gratia gratis dana*, and had nothing to do with the pope's life or conduct. He could be thoroughly wicked—which was reprehensible—but this had no effect on the validity of the duties of his office. Páleč did not mince words about it, and it must be admitted that he was closer to the Church's ultimately dominant position than Hus. The latter indeed skated on the thin ice of Donatism, except for the saving fact that he acknowledged the acts of the wicked priests as valid, though unworthy. No wonder that Páleč's

[55] *Antihus*, p. 28.

thesis served as one of the principal charges against Hus at Constance, on the basis of which he was condemned. For the Council ignored the "saving exception" as completely and thoroughly as Páleč had done.

This basic difference in the position of the two antagonists is also clearly seen in the next topic, the controversy over the pope's title. Hus denied the propriety of calling the pope "most holy" [*sanctissimus*], since only God is *most* holy. At best the pope should bear the title "holy," if he deserves it. If by reason of office the pope is called most holy, as Páleč argued, why is not the Roman emperor called the same by reason of his office? For a king, according to Augustine, reigns in place of Christ's deity, having authority over all temporal affairs, while the priest ministers in place of Christ's humanity, for in this nature Christ's kingdom is not of this world, but only spiritual. Why then should not justices and lawyers, even executioners and public criers, be called holy, for they officiate for the benefit of Christ's Church? "Indeed, even the devil should be called holy, for he is an official of God and a minister deputized by God to torture the condemned, as appears from Christ's words in Matt. 7:18, 22."[56] This is indeed *argumentum ad hominem*, which his enemies later utilized to his harm.

Páleč, on the contrary, argues that since Saul could be called the head of the kingdom, so much more the pope. Hus replies that Saul was rejected from the rule because of his disobedience, therefore the pope should be rejected for the same cause. Saul was chosen king because of his moral qualities as the best available leader of the people of Israel. "Therefore, if the pope is of the elect and good, than whom no better man exists among the Christian people, then he is most holy among them,

---

[56] *Contra Paletz*, pp. 322-323. The biblical quotation should be Matt. 17:18.

a good shepherd and the head of the multitude whom he rules by the example of his life and the word of doctrine. But this the *Fictor* [the liar, i.e., Páleč] will not prove about every pope till the Day of Judgment. . . ." Indeed, "if the pope lives contrary to Christ he is the Antichrist."[57]

In his reply Páleč first of all turns upon Hus' statement that a pope living contrary to Christ is the Antichrist. "The ecclesiastical authority ever remains holy even in a wicked pope . . . since such power is the spiritual light granted to the pope by God for the advantage of others."[58] He denies that the unction given to Saul is not the same as that bestowed on the pope, for "the sacrament of unction to the papal, episcopal, or priestly dignity is not lost by their wickedness. . . ." Hus' argument that if the pope is called most holy because of office, the same should be true of kings and secular officials, and even of the devil, is fallacious. Their office does not deal with the sacraments which confer grace. He chides Hus who, being a *baccalarius formatus* (would it were not *deformatus*, he adds!), should know such distinctions. For to compare the papal office to that of executioners, public criers, and the devil amounts to an extreme abuse of it. In towering rage Páleč breaks out into a tirade that Hus calls shoemakers and tailors, his adherents, saints rather than the most holy pope. He had "sanctified" the three young men decapitated because of their denunciations of the indulgences. Páleč does not shrink from distorting the description of that event in order to prove his point. He also taunts Hus for having addressed John XXIII, in writing to him of the presumed concord established between him and Archbishop Zbyněk in 1411, as "the most holy father." Actually, Hus addressed the pope as "the supreme vicar

[57] *Ibid.*, p. 323.     [58] *Antihus*, p. 54.

of Christ," and "Your Holiness."[59] Páleč concludes this tirade by retorting to Hus' statement that the pope should be the man "than whom no better existed among the Christian people," that in that case we would need a revelation for the pope's election. (That would indeed be true.) Páleč, however, ignores the fact that Hus' statement paralleled the biblical description of Saul's election. Moreover, Hus' normal criterion and a presumptive proof of predestination was the man's conduct. Thus no divine revelation was necessary if the pope's life were consonant with Christ's precepts.

To return to Hus' further argument in his *Contra Paletz*: he quotes "the *Fictor*" as asserting triumphantly that all the previous proofs offered by him show that "the pope is the head of the Roman Church and the cardinals its body." To this Hus bluntly responds that "in all this mud [*brodium*] there is not a glimmer of Scriptural proof." "I should like to know from him how he would prove this sequence: Apostle Peter was constituted by Christ bishop and pastor of the sheep, therefore John XXIII [was so constituted]."[60] To Páleč's assertion that a legitimate election makes a legitimate pope, Hus answers that no one who has not ascended into the sheepfold of the sheep through Christ, that is, not merely by a legitimate election according to the human right but by one "principally effected by God," has ascended rightfully. To this Páleč retorts that it may happen that a pope elected by a legitimate election may at first live in conformity with Christ, but later turn contrary to Him. Thus he did not ascend otherwise. Hus again refers to his demand that it is not a legal election but the spiritual state of the pope-elect which is determinative of the rightness or wrongness of the election. "If the pope or another prelate lives in a manner contrary to Christ, in pride, avarice, vengeance of

[59] Palacký, *Documenta*, p. 20.    [60] *Contra Paletz*, p. 323.

himself, and voluptuousness, then he has ascended otherwise than through Christ."[61]

Responding to this in his *Antihus*, Páleč holds stubbornly to his argument that because Peter was appointed
by Christ bishop and general pastor of the sheep, "so
likewise is John XXIII constituted by Christ bishop and
general pastor of the sheep; therefore he is the head of
the Church militant."[62] It is proved by his election in
which all the cardinals concurred. This is of the faith
[*est fides ecclesie*], having been many times so defined in
the law. It is the duty of the cardinals participating in
an election to testify to its validity. Their word is trust-
worthy, for they are men of dignity and authority. Since
they have so testified concerning the election of John
XXIII, the Church should recognize it as a fact constituted by Christ. "Unless you agree with the Church in
this faith," Páleč admonishes Hus, "it is to be feared
that you will be burned as a heretic."[63] Kybal remarks
that it is a pity that at the Council Páleč did not repeat
this sentiment, that whoever does not believe that John
XXIII was appointed pope by Christ should be burned!
He calls it blasphemy to assert that an official pronouncement of the cardinals is *de fide*![64]

Turning again to *Contra Paletz*, we further note that
Hus quotes Páleč's statement that Wyclif's forty-five
articles were condemned because none of them was
catholic, but every one was either heretical, erroneous,
or scandalous. Hus exclaims:

> O doctor, where is the proof? You are a fiction-monger,
> inventing charges you do not prove. . . . Show the
> scriptural proof, assign the true reason for it. We
> came to the public place designated for disputations
> about the sacred Scriptures and we spoke and wrote
> openly that your condemnation of the articles is with-

---

[61] *Ibid.*    [62] *Antihus*, p. 67.    [63] *Ibid.*, p. 68.
[64] Kybal, *Jan Hus, Učení*, II, p. 238.

out reasonable foundation and unfair, offering no sacred Scripture to the contrary. . . . Do you not remember the arguments of your colleague Stanislav in which he argued before the university gathering that the articles should not be condemned? Do you not remember how you praised the article saying that you would not be able to contradict it? But now, along with Stanislav, you turned to the opposite side, and contradict everything. Now you would not throw down a book of Master John Wyclif in a university meeting of the masters with the challenge: "Let anyone who wishes rise and impugn one word of it, and I will defend it! . . . Once you were realists, now you are "terminists" [i.e., nominalists].[65]

Furthermore, to the charge that Hus and his party denied the faith of entire Christendom and of the mother of all churches, the Roman Church, in their teaching and writing, and dared to call themselves the evangelical clergy, Hus retorts that it is a lie.

I trust that by God's grace I am a sincere Christian, not deviating from the faith. I would rather suffer the dire punishment of death than to put forth anything contrary to the faith or to transgress the commands of the Lord Jesus Christ. . . . Hence I wish that the *Fictor* would show me today one precept of sacred Scripture that I do not hold. . . . And if I ever taught anything I should not have taught, I am ready humbly to revoke it. But I trust that I shall sooner appear before the tribunal of Christ before he finds me to deny one jot of the law of the Lord![66]

In his *Antihus*, Páleč divides his rebuttal into six parts. First of all, he maintains that when Hus had been cited to Rome he took no steps to obey, but remained

[65] *Contra Paletz*, p. 324.     [66] *Contra Paletz*, p. 325.

obdurately in his excommunication. He further asserts his belief that "the judges to whose judgment you would dare to submit do not exist in all the world; for you regard no catholic prelate in all the world as judging according to God's law. This is great blindness that you consider all others to err. . . ."[67]

In the third and fourth points he declares that Hus and his accomplices have brought shame upon the kingdom of Bohemia by defending Wyclif's articles "condemned by three famous communities." This condemnation was just and *ex causa*. He and Stanislav proved the articles false in their sermons preached at the Týn church and submitted them to Archbishop Zbyněk. However, Páleč again deliberately omits to acknowledge—for he must have known it if he had read Hus' own text of his defense of the articles—that Hus defended a greatly amended version of the theses presented in their "acceptable" sense. Thus Páleč condemns what Hus did not hold.[68]

In his fifth argument Páleč recalls to Hus' memory that Hus consented to the prohibition of the teaching of Wyclif's articles at the meeting of the Czech university masters at the "Black Rose" house.[69] As in the previous points, he fails to mention that this prohibition applied to the teaching of these articles "in their wrong sense." The very phrase used implied that the articles had a correct sense. It was in that correct interpretation that Hus used them. As for Hus' charge that Páleč himself defended Wyclif, he excuses himself lamely by saying, "Who does not ever fail in speech" [*qui verbo lapsus non est*]?

In his sixth argument Páleč repeats the charge that Hus refused to hold "the three truths" which the whole Christendom and the Roman Church believe. On that account he curtly asks:

[67] *Antihus*, p. 75.    [68] *Ibid.*, pp. 76-77.    [69] *Ibid.*, p. 79.

How then do you dare to profess yourself a sincere Christian, not deviating from the faith . . . ? For on the forementioned three truths the whole Christian religion depends, and they have been for many centuries firmly held by learned and unlearned Christians; . . . and yet you have attempted and are still persistently attempting to annul them; how can you declare yourself to be a sincere Christian, in no way deviating from the faith? . . . If you opened the blinded eyes of your mind, you would find yourself with your master Wyclif the most dangerous assailant of the Christian faith and religion.[70]

This ruthlessly savage attack upon Hus' Christian character and profession is perhaps not exceeded in any other document from the pens of his adversaries!

Finally, Páleč strenuously objects to his opponents' assumption of the term "evangelical clergy." He finds, quite properly, the reason for it in their "contempt for the canons" and their professed desire to be governed solely by the law of Christ, rejecting all that is not taught in it. He insists that "it has never been Christ's law to disobey the Roman Church and its supreme pontiff," to refuse its censures, to deny the use of the keys, to repudiate the indulgences, and to blaspheme the supreme pontiff's authority.[71] Nor is it in accordance with Christ's law to preach contrary to papal prohibition and thus to sow discord among the people. It follows, therefore, that Hus' party "is not evangelical but rather diabolical clergy."[72]

Hus further comments in his *Contra Paletz* on Jesenic's denial of the doctors' statement that all Christendom shares the faith of the Roman Church. Jesenic maintained that the Schism rent the Roman Church into three parts under the three popes, while the fourth part [the non-Roman Christendom] was neutral. Páleč vehemently

[70] *Ibid.*, pp. 79-80.    [71] *Ibid.*, p. 82.    [72] *Ibid.*, p. 85.

denies this. Hus thereupon explains his own federalist view of the Church: that it is not only tripartite but actually divided into a multiplicity of particular churches which together constitute Christendom. It has its members in Spain under Benedict XIII, in Naples and the Rhine valley under Gregory XII, and in Bohemia under John XXIII. "God forbid that Christ's faith be extinct in Christ's simple believers and that the papal grace be absent in infants because of the three beasts who contend about the papal dignity out of arrogance and avarice."[73] For Christ said: "Wherever two or three are gathered in my name, there I am in the midst of them."[74] "If two or three or more people in India, Greece, Spain, or any other part of the world are gathered in the name of Christ, how will the *Fictor* bar Christ from being among them and consequently prevent them from being the most faithful Christians and thus an integral part of Christ's Church militant?"[75] Hus further cites Jerome's testimony that the Roman Church should not be esteemed as above all the other churches in the world. The faithful in Gaul, Britain, Africa, Persia, the East and India, and all the barbaric nations adore one and the same God and observe one rule of truth; "orbis est major urbe."[76] Even though the Church is outwardly divided, it is one in Christ, united by faith, hope, and love. Unity of the Church is spiritual, not organizational. Hus therefore rejects Páleč's argument that as there is only one Christ there must be only one vicar of Christ. All Christ's apostles were Christ's vicars, even Paul, who received his apostolic authority not from Peter and the other apostles, but immediately from Christ.[77]

---

[73] *Contra Paletz*, p. 325. The phrase "papal grace" is in the text, although it may be a mistake.

[74] Matt. 18:20.      [75] *Contra Paletz*, pp. 325-326.

[76] Gratian's *Decretum*, dist. 93, c. 27; *Legimus* (Friedberg, *Corpus juris canonici*, I, pp. 328f.).

[77] Gal. 2:6-8 and 1:11-12.

These are indeed far-reaching ideas and sentiments in which Hus anticipates the present-day ecumenical aspirations. In fact, his thinking on this matter is clearer and more cogent than that of many of the contemporary ecumenical leaders. He has firmly grasped the nature of true ecumenicity as consisting of those who possess the Spirit of Christ; they are already one, no matter to which of the numerous organized bodies of Christians they belong.

In his *Antihus* Páleč admits that the Church militant is not only divided into three but into many more parts. But he denies that this applies to the Roman Church of which he and his fellow-doctors wrote. They referred to the mystical-ecclesiastical synthesis of the pope and the cardinals, which is not and cannot be torn into parts. The Church militant, however, can be so torn. It is utter falsehood to maintain that the Roman Church in the sense defined by the doctors could be tripartite, as well as to assert that there could be three popes. Schismatics possess neither Church nor pope, for they are as pagans. The only Church in the sense defined above is the Roman Church. Hus and his fellow-partisans are schismatics: ergo, they belong to no Church. The statement that because Christ is only one, therefore the pope also is only one, is catholic. Even though there might be several putative popes as to persons, there is only one as to substance [*formam*]. It is not true that this unity and oneness of the Church did not obtain at the time of the apostles. "I call the immediate vicar of Jesus Christ on account of his supreme authority and the power bestowed on him by Christ, which was solely in Peter."[78] The Church has never been absolutely acephalous, since Christ is its primary head.

Resuming our analysis of Hus' *Contra Paletz*, we note that he next deals with Páleč's accusation that the party

[78] *Antihus*, p. 96.

of Hus refuses any other judge but Scripture. Hus repudiates this assertion as untrue, for he and his fellow-reformers have been willing to have the pope as judge. In
fact, they have repeatedly but vainly appealed to him.
He again declares that they are willing to submit not
only to the pope's judgment, but to that of any other
man willing to judge them by the law of God. Páleč
furthermore maintained that Scripture "is an inanimate
thing, not itself capable of speaking." This Hus energetically and indignantly denies. "Do you not know, good
*Fictor*, that sacred Scripture is a book of life, itself passing
judgment?" It is "truth dictated to men by the Holy
Spirit," by which Scripture and Christ "both I and the
*Fictor* shall be judged in the Day of Judgment." Hus
adds that in this matter Páleč, "having abandoned
realism, was converted to nominalism, crawling like a
lobster backward."[79]

In rebuttal, Páleč merely repeats the well-worn formula
that in "matters catholic and ecclesiastical" which are
committed to the pope and the cardinals, Hus and his
"accomplices" insist on having Scripture alone as judge.
He again denounces Hus for regarding the whole Christian community as his enemies. Hus has not proved, he
asserts, that Scripture alone shall be the judge when he
refers to the Day of Judgment; for it is the Lord who
will judge all people. (He thus ignores Hus' statement
that Scripture and Christ shall judge, and his previous
statement that he would have "God and Christ principally as judges.") Páleč again asserts that the Church has
passed on to the faithful in its canons, decrees, and
Councils many things not contained in Scripture. These
pronouncements should be regarded as law. The decisions
of the Roman Church, if they are not contrary to Scripture, should be received as true. This concession is, however, completely cancelled by the flat statement follow-

[79] *Contra Paletz*, p. 327.

ing thereafter that "whatever decisions the Roman Church has delivered to the faithful to be believed and held are not contrary to, but truly and correctly consonant with, the holy Scriptures."[80] Anyone denying this subverts the gospel and commits a grave error and an enormous folly.

Resuming again his criticisms, Hus calls attention to the approbation granted to the French delegation by the Council of Pisa despite its previous schismatic adherence to the Antipope. He also protests against the defamatory charge that he attempted to incite the populace to disobedience of the prelates and to irreverence of the papacy. He justifies himself by the example of Christ who likewise denounced the scribes and the Pharisees, who thereupon said: "You have a demon."[81] As for the incitation to disobedience, he protests that he has ever taught the people to obey the prelates in all things lawful and to show them reverence. In regard to Páleč's statement that the bulls of Pope Boniface IX deposing King Wenceslas and Sigismund prove nothing against the doctors, Hus insists, on the contrary, that they prove them guilty of disobedience of papal orders. The same applies to the command of Pope Innocent VII ordering the theological faculty to receive Maurice Rvačka into their ranks. The doctors say that the pope must be obeyed when he commands something not wholly evil. The pope's command in that instance was not evil. Hence Páleč and the doctors contradict what they themselves declared to be "a catholic verity."[82]

Páleč's disclaimer is not very convincing. As for the French at the Council of Pisa, he maintains that the pope, out of the plenitude of his power, received them because such a conciliatory act facilitated unity of Christendom. In regard to Hus' profession that he has

---

[80] *Antihus*, p. 107.     [81] John 8:48.
[82] *Contra Paletz*, p. 329.

ever taught obedience to the prelates, he retorts that his deeds belie his words. Further, how does he dare to compare himself to Christ? Since he has rebelled against the Church universal, he is not in Christ but rather has rejected Christ.[83]

Hus further complains that Páleč wrote that many men of probity are enemies of the Wyclifites but offered no proof of it.

> I marvel at the *Fictor* that he formerly was irritated [*stomachabatur*] when someone called him and his colleague Stanislav Wyclifites, and now he dubs others as such. How has he been turned around [*in arcum curvum est conversus*]![84]

To the charge that some notorious adulterers and simoniacs are protectors of Wyclifites and vice versa, Hus indignantly retaliates in kind. He retorts that Páleč should open his blind eyes to discern to which party the proud, fornicating, avaricious, and simoniac clergy belong—his or Hus'. "Our supporters are the poor and beggarly priests. The *Fictor*, however, and his colleagues glory in claiming as theirs the clergy of the whole kingdom of Bohemia and the entire Christendom!"[85] If he were to confess the truth, Hus adds, the wicked clergy would be found among his party, not among the "Wyclifites." Páleč indiscriminately lumps all his opponents together as wicked.

> I, however, hope that there are many good men in both parties and also think that sinners are in both parties. Nor did I approve or ever shall approve that some call the doctor's party Mohammedans and seducers. Neither do I approve that the doctor calls us Wyclifites in a bad sense. For I confess that I hold the true tenets taught by Master John Wyclif, pro-

[83] *Antihus*, p. 128.     [84] *Contra Paletz*, p. 329.
[85] *Ibid.*, p. 330.

fessor of sacred theology, not because he declared them but because Scripture or the infallible reason declare them. If he taught some error, I do not intend to imitate in any way whatever either him or anyone else in the error.[86]

Brave words, indeed! But they were certainly to add fuel to the already raging fire! Nevertheless, they should ever be kept in mind when one speaks of Hus' "Wyclifism."

Hus furthermore asserts that it was the sale of indulgences and the crusading bull of John XXIII "which first separated me from that doctor. For if he would confess the truth, he would admit that he had said concerning the articles of indulgences, which he himself handed me with his own hand, that they contain 'palpable errors.' "[87] When accused of obstinately remaining in heresy, Hus declares that he follows the gospel of Christ "and will follow its doctrines, declining to turn either to the right or to the left. Whoever would teach me according to the law of Christ, whether he be a superior or not, even the *Fictor*, I am willing humbly to accept it. For thus the law of God shall be the guide and judge above him who teaches, the guide and judge whom the pope with the cardinals and the *Fictor* with his adherents should follow. Amen."[88]

Nonetheless, in his *Antihus*, Páleč again sings the old refrain that the cause of the dissension are "the three truths," the rejection of which constitutes "all the errors of the Wyclifites." On the other hand the adherence to these truths constitutes the *iusticia fidei*; those holding them, even though their lives be wicked, are nevertheless *iusti*.[89] Even those who live wickedly will be saved if they observe all that the Roman Church teaches. The criterion is not morality but the right faith. He facetiously thanks Hus for his testimony that he, Páleč,

---

[86] *Ibid.*
[87] *Ibid.*
[88] *Ibid.*, p. 331.
[89] *Antihus*, p. 136.

was irritated when anyone called him a Wyclifite. It proves that he has never been one nor wished to be one. But Hus and his "fellow-apostles" defend the "pestiferous" Wyclif to this day. Of him Páleč said, "No heretic had been more dangerous to the Church than he since the birth of Christ until now."[90]

As for Hus' statement that it was the sale of indulgences that first separated him from Páleč, the latter flatly denies it. He claims that it was Hus' disobedience of the pope and other superiors and his denial of the Church's power of the keys, and the slander heaped by him on the Church and its clergy, which caused the rupture between them. However, he acknowledges that he showed Hus the articles of absolution and said that they contained palpable errors. He insists that these errors were not in the papal bull but were invented by the indulgence sellers.[91] That being the case, he is ready to denounce them as errors to his dying day. In the conclusion of his very extensive treatise he requests to be excused if he wrote vehemently (as indeed he did!), for he wrote "out of zeal, as professor of theology, and in behalf of the truth which I swore to defend."[92] He even professes to have been moved by a desire to save Hus from his heresy and induce him to recant.

Thus the great controversy, this theological slugging match between the former close friends, comes to a close. Hus had no time to answer this diatribe until he faced his adversary at the Council of Constance.

There were other opponents who took part in this tournament, such as Dr. Maurice Rvačka who has been mentioned several times before. He wrote a treatise on indulgences[93] which Hus did not answer. He is also contingently identified as the author of the treatise which

[90] *Ibid.*, p. 139.    [91] *Ibid.*, p. 147.    [92] *Ibid.*, p. 156.
[93] "Magistri Mauritii Tractatus de Indulgentiis," in Jan Sedlák, ed., *Hlídka* (Brno, 1911), pp. 25-45.

Hus answered in his *Contra occultum adversarium*.[94] Rvačka severely upbraided Hus for denouncing the priests for their evil lives as being destructive of the office of priesthood altogether and contrary to God's law. He also objected to Hus' subjection of the priesthood to secular rulers in civil matters and to the criticism of priests by lay people. He censured Hus for not denouncing the priests disobedient to their superiors (undoubtedly meaning Hus himself) while he poured out his wrath on priests living in concubinage. Hus replied that Jesus did not destroy the law of God when he denounced the Pharisees. As for the duty of priests to submit to secular rulers in matters secular, he cited Paul's injunction in Romans 13:1-7 and Peter's command in I Peter 2:13. He also pointed out that Emperor Charles IV had punished disorderly priests. As for his disobedience of superiors, he indignantly denied it. "I expressly stated that priests disobedient to their bishops in lawful commands and spurning them in those things which pertain to God's law, profane, violate, and pollute their souls."[95] He further declared that among the vicars of Christ there are both true and false popes. The true are those who follow Christ; the false are those who by their conduct deny Him. Christ commanded His disciples to follow Him not only in power but also in knowledge of His law and the purity of His life. Hus thus refused to acknowledge as a *veritable* vicar of Christ or priest anyone who failed to fulfil the moral conditions of his office. He did not, however, deny his jurisdiction.[96]

Another opponent of Hus was an anonymous writer whose treatise against Hus' *De ecclesia* was found by Dr.

[94] *Historia et monumenta*, I, pp. 168-179. Cf. also Bartoš, *Literární činnost*, No. 68.

[95] *Ibid.*, p. 175.

[96] Paul de Vooght, *L'hérésie de Jean Huss* (Louvain, Publications universitaires de Louvain, 1960), p. 174.

Sedlák in the Benedictine monastery at Seitenstetten.[97] It was written between the middle of 1413 and the early part of 1415, for John XXIII is mentioned as pope. The author, usually referred to as the Anonymous, has not as yet been ascertained. Both Sedlák and De Vooght regard it as the best answer to Hus' treatise, since it is more systematic than the writings of Stanislav and Páleč. De Vooght characterizes it as "les notes classique de l'Église."[98] Actually, there is little in it which is essentially new, as after the exhaustive controversy described above there hardly could be. Nevertheless, for "good measure, pressed down, shaken together, and running over,"[99] we shall give the gist of the treatise in the briefest form.

The author defines the Church in the classical terms of the Apostles' Creed as "una, sancta, catholica et apostolica ecclesia." It is one because it consists of all who have received baptism. It comprises both the predestinate and the foreknown. Hus, of course, differed from this definition insofar as he would ascribe the "mixed" character to the Church militant, not catholic. The Anonymous, however, continues by asserting that because the Church contains both the good and the wicked, it needs to be governed in faith, laws, and morals. This authority was granted by Christ to Peter and his successors, and it is to last as long as there is need for the rule of the varied multitude, i.e., to the end of the age. Therefore, the Church is apostolic. The author proves the need of the monarchical rule not only by Scripture, but by Aristotle. He calls "satanic" any attempt to cast doubt on the apostolic character of the Church. He turns directly upon "quidam modernis temporibus"

[97] "Hic tractatus editus est contra Huss hereticum et contra eius tractatum, quem de ecclesia appellavit," J. Sedlák, ed., "Anonymous, *De ecclesia*," in *Studie a texty k náboženským dějinám českým*, 2 vols. (Olomouc, 1913-19), I, pp. 312-348.

[98] Paul de Vooght, *Hussiana* (Louvain, Publications universitaires de Louvain, 1960), p. 149.

[99] Luke, 6:38.

(in the margin Hus is named) who says that the Church catholic consists only of the predestinate. This is, of course, the characteristic confusion between the Church catholic and the Church militant constantly indulged in by Hus' opponents. It is difficult to believe that they did this unknowingly. Hus after all, asserted in season and out of season and times without number that the Church militant contains *both* the predestinate and the foreknown. Nevertheless, his opponents, by ignoring this distinction between the Church catholic and the Church militant, persisted in their perverse accusation.

The Anonymous further charges Hus with asserting that the prelates are "neither in unity, sanctity, catholicity, nor in apostolicity, unless they are predestinate." He declares that it is not predestination but the legitimate election to office which constitutes them true prelates. He offers ten arguments to prove his case, most of which rest on the above-mentioned premise confusing the Church catholic with the Church militant. It is really remarkable that he, apparently a well-instructed, theologically-trained person, could not discover for himself the contradiction on which most of his arguments rested. For instance, his fifth and sixth arguments stated: "The Church militant is an instrument of the Church triumphant." "Although all members of the Church militant are instruments of the Church triumphant, not all are members of the Church triumphant."[100] The latter proposition is exactly what Hus taught, although he also gave the reason for it, namely predestination! The Anonymous, like Stanislav, further likens the Church to the human body in which the soul governs and regulates all other senses. As the soul constitutes the *sensus communis*, so the Roman Church governs the entire Church universal by its authority. The author asserts that the supreme authority, in the absence of the

[100] Anonymous, *De ecclesia* (see n. 97), p. 335.

pope, resides collectively in the bishops, inasmuch as they represent the universal Church.[101] This conciliar authority of the episcopate is, however, still only *particular*, not general, for the latter is exercised exclusively by the pope and the cardinals. This, of course, falls far short of Conciliarism, whose proponents claimed for the general Councils the supreme authority over the Church militant, including the popes. The Anonymous then argues that since the Roman Church represents the *sensus communis*, it cannot err in judging any ecclesiastical matter. All must, therefore, submit to its authority. Moreover, the Roman Church itself is permanent, even though the office-holders are not. He likens it to the River Vltava in Prague or the Tiber in Rome, which are the same although the water-current constantly changes. Furthermore, as the particular senses cannot judge the general truth, so the members cannot judge the pope. The rule of the Church must be visible; therefore, it is held by the successors of Peter, at present Pope John XXIII.

This treatise, which Hus either had no time or desire to answer, concludes the long-drawn out, bitter struggle between Hus and his opponents, or to put it into a broader perspective, between the papalist and the evangelical parties. Its unavoidably repetitious character has already yielded us abundant material for understanding the essential position of both the warring camps. Although we have thus learned, in a somewhat unsystematic way necessitated by the exigencies of the controversy, a great deal about Hus' concept of the Church, we must

---

[101] *Ibid.*, p. 340: ". . . illa auctoritas universalis in ecclesia habet appropriate residenciam in ecclesia romana . . . alie vero particulares in episcopatibus, in diversis distributive, in collectis autem episcopis synodaliter eciam sine papa residet illa potestas uberius, de quanto representant universalem ecclesiam, cum qua illa potestas manet inseparabiliter (Mt. 18 et in fine evangelii)." Cf. also De Vooght, *Hussiana*, p. 151.

now turn to a more systematic exposition of it. This we shall endeavor to do in an analysis of his chief work dealing with the subject, the *De ecclesia*, and supplement it from his remaining writings, both Czech and Latin, as far as they deal with our chosen theme.

## CHAPTER VIII

## HUS' *DE ECCLESIA*

IT is to be regretted that the treatment of this important work of Hus, which served not only as the target of Páleč's polemics during 1413-14, but above all as the source of the majority of the charges against Hus at the Council of Constance, is placed so late in this study. The choice, however, was narrowed down to placing it between the polemical treatises of Stanislav of Znojmo and of Páleč, thus interrupting the analysis of the controversy mounted by Hus' chief opponents, or treating Hus' writings of the same period as a unit. I decided for the latter course as the less objectionable. I admit that this choice can easily be subjected to the obvious criticism that I placed the cart before the horse. But to choose the other alternative is certainly also not without its objectionable features.

Hus began writing *De ecclesia*, his principal work, in exile, perhaps toward the end of the year 1412 or the beginning of the next, and finished it in May 1413. It was read at the Bethlehem Chapel before eighty persons on June 8, 1413. Since the attack of his opponents centered upon his concept of the Church, he rightly decided to answer it as fully and systematically as possible. He wrote the first ten chapters, a calm, academic discussion of the subject, prior to his knowledge of the result of the meeting held by the king's order at the Town Hall of the Old Town on February 6, 1413. This meeting resulted in the adoption of the *Consilium* of the theological faculty which initiated the polemic concentrated on its terms. When the text of this document reached Hus, he changed the plan hitherto followed and devoted the remaining thirteen chapters to his reply to the *Consilium*. The first part was written at Kozí

Hrádek, where he had found refuge. Many scholars regard the book as indicating a radical change in Hus' thinking, as if he were now adopting Wyclif's ideas to an unprecedented degree. This interpretation, for instance, was adopted by De Vooght,[1] who argues that Hus continued until 1413 to define the Church as the *congregatio fidelium* composed of all who have been baptized, profess the catholic faith, and partake of the sacraments, whether or not they are of the predestinate. He claims that in writing the *De ecclesia* Hus adopted, for the greatest part, Wyclif's concept of the Church catholic as the *universitas praedestinatorum*. This is not so. In our study hitherto we have seen convincing evidence that Hus from the beginning consistently held the views expressed in this work. It is true that he now relied very considerably on Wyclif's writings, although always freely and critically. It is emphatically not true that the work "contains hardly a line, local coloring apart, which does not proceed from Wyclif," as Loserth declared.[2] De Vooght also repudiates Loserth's thesis most decisively. Sedlák, who is usually hypercritical and not always fair toward Hus, after comparing Hus' treatise with Wyclif's works, declares that although Hus is dependent upon Wyclif, it "cannot be called plagiarism. Hus did make excerpts from one or two of Wyclif's treatises (*De ecclesia* and *De potestate papae*), but selected from Wyclif's writings all which deals with the subject and arranged it in a relatively independent whole. . . . And that is surely a literary work not to be underestimated!"[3] Such borrowings as are found in Hus' work were not only the ac-

[1] Paul de Vooght, *Hussiana* (Louvain, Publications universitaires de Louvain, 1960), pp. 34, 45, 54-56.

[2] J. Loserth, *Hus und Wiclif: zur Genesis der Husitischen Lehre* (München and Berlin, 1925), pp. 156, 210; also his edition of Wyclif's *De ecclesia* (London, The Wyclif Society, 1886), pp. xxvi f.

[3] "Husův traktát De ecclesia," in Jan Sedlák, *Studie a texty k náboženským dějinám českým*, 2 vols. (Olomouc, 1913-19), II, pp. 526-527.

cepted but even the approved scholarly method *more academico*. S. Harrison Thomson, who has recently prepared the critical edition of Hus' *De ecclesia*,[4] estimates that Hus in composing the work "borrowed" about one twelfth from various works of Wyclif, chiefly from the latter's own *De ecclesia*. This, however, included Wyclif's own quotations from Scripture, the Fathers, chronicles, and canon law. Were these deducted, Wyclif's own material would amount perhaps to one twentieth of the whole. "The borrowed material, moreover, is so selected and ordered as to make it clear that the argument and the convictions behind it are Hus' own property. . . . He has drawn upon Wyclif's many treatises for substantiation and elaboration."[5] A recent estimate by a Czech scholar who has made an independent study of the subject places the proportion at twenty-three percent; the excerpts were taken from at least fourteen works of Wyclif.[6]

De Vooght, although he finds much to criticize in the treatise, yet gives it as his over-all estimate that "*De ecclesia* is, of all Hus' writings, the one which expresses most eloquently, but also most passionately, the reformist sentiments: the revulsion against the simoniac curialist disorders and the nostalgia for the purity of the Church. *De ecclesia* has expressed these sentiments with eloquence."[7]

Nevertheless, it is remarkable that Hus, who was defending himself against the aspersion of Wyclifism foisted on him by his powerful foes, would copy even the amount

[4] S. Harrison Thomson, *Magistri Johannis Hus Tractatus de ecclesia* (Boulder, Colo., University of Colorado Press, 1956); F. M. Dobiáš and Amedeo Molnár, transl., *Mistr Jan Hus, O církvi* (Praha, Československá akademie věd, 1965).

[5] *Ibid.*, p. xxxiii.

[6] F. M. Dobiáš, "Jubileum Husova spisu o církvi," *Kostnické Jiskry* (Praha), Oct. 31, 1963.

[7] De Vooght, *Hussiana* (see n. 1), p. 65, n. 221.

of Wyclif material ascertained by the scholars mentioned above. One would suppose that he would have avoided any such obvious link with Wyclif, knowing that his adversaries could easily detect it and utilize it for their purposes—as they indeed did! After all, he could have expressed all such "borrowed" passages in his own words as easily as he could copy them from Wyclif. Did he think they would thus be more effective? Or was it again that stubborn consciousness of his own integrity that made him feel, in quoting from Wyclif only such material as was in his opinion doctrinally unobjectionable that it would be so recognized by others as well? Or did he hope to demonstrate to the world that Wyclif, despite all the calumny and slander heaped on him, was "an evangelical doctor"? Undoubtedly, he felt that an abandonment of Wyclif at this stage would verge on a craven betrayal of truth.

Let us now turn to the text of the *De ecclesia* itself. Hus begins by stating three meanings of the word "Church": first, it is the house of God in which He is worshipped; secondly, it includes the priests ministering in it. Hus thus repeats two of Páleč's six definitions given in the latter's *De aequivocatione nominis ecclesia.* In the third place, according to the meaning of the Greek term *ecclesia*, it is the congregation of all men under the rule of Christ. But to Hus it is the third which is the real meaning of the word. He then immediately goes on to point out that since not all men are under the rule of Christ, there exist two churches, of the sheep and the goats, of the predestinate and the foreknown. The former alone is the Church catholic, universal in the widest sense of the word. But it comprises the predestinate in the particular churches as well, such as the saints of the church of Prague. The Church catholic, then, is the totality of the predestinate, *omnium praedestinatorum universitas*, past, present and future.[8] This basic Pauline-Augustinian-Wyclifite definition is used by Hus through-out the treatise as he had used it ever since the beginning of his ministry. Quoting Augustine on John, Hus com-ments that the Church has remained the same from the time of Abel, through the time of the prophets and of the apostles and the martyrs, and will continue the same to the end of time. Even the angels are part of it. Thus the Church is one, although the full number of the saved will not be reached until the end. This concept of the predetermined number of the saved is distinctly Augus-tinian. Hus then includes his favorite definition of faith, that we should not believe *in* the Church, for it is but a creature of God, not God Himself; we should believe *in* God alone. This universal Church is Christ's mystical body of which He alone is the head. As such "Christ loved the church and gave himself for it that he might sanctify it, having cleansed it by the washing of water in the word of life, that he might present it to himself a glorious church, not having spot or wrinkle or anything of the kind, but that it be holy and immaculate."[9] Of *this* Church necessarily only the elect are members. But even they have not yet reached the goal of sanctity, but are on the way toward it. They are thus the *salvandi*, as the phrase of the text indicates, "that he might sanctify it." Consequently, even the Church of the predestinate needs constant edification in virtue and growth in sanctity.

It might be remarked that this lofty concept of the Church "without spot or wrinkle" had been for Hus the abiding ideal at which all his reformatory zeal and

[8] *De ecclesia* (see n. 4), p. 2. De Vooght argues that this concept is not Augustinian, for he operated with three definitions of the Church, not one. In his view, the Church is composed of the *con-gregatio fidelium*, of the *sancti*, and of the *praedestinati. Hussiana*, p. 88.

[9] Eph. 5:25-27.

effort had aimed. Unless one keeps this in mind, no proper or adequate apprehension of his life-work can be gained. If this ideal seems "visionary" and impractical, so was Paul's. No wonder that it collided head on with the concept of those who sought to justify the Church as it then existed!

In chapter 2 Hus deals with the familiar division of the Church into three parts—triumphant, militant, and dormient. The important thing to notice here is that all three are composed of the predestinate, although the Church militant also comprises the foreknown. The latter are, however, in the Church without being of it. In the Day of Judgment all these three parts will be united into one—the Church triumphant. Hence, "the unity of the Church catholic consists in the unity of predestination. . . ,"[10] a statement, as we have seen, violently repudiated by Stanislav and Páleč. He further declares that the Church is called "apostolic" "because the apostles are full participants of this same mother Church, fully purged in the spirit, which Church they planted by the teaching of Christ and with their blood, and by which teaching and authority their vicars now rule the young damsel seeking the bridegroom of the Church."[11] This passage then acknowledges the function of the vicars of the apostles: it is conceived as the continuation of the work of the apostles themselves—planting the Church by teaching the apostolic doctrine and even shedding their blood. Their authority to rule is also recognized.

In the third chapter Hus deals with the extremely important consequence of his doctrine that the Church catholic consists only of the predestinate, namely, the place of the foreknown in it. His opponents to the very end charged him with denying the foreknown any place whatever in the Church militant, and he was finally con-

[10] *De ecclesia*, p. 10.   [11] *Ibid.*

demned on account of this accusation among others.
His foes, however, could not have been in doubt about
or in ignorance of his real teaching. He explained it ful-
somely both in this and in many other of his treatises,
and at the Council of Constance. He repeatedly asserted
that as for the Church militant, it is of a mixed character, comprising both the good and the wicked, the predestinate and the foreknown. He had cited Scriptural
passages proving this point, such as the parables of the
net cast into the sea and catching fish both good and
bad,[12] or the feast to which the guests were brought in
from highways and byways,[13] or the field which yielded
both wheat and tares.[14] He quotes the concluding words
of the last-mentioned parable: "Let both grow until the
harvest. . . ." He also likens the Church to the human
body, where all the particular members and senses are
governed by the head. The mystical body of Christ is
similarly constituted, the different members having different functions, as described by Paul: "though they are
many, they are one body; . . . so also is Christ."[15] Furthermore, the human body contains elements that are
foreign to it, such as spittle, phlegm, excrements, and
urine. They are eliminated from the body. Similarly the
foreknown: although they are *in* the Church, they are
not *of* the Church [*sic aliud est esse de ecclesia, aliud
esse in ecclesia*].[16] Ultimately they will be purged from
the Church militant, although only at the Day of Judgment. The predestinate alone will remain, being bound
to the head, Christ, by predestinating love. Hus quotes
Paul's exultant cry, "I am persuaded that neither death
nor life, nor angels, nor principalities, nor powers, nor
things present, nor things to come, nor might, nor
height, nor depth, nor any creature can separate us from
the love of God in Christ Jesus our Lord."[17] Emphasizing

12 Matt. 13:47.          13 Matt. 22:10.          14 Matt. 13:24-30.
15 I Cor. 12:12.          16 *De ecclesia*, p. 15.          17 Rom. 8:38ff.

once more predestination as the cause of salvation, Hus declares that "neither position nor human election makes a person a member of the holy universal Church, but divine predestination of everyone who persistently follows Christ in love."[18] He distinguishes, however, between two kinds of grace: "according to predestination to life eternal by which all finally holy are of the holy mother Church; and according to predestination solely to present righteousness. . . ."[19] These latter lack perseverance; hence, they shall not finally obtain salvation. Thus Paul, who was at first blasphemer became in the end a true member of the Church; while Judas, who for a time possessed a measure of present righteousness, was not a member because he lacked perseverance. Both, however, for the time being continued as members of the Church. Thus the separation from the Church may be impermanent [*deperdibilis*], as in the case of Paul and other sinners who by the grace of God were brought back into the fold; or permanent [*indeperdibilis*], as in the case of Judas.

Hus continues in the next chapter to deal with the theme of Christ as the only head of the Church. No one, a mere man, can occupy that position in the same sense. Strangely enough, Hus cites in support of the thesis, Pope Boniface's notorious bull *Unam sanctam* (1302),[20] asserting that as the Church is one, "of this one and only Church there is one body and one head—not two heads as if it were a monster." Nevertheless, the pope immediately thereafter asserts that the head is "Christ and the vicar of Christ, St. Peter, and the successors of Peter." Thus there are two heads of the Church, after all! Hus does not quote the sentence added above. Moreover, the pope without any doubt had the Roman Church

---

[18] *De ecclesia*, p. 16.   [19] *Ibid.*, p. 17.
[20] E. F. Henderson, *Select Historical Documents of the Middle Ages* (New York, 1892), pp. 435-437.

in mind, while Hus applies the phrase to the Church catholic. He flatly denies that the Church has two heads. No apostle ever claimed to be the head of the Church, but only a servant of the head, Jesus Christ. Displaying a flair for making distinctions, as was the custom of the times, Hus defines the term "head of the Church" as inward and outward. Christ has been both: from the beginning of the world to his incarnation he had been the outward head, while from his incarnation onward to all eternity his headship has been inward. Thus the Church universal has ever had Christ as its head and will have him to all eternity. At first he had been present with the Church by reason of his divinity and, after his incarnation, by reason of his humanity. Moreover, since he chose each member from all eternity and is bound with him by love, no such elect can ever fall away. For "love never faileth."

Chapter 5 deals with the mixed character of the Church militant and with Christ as the head of the elect within that Church. It thus develops further what has already been said. All members of the Church militant are divided into the predestinate and the foreknown. Thus they hold membership in different ways. Some are in the Church by present faith and grace but not by predestination to eternal life. Others are there by predestination, as unbaptized infants, pagans, and Jews, who will perhaps become Christian later. Others belong to the Church by predestination and present grace, although they could fall away from grace. Others possess only unformed faith and will attain to faith formed by love later. Finally, others are now members of the Church triumphant, confirmed in grace.[21] It is abundantly clear, therefore, that Hus recognizes the foreknown as being members of the Church militant. They differ from the predestinate only in relation to their ultimate destiny.

[21] *De ecclesia*, p. 30.

The teaching of the parables mentioned in chapter 3 is thus fully confirmed. The identity of the members of these groups cannot be positively and securely known, but may be inferred from their actions. "By their fruits ye shall know them," is Hus' favorite way of answering the problem. Those who "sit in Moses' seat," if they live in a manner contrary to Christ, are to be deemed, for the time being, as either belonging to one of the classes mentioned above, or to the reprobate. Hus exclaims:

> Let the disciples of Antichrist blush who, living contrary to Christ, speak of themselves as the greatest and the proudest of God's holy Church. They, polluted by avarice and arrogance of the world, are called publicly the heads and body of the holy Church. According to Christ's gospel, however, they are called the least.[22]

This is an unmistakable reference to the papalists' everlastingly reiterated declaration that the pope is the head and the cardinals the body of the Church. Hus, on the other hand, reaffirms his conclusion that "predestination makes a man member of the holy catholic Church, which is the preparation of grace in the present and of glory in the future time. No position of dignity or of human election or any other outward sign [can be so regarded]."[23] Yet no one can, without divine revelation, declare himself a member of that holy Church. Hus calls it a shocking effrontery on the part of worldlings living vicious and barren lives to call themselves heads, or body, or the chief members of the body of Christ! Answering the common objection that every cleric, because of his ordination, should be honored by laymen as part of the holy mother Church, Hus declares that "a layman is not bound to believe anything about his superior but the truth. It is clear that no one is obliged to believe any-

22 *Ibid.*, p. 33.　　　　　　23 *Ibid.*, p. 35.

thing unless God has moved him to believe it. But God does not move a man to believe what is false."[24] The prelate or the priest must prove by his holy life that he is truly a member of the holy Church. If, however, the superior is a manifest sinner, the layman should conclude that he is an enemy of Christ. Hus judges that many are reputedly considered members of the Church who are not such according to predestination to glory.

In chapter 6 Hus stresses the separate existences of the Church of the predestinate and the church of the reprobate. He copied this short chapter largely from Wyclif's *De ecclesia*.[25] Since Hus unmistakably taught that the Church militant consists of these two groups commingled but not separated, the concept of the two independent churches of the predestinate and the reprobate is admittedly confusing. Kybal, for instance, was misled into assuming that the thesis of the *two* churches existing side by side contradicts Hus' previously stated teaching concerning the mixed character of the Church militant. Strangely enough, this error was caused by his overlooking the sentence affirming that in the Day of Judgment "the bipartite body" will be separated and dissolved.[26] This clearly implies that Hus, as he has done before, includes under the confusing terminology both the Church of Christ and of Antichrist within the Church militant. He had made the same distinction between these two "churches" in 1404-05 when he preached on Gal. 4:30, dealing with the son of Sarah and the son of Hagar.[27] On that occasion he clearly stated that he speaks of the mixed membership of the Church. In his

[24] *Ibid.*, p. 38.

[25] Wyclif's *De ecclesia* (see n. 2), pp. 102-104, 57-58.

[26] Hus' *De ecclesia*, p. 41; V. Kybal, *Jan Hus, Učení*, 3 vols. (Praha, Jan Laichter, 1923-31), II, p. 177.

[27] Anežka Schmidtová, ed., *Magistri Joannis Hus, Sermones de tempori qui Collecta dicuntur* (Praha, Československá akademie věd, 1959), pp. 150-151.

*Super IV Sententiarum* he also makes the same distinction, calling the reprobates *ecclesia malignantium*.[28] But again both groups are comprised in the Church militant. Resuming our consideration of his *De ecclesia*, we note that Hus, following Wyclif, recognizes within the church of the reprobate a difference between its "outer form" and "inner deformity." The former is God's foreknowledge of what the particular individual will do, while the latter is the man's self-willed final disobedience, the sin against the Holy Spirit. Thus the foreknown are condemned for their own sin of final impenitence, not by an arbitrary *fiat* of God. Hus answers the objection based on Aquinas' statement that Christ is the head of all men by distinguishing between Christ's benefits granted to all men and His being the head only of the elect by the grace of predestination.

In chapter 7, largely independent of Wyclif, Hus undertakes to deal with the explosive question of whether the Roman Church is identical with the Church universal. This question also bears on his opponents' definition for whom the Roman Church consisted of the pope as its head and the cardinals as its body. After admitting for argument's sake that according to Boniface's bull *Unam sanctam* the Roman Church is the Church universal because it is said to be one, he immediately counters by pointing to the Greeks and others who do not profess or practice obedience to it. Thus it is not one, and therefore not universal. He argues further that the bull declares it "necessary for salvation" that all men be subject to the Roman pontiff. Since, however, the Roman Church is said to consist of the pope and cardinals, it obviously is not the totality of the membership of the Church, not to say of the elect. Therefore, "that Church is not the holy catholic and apostolic Church."[29]

28 V. Flajšhans, ed., *Spisy M. Jana Husi*, vols. 4-6, *Super IV Sententiarum* (Praha, Jaroslav Bursík, 1904-06), pp. 36-733.

29 *De ecclesia*, p. 44.

Hus then passes on to the discussion of the crucial text in Matt. 16:16-19, stating that "Simon Peter answered and said, Thou art the Christ, the Son of the living God. And Jesus answered. . . . And I also say unto thee, Thou art Peter, and upon this rock I will build my Church. . . ." Hus declares that "in this gospel passage Christ's Church, its faith, its foundation, and its power are designated." These four topics constitute the subject matter of chapters 7 to 10. In chapter 7, on Christ's Church, he distinguishes three senses in which this verse is interpreted: (1) The Church is the congregation of the faithful in respect of present righteousness, including the foreknown who are at the time in grace. This is not Christ's mystical body. Special attention should be paid to this statement as being particularly important, since the *congregatio fidelium* was commonly regarded as the Church catholic. (2) It is an admixture of the predestinate and the foreknown while they both are in grace. In this sense it partially corresponds to the Church universal by reason of the predestinate. (3) It is the congregation of the predestinate, whether or not they are in grace at the time. This, then, is the mystical body of Christ and "in that sense the Church is an article of faith"[30] according to Eph. 5:25-27. It is this Church that the Savior meant when he said that "on this rock I will build my Church." It was built not on Peter but on his confession that Christ is the Son of the living God. This the wisdom of this world (flesh) or philosophical knowledge (blood) does not reveal, but only God the Father. "The conclusion therefrom is that the holy Church of Christ is one, called catholic in Greek and universal in Latin. It is also called apostolic because it was established by the words and deeds of the apostles and founded by Christ the Rock. . . ."[31]

How then is the Roman Church related to this Church

universal? Again, *more scholastico*, Hus at first seems to admit the identity of the two. But he quickly follows with a positive denial on the ground that the ascription to the Roman Church of having no spot or wrinkle cannot be applied to the pope and his cardinals. Again when the *Decretum*[32] speaks of the Roman Church as never having erred or succumbed to heresies, Hus counters that this cannot be said of every pope and his domestics. "For it is certain that the pope and his college of cardinals can err, for they are often polluted by deception and sin, as at the time of Pope John, the Englishwoman who was called Agnes."[33] Other popes were heretics and as such were deposed. Nevertheless, Hus admits that the Roman Church is the principal [*principalissima*] among all other churches; likewise the pope with his cardinals "are the chief part of its dignity," if they follow Christ closely and serve the Church humbly and diligently. Originally, the designation of the Roman Church was applied to Christ's faithful under the authority of the Roman bishop, just as the Jerusalemite, Antiochene, Alexandrian, and Constantinopolitan titles were borne by those living under the rule of their own bishops. Historically, the Church of Jerusalem ranked first and that of Antioch second. The Roman Church is not, therefore, preeminent on the historical account. Nor is it to be regarded as preeminent because emperors endowed it with territorial possessions and power over the other churches. The real reason for the choice of Rome was Christ's foreknowledge that the gentiles would take the place of unbelieving Jews, and the fact that a greater number of martyrs triumphed there than in any other city. Nevertheless, Christ's Church does not depend on any locality or antiquity, but on its faith in Jesus Christ.

[32] E. Friedberg, ed., *Corpus juris canonici*, 2 vols. (Leipzig, Tauchnitz, 1879), I, p. 970.
[33] *De ecclesia*, pp. 47-48.

Hus infers, after some inconclusively formulated arguments, that the Church defined as consisting of the pope and the cardinals, even if they were holy, is not the entire holy catholic and apostolic Church, but only a part of it. Christ alone is the head of that Church and the predestinate everywhere and in all particular churches are its body. This concept links Hus with the best thought of the modern ecumenical movement.

The second deduction from the words of Christ in the verse under consideration concerns the faith by which the Church confesses Christ as the Son of the living God. It is this faith, not Peter, on which the Church is built. Hus reiterates his definition of faith as twofold: the unformed, possessed even by demons, and the faith formed by love. The latter, as the "faith formed by love accompanied by the virtue of perseverance, suffices for salvation."[34] Hus thus shared the orthodox view then current that not *sola fide* but *fide caritate formata* is the saving faith. It is infused by God into the hearts of men. Those who vacillate in it or do not persevere to the end, or those who do not believe all that ought to be believed, or who by deeds deny the faith, lack faith. To believe rightly is to put trust in all that is necessary for salvation and to adhere to it firmly even by braving death on its account. These necessary truths are found in Scripture which the faithful are bound to believe. Whatever is beyond or contrary to Scripture, whether it be sayings of the saints or the papal bulls, is not to be believed. Papal pronouncements may be accepted as probable, for the popes and the curia may be mistaken or misinformed. The same applies to the pronouncements of civil authorities. But "it is not lawful to disbelieve or to contradict the sacred Scriptures. . . ."[35]

As for the third deduction from the text, namely, that the Church is founded on Christ the Rock, Hus repeats

[34] *Ibid.*, p. 53.  [35] *Ibid.*, p. 56.

what he has asserted many times before, that Christ and
not Peter is the foundation of the Church. He quotes
Paul: "Other foundation can no man lay than that which
is laid, which is Christ Jesus."[36] The word rock [*petra*]
does not derive from Peter [*Petrus*]. Peter himself spoke
of Christ as "the living stone, rejected by men but by
God chosen and honored. . . ."[37] The apostles are to be
regarded as the foundation of the Church in a sense different from Christ. Since He is the principal foundation
and "the foundation of foundations," so they may be
spoken of as foundations because they strengthen and
fortify our faith in Christ. Peter was chosen by Christ
because of his preeminent steadfastness of faith as well
as his humility and love. He was not higher in dignity
than Christ's mother, or equal to Christ, or the ruler
of angels. He never dared to claim to be the head of the
Church universal. Hence, he is not even now "the head
of the holy catholic Church." Hus adds significantly:
". . . it would be the greatest presumption and folly for
any man, Christ excepted, to call himself the head and
bridegroom of the holy catholic Church."[38]

Hus then expatiates on the reasons why Christ appointed Peter to be "the captain and shepherd" of the
Church, namely, his virtues. Hus thus indirectly indicates
what the grounds for papal election should be. First
of all comes Peter's firmness of faith and his confession
of Christ as the Son of the living God; it is likewise
the task of Peter's vicars to preach this faith. Christ
joined to Peter's faith the primacy of office by giving him
the keys of the kingdom of heaven, consisting in the
spiritual power of discerning sins and either absolving
or retaining them, not in juridical or monarchical rule.
Hus states that in the second place, Peter excelled in
humility. This is in sharp contrast to the modern "image"
of Peter as a blunt, dominating if not domineering sort

[36] I Cor. 3:11.    [37] I Peter 2:4.    [38] *De ecclesia*, p. 66.

of person. Nevertheless, Hus cites some examples of this virtue which, it must be confessed, do not sound very convincing. One has the impression that Hus had his eye more directly on the popes than on Peter and was obliquely criticizing them for their pomp and excessive pretensions. Much more convincing is Hus' ascription of preeminence of love to Peter. This is, of course, based on Jesus' own three searching questions, "Simon, son of John, lovest thou me more than these?"[39] Finally, Peter is said to possess preeminence of poverty and endurance. What is important to note is that Peter was chosen for his leading role in the Church for his virtues; he was not merely appointed to the office irrespective of his ethical qualifications. Hence, it logically follows that "if he who is called Peter's vicar follows in the way of virtues just mentioned, we believe that he is his true vicar and the preeminent pontiff of the Church he rules. If, however, he walks in contrary ways, then he is the representative of Antichrist, opposed to Peter and the Lord Jesus Christ. . . . For no one can truly and acceptably to Christ occupy the place of Christ or Peter unless he follows him in behavior [*moribus*], for no other following is suitable except he receive the procuratorial power from God subject to this condition."[40]

The tenth chapter is devoted to the last of the deductions from the text we are considering, namely, to the authority granted by Christ to his vicars. This power is spiritual, restricted to the administration of the sacraments and the *sacramentalia*. Every priest has the power to "teach, counsel, punish, console, remit sins, bear the infirmities of others, and pray for all." It is not coercive. The civil power, on the other hand, is coercive and authoritative. It belongs only to the civil lords. Nevertheless, the spiritual power excels the secular both in antiquity and in dignity. For God instituted priesthood prior

[39] John 21:15.     [40] *De ecclesia*, p. 70.

to royalty. Above all, the spiritual power deals with things eternal rather than temporal. The keys of heaven were granted to Peter, who on that occasion represented in his person the whole Church. They consist of the knowledge or discernment of truth and the power of judging of right and wrong, or virtue and sin, and of the consequent remission or retention of sins. God alone has this power supremely. Even Jesus Christ possessed it to a subordinate degree, since he was both divine and human. Ministers of the Church possess it only *ministerialiter*. Hus then castigates the superstitious fear some lay people have of the sacerdotal power, as if it depended on the caprice of the priest whether or not he would grant them remission of sins. He explains that such binding and loosing of sins first takes place in heaven and is only declared by the priest, if all the conditions governing it are fulfilled by the repentant sinner. These conditions comprise contrition, confession, and satisfaction. In case of necessity, if a priest is not available, contrition alone suffices. For it is God who forgives sins, not the priest. Even the pope has no power to forgive sins unless God has first remitted them. "Therefore, the priests who think or say that they can of their own will loose or bind without the previous absolving or binding by Jesus Christ, are ragingly insane."[41] It is blasphemy to assert that a mere man can remit sins against God without God's own previous consent. To ascribe such power to the pope is tantamount to making him sinless. Nor can the sins truly repented of be retained by a priest out of malice or because of non-payment of money demanded by him. Similarly, if an impenitent sinner is willing to pay money for absolution without contrition for his sins, he is not forgiven by God, even though the pope himself declares him forgiven.

Hus probably received the text of the *Consilium* of

41 *Ibid.*, p. 81.

the doctors while he was working on chapter 11, for he mentions it toward the end. In the early part of the chapter he deals with the abuse of Scripture for the upholding of priestly authority. He charges the clerics with appropriating and exaggerating everything which exalts them, and ignoring or spurning whatever calls for their self-abnegation and emulation of Christ, such as poverty, humility, chastity, and labor. Christ said to his disciples that they were not to rule as the gentile rulers do, but to minister to all. The prelates and priests abuse their power by committing simony in buying and selling sacred orders, episcopates, canonries, and parishes, as well as by charging fees for the sacraments. They profess to believe in God but deny Him by their deeds. They crucify the Son of God afresh when they unworthily administer the sacraments. He quotes Jerome, "A priest who is besmirched by any stain of sin should not approach the table to offer sacrifices to the Lord."[42]

It is at this point that Hus introduces a reference to the *Consilium* by protesting the statement of the doctors that the "pestiferous clergy" caused the dissension in the Church of Bohemia. He counters by asserting that the doctors denounce as heretical all who by their preaching rebuke clerical corruption.

In the next chapter Hus plunges again into a discussion, much of which is based on Wyclif, concerning Christ's headship of the Church. He refers once more to Boniface's bull, *Unam sanctam*, and its declaration that it is necessary for salvation that every human being be subject to the Roman pope. But instead of treating this declaration as it was undoubtedly intended by Boniface, namely, as applying to the pope as the vicar of Christ, Hus applies it to Christ himself. Since Christ is the head of the universal Church, he is the head of

[42] *Corpus* (see n. 32), I, p. 391.

that portion of the Roman Church, which is part of the Church catholic. He even calls him "the Roman pontiff." Boniface's declaration is therefore true (of course, on Hus' interpretation), for all men must be subject to Christ in order to obtain eternal salvation. Christ was not subject to any pope, nor was his mother, John the Baptist, or even Peter and other saints now in glory. "For none of these was it necessary to be subject to any other Roman pontiff but Christ, since they are already saved."[43] He then recounts the case of several popes who acted in ways unworthy of their office. About Pope Clement he says that he commanded the angels to conduct to heaven the soul of a pilgrim who died on the way to Rome to secure indulgences there and whom he absolved from purgatory. He commanded that the powers of hell "should bow at his mandate."[44] Hus remarks wryly that when John on the island of Patmos was ready to fall at the angel's feet, the latter forbade it saying, "Worship God!" The angel was surely greater than Pope Clement! The apostles did not call themselves "most holy popes." Pope Gregory the Great in his famous letter to Patriarch Eulogius of Alexandria repudiated the title of "universal pope," declaring that he sought to be distinguished by good life alone.[45] The modern popes, on the contrary, "shake with anger" if one omits their "pompous title." Finally, he cites the decree of the Council of Carthage which forbade that the Roman pontiff be called universal bishop.[46]

In chapter 13 Hus takes up the doctors' basic definition

[43] *De ecclesia*, pp. 97-98.

[44] This was a spurious bull, referred to in M. H. Dziewicki, ed., *John Wyclif De blasphemia* (London, The Wyclif Society, 1893), p. 16; see Thomson, *De ecclesia*, p. 98, n. 3.

[45] H. Wace and P. Schaff, transl., *A Select Library of Nicene and Post Nicene Fathers of the Christian Church*, 2nd series, 14 vols. (New York, 1890-1900), XII, p. 241.

[46] The third Council of Carthage, 397. Friedberg, *Corpus*, I, p. 350.

of the Church as consisting of the pope as the head and the cardinals as its body. In that capacity they are said to be the "true and manifest" successors of Peter and of the other apostles. No other such successors exist or can be found on earth. Hus declares it an *abusio termini* if any person elected to the office is to be recognized as pope, even though he be a female, a heretic, an unlettered rustic, or Antichrist. He cites the notorious cases of the alleged female Pope John,[47] of Pope Constantine II, a rough and illiterate layman,[48] of Pope Gregory,[49] and of Pope Liberius who adopted Arianism.[50] Further, any pope living contrary to Christ is Antichrist. Hus traces the papal supremacy over all ecclesiastical dignitaries to the endowments granted to Pope Sylvester by Emperor Constantine, allegedly as a reward for healing the emperor of leprosy and baptizing him.[51] Emperor Phocas confirmed the grant. The Council of Nicaea allegedly approved the Roman pope's supremacy. (Of course, it did nothing of the sort!) Hus then summarizes his opponents' concept of the Church in six points and declares that none of them is true according to reason, revelation, or Scripture. No one of them is part of the doctrine of Jesus Christ. Yet, the doctors hold their

[47] Although this is a discredited legend, it was generally accepted in the Middle Ages. Hus uses it in season and out of season.

[48] He held office during 767-768 (not 707 as Hus' text states), having been made pope by the influence of his brother, Duke Toto of Nepi.

[49] Gregory VI (1045-46) bought the see from Boniface IX. He and Sylvester III were deposed under pressure from Emperor Henry III at the Synod of Sutri.

[50] Liberius (352-366) with an interval of three years.

[51] "The Donation of Constantine," the most successful forgery of the Middle Ages, was in Hus' time generally received as genuine. It allegedly granted the pope rule over Rome, Italy, and all the West, and the supremacy over the patriarchates of Antioch, Alexandria, Jerusalem, and Constantinople. Constantine never had leprosy and was baptized on his deathbed by the Arian bishop Eusebius of Nicomedia. Constantinople and Jerusalem were not patriarchates in 301.

concept as being *de fide* which must be held on pain of
anathema. They thus make their own pronouncements
as if they were the authoritative decrees of the Church
catholic. Consequently, "since those doctors are not the
authors of the sacred Scriptures," the faithful are "not
to think it is true because the doctors feel it to be true,
unless they prove by other writers of Scripture or for
canonical or probable reasons that these points do not
deviate from the truth."[52] Furthermore, "no pope is the
head of the Church catholic besides Christ," the Church
of which he said that "the gates of hell shall not prevail against it."[53] Since no one can tell whether or not
he is of the predestinate, "no one without revelation
can reasonably assert about himself or another that
he is the head of a particular holy Church, although
if he lives well he should hope that he is a member of
the holy catholic Church, the bride of Christ." "If the
acts of the Roman pope do not contradict the assumption, it should be supposed that he is the head of that
particular Church."[54] This is as far as Hus would go
in conceding the claim of the doctors that the pope is
the head of the Church. He has consistently held that
view and continued to hold it to the end. He challenges the doctors to declare openly whether they believe that Agnes was really the head of the Church. He
boldly concludes that it is not necessary for salvation
to believe specifically that anyone is the head of any
Church unless he possesses the ethical qualifications that
constitute a presumptive proof of it. As for the argument of the doctors that a visible head should always
be present with the Church, he replies that Christ *is*
present by means of his grace and in the sacraments.
He asks sarcastically what good does the "visible" pres-

---

[52] *De ecclesia*, pp. 106-107.
[53] *Ibid.*, p. 107.          [54] *Ibid.*

ence of the pope do us when he is two thousand miles away.

In the next chapter Hus deals with the second half of the doctors' definition—that the cardinals are the body of the Church. The reasoning he applies to the cardinals is essentially the same as that relative to the pope. To constitute the mystical body of Christ which is the Church, the cardinals would have to be of the predestinate. The doctors have no possibility of knowing and therefore of proving the point. Moreover, although the predestinate are the real body of the Roman Church, the cardinals do not comprise all of them. Therefore, as Hus has stated so many times before, the only correct and adequate definition of the Church is that Christ is its head and the predestinate are its body. Surely, it is not the pope with his cardinals against whom the gates of hell shall not prevail! The doctors further declared, although without offering any proof, that the pope and the cardinals are the manifest successors of Peter and of the other apostles. Vicars ought to occupy the place of those from whom they received the procuratorial powers. The doctors did not prove that the present vicars truly occupy the place of Peter and the other apostles by following them in their behavior, in humility, poverty, and labors. The cardinals live in pomp and luxury, devouring the alms actually belonging to the poor. They heap up livings one upon another, but seek not the things of Christ. Reverting again to the pope, Hus castigates him for allowing himself to be adored on bended knee and by having his feet kissed. Some of these crass adulators bow to the pope and kiss his feet more devoutly than they do the sacrament of the body of Christ! Our Lord after His resurrection did not allow Mary Magdalene to kiss His feet; yet those who presume to be His vicars do! Hus further denounces the pope for calling himself the most holy father [*sanctissimus*

*Pater*]. This title derives not from his actual personal sanctity, or from the fact that he occupies the place of Peter, but from Constantine's donation.

This being so, Hus concludes in the next chapter that the Church has no absolute necessity of the pope and the cardinals. In fact, "no one does more harm to the Church than he who acts perversely, having the name and order of sanctity."[55] As for the assertion of the doctors that no other successors of Peter or the apostles are to be found on earth, Hus replies that during the first three hundred years the Church prospered under the rule of Christ through devoted priests and bishops who administered it by His law. St. Augustine was more profitable to the Church than many popes, and his teaching has ever since been more valuable than all the cardinals who have ever held office. He pointedly inquires why St. Augustine, St. Jerome, St. Gregory, and St. Ambrose are not regarded by the doctors as the true and manifest successors of the apostles rather than any modern pope or cardinal. This should put a stop to any accusation either that Hus limited himself to Scripture or that he interpreted it "according to his own head." Hus then mentions in the second place that such Fathers as John Chrysostom, John of Damascus, and even Dionysius the Areopagite also taught by the Holy Spirit and illuminated the Church by their knowledge and piety. It was Constantine who instituted the pope as head of other patriarchs and endowed him with imperial honors and territorial rule. In the same way, Emperor Lewis endowed Pope Pascal with rule over "the Roman state."[56]

Hus then turns to the objection that the pope re-

[55] *Ibid.*, p. 120; the passage is quoted from Gregory's *Liber pastoralis*, J.-P. Migne, *Patrologia latina*, 221 vols. (Paris, Garnier Fratres, 1896), LXXVII, pp. 15f. and the letters 40-41.

[56] *Ibid.*, p. 122. The alleged pact between Lewis and Pascal (817-24) is a forgery. The text is in Friedberg, *Corpus*, I, pp. 244f.

ceived his primacy from God, as Anacletus, the supposed first successor of Peter as bishop of Rome, is alleged to have said. He counters it by somewhat obscure arguments. Following Wyclif in this whole matter, Hus concludes that Anacletus meant the primacy of virtues rather than of civil rule. Peter and Paul had no such primacy as Sylvester received, and therefore could not pass it on to Anacletus. Nevertheless, Hus concedes that "the pope has the excellency of his dignity immediately from God and not from man who is not God or from mere man,"[57] on condition that he live humbly and without pomp. The dignity bestowed on him by Caesars is incongruous with this requirement of humility. De Vooght calls it undoubted heresy that "Hus did not consider primacy as an immutable divine institution. If he did not hold the idea that one could be saved without faith, the sacraments, and the priest, he was certain that one could be saved without the pope and, therefore, without the papacy. The Church without it would not be diminished by anything essential."[58] It is for this reason primarily, if not altogether, that he held Hus a heretic, despite the very high opinion he entertained about him otherwise. The disturbing feature of this fair-minded, scholarly monk's verdict is that he ignores, passes over in silence, and thus in reality negates the statement made by Hus not only on the occasion referred to above, but on numerous other occasions, that the spiritual functions of the pope are indeed derived from Christ. Only the supreme rank, material possessions, and the territorial rule, were be-

[57] *Ibid.*, p. 125. Kybal says (*Jan Hus, Učení,* II, p. 193) that "Hus explicitly denies the divine origin of the Roman primacy as such (*per se*) and derives its origin from the Roman emperors. The sentence quoted certainly does not bear him out. I understand Hus to say that the spiritual office of the pope is immediately from God, but his temporal honors are from the Caesars.

[58] De Vooght, *Hussiana*, p. 59.

stowed on him by the emperors. Surely the learned Benedictine knew that as well. How is one to account for his patent refusal to credit the plainly expressed opinion of Hus?

The assertion of the doctors that the pope can do as he pleases and nobody can say him nay, Hus brusquely rejects as mendacious rhetoric, leading the common people astray. The pope should be believed only to the extent that he agrees with Scripture. The Christ-loving bishops are the successors of the apostles as well, not the pope and the cardinals alone. Priests are ordained and guided by the Lord Jesus Christ directly, the bishops serving in this rite only in their ministerial capacity. Hus cites Jerome's letter to Evagrius[59] as declaring that formerly there was no difference between bishops and presbyters, and that Rome is not to be extolled above the other churches of the world—those of Gaul, Britain, Africa, Persia, India, the Orient, and the barbarous nations. For "they adore the same Christ and observe the same rule of truth. If authority is sought, the world is greater than the city [*orbis maior est urbe*]. Wherever there are bishops, whether at Rome, Eugubia, Constantinople, Regium, Alexandria, or Thamis, they are of the same merit as the priests."[60] I agree with Kybal, who concludes that Hus' ideal of the Church is a federalist episcopal organization comprising bishops and priests living Christlike lives, and having Christ alone as their common head.[61] Nevertheless, he regards the idea as wholly unrealistic. I do not. He forgets that Eastern Orthodox Churches are so organized to this day.

In chapter 16 Hus takes up the doctors' charge that the evangelical party wishes to have holy Scripture alone as judge; but that they interpret it "according to their

---

[59] Friedberg, *Corpus*, I, pp. 328, 332.
[60] *De ecclesia*, p. 127.
[61] Kybal, *Jan Hus, Učení*, II, p. 193.

own heads," rather than accepting the interpretation of "the wise men of the Church." This accusation Hus disposes of easily. In the first place, he denies that his party wishes to have Scripture alone as judge. Tracing this charge to Páleč, who further claims that Hus' party would have "neither God, nor the apostles, nor the holy doctors, nor the holy Church universal as judges," Hus calls it a lie.[62] Páleč bases it on a certain disputation they had some time ago. Hus repeats that the doctor should know "that in matters of faith we agree with him or his adherents only insofar as they ground themselves on Scripture or reason."[63] He then turns the tables on his accusers by charging that it is the doctors who do not wish the Scriptures to be the judge so that their own opinions will prevail and whatever they condemn or approve be accepted.

The second lie consists of the "recalcitrants'" alleged private and hence erroneous interpretation of Scripture. Hus vehemently denies that he and his party rely in this matter "on their own heads." And well he might, since he has ever and most copiously quoted the Fathers in support of his tenets or the interpretation of Scripture. He challenges Páleč: "I wish that that doctor and all his colleagues would show which Scripture we expound wrongly." However, the biggest lie Hus declares to be the argument based on a passage in Deuteronomy asserting that every uncertain or difficult case should be referred to the priests;[64] implying, of course, that this means the pope and the cardinals. He points out that even the apostles fell into heresy, and ironically asks "whether the pope and the cardinals received greater gifts of the Spirit and cannot blunder to the same or greater degree?"[65] He does not doubt that the pope and the cardinals should be obeyed in all matters consonant

[62] *De ecclesia*, p. 132.
[63] *Ibid.*, p. 133.
[64] Deut. 17:8-12.
[65] *De ecclesia*, p. 136.

with God's law. If they should command anything besides the truth, however, the faithful should not obey even though the whole Roman curia should command it. Hus declares that the doctors aim to make the pope judge in all cases and declare that whoever should refuse to obey, should die. Christ did not judge and bade his disciples not to judge. The doctors, however, not only condemn anyone in Bohemia acting against their opinions, but should he refuse to yield to ecclesiastical censure, they declare that he be "turned over to the secular tribunal," i.e., to be punished by death. In this they follow the Jewish authorities who turned Jesus over to Pilate, thus becoming "worse murderers than he." As examples of wrong papal judgments, Hus cites sixteen cases gathered from the *Chronicles* of Martinus Polonus (d. 1278), the Cestrensis (Ralph of Higden), and Rudolf Glaber, a monk of Cluny; they deal with various schisms and illegal elections of several popes. He finally describes the "Great Schism" of 1378 and its aggravation caused by the Council of Pisa.

Chapters 17-21 are devoted to the concept of obedience to papal and prelatical authority. The doctors claimed that obedience is due to the pope and the prelates in all things whatsoever where the purely good is not prohibited or the purely evil commanded. They charged that some clergy refused obedience and seduced the people to do likewise. Hus retorts that the "evangelical" clergy endeavor to live in accordance with Christ's law and instruct the people in the same way. He further asserts that "our side" desires that the three estates, clergy, nobility, and lay people, be properly commingled in the Church militant, a statement showing his traditional concepts of social organization. All three estates should be recognized as members of the Church and accorded their proper share in its administration. Obedience is due to that which is good, disobedience to that which is evil. Thus no superior should expect or demand an unconditional and unquestioning obedience. The subjects have the right and duty of judging of the commands whether they be right. Thus obedience involves understanding, judgment, and decision. Apostle Paul teaches[66] that obedience is due to superiors, both secular and spiritual, for they are ordained to encourage the good and punish the evil. But no one should be obeyed when he commands anything contrary to "the divine will, good morals, or the necessities of life," or in anything which conflicts with the commands and counsels of the Lord Jesus Christ.[67] Hus sums up by writing that obedience is three-fold: spiritual, secular, and ecclesiastical. Spiritual obedience is due to God's law; the Savior and the apostles lived under it and so should we. Secular obedience is due to secular rulers provided that their laws do not conflict with those of God. Ecclesiastical obedience has to do with "the regulations of the priests of the Church aside from the express authority of Scripture."[68] It is apparent that Hus was no social revolutionary as Jean Gerson then and the Czech communists now portray him. In fact, Peter of Chelčice, the spiritual father of the *Unitas Fratrum Bohemicorum*, differed from Hus on this point by denying the threefold division of society. For him all men were equal before God. Thus he was more "revolutionary" than Hus.[69]

Applying these principles directly to the Apostolic See, Hus first of all defines the word "apostolic." After enumerating several connotations which do not go to the root of the matter, he explains the original meaning of the Greek word as the "one sent." Christ was

[66] Rom. 13:1-7.
[67] *De ecclesia*, p. 154.        [68] *Ibid.*, p. 156.
[69] Matthew Spinka, "Peter Chelčický, Spiritual Father of the *Unitas Fratrum*," *Church History*, December 1943, pp. 271-291; also Alois Míka, *Petr Chelčický* (Praha, 1963).

sent by God to reveal Him. No one who was not sent by God should hold either the "apostolic" or any other office in the Church. The pope is apostolic if he teaches the apostolic doctrine and follows the apostles in his behavior. Otherwise he should be called "pseudo-apostolic or an apostate." Any pope elected simoniacally, or by human favor, or by military force, is not to be considered apostolic. Hus then explains Christ's words, "The scribes and the Pharisees sit on Moses' seat; whatever they tell you, observe and do, but do not act according to them. For they teach but do not practice."[70] The Apostolic See has, therefore, the authority to teach and judge according to Christ's law. But Hus accuses the Roman curia of teaching erroneous doctrine in its bulls or of vaunting haughtiness in seeking first places, or of striving for honor and the genuflections of the people: "one wants to be a cardinal, another a patriarch, another an archbishop."[71] In case they teach rightly, they do not practice what they teach. "Even worse are those who neither teach nor practice. Worst are those who prevent teaching of good doctrine. The ultimate degree of wickedness is manifested by those who forbid good teaching and command their own." Such men must not be obeyed but rather opposed. Hus cites the case of Bishop Robert Grosseteste,[72] who refused to give a stall in the Lincoln cathedral to Pope Innocent's nephew. Hus then justifies his own refusal to obey the papal order forbidding preaching in chapels, and his appeal "from Alexander misinformed to Alexander better informed." He also refers to his protest against the indulgence bull of Pope John XXIII and, finally, to his appeal to Christ, as Grosseteste had done after he had been excommuni-

---

[70] Matt. 23:2-4.     [71] *De ecclesia*, p. 161.

[72] Robert Grosseteste, bishop of Lincoln (1235-53), who refused to grant a place to the nephew of Pope Innocent IV. He protested the request in several letters. Hus knew of the case either from Wyclif's writings, or directly from Grosseteste MS in Prague.

cated. Accordingly, Hus asserts that "to rebel against an erring pope is to obey Christ the Lord. . . ."[73] He then concludes the chapter with the bold declaration:

I do not, however, say that the city of Rome is the Apostolic See and so necessary that without it the Church of Jesus Christ could not stand. For if it should happen that Rome were destroyed like Sodom, the Christian Church could still survive. Nor is it true that where the pope is there is Rome. Nevertheless, it is true that wherever the pope shall be so long as he is here on earth, there Peter's authority abides in the pope, so long as he does not depart from the law of the Lord Jesus Christ.[74]

Let it be noted that Hus does not repudiate the papal office absolutely, but recognizes it as possessing Peter's authority. Nevertheless, this authority is grounded on ethical requirements and not merely on the vicissitudes of the papal election. One can imagine how offensive such bold denial of the absolute necessity of the papacy must have sounded to a convinced and devoted papalist.

In chapter 19 Hus continues to deal with this important subject. Specifically, he considers the doctors' dictum that the Apostolic See must be obeyed in all things "intermediate." Hus cites Bernard (from whom the doctors derived the definition) as giving examples of a hypothetical command that a person marry or possess property, both of which are permissible to a layman but not to a monk. There being the three kinds of commands specified in the doctors' definition, every man, cleric or layman, has the duty of distinguishing among them. This implies the necessity of judging the acts of the prelates and even those of the pope himself. Every man must be on guard lest he believe that their commands must be obeyed as if they were God's mandates or as if

[73] *De ecclesia*, p. 169.     [74] *Ibid.*, pp. 172-173.

the prelates could not err. "For no superior is above correction." If they command something which is of no benefit to the Church and which is not contained either explicitly or implicitly in Scripture, no faithful Christian is bound to perform it. "God commands us to do nothing except what is meritorious and reasonable for us and consequently profitable for salvation. . . . Subjects are bound to obey willingly and cheerfully virtuous and, indeed, even harsh superiors when they demand the fulfillment of the mandates of the Lord Jesus Christ."[75] But no one should obey them even in the least thing when their command is contrary to these mandates. The wise subject, cleric and layman alike, must examine the acts of his superior. Let no priest or prelate say to his people: "What business is it of yours to pay attention to our lives or acts?" It is indeed the concern of the people whether the clerics teach and live aright.

In the next chapter Hus continues to discuss the same subject, commenting on the doctors' requirement of obedience as if it were mortal sin not to obey or pay reverence to the prelates. He reminds his readers that he was excommunicated because he disobeyed the Holy See. But no one is to be excommunicated except for mortal sin. Furthermore, it would be presumptuous of the Roman curia to demand, under pain of excommunication, what Christ neither commanded nor counselled. Hus then scores two hits, already familiar to us from previous references to them, against the doctors: he points out that Pope Boniface IX ordered Kings Wenceslas and Sigismund to resign their rule, the former over the Roman Empire, the latter over Hungary.[76] Neither of the kings obeyed and both were excommunicated, and have never since been absolved. Thus, according to

[75] *Ibid.*, p. 177.
[76] Boniface IX acknowledged Ruprecht of the Palatinate as Emperor (1403).

the doctors, they are still continuing in mortal sin. The second case is even more pertinent. Pope Innocent VII ordered the Prague theological faculty on pain of excommunication to give a place to Master Maurice Rvačka.[77] Since the faculty had steadfastly refused to do so, Stanislav and Peter of Znojmo, John Eliášův and one other master were placed under the papal ban. Since they have not hitherto been absolved, they are still excommunicates. Hus refers to both of these cases fairly often, for they are indeed telling examples of disobedience, on the part of the doctors, which they condemned in others. He finally concludes that when a man is unjustly excommunicated (i.e., not for mortal sin), he should bear it patiently and, if a priest, should continue to perform his duties. It is wrong for a priest to stop preaching. Augustine wrote that such priests "may not be excused from the guilt of keeping silence, since they ought not to have a place of authority who do not know how to preach, nor should they who do know how to preach keep silent. . . ."[78] Preaching is a matter of obligation, not of choice. For that reason, Hus says, he did not obey the papal order to desist from preaching at Bethlehem.

Next Hus discusses the clause in the *Consilium* which asserts that the Roman Church and its prelates must be obeyed in all things. The doctors base this opinion on Christ's injunction about the scribes and Pharisees that "all they bid you do, these observe and do." Hus wonders why the doctors left out the following clause, "but do not do according to their works." Moreover, Christ adds, "They lay heavy burdens and grievous to be borne"; he thereby as much as asserts that these burdens should not be borne. Thus not all that the author-

[77] He never secured the place.
[78] Augustine, Prologue to his *Sermons*, in *Patrologia latina*, XXXVIII.

ities command should be done. No one can be neutral in matters of right and wrong. One must judge whether the commands are proper. The decisive factors in the judgment are the possibility, reasonableness, time, place, and the person who issues the command. If one were ordered something impossible or unreasonable, he should not obey. As an example of an unreasonable command Hus offers a hypothetical order of "a dull and fat" bishop that a priest should feed swine instead of Christ's sheep. Likewise as to the time and place, Hus argues, on the ground of a number of canonical provisions, that an accused person can rightfully refuse to appear before a tribunal composed of his enemies. Since this is the provision of secular courts, how much more it should apply to ecclesiastical trials! Moreover, the trial should be held where the alleged crime was committed. As a proof he offers Gratian's provision that no man under any circumstances should be summoned to a trial outside the province in which the crime he is accused of took place.[79] This was, of course, the reason why he himself refused to obey the citation to appear before the Roman curia. He pleaded the distance from Rome, the roads infested by his German foes, the neglect of his own duties, and the hopelessness of expecting a just verdict from his judges, particularly when he had no money. For without money, no justice could be obtained in Rome. He insisted that Prague was the proper place for the trial, a position shared by the king and the queen. He concluded from these premises that the excommunication imposed on him was invalid, "because hostile judges and witnesses dwell in Rome." He argues further that it would be unreasonable if a prelate ordered a man to give alms that would necessitate letting his own children go hungry, or a man physically incapable of it to fast. This is "laying on insufferable burdens," which no

[79] Friedberg, *Corpus*, I, p. 519.

one is in duty bound to bear. Although these matters are "intermediate," they need not be obeyed because a command "must be reasonable in the sight of God."[80]

Furthermore, Hus answers the objection that the pope occupies the place of Christ on earth and, therefore, it is not permissible to criticize him or to point out any fault of his. Hus reminds his foes that Christ called Peter Satan when the latter presumed to dissuade him from going to Jerusalem to his death. Certainly a pope is not sinless as Christ was; therefore, he is subject to correction and reproof for his sins and faults just as any other mortal. The same applies to any other prelate.

In the last two chapters Hus deals with excommunication, suspension, and interdict. He answers the doctors' statement that the clergy of Prague accepted the result of the trial of Hus and that it should for that reason be obeyed. Further, that "it is not the business of the clergy of Prague to pronounce judgment on the question of whether the excommunication of Master John Hus is just or unjust. . . ." The fallacy of the pronouncement is so obvious that Hus comments with biting scorn that "the doctors of theology, particularly Stanislav, who is the ablest logician among them, should be ashamed of arriving at such a conclusion."[81] What the doctors' thesis amounts to, he says, is that the Prague clergy cannot err. For only on the supposition of their infallibility can their conclusion be regarded as valid. Moreover, since they accepted the papal excommunication of himself, they must have judged it right, contrary to their protestation that it is not their business to express an opinion concerning it. Thus their deed contradicts their word. Further, since they say that because the Prague clergy accepted the judgment as the one that should be obeyed, and the doctors themselves belong to the Prague clergy, they therefore share in the judg-

[80] *De ecclesia*, p. 204.    [81] *Ibid.*, p. 209.

ment. This contradicts the assertion that it is not for them to judge whether or not the verdict is right. Furthermore, since the doctors say that the excommunication of Hus should be accepted, they affirm thereby that it is just. Hus, on the contrary, relying on the opinion of John of Jesenice, doctor of canon law and his legal representative, concludes that the sentence fulminated against him is unjust and therefore null and void.

Hus then undertakes to deal with the concepts of excommunication, suspension, and interdict. As for the first, he defines it as a fourfold separation: from the participation in divine grace [*gratia gratum faciens*] which is the communion of saints; from worthy participation in the sacraments; from the participation in the aids [*suffragiorum*] conducive to eternal life; and from intercourse with all Christians. Excommunication of the first three kinds should never be inflicted except for mortal sins, which alone separate the sinner from the Church as well as from God. So long, however, as a man is in grace, he partakes of the three benefits of communion. No one can, therefore, be excommunicated unless he excommunicates himself by his own sinful acts.

A further distinction is to be drawn between the major and the minor excommunication. The minor deprives one of the sacraments, the major separates him from the communion of the faithful. Moreover, the major excommunication should be remedial, aiming at restoring the sinner to spiritual health and thus to a return into the communion of the Church. Hus declares that by the excommunication imposed on him he is cut off from all human communion. But it cannot prevent God from succoring him if he bears this unjust sentence with patience and humility. Indeed, it aids in purifying him and thus in increasing his reward. He professes to fear more the Pauline warning, "If any man love not our Lord Jesus Christ, let him be anathema,"[82] than the papal excommunication. This would greatly exceed the major excommunication imposed on him by Cardinal Stephaneschi. Any unjust excommunication rebounds on the man imposing it. For no man should excommunicate anyone unless he first knows that the person is excommunicated by God. Hus had this thesis inscribed on the walls of Bethlehem Chapel.

Suspension is the term used in the old decretals for what is called interdict in the new canon law. Just as in the case of excommunication, it should not be inflicted unless it has first been decreed by God. Hus cites Old and New Testament examples of divine suspensions from priestly[83] and from (of Saul) kingly[84] office. The suspension is incurred for a manifest sin. The prelates nowadays, Hus says, suspend for their own advantage or from avarice rather than for men's sins. He declares that such prelates should themselves be suspended from office because they lack knowledge of Scripture and neglect the task of evangelization. Furthermore, they fail to punish their spiritual sons as Eli failed to punish his natural sons.[85] Prelates show more favor to God's enemies than Saul showed to Amalek, for which he was rejected by God.[86] Were the doctors to speak truly about the prelates, they would have to confess their iniquity. They would find in how many cases the prelates cooperate with, defend, and condone open sins. Moreover, they excommunicate or suspend from office all who dare to resist their will. The prelates' censures of the preachers of Christ's law proceed from Antichrist, "who has usurped the clergy in the largest measure for himself."[87]

Hus condemns the interdict imposed on a whole community of Christians on account of the transgression of one person. Why should faithful Christians be deprived

[82] I Cor. 16:22.
[83] Hosea 4:6; Isa. 1:13; Mal. 1:10; I Cor. 11:27.
[84] I Sam. 15:23.  [85] I Sam. 2:12, 22.
[86] I Sam. 28:18.  [87] *De ecclesia*, p. 226.

of the preaching of the Word and the sacraments—baptism, communion, confession, and extreme unction in case of mortal illness? There is no Scriptural authority for such an arbitrary action on the part of the pope or bishops. Gratian declares that an excommunication suffered on account of another man's sin is illegal. St. Augustine also condemned the practice. Let the doctors prove that a general interdict is a thing intermediate, something between absolute good and total evil! Hus then cites the extremely harsh terms of his own aggravated excommunication:

> Every place, city, walled town, villa, or castle, privileged or unprivileged, to which the said John Hus may have gone and, how long soever he may remain and how long soever he may tarry, and for three natural days after his departure from such places we, by these writings, do put them under the great ecclesiastical interdict and desire that the divine ministries be stopped in them.[88]

He then asks where such terms are found in the Scriptures or in the example of Christ or of his apostles. In conclusion, he thanks God that the Church does not depend on the pope for its life, having Jesus Christ for its head. As a parting shot he asks ironically through which of the three existing popes does the Roman Church speak. This tripartite papacy is but a feeble foundation for the doctors' claim that anything declared by the Roman curia should be held inviolable!

Such, then, is the most important of Hus' works expounding his concept of the Church. All in all, *De ecclesia* has remained the work with which, above all others, Hus' name is associated and his fate bound.

[88] *De ecclesia*, p. 232; quoted in F. Palacký, *Documenta Mag. Joannis Hus* (Praha, F. Tempský, 1869), p. 462, where the interdict is said to continue one day after Hus' departure, not three.

## CHAPTER IX

## HUS' CZECH TREATISES

DEPRIVED of the opportunity of preaching to his
beloved congregation at the Bethlehem Chapel,
Hus in his exile devoted much time to writing
Czech treatises for them.[1] In this he continued the grand
tradition of Thomas of Štítné (1331-1409),[2] whose fairly
numerous works in Czech represent an outstanding accomplishment of a lay religious thinker. Many of Hus'
Czech works are either purely hortatory or instructional,
but some are polemical. All contain references to the current controversies either with his curial judges or the members of the Prague theological faculty. One could thus du-
plicate from these extensive works most of the material
dealt with in his Latin works of the period. It would,
however, be inexcusably redundant to reproduce even
in the briefest form the content of each of these treatises.
We shall, therefore, organize the material under subjects bearing on the concept of the Church and, as much
as possible, include only such aspects of it as are either
supplementary to the Latin works or afford new insight
into them. We shall also include the doctrinal references found in his earlier sermons, particularly those
preached in Bethlehem during the years 1410-11.

Among the most important of Hus' Czech literary
works is his revision of the Czech Bible comprising practically the whole New Testament, part of Ecclesiastes,
all of the Song of Songs, Ecclesiasticus, and the Psalter

---

[1] The dating and other information is based on F. M. Bartoš,
*Literární činnost M. Jana Husi* (Praha, Česká akademie věd a
umění, 1948), pp. 101-118.

[2] Cf. Paul de Vooght, *L'hérésie de Jean Huss* (Louvain, Publications universitaires de Louvain, 1960), pp. 35ff.; Count Francis
Lützow, *A History of Bohemian Literature* (London, 1909), pp.
65-79.

(to Psalm 134).[3] The most popular work was his *Postil*, comprising sermons for a year. It was completed at Kozí Hrádek in 1413, and is regarded as the crowning masterpiece of his preaching career. The original edition was published in Nuremberg in 1558. The latest edition is that of J. B. Jeschke, published in 1952. The principal doctrinal treatises are the three *Expositions* consisting of an *Exposition of the Faith* [*Výklad víry*]; of the *Decalogue* [*Výklad desatera*]; and of the *Lord's Prayer* [*Výklad modlitby Páně*]. They are in two recensions, major and minor.[4] These treatises are intended to teach the common people what to believe, what to do, and how to pray. The smaller treatises bearing on our subject were written mostly in 1412. The *Treatise on Simony* [*O svatokupectví*][5] is a sharp attack on the most prevalent sin of the time, which was undermining the very foundations of the whole Church, from the pope to the lowest cleric, as well as the lay people. *The Three-stranded Cord* [*Provázek třípramený*] deals skillfully with faith, hope, and love. *The Daughter* [*Dcerka*], a beautiful little tract, is addressed to the pious women living in the immediate neighborhood of the Bethlehem Chapel in a semi-conventual manner. Thomas of Štítné's daughter was among them. If Hus' attitude to women has often seemed to verge on Bernardian sharp critique,

[3] *Historia et monumenta Joannis Hus atque Hieronymi Pragensis, confessorum Christi*, 2 vols. (Norimberg, 1715), II, pp. 131-511. This, however, actually comprises Hus' lectures on these Scriptural books. The translation itself was made in 1406 and thereafter. Cf. particularly F. M. Bartoš, "Husitsví a česká bible," *Křestanký Revue* (Praha, 1954), pp. 79-85.

[4] All these Czech works are to be found in K. J. Erben, ed., *Mistra Jana Husi Sebrané spisy české*, 3 vols. (Praha, 1865). Also in F. Žilka, ed., *Vybrané spisy Mistra Jana Husi*, 2 vols. (Jilemnice, n.d.), II, pp. 1-529.

[5] V. Novotný, *M. Jana Husi O svatokupectví* (Praha, 1907). My translation of the text with minor deletions is found in *Advocates of Reform* (Library of Christian Classics, XIV, Philadelphia, Pa., The Westminster Press, 1953), pp. 196-278.

this little book should suffice to correct all misapprehension of his position. It shows him at his best in dealing with genuine and fervent piety inspired and guided by him in a group of devoted women. *The Mirror of a Sinful Man* [*Zrcadlo člověka hříšného*] aims at self-knowledge. *The Kernel of Christian Doctrine* [*Jádro učení křesťanského*] is a catechetical handbook. The *Nine Golden Theses* [*Devět kusův zlatých*] and *The Six Errors* [*O šesti bludich*] are antithetical tracts, one dealing with particularly notable virtues and religious doctrines and the other with six heinous errors. The Wyclifite influence on the composition of *Simony* and the three *Expositions* is considerable. In the former, Hus obviously made use of Wyclif's *De simonia*; in the latter, his dependence on Wyclif's works is clearly discernible. Nevertheless, as was Hus' usual practice, he avoided all abstruse speculation and doctrinal deviation. The stamp of Hus' own personality and independent thinking are indelibly imprinted on all his works. De Vooght says of the *Expositions* that they are to Hus what the *Cid* is to Corneille.[6]

The definition of the Church as the totality of the predestinate having Christ alone as the head is repeated frequently in these Czech writings. Since it differs in no way from the previously discussed formulations, it would be redundant to repeat it. Hus writes in the *Exposition of the Faith* that we should not believe that the Church is a building made of stones or of beautifully carved wood, or is the pope with his cardinals, or all the clergy, or every congregation of the faithful, or the totality of them all, but that "the holy catholic Church is the congregation of all the elect which is called Christ's spouse. . . ."[7] It seems obvious that Hus here has in mind such definitions as Páleč piled up in his *De aequivocatione*

---

[6] De Vooght, *L'hérésie*, p. 234.

[7] "Výklad víry," in Žilka, *Vybrané spisy* (see n. 4), II, pp. 38-41.

*nominis ecclesia.* In this Church catholic there is only "one Lord, one faith, one baptism . . . one kingdom, one law, one membership, one food which is Christ's body, and one drink which is His blood, one raiment, love, one Father, one mother [the Church] whom we should know by faith and embrace by love and whom we should obey, rightly believing about her but not in her."[8] For we should believe only in God, as has been said before, and the Church is not God.

The basis of membership, the ultimate ground of man's salvation, is divine predestination. No one without revelation knows whether he was chosen by God in eternity or whether he will persevere to the end. In this regard the pope is no better informed than the least peasant.[9] Moreover, the number of the predestinate is small, for Christ testified that "many are called, few indeed are chosen."[10] Accordingly, the Church militant consists of both the predestinate and the foreknown. Hus sometimes speaks somewhat misleadingly of this mixed membership as constituting "two churches." He writes that "all people are divided into two groups: the sons of God and the sons of the devil." Thus every man from the beginning of the human race belongs to one of these groups. He is God's by having been elected to salvation and now in time existing in grace; he is the devil's by reason of mortal sin and especially by his final non-repentance.[11] And yet, Hus insists, God does not foreordain anyone to damnation but only foreknows what each man is going to do with the offer of grace. He goes so far as to say that God has called all, both the predestinate and the foreknown, but not all have accepted the call "because they did not want to." He writes further:

[8] *Ibid.*, p. 41; reminiscent of Eph. 4:6.

[9] J. B. Jeschke, ed., *Mistr Jan Hus, Postilla* (Praha, Komenského ev. fakulta bohoslovecká, 1952), p. 174.

[10] Matt. 22:14.   [11] *Postilla* (see n. 9), p. 137.

. . . and because every sin depends on freedom, it is evident that if the reprobate wished to turn to the Lord God in real penitence, God would accept him into grace; but because he does not want to do so, because consummate pride of the reprobate is his greatest passion, there is nothing outside or inside him to incite or move him to genuine repentance.[12]

It follows that a man does not sin mortally, who does not consent to sin. . . . Accordingly, Czechs have a proverb, "One's will is both the paradise and hell."[13]

God wills that all men be saved, "but we do not act according to his will when we do not keep his commandments; . . . for it is God's will that we never transgress his commandments. And his commandment is that we never sin but keep ourselves entirely free from sin."[14] An awesome requirement, indeed!

The separation of the sheep from the goats, the saved from the damned, will take place only at the Day of Judgment. It is only then that there will be "one sheepfold" consisting only of the predestinate. Until then, their number is not complete.

Passing on now to the subject of the pope and the cardinals, let us note that Hus does not reject the office entirely and demand its abolition, as Wyclif did. In fact, if the pope, bishop, and priest serve the Church well and devotedly, as spiritual fathers, they are to be honored above the natural fathers. This is true also of the mother-Church, the congregation of all saints, which is to be honored above the natural mother.[15] But those who neither care for the Church nor minister in the Word of God or the sacraments, thus wrongly occupying the Apostolic See, wrongly call themselves fathers. For

---

[12] "Výklad modlitby," in Žilka, *Vybrané spisy*, II, p. 411.
[13] "Výklad desatera," in Žilka, *Vybrané spisy*, II, pp. 265-266.
[14] *Výklad modlitby* (see n. 12), p. 454.
[15] *Výklad desatera* (see n. 13), p. 211.

"similarly those who do not live saintly lives wrongly call themselves saints."[16] This is Hus' ever-iterated demand that all ecclesiastics should live lives of exemplary virtue, exceeding in this regard the lay people. The ethical standard is his criterion of the rightness of their possession of the office. His favorite simile is that of "entering the sheep-fold by the lowly gate of Jesus Christ." Any cleric or prelate who lives in pride, luxury, or immorality, whether or not he was rightly elected or appointed to his office, is not a shepherd but a thief and a robber. He has not entered through Christ.

The pope is not the head of the Church universal but at best of the particular church under his jurisdiction. If the pope were of the foreknown and we, his members, were obliged to obey all his commands, we would have to follow him to hell.[17] In the early Church, bishop and presbyter did not differ from each other except that the former ordained the priests.[18] Hus asserts the same concerning the pope: "he is no more than a priest, even the least priest, except that he is richer, that people look up to him more, he is more esteemed by the world, and exercises greater rule with the power he has."[19] If the bishop or other prelate does not personally do the work of his office but relegates it to a vicar, the vicar, not he, receives the reward: "Therefore you should know that even if you appointed in your prelatical office a thousand vicars and you yourself would not work, they all would receive the reward and you would remain forever unrewarded. Thus the assertion of the canonists that another man's work can be substituted for one's own is invalid."[20] Moreover, Hus denounces the pre-

<hr>

[16] *Ibid.*, p. 193.

[17] V. Flajšhans, ed., *Mag. Io. Hus, Sermones in Bethlehem, 1410-11,* 5 vols. (Praha, Královská česká společnost nauk, 1938-42), I, p. 88.

[18] *Ibid.*, II, p. 53.      [19] *Výklad desatera*, p. 371.

[20] *Sermones in Bethlehem* (see n. 17), II, p. 238.

occupation of popes, cardinals, and prelates with material affairs, particularly the selling of benefices. The archbishops and bishops do likewise. He declares that the endowments willed to churches as well as offerings are alms given by their donors for the salvation of their souls. They are not the Church's property in an absolute sense but a trust set up for pious purposes or for the poor. Hus continues his complaint: "The canons care for themselves; the altar-priests who do not preach, having finished the masses, usually sleep, play, or stay in a tavern; and the rich monks, locking themselves in, feast well or, if they are mendicants, roam around in order to beg as much as possible from the people."[21] In a direct apostrophe to the three popes, in language unusually harsh, he excoriates them for causing the schism:

> Well, you apostolic vicars! see whether you have the Holy Spirit, which is the spirit of unity, peace, and grace. For then you would live as the apostles did. However, because you quarrel about dignity on account of possessions, murder people and cause contention in Christendom, you show by your deeds that you possess an evil spirit, the spirit of discord and avarice which has been a killer or murderer from the beginning.[22]

Hus denounces particularly vigorously papal adulation and flattery on the part of avaricious sycophants begging for benefices. He says of them that they regard the pope "as an earthly god"[23] and "crawl to the papal court praying and bowing before him more than before the Lord God."[24] Preaching on Jesus' humble entry into Jerusalem, he writes:

> I know not how well the pope or bishop could read . . . [the story], although perhaps he could. For many

21 *Postilla*, p. 83.  22 *Ibid.*, p. 236.
23 *Ibid.*, p. 21.  24 *Ibid.*, p. 30.

have been popes, archbishops, cardinals, bishops, canons and priests who could not read books. How could he read it, since it all contradicts him? Christ on a little ass, he on a large white horse or *hengst* [war horse], which is accoutred with gold-studded bridle, the breast strap and the stirrups covered with precious stones, the colored hat tassels reaching to the ground, and the coverings of the horse dragging on the ground. They drive before him a she-ass or a mule carrying God's body, while she is cropping the grass along the road. They pay no attention to her or the Christ's body, but kneel before the pope, calling him the most holy, while he rides under a baldachin. They push themselves forward begging for benefices, and kiss his feet, if the guards permit it. For they beat back with silver cudgels the poor from his feet. The pope, sitting on that war horse and laughing at it, enjoys such high praise. And our dear, silent and humble Savior rides with great weeping on a little ass![25]

Hus certainly did not lack the power of description or of apt vocabulary! He denounces with equal vigor the pomp and ostentation of the cardinals who accompany the pope, although they do not rate the baldachin and the golden slippers. Nevertheless, they do not go afoot as the apostles did when they accompanied Jesus on his entry into Jerusalem. He remarks that they and all the people regard this adulation of the pope as right and proper and adds ruefully: "As I also had regarded it as right before I knew Scripture and the life of my Savior well. But now He has granted me to know that this is a veritable blasphemy of Christ and repudiation of His Word and the following of Him; as such it is truly antichristian."[26]

Commenting on Christ's saying that "whoever trans-

[25] *Ibid.*, pp. 146-147.          [26] *Ibid.*, p. 147.

gresses the least of the commandments and teaches men so shall be called the least in the kingdom of heaven,"[27] Hus applies it to the "great" in the Church:

> Whoever considers this saying of the Savior, discerns who are the great in Christ's holy congregation. He finds that those who are called the highest and the most reverend, as are the popes, bishops, cardinals, and other such great ones, are called the least in Christ's congregation. For they command much but they themselves do not fulfill the Lord's commandments. . . ."[28]

Hus teaches, as Dante did in his *De Monarchia*, that the Church possesses "two swords"; but the material sword is wielded by the magistrates and nobility for the protection of the Christian faith and truth. Only the spiritual sword belongs to the clergy. As the nobles should not interfere in the spiritual ministration of the Church, so likewise the clergy should refrain from using the material sword. If the nobles wished to administer the mass, to baptize, preach, and grant absolution, priests would instantly raise the cry of heresy. The kings and princes should likewise tell the bishops and priests "not to interfere in their office."[29] Hus bases himself on the well-known passage in Paul's letter to the Romans 13:1-4. He denounces the fighting bishops and popes as misusing the spiritual power they possess.

> Go to the Rhine and there you will find bishops accoutred in breast-plate, coat of mail, swords, spears, shields and hauberks. They guard themselves well with iron so that they will not be wounded in hands, side or feet, as Christ was. Christ on a high cross, they on a great war-horse; Christ with a crown of thorns on his head, they with a crown covered with precious stones

[27] Matt. 5:19.    [28] *Výklad modlitby*, p. 401.
[29] *Výklad desatera*, p. 250.

and pearls; Christ let his side be pierced by a spear for our sake; they want to kill their fellow-men for the sake of the refuse of this world.[30]

This applies equally to priests who do not preach peace but counsel war. Such conduct makes them unworthy of priesthood. "If they say that they fight in defense of the faith, surely they have no such example in Scripture or in Christ's life!"[31]

Hus concludes that it is right to preach against wicked prelates and priests whose lives scandalize the people. One should, however, "speak the truth with love" with a view to bringing about the man's correction, not condemnation. It is equally right to praise the priests when they strive to follow Christ and thus to encourage them in well-doing. On the other hand, he stresses the duty of the prelates to correct the sins and misdeeds of their inferiors in a kindly personal interview, in order to promote their improvement rather than to dishonor and rob them.

Hus was understandably reproved for non-obedience of ecclesiastical superiors. In the *Sermones in Bethlehem* he writes that someone may well object to him that he disdains to obey the prelates and even his own archbishop. He replies that he wishes to play the rôle of Balaam's ass which refused to go forward when she saw her way barred by an angel with a sword, although Balaam perceived nothing.[32] Hus says that "because the Balaam-prelates sit on me and want to drive me against the Lord's command that I preach not, I will squeeze the feet of their desires and will not obey. Nevertheless, in all things lawful and honorable I am willing to submit to all for God's sake. . . ."[33]

Hus further distinguishes between good and bad obe-

30 *Ibid.*, pp. 220, 243-244.
31 *Ibid.*, p. 344.    32 Num. 22:20-35.
33 *Sermones in Bethlehem*, ii, p. 102.

dience. All rational creatures, angels included, ought to obey God. But we should not obey anyone in anything evil, be it even the least thing. When prelates or secular rulers command anything in accordance with Christ's teaching, we ought to obey. But many teach that we must obey our superiors in all things whatsoever, whether they be good or bad. This he absolutely repudiates, as he did when forbidden to preach. No priest who is capable of preaching and who desires to serve the people should obey when prohibited to preach, even when the mandate is issued by the pope. It is more meet to obey God than men. "Thus it is right sometimes not to obey the prelates or our elders."[34]

Hus further distinguishes among spiritual, secular, and ecclesiastical obedience. Only the first of these, being obedience of God's law, requires our absolute submission. The other two—obedience to secular laws and ecclesiastical regulations—are conditional, depending on their conformity to the law of God in Scripture.[35] In this connection we may include Hus' view of excommunication. He does not repudiate it as wrong in principle but discriminates between just and unjust excommunication. It is just, when God and Church authorities exclude someone for sinning mortally and openly. Even in such a case, however, he must first be warned and admonished three times, according to Christ's instruction to the disciples.[36] Only when he stubbornly refuses to abandon his sin is he to be declared cut off from the Church and its ministrations and from the Christian community as long as he remains obdurate. Excommunication, therefore, should be imposed only for mortal sin by means of which the man cuts himself off from God and the Church. The current custom of declaring the

[34] "O šesti bludiech," in B. Ryba, *Betlemské texty* (Praha, Orbis, 1951), p. 79.
[35] *Výklad desatera*, p. 130.     [36] Matt. 18:15-17.

man excommunicated by extinguishing candles, ringing bells, throwing stones in the direction of the man's dwelling, turning the image of Christ's death to the wall, goes beyond the Scriptural instruction to which it should be limited. Moreover, excommunication should be remedial in intention, not punitive. An unjust excommunication does not harm the one upon whom it is imposed, although the prelates and priests teach that every excommunication is valid. Hus declares this "a gross lie."[37] He cites the authority of Augustine, Jerome, Chrysostom, and Gregory in support of his position. Since he himself was under aggravated excommunication, this subject was no mere academic tenet for him, but a matter, as it ultimately proved, of life and death importance.

Hus also has a word of warning to the university masters who neglect their spiritual condition for intellectual concerns. He speaks of them that they strive day and night to acquire mastery of their specialized branches of knowledge but pass over the study of eternal truths. They devote themselves to the study of the stars and to prognostication of the future from their courses, while they ignore their own eternal destiny. "This happens when a cleric is more enticed by the teaching of Aristotle and the Physicists, by laws and statutes, than by the teaching of Jesus Christ. . . ."[38]

In dealing with priests Hus first of all speaks of their ordination. He objects to the custom of the bishops of breathing on the ordinand while pronouncing the words: "Receive the Holy Spirit." He cites against it St. Augustine's oft-repeated assertion that no one can grant the Holy Spirit but God. The bishop can place his hands on the ordinand's head and pray that God will grant him

[37] *O šesti bludiech* (see n. 34), pp. 83-86; *Postilla*, pp. 225-230; *Výklad desatera*, pp. 348-349.
[38] *Sermones in Bethlehem*, II, pp. 158-159.

His Holy Spirit; but he has no power himself to bestow it. Moreover, both the bishop and the ordinand may be in mortal sin, which condition excludes the presence of the Holy Spirit.[39] Nevertheless, the ordination even by a wicked and unworthy bishop is valid, provided the ordinand himself is in the state of grace. If the latter receives it with the right and pious intention, he receives the Holy Spirit not from the bishop, but from Christ.[40]

Hus has a high regard for a good priest. He is a servant of Christ and occupies the highest office on earth after Christ, the apostles, and the Virgin Mary. "In his spiritual office he is, therefore, of greater dignity than the secular king. The king, however, being anointed equally as the priest, is of greater dignity in the secular rule than the priest. Therefore the king should obey the priest's counsels in matters spiritual, while the priest should obey whatever lawful commands the king issues in matters secular. But any old granny observing all God's commandments not from official duty but from the sanctity of her life possesses greater dignity before God than any who do so from a sense of duty."[41] He recommends, to the good priest, Paul's exhortation to wear the "whole armor of God,"[42] with which he should be equipped. He declares that in accepting the priestly office the priest voluntarily takes on himself the obligation to perform all that belongs to that office. Its duties consist of preaching, celebrating the mass and dispensing the other sacraments, chastity, and voluntary poverty.[43] Hus wryly remarks that in caring for the sacramental utensils, the priests attend to it more assiduously than to all the duties enumerated above. He likens a good priest somewhat inelegantly to an ox[44] who plows the human hearts

---

[39] *Postilla*, p. 179.　　　　[40] *Ibid.*, p. 180.
[41] *Sermones in Bethlehem*, IV, p. 334.
[42] Eph. 6:10-18.
[43] *Výklad desatera*, p. 371.　　　[44] Isaiah 1:3.

in order to uproot all sin; the farmer then sows the seed of the Word of God into them and plucks out all the weeds. This latter signifies the separating of truth from human inventions.[45] "God ordered us priests to preach and to witness. In that indeed consists the mandate of the preachers, excluding no one. For they have no different commands from the common people, except to preach the Word of God."[46] The true preacher must be firm in preaching the truth of Christ without fear of the threats of Antichrist. For he must render account at the judgment seat of God of the care of all souls committed to him.

But if Hus is generous in his praise of the good priest, he is severe in his condemnation of the bad. He exclaims: "Behold, the world is full of priests, but hardly a worker can be found for God's harvest! We accept the priestly office, but do not fulfill its duty, namely, preaching."[47] He complains bitterly: "We, today's shepherds, do not know our sheep, except those which have wool more abundantly. The sheep which bring more wool and offering we regard higher and know them better; those, however, which bring less, we know less."[48] He denounces priests for having entered upon their office not to follow Christ and to feed his sheep, but "that they might feed themselves and fill their purses and bags with money of the poor, like Judas Iscariot."[49] He declares that he has learned by his own personal daily observation that no other group of men is so avid for entertainment and amusement than the clerics. Moreover, most of these frivolities are provided for them. He denounces their wasting time in playing chess and in attending jostling shows, theatricals, hunting with falcons and dogs, and breeding horses. Their luxury and

---

[45] *Sermones in Bethlehem*, IV, p. 226.
[46] *Ibid.*, IV, p. 160.      [47] *Ibid.*, V, p. 133.
[48] *Ibid.*, IV, pp. 168-169.      [49] *Ibid.*, II, p. 157.

gluttony are notorious and are contrary to Christ's law; for having enough to eat and to wear should suffice them. They should share the rest of their resources with the poor, to whom they belong by right.[50] Whatever they spend beyond their necessities is a theft. He denounces the beneficed priests for hiring miserably paid substitutes to do their work while they themselves live in idleness and unbridled luxury. He asserts that the substitute will receive God's reward, not they. There existed at the time such an overabundance of clerics that a great number of them could not be beneficed, particularly when the richer and more influential clerics and prelates were pluralists, holding several benefices.

Among the sins of the clergy Hus never fails to include immorality, especially adultery. He writes that if Paul were to send an epistle to the Praguers and to all the Czechs, he would surely censure them, particularly the clergy, for adultery. Paraphrasing Christ's lament over Jerusalem, Hus exclaims poignantly: "O Prague, Prague . . . which killest thy prophets . . . Milíč, Conrad, and Matthew, and stonest them!"[51] He accuses priests of readiness to denounce anyone who opposes their avarice and adultery. They seize and jail him, "shouting that according to their rules he should die and not by a light death, but by burning!"[52]

[He who preaches] that priests are gods, God's creators, and that they have the power both to save or condemn whomever they want; that no one can be saved without them; that no one ought to punish them; and that they should eat, drink, and wear nothing but the best—he who preaches thus is a reverend preacher and should preach; but whoever preaches that priests should not commit adultery, rob people by avarice and simony, leave other men's wives alone, and be

[50] *Ibid.*, II, pp. 158-159; also *Postilla*, pp. 224, 246-247.
[51] *Ibid.*, II, p. 147.      [52] *Postilla*, p. 223.

content with one benefice . . . him they immediately
dub a slanderer of the holy priesthood, a destroyer
of the holy Church, and a heretic who should not be
allowed to preach. They drive him [to court] and
condemn him. And when that devil's net does not
suffice, they stop the services.[53]

He preached in the same vein in one of his previous
sermons that some pompous priests say to their parishioners: "You rascals, we can send you to hell or give
you the Holy Spirit!"[54] He also opposes those who
affirm that an excommunicated priest cannot transubstantiate the bread and wine at the mass. He declares
that "even the worst priest consecrates and transubstan-
tiates the body of Christ as well as the best," although
he does it to his own damnation.[55] Preaching on Matt.
18:6, dealing with Christ's saying that it would be
better for him who would offend one of the little ones
if he were thrown into the depths of the sea, Hus exclaims:

O, thou dear Christ! If every one who offends others
by evil example were thus to be drowned, there would
remain but few priests and lawyers, beginning from
the pope down to the least of them who are not guilty
of avarice, pride, and adultery! And what would we
do with the priests and monks living with concubines,
since we have no sea?[56]

[53] *Ibid.*, p. 197. In the reply written by Hus to the people of
Plzeň he explicitly states that he received a letter from some citizen
of the town who had heard a priest preach at another's ordination
that the ordinand is now "the father of God and creator of God's
body." Hus declares in his answer that such a priest sows heresy.
"Let him take all his fellow-priests and create a single louse; then
shall I admit that he is creator." V. Novotný, ed., *M. Jana Husi
Korespondence a dokumenty* (Praha, 1920), pp. 106, 108.
[54] *Sermones in Bethlehem*, IV, p. 171.
[55] *Ibid.*, IV, p. 223; also *Výklad desatera*, p. 181.
[56] *Postilla*, p. 312.

Hus sharply upbraids priests for conducting the worship services in such an irreverent and careless manner that the worshippers cannot understand what is going on. In antiphonal singing or reading they recite their parts without waiting for each other to finish. "What good does it do when we howl like puppies in a sack, not understanding what we howl?"[57] He sharply berates the customary mummery when pupils elect one of their number a mock bishop, seat him on an ass backward, and lead him into a church. They place a plate of soup and a jug of wine before him which he gulps down. Then he swings incense before the altar, lifts his leg in an indecent gesture, and cries "Boo!" while the pupils dance before the altar. People laugh and regard this blasphemy as all quite innocent and proper fun! Hus deplores the fact that he himself had taken part in such sacrilege when he was young.[58] He confesses that as a youth he used to sing the vigils with other poor pupils just so they would get it done as quickly as possible: "for others took the money while they used us to do the work."

Hus criticizes the priests for diverting the common people from worship and prayer by excessive and elaborate ceremonialism of the services and the splendor of the churches.

> [They gape] at the pictures, the vestments, chalices and other marvelous furnishings of the churches. Their ears are filled with the sound of bells, organs, and small bells, by frivolous singing which incites to dance rather than to piety. The minds of the people are filled with observing how irreverently the priests pray, walking, talking and laughing in the church. They are clad in sumptuous robes, hoods, caps with pearl knots, silk tassels, as well as capes variously ornamented;

[57] *Výklad modlitby*, p. 417.     [58] *Ibid.*, pp. 419-420.

they carry crosiers, staffs and silver crosses, ampullas and gilded sprinklers. Thus a simple man wastes his whole time in church and returning home, talks about it the whole day while he says not a word about God.[59]

Finally Hus condemns the priests who abandon their sacred office for some secular employment. This is particularly the burden of a small treatise written in reply to a certain priest-cook in a lord's employ. The latter severely criticized Hus for not obeying the papal citation to appear in Rome after he had been excommunicated. The cook called him "worse than any devil."[60] Hus replies to the heresy charge by citing Augustine's definition already familiar to us that he alone is a heretic "who obstinately holds an error contrary to Scripture." He declares that he holds no such error. He then turns upon his would-be critic and denounces him for having abandoned his priestly duties for secular employment. He includes in this charge many high-placed prelates as he exclaims:

Behold, the sub-camera judge [*purkrabí*] is priest, there is priest at the land-office, priest is judge, priest rules commerce, priest is a cook, a scribe; and if the catchpole's job paid well enough and were not despised and laborious, priest would be even catchpole. Alas! even the pope receives a gulden a month from prostitutes, of whom there are many in his city.[61]

Although Hus has rarely failed to include simony among the chief clerical sins, yet because he devoted an extensive treatise[62] to this cancerous malady with which

---

[59] *Výklad desatera*, p. 110.

[60] "Knížky proti knězi kuchmistrovi," in Erben, ed., *Sebrané spisy* (see n. 4), III, p. 241.

[61] *Ibid.*, p. 246.

[62] Novotný, *O svatokupectví*. My translation, in *Advocates of*

the Church of his time was fatally infected, it deserves to be treated separately. The work is based, among other authorities, on Wyclif's *De simonia*. Sedlák estimates that Hus excerpted about one-ninth from the treatise of the Oxford reformer.[63] But where Wyclif's book is couched in technical language, Hus uses pungent plain language most effective for popular exposition. Moreover Wyclif restricts his argument largely to the papal, episcopal, and monastic simoniacal practices, while Hus includes the parish clergy, academic circles, secular nobles, and laymen.

Hus begins his work by restating again Augustine's definition of heresy[64] given above. He deduces from it that whoever stubbornly persists in an opinion or deed contrary to Scripture, commits a mortal sin and as such is a heretic. He distinguishes three kinds of heresy: apostasy, blasphemy, and simony. Priests who declare that they are creators of God or that they can save or damn whomever they please are guilty of blasphemy. To declare that the pope is an earthly god who can do as he pleases, is blasphemy. Christ was put to death on a pretended charge of blasphemy. As for simony, Hus defines it as "trafficking in holy things."[65] It comprises both buying and selling them. This was a generally shared opinion among the most eminent theologians, so that Hus was in most respectable company in expressing the tenet.[66] Hus applies it to popes, bishops, and priests as well as to lay members of the Church.

He then explains the origin of the term "simoniac"

---

*Reform* (see n. 5), pp. 196-278. Cf. also Paul de Vooght, *Hussiana* (Louvain, Publications universitaires de Louvain, 1960), pp. 379ff.

[63] J. Sedlák, *Studie a texty k náboženským dějinám českým*, 2 vols. (Olomouc, 1913-19), I, p. 179.

[64] Augustine, "De utilitate credendi," in J.-P. Migne, *Patrologia latina*, 221 vols. (Paris, Garnier Fratres), XLII, pp. 64ff.

[65] *On Simony* (see n. 5), p. 201.

[66] De Vooght, *Hussiana* (see n. 62), pp. 379-399.

by tracing it to Simon who offered money to the apostles for the power of conferring the Holy Spirit by the laying on of hands.[67] He also includes in it Gehazi who took money from Naaman for the cure of leprosy.[68] Consequently, all who receive payment for ministerial acts are sinning Gehazi's sin. The simoniacs are those who buy or sell the gifts of God.[69]

In respect of the pope, he refutes those who say that the pope cannot be a simoniac "since he is the lord of all the world who by right takes whatever he wishes and does as he pleases."[70] Hus curtly rejects this position on the ground that God alone is such a Lord. Nor will he acquiesce in the plea that the pope is "the most holy father." He repudiates it by the ever-iterated statement that the pope would be such only if he lived the most holy life. He makes short shrift of the argument that the pope is most holy on account of his office. Position does not make a man holy: hence, the pope may be a simoniac. He commits simony, first of all, if he desires the papal office on account of worldly possessions and preeminence of rule. "There is no estate in Christendom more liable to fall. . . . Therefore, everyone who runs after and strives for that dignity on account of material gain or worldly eminence is guilty of simony."[71] The pope is likewise guilty of simony when he appoints unworthy men to ecclesiastical offices for profit. "For is it not against God's order when he commands that his cooks, doormen, grooms, and couriers be accorded the first claim upon benefices of great dignity in lands the language of which they do not know?"[72] Or that the money for the appointment be first paid? The appointment of bishops and priests for money is an obvious instance of simony, as the sale of the archbishopric of Prague proves.

[67] Acts 8:18.
[68] II Kings 5:20-23.
[69] On Simony, pp. 205-209.
[70] Ibid., p. 211.
[71] Ibid., p. 213.
[72] Ibid.

Since the pope commonly does not even know the people he appoints, how can he know whether they are worthy of the dignity? Nor can the pope retain the income of a vacant bishopric or benefice as long as he pleases, for it does not belong to him. Moreover, if it be objected that the pope appoints only worthy men and without a financial agreement, it is plainly contrary to facts; ". . . it is known even to simpletons that many bishops are unworthy and are not fit even to herd swine properly! Moreover, who has ever been granted a bishopric without an agreement that he first pay for the pallium?"[73] Hus then cites the actual circumstances by which the Prague archbishopric was secured. He also points out that it was the "miserly" Pope John XXII who first decreed that he must be paid annates from all benefices. The pronouncement of the canon law jurists that "whatever the pope decrees no one should contradict" would be admissible if he never decreed anything wrong. But can such a miracle be expected from any man, the pope included? Moreover, the statement is contradicted by what the same jurists teach in their own schools. Hus cites again the prohibition of preaching in chapels and asks, "what faithful man would approve it as good?" Finally, he asserts that papal power "is limited by God's law, the law of nature, and the pronouncements of saints which are grounded in God's Word."[74] The pope must do nothing contrary to Scripture, which bids him to confer the spiritual gifts freely. Reason also asserts that he should do nothing unworthy in itself. The saints likewise confirm what Scripture teaches.

---

[73] *Ibid.*, p. 217. Hus cites as examples the sale of the Prague archbishopric to Nicholas Puchník (1402) who not only promised to pay 3,300 gulden for his own appointment but also the arrears of his two predecessors amounting to 1,480 gulden. When he died before he was confirmed, his whole "debt" was passed on to Zbyněk Zajíc of Hasenburg, who promised to pay the arrears as well as his own payment of 2,800 gulden. He paid only the latter.

[74] *Ibid.*, p. 218.

The next section deals with the episcopal simony. A bishop may be guilty not only of selling but of buying holy things. Just as the pope, he may commit simony upon entering his office, if he does so not for God's glory but for his personal gain, power, and dignity. He may, of course, enter it worthily. "But the Prague bridge is more likely to fall down than that a candidate for the Prague bishopric should secure it by such a holy course!"[75] Having entered upon his duties, a bishop may be a simoniac by neglecting his duties, by squandering the revenue on himself, or by bestowing it on his friends. Hus cites the rule of Nicaea that simoniacs should be damned eternally. In the third place a bishop may become a simoniac by accepting money for the consecration of churches, altars, or for ordaining clerics, particularly if he makes demand for a payment prior to the act. He cites prohibitions of this practice by Pope Gregory and by the canon law, but ruefully admits that "that holy provision has died out among the bishops." He quotes the rates stipulated by bishops for their various functions. To the excuse that these charges are made for the physical labor, not for consecration, Hus retorts that these functions are part of the episcopal office. The bishop has the usufruct of the land for his support in order that he exercise his spiritual functions free of charge. Nor does it excuse him if he does not receive the payment personally, but through an official. Further, he should not confer ordination by reason of favoritism but only to such as are worthy of it.

In connection with the ordinations, it is not only the bishop but also his numerous clerks who profit. They charge varying amounts for the certificate without which no ordination can be performed. To the objection that the notary cannot work for nothing, Hus replies that his salary should be provided by the bishop whom he serves.

[75] *Ibid.*, p. 222.

The titular bishops, who sometimes complain that their charges for ordination are their only source of income, should likewise be cared for by the diocesan bishops, since they are his substitutes. Moreover, all bishops should live frugally, distributing the surplus of their income to the poor.

Hus then undertakes to deal with monks. They too may become simoniacs by the way they enter the Order. If it is done for money or some other benefit, then both he who receives the candidate and the candidate who is received commit simony. If they enter in order to secure higher dignities, or on account of a comfortable livelihood, or a life of ease, they are simoniacs. Those already in the monasteries may commit simony by offering money to the pope or nobles for the enlargement of their holdings or privileges, or for mitres and croziers for their abbots. They pretend poverty, while in reality they have so much property that it would come between twenty or thirty *kopy* of revenue per monk![76] Moreover, they are guilty of squandering their revenue. Their gluttony in eating and drinking is notorious. "Kings, lords, and princes do not always have drink and food so wholesome and certain as they. The cellars of the lay people are sometimes exhausted; but theirs never! . . . . Cold does not bite them, for they have boots and greatcoats; heat does not scorch them, for they have cool cells and cloisters, that is, courts of paradise. Therefore

> Whoever wishes to live well
> Let him enter the monk's cell.[77]

As for the vow of poverty, the monks keep it "about as well as a prostitute does chastity." What, then, should a good monk do under these circumstances? Hus replies that he should refuse to participate in simony and

[76] *Ibid.*, pp. 235-236.          [77] *Ibid.*, p. 238.

should oppose it. Should he then be imprisoned for disobedience, he would suffer for truth's sake.

Next come priests. They too commit simony if they purchase their ordination and seek the office for gain. Evil intention constitutes simony. The bishops, of course, charge for the ordination and confirmation. They do wrong. They should examine the ordinand only as to his morals and his fitness for the cure of souls. Once ordained, the priest may commit simony by demanding payment for baptism, confession, funeral, marriage, the thirty masses, purification, consecrated oil, or any other ministerial act. Hus upbraids those who excuse this practice on the ground that it is an old custom. He counters that fornication is an old custom, too. He deplores the squandering of the revenue given for God's sake on priests' relatives, favorites, flatterers, or their own luxury. He cannot find words harsh enough for those priests who lavish the money on their "concubines, priestesses, or prostitutes more sumptuously than on the church altars and pictures, purchasing for them skirts, capes, and fur coats from the tithes and offerings of the poor."[78] Particularly does he denounce the superiors who do nothing to eradicate this evil; above all, he upbraids bishops who even receive an annual tax from priests for keeping a mistress or a cradle tax for having a child. He insists that no one should attend the mass celebrated by such a priest and should withhold the tithes from him. He quotes Paul in saying: "Cast out the old leaven!" "I know not how the holy Church can rid itself of them unless the community follow the order which Christ and St. Paul have established."[79] Priests may further commit simony by exchanging or renting parishes. A priest rents his parish to another and himself lives in idleness. Meanwhile, the renter "diligently

[78] *Ibid.*, p. 251.　　　　[79] *Ibid.*, p. 253.

shears and milks the sheep." All this constitutes priestly simony.

Having dealt with this kind of simony, Hus turns upon the lay people. The chief forms of simony among them are the granting of bishoprics and other benefices by kings and nobles for money, as gifts or service, or for the sake of kinship. "Many a noble grants such an office to incapable relatives who are not fit to keep swine!"[80] Fathers render services to nobles or buy papal bulls to secure an ecclesiastical office for their sons. Hus cites the case of the vacancy in the Prague archbishopric after Zbyněk's death when twenty-four contestants strove with each other to gain the place! He next discusses the duties of the lord possessing an advowson—the right of appointment to a benefice. If he bestows it upon any-one for money or as a gift, for service, favor, or relation-ship, he is guilty of simony. Advowson is not property but spiritual power, which it is not lawful to sell. He concludes the chapter by exhorting the nobles and other laymen who hold endowments in trust to use them for their designated use; otherwise if they alienated them for private profit, they would be thieves. However, he advises the rich to distribute their possessions during their lifetime, instead of leaving them in trust. Scripture commands that men ought to give alms to the poor, for thus alone will they receive reward for their good deeds. Once a man dies, whatever is done with the money he left behind is of no benefit to him. Hus writes: "Who-ever gives one heller for God's sake during his lifetime, honors the Lord God and profits his soul more than if he gave so much gold after his death as could reach between heaven and earth. The reason for it is simple: time is given before death to earn and secure God's

[80] *Ibid.*, p. 255.

grace. After death no one can do or earn anything, nor can he give away his goods."[81]

But one may share the guilt by consenting to another man's simony. This is especially true of superiors, ecclesiastical and lay, who neglect their duty in condoning the practice of simony and keeping silent about it. Furthermore, defense of another man's simony, be he pope, bishop or priest, constitutes guilt on the defender's part.

The treatise concludes with a chapter dealing with the best means of avoiding simony. He first suggests that only good men be elected bishops and priests. That would, of course, necessitate a radical reform of the papal system. Formerly, church leaders were chosen by the people. This right is denied them now, nor is there any chance of their regaining it. Avaricious men buy an appointment from the pope and thus "buy people from the pope as if they were cattle. . . ."[82] In the second place, the right of episcopal election was usurped by the pope from the cathedral canons. Hus has no great expectation that the prelates will reform the system. He trusts the secular princes and lords to forbid "the trafficking and the irregular appointments of unworthy prelates over the people."[83] The king should banish simony by the exercise of his secular powers, since priests are subject to his jurisdiction in matters civil. Thus Hus acknowledged the dependence on the secular rulers just as Luther did a century later. For himself, this was a forlorn hope, since his break with King Wenceslas precluded any really effective help from the royal quarter. There was more chance that the nobles would take a hand in effecting a reform, as it actually turned out to be the case later. Hus thinks that the most effective

[81] "Devět kusův zlatých," in Erben, *Sebrané spisy* (see n. 4), III, p. 147.
[82] *On Simony*, p. 269.      [83] *Ibid.*, p. 272.

remedy lies in the hands of church communities, who could withhold tithes and other revenues from the simoniacs. This radical measure would have produced results, since the clerics were most sensitive in respect of their income. But one wonders how practical such a proposal would have proved in practice. Suppose that a lay member or a whole community would resort to such means of bringing their priest to reform. The indubitable and invariable result would be a swift reprisal by every means at the disposal of the authorities, ecclesiastical and secular. For the law was on their side. One could easily anticipate that were not such a measure accompanied by a successful armed revolt, as for instance that of the Taborites under the leadership of Žižka, the measure proposed by Hus would have collapsed in utter defeat. Yet Hus did not advocate an armed revolt. After making this earnest appeal to lay members, however, Hus seemed to have exhausted the remedial measures he could suggest. That he himself did not have much hope of success of any reform may be judged from his concluding remarks: ". . . I have decided that it is better to suffer death for the truth than to receive material reward for flattery."[84] Martyrdom is admirable when it serves to win a noble cause. Hus' martyrdom ultimately did contribute to such a victory, but only a long time, even centuries, later.

In this treatise Hus pointed to the very root of evil in the contemporary Church. Simony was the all-pervasive malady of the time. Only desperate and heroic efforts could cure the evil. For that reason Hus' radical proposals were justified, even though they were not immediately effective.[85] In urging voluntary poverty for the whole clerical estate, Hus' proposals were less extreme and more moderate than those advocated and practiced

[84] *Ibid.*, p. 278.

[85] V. Kybal, *Jan Hus, Učení*, 2 vols. (Praha, Jan Laichter, 1923-31), II, p. 445.

by Francis of Assisi and his small band of lovers of the Lady Poverty. Hus did not advocate that the clerics call absolutely nothing as their own; he only urged that they be satisfied with the necessities.

We now return to the discussion of the Church in general. After having considered the evils of simony and the efforts to eradicate it, Hus turns to the lay people. He describes a good Christian as one who, first of all, knows his own spiritual condition. In a short treatise, *The Mirror of a Sinful Man*,[86] which is basically a reworking of St. Bernard's *Meditatio de humana conditione* and of *De interiori domo*, Hus deals with the theme of *de contemptu mundi*. In a truly ascetic spirit, for he is expressing Bernard's ideas, he exhorts the sinner to know himself as he is as well as he should be. Then alone will he be able to lift himself to know God. To love God supremely one must renounce the world. The worldly joys consist of possessions, delights, beauty, human favor, honor, praise, power, and dignity. "I warn you that if you will love this world you will perish; but if you will love the Son of God, you will reign with him and his saints forever." In this spirit of rigorous renunciation of the world and the fulfillment of all divine commands man must see his salvation. One really hears the voice of Bernard rather than that of Hus. He was no fanatical ascetic; his piety was fervent but sober. At most, one may regard this Bernardian protest as a warning against excessive worldliness. As such, it may be considered an authentic expression of the reformatory strivings of Hus himself. It is more characteristic of Hus to urge that Christian life consists in a lifelong changing of "unformed" faith, which does not save, into the faith formed by love, which alone is the saving faith. How then is a man to know whether he has ful-

---

[86] "Zrcadlo hříšníka menší," in Erben, *Sebrané spisy* (see n. 4), III, pp. 142-146.

filled the commandments? "I say that when a man firmly resolves in his heart that he would rather die than transgress a commandment of God and perseveres in this resolve, he possesses a great sign that he is fulfilling God's commandments. . . . For he cannot have a greater sign that he loves God except by divine revelation."[87]

Hus teaches that man, having free will, is responsible for his moral acts. Every sin has its origin in man's will, which cannot be forced to choose what he does not want to do. He writes: "Now you understand that God gave every man his soul into his keeping, that is into the power of reason, that he might be directed by his reason, observing the commandments of God. If he perseveres in keeping them till death, then they will preserve him eternally."[88] He cites Bernard (possibly his *Steps of Humility*): "The first degree of freedom of will concerns freedom from external compulsion. . . . The second is freedom from mortal sin, which man has here on earth; the third is freedom from all sin. But that degree has none but the blessed already enjoying the eternal joy; for he alone can be fully free."[89]

This is followed by an exposition of faith. In the first place, Hus places the prevenient grace as the ground of the entire spiritual life. This is the consequence of divine predestination, as we have seen previously. He defines it sometimes in intellectual terms, as when he writes: "What are we to build on? On the foundation of the most holy faith, so that our faith will likewise be holy. To believe, then . . . is to agree with the truth which we do not see. . . ."[90] He refers often to the definition of faith in Hebrews 11:1, "Faith is the assurance of things hoped for, the conviction of things not seen." The apprehension of things unseen by faith is stressed

[87] "Dcerka," in Erben, *Sebrané spisy*, III, p. 128.
[88] *Postilla*, p. 328.      [89] *Výklad modlitby*, p. 493.
[90] *Sermones in Bethlehem*, I, p. 89.

because things visible need not be believed, since they are seen. Faith is twofold: living and dead. The former is "adorned by good works"; the latter is without them. He quotes James in support of the latter: "Faith without works is dead."[91] Christian faith is a living faith because "a just man shall live by faith." As has already been mentioned, to Hus this implies "faith formed by love." The lifelong effort to acquire that degree of faith by virtues of every sort, by keeping God's commandments, ultimately resulting in the supreme love of God, is the only means of attaining the goal. Hus likes to quote Augustine's saying: "In vain does a man own the name of Christian who does not follow Christ the Lord." Most often does Hus refer to the Augustinian distinctions as to believing about God, believing God, and believing in God. The first implies that one believes that God is and will be eternally; the second connotes the faith in Scripture as containing absolute and inerrant truth about God. Only the third is true faith, for it involves supreme love of God and incorporates us in Him by love. We must love Him with all our heart, mind, and might. The first two kinds of faith are shared by all Christians, even those in mortal sin, as well as by the devil. Only the third is the saving faith.[92] He concludes therefrom that with the third kind of faith we should believe in no man or thing but only in God.

Hus further subdivides faith in accordance with its degrees. The first is mixed with doubt; the second is free from all doubt; the third is characterized by utter conviction of its reliability. With the faith of the first degree one believes another man's assertion of a proposition aside from Scriptural proof. With the second degree of faith one believes papal pronouncements not based on Scripture.

[91] James 2:17.
[92] *O šesti bludich* (see n. 34), pp. 67-104.

> With the third degree I believe the holy Scriptures, for they securely show the truth for which every Christian should be ready to offer his life. The third degree is called the catholic faith, for the entire Christian community is bound to hold it on pain of damnation. . . .[93]

Thereupon Hus penned a memorable passage which has been cited numberless times as best expressing the deepest motivation of his own life:

> Therefore, faithful Christian, seek the truth, hear the truth, learn the truth, love the truth, speak the truth, adhere to the truth, defend the truth to death; for truth will make you free from sin, the devil, the death of the soul, and finally from eternal death. . . .[94]

Passing on to the consideration of the sacraments, Hus of course recognizes all seven: baptism, confirmation, marriage, priestly ordination, penance, eucharist, and the extreme unction. Baptism is absolutely essential to salvation. Without it no one can be saved. He recognizes baptism with water, Spirit, and blood. The first-named is the usual form of baptism administered to infants or adults. It cleanses of all sins, both original and acquired. Infants, who possess only the original sin, are cleansed of it on account of their parents' faith. Hus remarks that infancy lasts up to the seventh year during which time the infant "does not sin gravely, because he does not possess reason."[95] Baptism does not, however, necessarily imply that baptized persons are of the elect. For that status it is necessary that they receive the baptism of the Spirit, "which God grants by His gift to His baptized faithful."[96] Men are saved by the baptism of water and the Spirit, not by water alone.[97]

[93] *Výklad víry*, p. 14.     [94] *Ibid.*, p. 15.
[95] *Sermones in Bethlehem*, II, p. 237.
[96] *Ibid.*, IV, p. 36.     [97] *Postilla*, p. 258.

Martyrs are baptized by the baptism of blood, even those who had not been baptized by water. This applies to the saints of the Old and New Testaments who suffered death "for Christ, . . . for instance the holy youth and many others who, having believed the apostles or other saints, immediately and voluntarily went to their death without the baptism of water."[98]

The sacrament of penance consists of contrition, confession, and satisfaction or restitution. Contrition is defined as a heart-felt sorrow for sins committed and a firm resolve to sin no more, but to observe all God's commandments. The present life is the time for repentance, even though the sinner is moved to it on his death-bed. No one who sincerely repents will be rejected. Hus writes in a beautiful little treatise entitled *The Nine Golden Theses*:

> Whoever sheds a single tear for his sins [during his lifetime] honors the Lord God and benefits his soul more than if after his death he were to weep so much that two rivers were to flow from his eyes. That is so because the time and place for repentance, for securing grace and deserving of eternal salvation, is here. For there [after death] is no deserving act, nor wisdom, nor the capacity. . . .[99]

The second part of the sacrament consists of confession of one's sins before God and the priest, if a priest is available. Hus confirms that such auricular confession to a priest is proper and commendable. "Confession should be voluntary, undelayed, open, to a priest, and inclusive of all sins."[100] The priest's function, however, in granting absolution for sins is only declaratory, ministerial, as even Lombard taught. It is God and

[98] *Ibid.*
[99] *Devět kusův zlatých* (see n. 81), p. 149.
[100] *Postilla*, p. 375.

Christ who forgive sins, while the priest merely declares
that if the sinner is truly contrite and resolves to sin
no more, God has forgiven him his sins.[101] Hus reproves
the pope or those priests who claim that they can of
their own authority either forgive or retain sins. He
writes: "Therefore let the pope, bishop, or another priest
declare as he will to a man: 'I forgive you your sins and
free you from both the sins and punishments.' If the
Lord God does not free the man, provided he heartily
repent of his sins, their declaration will not save him!"[102]
Even if the priest declares the sin forgiven, the declaration is of no effect unless the sinner had been genuinely
contrite for them and God had already forgiven them.
He quotes Lombard that God does not follow the
priestly judgment but judges according to truth when
He forgives or retains sins. Hus also severely censures
priests for demanding payment for absolution.[103] He denounces the indulgence bull of Pope John XXIII which
declared forgiveness of all sins and their punishment,
although neither he nor his indulgence sellers knew
who had truly repented of his sins. He further upbraids
some priests for demanding that people come to confession seven times, or three times a year and pay for it.
He sarcastically berates such priests, saying that "what
neither the lord seized by force nor a footpad or thief
stole by night, that the simoniac coaxes out by asking
this much for confession, that for the mass, or sacraments,
or indulgence, or churching, or blessing, funeral, sprink-
ling, or prayers. The last heller that an old granny has
tied in her handkerchief lest a footpad or thief steal it,
the enticer and thief coaxes out of her. . . ."[104] The
priests who excuse or minimize the sins of some
out of favoritism, on the ground that they are insignifi-

101 *Ibid.*, p. 183; *Výklad modlitby*, p. 473.
102 *Postilla*, p. 183.      103 *Ibid.*, pp. 373-374.
104 *Výklad desatera*, p. 304.

cant, saying to them, "It is not a sin to you; or if it is, it is but a minor one; you can make it right by giving alms or by ordering mass; give the priests two *kopas* of pay and they will sing vigils in your behalf forever,"[105] he denounces as unworthy of their office. He further declares that the satisfaction for sins imposed by the priest should consist of prayer, fasting, alms, and other good works. Prayer is particularly effective against pride, fasting against adultery, alms against avarice, and the other good works against other sins. If the restitution imposed by the priest cannot for some reason be fulfilled, it can be changed into some other form. This is, properly speaking, called indulgence. Hus has no objection to its proper use. He remonstrates only against its frequent abuse. The most notorious example of such an abuse is, of course, Pope John's bull of indulgences. He points out that according to that document, the man who bought the indulgence is under no obligation to make satisfaction by prayers, fasts, or alms, or restitution for the evil done to his neighbor. His sin, guilt, and punishment are already forgiven. Any such man, were he to die then, would go directly to heaven![106] He also cites the doctors' argument that the man who gives as much money as would be required for a journey to Rome is forgiven. This is proposed as if it were a great concession on the pope's part that he frees the man from such an arduous and long journey![107]

The third sacrament we need to include in this discussion is the eucharist. Since Hus had been constantly accused of teaching remanence, he had special reason to deal with this subject fully and adequately. First of all, he asserts unequivocally that the bread and wine in the sacrament of the altar are transubstantiated into the body and blood of Christ.[108] Commenting on the pas-

---

[105] *Postilla*, p. 390.
[107] *Ibid.*, pp. 174-175.
[106] *Ibid.*, p. 173.
[108] *Ibid.*, p. 92.

sage in John 6:54-56, he distinguishes three ways of partaking of the sacrament. In the first mode, it is partaken of only spiritually; in the second, only sacramentally; and in the third, both spiritually and sacramentally. The first mode is enjoyed only by those free from mortal sin, for then God resides in them and they in Him. The sacrament thus unites them with Christ. The second is partaken of by men in mortal sin who eat it to their damnation. The third denotes those without mortal sin who eat it to their salvation: "et sic sumunt aliter boni et aliter mali."[109] Hus stresses the tenet that the transubstantiated host is not materially the body of Christ which is broken and eaten. He quotes Augustine as saying that such a notion was the first heresy concerning the eucharist. Even the Jews did not break Jesus' bones on the cross, for it was forbidden to break the bones of the paschal lamb.[110] To quote his very words:

> The true body of Christ and true blood of Christ are truly eaten and drunk, not under the visible aspect of themselves but under the visible aspect of the sacrament. For we do not see with our bodily eyes the body of Christ or his blood, but we see the sacrament, touch, handle, and break it, not the body of Christ. Therefore you must refer all these things, i.e., seeing, breaking, touching, to the sacrament.[111]

He repeats this explanation in the *Postil*, where he reprobates those who wish to see the body and blood of Christ in the wafer and calls it an error. He cites the frauds which had been perpetrated in the bishopric of Litomyšl and elsewhere, where the priests had sprinkled blood on the host and exhibited it as a miracle. Under strict examination they confessed what they had done.[112] Hus does not follow Matthew of Janov in urging

---

[109] *Sermones in Bethlehem*, IV, pp. 192, 195.
[110] *Ibid.*, p. 190.  [111] *Ibid.*  [112] *Postilla*, p. 207.

daily communion. However, he exhorts the faithful to frequent communion as a good practice, without demanding it. Whether a man should communicate several times a year or every month or week depends on the promptings of the Holy Spirit governing the man.[113] In this connection he quotes St. Augustine's familiar saying: "Believe and thou hast eaten!"

Having considered this important element of Hus' faith and practice, we may next turn to his views concerning the saints and the Virgin Mary. He exhorts the faithful to venerate them as examples of pious living, and advises prayers to them for their aid in heaven, although not for temporal benefits. He reprobates prayers such as "St. Nicholas, guard me from drowning!" or "St. Erasmus, protect me from poverty!" Our prayers should be "Not my but Thy will be done!" Moreover, he warns against excessive veneration of saints verging on worship: only God is to be worshipped. He reproves those who buy the relics of saints and importune the pope to canonize saints. He quotes Chrysostom as condemning those who lavish money on honoring the saints while the poor weep for hunger. Concerning the traffic with the bones of saints he, quoting Bernard, cries out: "What a great abomination and perversion it is when the bones of saints are exposed for profit, when those saints who while living had renounced all possession are forced to beg for them when dead!"[114]

As for the Virgin Mary, Hus held her in extraordinary honor. He declares her to be superior to all the apostles, patriarchs, and the angelic choirs. He professes belief in her resurrection and ascension to heaven, where she intercedes for us. After Christ, "she is our foremost helper . . . appointed to be our advocate."[115] Neverthe-

[113] *Výklad modlitby*, pp. 460-461.
[114] *Výklad desatera*, p. 113.
[115] *Výklad modlitby*, pp. 488-489.

less, "whoever regards God dearly above all creation and submits himself to Him completely, he thereby honors God and profits his soul more than if the Mother of God with all the saints prayed for him."[116]

The last item to be considered is Hus' view of Scripture. Enough has already been said about his acceptance of it as the absolute source of all Christian doctrine and his demand that his enemies prove their charges Scripturally. This aspect of the subject need not therefore be repeated. Like Wyclif, Hus earnestly advocated its use in the vernacular for the benefit of the common people. In a letter to the people of Plzeň in 1411, when he had learned that the use of the Bible in Czech and German had been forbidden them by the ecclesiastical authorities, he attacked this ruling. He wrote that everyone has the right to read the Scriptures, if he is able, "either in Latin, as St. Mark wrote it, or in Greek, as St. John wrote his gospel, canonicals, and epistles; or in the Jewish tongue, as St. Matthew wrote his gospel; or in Syriac, as St. Luke wrote his gospel; or in Judean [Aramaic or Hebrew?], as St. Bartholomew did; or in any other language. How is it that you allow the priests to oppose the reading of the law of God by the people in Czech or German?"[117] Hus had an astonishingly competent knowledge of the Bible and could quote much of it from memory, although occasionally he failed to do so absolutely accurately. He was aware of some of the difficulties which modern biblical scholarship has made exceedingly evident. Nevertheless, he declared that he remained firm in the conviction that "every word of Christ is true;

[116] *Devět kusův zlatých*, p. 149.

[117] Novotný, *Korespondence*, p. 107. Bartoš supposes that St. Bartholomew's version was Hindu, not Jewish, and comments that it was Florentius Radewyns who found the statement in Bishop Dorotheus' writings. The bishop had been martyred under Julian the Apostate. Novotný's text, however, asserts that it was "Judean." F. M. Bartoš, *Ze zápasů české reformace* (Praha, Kalich, 1959), pp. 42-43.

if I do not understand some, I commit it to His grace in the hope that I shall understand it after I die."[118] On the whole, however, he insisted that Scripture may be comprehended by reason. He accused the masters and priests of deliberately excluding the common people from understanding it and denouncing those who sought to teach it. They immediately raised the cry: "He is one of them! A Wyclifite! He does not obey the holy Church!"[119] implying, that he does not do as they wish. Such prelates and masters oppose the reading of Scripture and "desire that no ordinary man should know it." He recounted an incident told him by Nicholas Faulfiš who had studied at Oxford and had brought some treatises of Wyclif to Prague. A certain cook with whom Nicholas boarded was called before the bishop, who asked him why he, contrary to the prohibition, had read the Scriptures in English. When the cook defended himself, the bishop indignantly retorted:

> Do you know with whom you are speaking? The cook answered that with a man, a bishop. The bishop then angrily shouted: "How dare you, a miserable layman, quote Scripture to me?" Then the cook: "I know that you are no greater than Christ and hope that I am no worse than the devil. Since the gracious Christ quietly heard the Word from the devil [in the temptation], why would you, being less than Christ, not hear it from me, a man?"[120]

Hus warns the lay people who, because their priests oppose their hearing the Word, and fearing to lose their livelihood, stop listening to it, that they might be eternally condemned for having abandoned the truth on account of a slice of bread. He asserts that he was excommunicated because God had given the bread of the Word through him. He summarizes the benefits accru-

[118] *Postilla*, p. 86.   [119] *Ibid.*, p. 111.   [120] *Ibid.*, p. 112.

ing from hearing the Word of God as sixfold: enlightening the reason, regulating the desires, extinguishing the evil promptings, destroying the obstinacy in evil-doing, eliminating sin, and engendering God's grace.[121] Therefore, it should be freely preached all over the world. It is the first and foremost duty of all bishops and priests, according to Christ's command: "Go ye into all the world and preach the gospel to every creature."[122]

In conclusion it may be said that although the Czech treatises are less polemical, their chief purpose having been the instruction of the common people, they are by no means less expressive of Hus' doctrinal views. In fact, it may be asserted that they constitute a moderating balance to the Latin works. The reader is able to reconstruct Hus' theological stance even more clearly from these writings than from the learned polemics. Not being obliged to deal point by point with his opponents' arguments and accusations, Hus was able to write more systematically. It is a pity that being written in the language of a relatively small nation, they are not easily accessible to the wider circle of scholars. To base one's judgment of Hus' views exclusively on the Latin polemical works is to invite almost certain misunderstanding of them.

[121] *Ibid.*, p. 28.  [122] Mark 16:15.

## CHAPTER X

## HUS' TRIAL AT THE
## COUNCIL OF CONSTANCE

ALTHOUGH Hus was under an aggravated excommunication and interdict, he not only continued to live under the protection of his powerful noble friends at various castles—Kozí Hrádek, Sezimovo Ústí, and finally Krakovec—but to carry on an exceedingly effective preaching and literary activity there. As we have seen, his most important works, such as the *De ecclesia*, and the Czech treatises *On Simony*, the three *Expositions*, and the *Postil*, were written in exile. Such flagrant defiance of the ecclesiastical condemnation, permitted or at least not interfered with by Archbishop Conrad of Prague and Patriarch Wenceslas Králík, administrator of the diocese of Olomouc, could not be condoned by the curia. Incited to action by Michael de Causis, John XXIII turned to Bishop John of Litomyšl, the energetic and ruthless enemy of Hus, to enforce the execution of the interdict. He empowered the doughty bishop to proceed, with force if necessary, against the two above-named highest dignitaries in the land (April 30, 1414). In June the pope ordered King Wenceslas to take effective measures against the Wyclifites. Should he refuse, the pope threatened, he must be prepared to take the consequences. Bartoš interprets this remark as implying that the pope was ready to incite a crusade against Bohemia as he had done against Naples.[1] The king did not seem to take the threat very seriously, and turned the whole matter over to the principal member of the royal Council, Lord Henry Lefl of Lažany. The

[1] F. M. Bartoš, *Čechy v době Husově* (Praha, Jan Laichter, 1947), p. 378.

latter owned the castle of Krakovec, where Hus was soon to find refuge.

In the meantime, Sigismund, king of Hungary and of the Roman Empire, was negotiating with the pope about the calling of a new Council which would at last settle the Schism in some definite manner. The pope was reluctant to do so, preferring "to let sleeping dogs lie." Nevertheless, since the Council of Rome (1412-13) had been provisionally prorogued for three months and the pope depended on the good will of Sigismund, he agreed, on October 31, 1413, to call the new Council for November 1 of the next year to meet at Constance.[2] Thereupon Sigismund entrusted two Czech knights, John of Chlum and Wenceslas of Dubá, who served in his army and were returning home in the Spring of 1414, with a message for Hus. They were to invite him in the king's name and under his safe-conduct to attend the Council in order to clear himself and Bohemia of the persistent charges of heresy. It appears that he believed, or at least thought it possible, that Hus could refute the charges. De Vooght supposes that Sigismund was influenced by the two above-named Czech knights with whom a third, Henry of Lacembok, was associated, to look upon Hus' case in such favorable light.[3] Bartoš does not interpret the situation as being so auspicious. In the first place, he names only John of Chlum as the messenger. Further, in marked dissent from Novotný's description of the event, Bartoš asserts that after consulting with his friends in Prague, Hus at first refused the king's offer as an obvious attempt on Sigismund's

[2] Louise R. Loomis, transl., *The Council of Constance: the Unification of the Church*, edited by John H. Mundy and Kennerly M. Moody (New York, Columbia University Press, 1961), pp. 70-83; the text of the papal and imperial proclamations is cited there.

[3] Paul de Vooght, *L'hérésie de Jean Huss* (Louvain, Publications universitaires de Louvain, 1960), p. 293.

part to seize him by guile.[4] When, however, the pope put pressure on King Wenceslas to exterminate Wyclifism from the land, and the king turned the whole matter over to Lord Henry Lefl, Hus consented to go to the Council.

Likewise the circumstances bearing on this yielding of Hus to pressure are interpreted quite differently by Novotný, Bartoš, and De Vooght. Novotný declares that when the two Czech knights brought Sigismund's message to Hus, "he did not refuse it in principle" but asked for further clarification of the terms of the safe-conduct. Sigismund sent his own courtier, Lord Mikeš Divoký of Jemništé (as Hus himself mentions in his letter of acceptance sent later to Sigismund),[5] whose assurances apparently satisfied Hus. They included a promise that under all circumstances he would be allowed to return to Bohemia. In a letter written from Constance on June 13, 1415, Hus specifically states, "Indeed, he [Sigismund] so informed me by Henry Lefl and others that he wished to procure for me an adequate hearing; and if I did not submit to the judgment, that he would send me back in safety." Nevertheless, in the same letter he remarks that Sigismund's emissary told him before Jerome of Prague: "Master, you may take it for certain that you will be condemned. I suppose that he knew the king's intention."[6] Novotný, therefore, is on solid ground (except for the last sentence) when he declares that he has "no doubt that Hus demanded a safe-conduct and Sigismund promised it, with the view to ensuring him a free journey, stay, *and return even if*

---

[4] Bartoš (see n. 1), p. 378. He cites in support of this interpretation the passage in Hus' treatise, *Knížky proti knězi kuchmistrovi* (K. J. Erben, ed., *Mistra Jana Husi Sebrané spisy české*, 3 vols., Praha, 1865-68, III, p. 253), "that he will await to be seized by the papal emissaries." But this passage refers to Hus' refusal to obey the citation to go to Rome.

[5] Matthew Spinka, *John Hus at the Council of Constance* (New York, Columbia University Press, 1965), Part II, No. 5.

[6] *Ibid.*, No. 14.

*an agreement were not reached*; the form of the safe-conduct issued to him later sufficed for that purpose."[7]

Bartoš agrees that Sigismund indeed promised, through Mikeš Divoký, to grant Hus a safe-conduct guaranteeing his safe journey to and from Constance, but in the end did not keep his promise. He interprets this, however, as a concession to Lord Henry Lefl which went beyond the promise delivered to Hus by John of Chlum, in order to secure King Wenceslas' consent to his coronation as emperor. The two brothers, Wenceslas and Sigismund, had agreed three years before to divide their rule; Sigismund was to reign as king of the Romans on condition that he would not be crowned emperor during Wenceslas' lifetime. Lord Henry Lefl now secured Wenceslas' consent to his brother's coronation in exchange for the latter's promise to secure a settlement of Hus' affair.[8] Nevertheless, in Bartoš' judgment, the legal case of Hus was already definitely lost, and Hus knew it. He went to Constance not in the hope of receiving a favorable verdict, but to present his defense before the tribunal of Christendom. De Vooght, on the other hand, denies altogether that Sigismund did, or intended to, guarantee Hus' return from Constance in case the judgment went against him. He regards the idea as absurd.[9] Hus himself, he writes, expected nothing else in such a case than "to die for Christ."

It is to be regretted that on such an important point, which vitally affects our judgment of the decision of the Council as well as of the character of Sigismund, there should exist a basic disagreement among the outstanding authorities dealing with it. Contrary to Novotný's position, it must be admitted that the safe-conduct actually

[7] V. Novotný, *Jan Hus, Život a dílo*, 2 vols. (Praha, Jan Laichter, 1919-21), II, p. 344; the safe-conduct obviously *did not* suffice for Hus' free return!

[8] Bartoš (see n. 1), pp. 379-381.

[9] De Vooght, *L'hérésie*, p. 292.

issued to Hus did not explicitly specify the guarantee of a free return from Constance. There is no doubt, however, that the two Czech nobles into whose care Hus was entrusted, as well as Hus himself, were convinced that Sigismund's promise did include a guarantee of his safe return. Hus specifically asserted that Sigismund had promised it to him through Henry Lefl and Mikeš Divoký. The university representatives and the numerous nobles, both Czech and Polish, who protested to the Council and the emperor the gross violation of the safe-conduct, also obviously so understood it. But at best it was Sigismund's verbal assurances rather than the text of the safe-conduct, to which they could point. Bartoš' and De Vooght's explanations have this in common that they deny the validity of the safe-conduct altogether. Bartoš regards the document granted Hus when he was already in Constance as a mere pass,[10] while De Vooght argues that the emperor could not grant a condemned heretic a safe-conduct guaranteeing his return from the Council.[11] Hus, however, before he left Bohemia, could not have anticipated that Sigismund would not keep his promise. Trusting that promise, he went to the Council, not as a condemned heretic cited there to receive the confirmation of his previous verdicts, but freely, confident of the justice of his cause and eager to "give reason for the faith he held." He was ready to submit to the Council and abandon whatever errors might be proved against him, provided they were proved on the basis of Scripture. He was not so naïve as not to consider the possibility of suffering death. But to assert, as Bartoš does, that Hus, "even though he knew that he was going to his death, only wished to secure a chance to die erect and by his death to aid the victory of the ideals for which he had fought all his life," goes beyond the

[10] Bartoš (see n. 1), p. 391.
[11] De Vooght, *L'hérésie*, p. 292.

evidence.[12] Bartoš' view of the *certainty* of death felt by Hus is contradicted by many of the latter's messages written from Constance in which he expresses hope of release and return to Prague. He expressed such a hope in the very letter of acceptance he wrote to Sigismund advising him of his willingness to accept the king's offer.[13] He wrote in a letter to John of Chlum immediately after the last public hearing (June 8), when his prospects looked anything but promising, "I still cherish the hope that the Almighty God may snatch me from their hands. . . ."[14] Even as late as June 25, about two weeks before his death, he wrote, "Why could not God still liberate me . . . from prison and death?"[15] Thus although he was ever ready to suffer death, he also sporadically entertained an amazing hope of release. On the other hand, De Vooght's view is contradicted by Sigismund's own declaration, made publicly during the second hearing (June 7), that he had granted Hus a safe-conduct. In fact, by a lapse of memory he asserted that he had done so "even before . . . [Hus] had left Prague . . . although some may say that I could not grant a safe-conduct to a heretic or one suspected of heresy."[16] It appears to me most probable that Hus decided to accept Sigismund's invitation because he was assured of defending himself freely before the Council. He was confident that he could prove his innocence. At least, he was ready to amend his views if he were convinced by Scriptural proof of error or heresy. If worse came to worst, he was prepared to suffer death. He went, however, with the hope of success, not with the *certainty* of defeat.

In his letter of acceptance, written on September 1,

[12] Bartoš (see n. 1), p. 384.

[13] Spinka (see n. 5), Part II, No. 5.

[14] *Ibid.*, No. 12.       [15] *Ibid.*, No. 26.

[16] *Ibid.*, Part I, pp. 179-180 ("Petri de Mladoniowicz, Relatio de Magistro Johanne Hus," in V. Novotný, ed., *Fontes rerum Bohemicarum*, VIII, Praha, Nadání Františka Palackého, 1932, p. 81).

1414,[17] Hus indeed stresses that "coming in peace to the Council I may be able to profess publicly the faith I hold," but also expresses the hope that the king "will bring the trial to a laudable end." He does not specifically mention the free return to Bohemia in case the presentation of his views did not end "laudably." Before he left for Constance, he had carefully prepared himself for all possible demands that might be made of him and for the proper presentation of his views. He had collected all the available evidence to be presented against the anticipated accusations and depositions of his enemies and witnesses. He had even secured a certificate of his orthodoxy from the Prague inquisitor, Bishop Nicholas of Nezero. John of Jesenice, Hus' advocate, was refused entrance into the archiepiscopal court and was thus prevented from securing Archbishop Conrad's declaration concerning Hus' faith. Nevertheless, the archbishop had declared in a plenary session of the Czech nobles that he knew of no error or heresy against the Master. Hus also wrote a sermon to be delivered before the Council,[18] as well as a short discussion on the theme *De sufficientia legis Christi*.[19] In this treatise he appealed to the Council to hear him first and then to judge him honestly on the basis of his own statement of his faith. "Therefore I, an insignificant man, preparing to speak before the assembly of the wisest of all the world (as I presume), beseech you by the mercies of Jesus Christ, the true God and true man, to hear me in peace. . . ." He then propounded the question, "Whether the law

[17] *Ibid.*, Part II, No. 5.

[18] "De pace," in *Historia et monumenta Joannis Hus atque Hieronymi Pragensis, confessorum Christi*, 2 vols. (Norimberg, 1715), I, pp. 60-71. "De pace" was recently published with a Czech translation by F. M. Dobiáš and A. Molnár, *Řeč o míru* (Praha, Kalich, 1963).

[19] "De sufficientia legis Christi ad regendum ecclesiam," in *Historia et monumenta*, pp. 55-60.

of Jesus Christ . . . suffices by itself for the rule of the
Church militant." He answers it affirmatively, for "we
cannot add or subtract anything from that law." He then
protests, "As I have formerly frequently declared, I now
again state that I have never asserted anything contrary
to the faith worthy of belief. On the contrary, I have
defended, now defend, and firmly desire to continue to
defend all truth worthy of belief. For I hope, with the
Lord's help, rather to suffer the punishment of dire
death than to defend any error contrary to the truth. . . ."
Although Hus was not permitted to present this declaration before the Council, the Czech nobles offered it in
his name to that body on May 30.

He had imagined, somewhat naïvely, that he might
be allowed to preach to the Council. For this purpose
he prepared a sermon, *De pace*, which he was *not* allowed
to deliver.[20] The most remarkable feature of this sermon is a critique of the vices of the clergy and the
prelates no less sharp than is to be found in his former
denunciations. He castigates the luxury of the clergy,
the struggle among the prelates and priests for the
highest and most lucrative places, and their repudiation
of voluntary poverty. If Hus had any idea of conciliation,
this was not the way of securing it!

Hus left Krakovec on October 11, 1414, in the company of the two knights assigned him for protection,
John of Chlum and Wenceslas of Dubá, and of John's
secretary, Peter of Mladoňovice. Master John "Cardinal"
of Rejnštejn, who represented the University of Prague,
and a few servants, completed the party. Hus had to
borrow money for the trip from some of his wealthier
friends, including John of Chlum. His inability to repay the debt worried him a great deal when he realized
his doom, as several of his letters poignantly testify. He
left without the promised safe-conduct; in the light of

20 *Ibid.*, I, pp. 65-71.

subsequent developments, this proved to be his first mistake. Since the other members of the party possessed such protective documents, he was nowhere challenged. The trip through Germany was almost a triumphant procession.[21] Hus travelled with his face uncovered, proclaiming everywhere by public notices his identity. He had friendly conversations with priests and officials along the way, even in such an important city as Nuremberg. Without any exception, his views were accepted as wholly orthodox. Nowhere was he treated as a condemned and excommunicated heretic, nor were the church services stopped on his account. When the party reached Nuremberg, Lord Wenceslas of Dubá left it to join Sigismund, who was awaiting his coronation at Aachen. Hus' safe-conduct was issued on October 18 at Speyer in the form of a mere pass, despite a reference to "return." It is indeed surprising that Hus had not been granted it before he left Bohemia, and not in the specific form promised him in Sigismund's name by Lord Henry Lefl of Lažany and Mikeš Divoký of Jemniště. Bartoš comments that since Sigismund got what he wanted—King Wenceslas' consent to coronation—he was no longer interested in fulfilling his part of the bargain.[22] Actually, since the pass was not delivered to Hus until two days after he had reached Constance, it was useless and superfluous in spite of the mention of "return."[23] If it was meant to protect Hus in Constance, it failed to accomplish even that, nor did it accomplish any other purpose.

Hus arrived in Constance on November 3, having decided at Nuremberg not to join the emperor and enter the city in his entourage. This was his second grave mis-

[21] For the description, see Mladoňovic, *Relatio* (see n. 16), pp. 31-32; cf. my translation (see n. 5), Part I, pp. 98-100, 102-104.

[22] Bartoš (see n. 1), p. 392.

[23] Mladoňovic, *Relatio*, p. 26; my translation (see n. 5), pp. 90, 100.

take. He was thus deprived of Sigismund's possible protection, for the latter did not arrive in that city until December 24. By that time Hus had already been in prison for almost a month. When later, on March 21, 1416, Sigismund wrote from Paris to the Czech and Moravian nobles, trying to dissuade them from any military action on account of Hus' death, he remarked that "had he [Hus] come to us first in order to proceed to Constance along with us, the matter might have taken a different course,"[24] i.e., he might not have been arrested. He added hypocritically: "God knows that we were so very sorry as to what happened to him that we could not be more grieved!" But we know from the record that he had a chance to rescue Hus from the prison, particularly after Pope John's flight, and did not avail himself of it.

Upon arriving in Constance, Hus and his guardians lodged in the house of a widow Fida in St. Paul's street (now called Hussenstrasse—the house still stands). Pope John, who had arrived about a week before Hus (October 28), suspended both the excommunication, and the interdict to save the city from their consequences. Thus Hus was free to move wherever he wished, although, in fact, he did not set his foot outside the house throughout the time he was free. The Council was solemnly opened on November 16. On that occasion Pope John delivered an address exhorting the members to work zealously for the peace of the Church.[25] When Cardinal d'Ailly joined

[24] F. Palacký, *Documenta Mag. Joannis Hus* (Praha, F. Tempský, 1869), p. 610.

[25] K. J. von Hefele–H. Leclercq, *Histoire de Conciles*, 10 vols. (Paris, Letouzey et Ané, 1916), vii/i, pp. 168-169. In describing the Council, we shall depend mainly on this authoritative work of Bishop Hefele, written in German and translated into French and considerably revised by the Belgian Dominican, H. Leclercq. The latter shows a hitherto most unusual understanding of Hus' case. He is thus a worthy predecessor of that other Belgian Benedictine, Paul de Vooght.

his colleagues the next day, he quickly assumed a leading position among them.

In the meantime, both Michael de Causis and Stephen Páleč arrived—Stanislav had died on the way—and lost no time in presenting the pope with the first list of accusations.[26] They charged that Hus advocated the granting of both bread and wine in communion and that he taught remanence. They further charged that he taught that no one in mortal sin could administer the sacraments validly; that the Church does not consist of the pope and the cardinals and other prelates; that the Church should possess no property; that the pope and the clergy in mortal sin lose all authority; that the secular lords have the right to install priests and that no one has the right to forbid priests to preach; and finally, that Wyclif's articles are orthodox. We already know from our previous consideration of Hus' teaching that all these charges were utterly false. Nevertheless, they had their intended effect.

Less than a month after his arrival Hus was visited in his lodgings by two bishops, the Constance burgomaster, and a knight.[27] They declared that they came by the order of the pope and the cardinals and that the latter desired to speak with him. Although John of Chlum immediately sensed danger in the invitation, Hus made his third mistake in consenting to go with them. When they arrived at the pope's residence, the cardinals spoke a few words with him and then left. Thereupon, a learned Spanish Franciscan theologian, Didachus de Moxena by name, pretending to be a simple ignorant friar, engaged him in conversation. He went straight to the heart of the matter by asking whether Hus believed in remanence. It is obvious that the cardinals were con-

[26] Palacký, *Documenta* (see n. 24), pp. 194-199; Hefele–Leclercq (see n. 25), vii/i, pp. 174-175.

[27] The events which follow are fully described in Mladoňovic, *Relatio*, pp. 37-41; my translation (see n. 5), Part i, pp. 104-114.

vinced that Hus was a thoroughgoing Wyclifite, for so his Czech enemies, they being "his fiercest foes," as Hus calls them in his letter of June 10,[28] had represented him. The friar repeated the question three times, each time receiving the same negative answer. Thereupon John of Chlum roughly interfered in the conversation, berating the friar for his persistence. Didachus then asked Hus about the two natures in Jesus Christ. Hus then perceived that he had to do with an *agent provocateur* and not a simple friar. Nevertheless, he answered the question, whereupon the friar left—no doubt disappointed. The armed guards standing about then told him that the visitor was one of the subtlest theologians in Italy.

When the evening came, Lord John was told that he could go home, while Hus must remain in custody. Incensed by this obvious treachery, he stalked into the pope's and cardinals' presence and loudly denounced the act, reminding the pope that he had told him at first that Hus was to be free "even if he had murdered his [the pope's] own brother!" He threatened to inform the emperor of this gross violation of the safe-conduct. The pope called upon the cardinals to witness that he had not ordered the arrest and even denied that his own servant Francis, who had apparently been instrumental in the affair, was a member of his court. Later, when he was alone with Lord John, he placed the responsibility for the act on the cardinals, as was indeed most probably the case. He pleaded that he himself was in their power and could not prevent the action. Mladoňovic, however, bluntly called this a lie. Later, in a letter to the University of Paris and the Duke of Orleans, Pope John admitted that he *did* order the arrest of Hus, but "did not proceed against him canonically because of the king

28 V. Novotný, ed., *M. Jana Husi Korespondence a dokumenty* (Praha, 1920), No. 129; my translation (see n. 5), Part ii, No. 13.

of the Romans, who demanded his release and even threatened to break the doors of the prison."[29] When Hus was arrested, Páleč and Michael danced around the room in high glee exclaiming that at last Hus "will not escape them!"

Hus then remained in custody, while Lord John could do nothing but go home alone. All his protests then and later were in vain. In the meantime, Hus was taken to the house of the precentor of the cathedral and after eight days was transferred to a dungeon in the Dominican monastery located on the island off the shore.[30] There he was kept in a murky, dank cell next to the latrine sewer. He fell ill and his life was despaired of. He remained imprisoned in that monastery until Palm Sunday.[31] Richental, who claims to be "an eyewitness," tells an absurd story that Hus was arrested because he had attempted to escape from Constance.[32] The story has absolutely no factual basis. In Hefele and Leclercq's *History* it is branded as a confusion with the later unsuccessful attempt of Jerome of Prague to escape from Constance.[33]

The third day after Hus' arrest, the Council appointed his judges—John de Rupiscissa, titular patriarch of Constantinople, Bishop Bernard of Castellamare, and John of Bořenice, bishop of Lubus. Not one among them was favorable to Hus. Thereupon the commission, still firmly convinced that Hus was an out-and-out Wycliffite, agreed that the simplest way to convict him would be to confront him with the forty-five articles of Wyclif, re-

[29] Hefele–Leclercq (see n. 25), vii/i, p. 200.

[30] It is now a magnificent hotel, the most luxurious in town. The round tower to which Hus was later transferred from the dungeon still stands.

[31] From December 6, 1414, to March 24, 1415.

[32] Ulrich von Richental, *Chronik des Constanzer Concils* (Hildesheim, Georg Olms, 1962), p. 58.

[33] Hefele–Leclercq (see n. 25), p. 173, n. 1.

peatedly condemned in Prague. They were presented to him on December 6 with the request that he state whether or not he held them.[34] When one remembers that the teaching of Wyclif had been declared heretical the previous year at the Council of Rome and all his books burned, one realizes the danger confronting Hus by reason of this demand. Were he to acknowledge the forty-five articles as held by him either in their entirety or for the greater part, his own condemnation would follow automatically. At first he refused to answer specifically, replying only with a general statement that he did not wish to hold any error. His judges, however, threatened to condemn him outright; thereupon he yielded. His request for a legal adviser was refused. He was ordered to put his replies in writing. In the specific answers which Hus now wrote he declared categorically that he did not hold thirty-two of the forty-five articles. As for the rest, three of them (Nos. 4, 8, and 15), which stated that a priest in mortal sin does not act validly, that a foreknown pope does not have power over the faithful, and that a secular or ecclesiastical lord in mortal sin does not hold his office, Hus modified them by adding the saving adjective "worthily." Concerning the first and second he added that even the worst priest acts validly and so does a foreknown pope; as for the third he stated that such lords hold the office *de facto*. About articles 5 and 11— the first denying that Christ established the mass and the second stating that no one should be excommunicated except God first does so—Hus answered that he did not know where Wyclif had written thus in his

[34] It is interesting that Peter of Mladoňovice does not include this examination in his *Relatio*. It is published by Jan Sedlák, "Několik textů z doby husitské," *Hlídka* (Brno, 1913), No. 15; also his "Proces kostnický," *Studie a texty k náboženským dějinám českým*, 2 vols. (Olomouc, 1913-19), II, pp. 1-19. The text of Wyclif's articles is found in Appendix I. The text with Hus' responses is published in Jan Sedlák's *M. Jan Hus* (Praha, 1915), supplement XVIII, pp. 304-310.

books. It is, of course, true that the mass as such was not established by Christ; nevertheless, Hus admitted that Christ "gave the priests the possibility of celebrating it." Excommunication should be imposed only for mortal sin. As for articles 13, 14, 16, and 17 he declared that they might have a correct sense, implying that in their present form they did not have it. Articles 19 and 23 were not formulated clearly. Articles 16, 18, and 33 he neither asserted nor denied. In connection with No. 18, dealing with tithes, he denied the second part which asserted that the parishioners might withhold them as they pleased.

These answers at several points were admittedly timid, although in no instance actually untruthful.[35] He had never defended Wyclif's theses *in toto*; he had defended seven which he reformulated in an acceptable sense. He objected to an indiscriminate condemnation of all of them because, in the first place, he did not regard them as correctly stating Wyclif's views and, secondly, no Scriptural proof of their erroneous nature had ever been produced. Some were notoriously perverted as, for instance, No. 6—"God should obey the devil." Much more basic, in my estimation, was the reason stated by Hus himself, that he came to the Council to defend *his own* views, not those of Wyclif, and to defend them before the whole Council, not before a few members of it. Thus his answers must be considered as a protest not only against his arrest, regarded by him as illegal, but also against being subjected to a trial. He came to the Council freely, not as one cited to a trial, but as one desiring to present his teaching to the Council. He refused to be

[35] Sedlák, in the article referred to (*Studie a texty*, II), accuses Hus of insincerity and of denial of his previous teaching. He bases this on the statement that his friends were "full of fear" that he had denied Wyclif (p. 3). On the contrary, John of Chlum writes that all his friends "praise your constancy profoundly and most appreciatively."

caught in the trap prepared for him by his judges—a practically automatic condemnation on the ground of the judgment passed on Wyclif—without being allowed a hearing before the Council. In his letter of acceptance sent to Sigismund, he had specified such a free hearing as his primary *desideratum* and he was determined to get it, instead of being condemned practically in secret! Hus' friends in Prague, particularly his legal representative, John of Jesenice, were disturbed by this examination in prison, as John of Chlum wrote Hus on January 4. Probably they shared Hus' own fears that he might be condemned without a hearing before the Council.[36] As for the commissioners, although balked of the easy victory they had counted on, they and the Council never gave up their firm belief in Hus' Wyclifism. In the end, the verdict was based primarily on this charge.[37]

On January 4, 1415, Hus "was again interrogated about each of the forty-five articles"; he wrote in his letter to John of Chlum:

> I replied with the same responses as previously. They questioned me about each article separately if I wished to defend it. I replied that I would abide by the decision of the Council, as I had declared before. To each of the articles I replied as I had done previously. About some I said: "This is true in such and such a sense." They said: "Do you wish to defend it?" I replied that I did not, but that I would abide by the decision of the Council.[38]

This new examination was held because someone had told the judges that Hus had informed the emperor that he wished to withdraw three or four articles. Hus had done nothing of the sort. At this same examination Patriarch John de Rupiscissa declared that Hus "had a

[36] Spinka (see n. 5), Part ii, No. 8.
[37] *Ibid.*, Part ii, No. 35.   [38] *Ibid.*, No. 9.

large amount of money, and an archbishop named the sum as amounting to 70,000 florins." Hus mentions Michael de Causis as the purveyor of this lie. Whether this was said in order to extort money from Hus he does not explicitly say.

In the reply of John of Chlum written on the same day (January 4), the noble lord announced to Hus: "The king spoke with the delegates of the nations of the entire Council about your affairs and especially concerning your public hearing. They all answered finally and conclusively that you will be granted a public hearing without fail."[39] This appears to have been the culmination of the efforts of John of Chlum and Sigismund in behalf of Hus. The noble lord, who had carried out his threat to denounce the arrest of Hus to the emperor, apparently was able to move Sigismund to action. The emperor was reported to have sent an order to his ambassadors at Constance ordering them to secure Hus' release and, if necessary, even to force the doors of the prison. If the ambassadors undertook any such violent action, it failed.[40] Lord John did not stop with the protest to Sigismund but posted placards throughout the city threatening the guilty persons with a dire punishment once the emperor should arrive. When at last Sigismund did enter the city (December 24), he had, according to his own testimony, several angry scenes with the Council "and even left Constance on Hus' account." Sigismund then states further that the Council sent him a message demanding to know whether he intended to deny it the right to carry on its work without his interference. Thereupon Sigismund capitulated (January 1, 1415), and gave up any effort to free Hus from prison "so that the Council would not come to naught on that

39 *Ibid.*, No. 8; De Vooght, *L'hérésie*, p. 335.
40 Hefele–Leclercq (see n. 25), VII/I, p. 179.

account."[41] Sigismund's surrender to the Council was tantamount to a repudiation of his promise made to Hus. To all intents and purposes he thus nullified his safe-conduct, depriving it even of the problematical significance it was supposed to have. The only thing he appears to have secured was the promise of public hearings, which took place early in June. In the meantime, the efforts of the commissioners to carry on the examination in private were not interfered with. Moreover, on April 8 Sigismund revoked and annulled *all* safe-conducts issued to anyone then in Constance. This was the final act of treachery vis-à-vis Hus.[42]

Having been disappointed with their first attempt, made on December 6, to convict Hus on the basis of Wyclif's forty-five articles, the judges entrusted Páleč with the task of preparing charges drawn from Hus' own writings. He produced forty-two articles,[43] which were presented to Hus for his written replies. Hus refers to this occasion by commenting that he had labored on the replies the whole previous night. Páleč, he writes, "labors directly for my condemnation. May God forgive him and strengthen me!"[44] It is a marvel that he was able to finish in one night the extensive answers which, along with Páleč's theses, comprise twenty pages of Palacký's *Documenta!* Since we have already examined Hus' *De ecclesia*, it would be repetitious to review these charges in detail. Suffice it to mention only some items which call

[41] Palacký, *Documenta*, No. 95; also Hefele–Leclercq (see n. 25), VII/I, p. 180. The letter is dated March 21, 1416, and is addressed to the principal nobles of Bohemia and Moravia, in an effort to dissuade them from an armed uprising on account of Hus' death. It is difficult to say whether the facts are stated correctly.

[42] Palacký, *Documenta*, No. 70.

[43] *Ibid.*, No. 9, pp. 204-224; De Vooght, *L'hérésie*, pp. 337-362; "Articuli e processu Mgri J. Hus Constantiensi" in Sedlák, *M. Jan Hus*, supplement XIX, pp. 311-317.

[44] Novotný, *Korespondence*, No. 104; my translation (see n. 5), Part II, No. 7.

for special comment. Páleč summarizes in article 36 the teaching of Hus as "false, erroneous, scandalous, temerarious, seditious, disturbing the peace of the Church, destructive of ecclesiastical jurisdiction, insane, contrary to sacred Scripture, the universal Church, conflicting with the conclusions and writings of the holy Fathers and otherwise heretical."[45] Rather a comprehensive charge! Hus replies mildly that if any of his tenets is demonstrated to be heretical, he is ready humbly to revoke it. He says that he requested and continues to request to be *shown* his errors from the holy Scriptures, but that no one has undertaken to do so. Among Páleč's charges (Nos. 41-42) was the old canard that Hus had stated in his sermons that even if he were induced to recant Wyclif's articles, he would do so with his mouth but not with his heart. Hus brands this charge as "full of lies." Even more absurd is the accusation that as soon as Hus arrived in Constance, he wrote home that "the pope and the emperor showed him consideration and received him with honor and that the pope sent two bishops to him in order that he would join him [the pope]." This is so insensate a lie that even the commissioners should have spotted it instantly! After all, they were most likely eyewitnesses of how the pope and the cardinals had received Hus! As Hus pointed out, instead of being received with honor, he was thrown into prison. As for the emperor, he was not in Constance until more than three weeks after Hus' imprisonment.

De Vooght characterizes Hus' answers as "chicanery," and cites as an example the first article: "The catholic or universal church is [composed] of the predestinate only." Hus' own version in the *De ecclesia* reads: "The holy catholic, i.e., universal Church, is the totality of the predestinate." De Vooght ridicules this as being

45 Palacký, *Documenta*, p. 222.

"bonnet blanc et blanc bonnet."[46] He conveniently chooses to forget that the concept of the Church universal held by the two antagonists is very different. Páleč includes in it the Church militant, while Hus does not, with the exception of the predestinate *in* the Church militant. Hence, Páleč drew the conclusion from *his* formulation of Hus' definition that Hus denied the very existence of the Church militant! This is not "bonnet blanc et blanc bonnet"! Páleč succeeded in foisting this false interpretation on the Council (and it appears on de Vooght as well), and it remained thereafter among the first articles of the charges on the basis of which Hus was condemned to death. Did that not make a difference? De Vooght also charges that Hus denied that article 22, "The pope is the beast which is mentioned in the Apocalypse," was in his book. He points out that Hus spoke of three beasts, i.e., the three popes disputing about the tiara.[47] In the first place, Hus' statement is not in the *De ecclesia*, from which presumably Páleč was quoting; it is found in his polemical work *Contra Paletz*,[48] where it is indeed applied to the three popes on account of their strife about "dignity, arrogance, and avarice"; but this reference does not identify them with the Apocalyptic beast. De Vooght himself admits that Hus never said that the pope is Antichrist.[49] That assertion was applied by Hus only to a pope living contrary to Christ.[50] De Vooght further concedes that Hus never held the view stated in article 17, "The power of the pope who does not imitate Christ is not to be feared." For de Vooght knew that Hus had taught just the opposite, namely, that the inferiors are in duty bound to obey their superiors, both good and bad, provided that their

---

[46] De Vooght, *L'hérésie*, p. 359.
[47] *Ibid.*, p. 360.
[48] *Contra Paletz*, in *Historia et monumenta*, I, p. 325.
[49] De Vooght, *L'hérésie*, p. 310.
[50] *Contra Paletz*, p. 323.

commands are in accordance with Christ's law.[51] Hus now added that if the pope abuses his power, the subjects need not slavishly fear him. After all, the cardinals of both Gregory XII and Benedict XIII had revolted against their respective popes and had at Pisa even voted their deposition! Strangely, De Vooght omits to mention article 27, "Christ obeyed the devil," and article 3, that the successors of the apostles should not possess property, which Hus certainly never taught. For the greatest part Hus explained the rest of the charges either by quoting his correct text or by giving a proper sense to the articles. That the commission itself recognized the majority of Páleč's articles as false or unproven is clearly shown by the fact that thirty-one of the forty-two were dropped and even the remaining eleven were thoroughly revised. Nevertheless, Páleč was not intimidated by this defeat and excerpted thirteen new articles from the polemics of Hus with Stanislav of Znojmo and himself.

On February 21,[52] Jean Gerson arrived at Constance bringing with him twenty additional articles, which he promptly offered to the commission. He had written, in May 1414, to Archbishop Conrad of Prague about the heresies rampant in Bohemia and urged him to extirpate them. The archbishop sent Gerson extracts from Hus' *De ecclesia*, asking for his opinion about them. Gerson and the Paris theologians set to work and in one month produced twenty conclusions.[53] They were not actually drawn from the text of *De ecclesia* itself, but merely

[51] S. Harrison Thomson, ed., *Magistri Joannis Hus Tractatus de Ecclesia* (Boulder, Colo., University of Colorado Press, 1956), p. 177.

[52] De Vooght in *L'hérésie* dates his arrival January 21 (p. 363). Novotný specifies February 25 (*Jan Hus, Život a dílo*, II, p. 392). Bartoš dates it February 21 (*Čechy v době Husově*, p. 410), and so does Hefele–Leclercq. The text of Gerson's twenty articles is found in Sedlák, *Jan Hus*, supplement XIX, pp. 318-326.

[53] Palacký, *Documenta*, pp. 523-528. The twenty articles are found in *Historia et monumenta*, I, pp. 29-30. De Vooght, *L'hérésie*, pp. 294-305, analyzes them in detail.

from the extracts sent by Conrad and "according to the sense" of it, as even Sedlák concedes.[54] It is doubtful if Gerson ever read Hus' treatise itself. The Parisians condemned the theses of Hus as "daring, seditious, scandalous, pernicious, and tending to the subversion of all government." They identified his teaching with Wyclif's without troubling themselves about any distinctions and differences. In his letter to Conrad, Gerson wrote:

> . . . the most pernicious error among others . . . seems to me this: that the foreknown or wicked existing in mortal sin has no dominion, jurisdiction, or power over others among the Christian people. It also seems to my insignificance that all rulers, both spiritual and temporal, should rise up against this error and exterminate it with fire and sword as fallacious. . . . For the political rule on earth is not based on predestination or love, because of their uncertainty and insecurity, but is stabilized according to the ecclesiastical and civil laws.[55]

This clearly shows that Gerson regarded Hus primarily as a rebel against the established order rather than as a theological thinker. In the Vatican manuscript of these articles it is added:

> It is clear that in respect of the daring, pertinacity, and the large number of adherents of the archheretic John Wyclif in England, Bohemia, and Scotland, they should be dealt with by judicial condemnation rather than by useless reasoning of which they are not worthy. For they extol themselves impudently against all ecclesiastical and secular dominion by holding the already many times condemned errors and by denying the principles of not only the positive law, both ec-

[54] Sedlák, *Studie a texty*, ii, p. 8.
[55] Palacký, *Documenta*, p. 528.

clesiastical and civil, but of divine and natural law as well. Finally, brutal and ignorant men who seduce and incite peasants to the vice of every kind of rebellion and sedition, as is known, would be corrected more quickly and effectively by punishment than by words.[56]

When Hus learned of Gerson's theses, he called them lies. In his letter written between March 6 and 18 he exclaims: "O that God would grant me time to write against the lies of the chancellor of Paris who so daringly and unjustly before such a large multitude was not ashamed to declare an almost complete untruth! Perhaps God will forestall my writing either by my death or his and so will decide everything better than I could have written!"[57]

Another aggravation of the case occurred when Hus' foes intercepted an inconsiderate and injudicious letter of Jakoubek's, thus adding to Hus' already serious situation another dangerous complication. It dealt with the granting of the cup in communion to the laity. Jakoubek of Stříbro had raised the question during the second half of the previous year. Hus agreed with him in principle but did not think the time opportune to make the demand public. He urged his more radical colleague to wait until he himself returned from Constance. Jakoubek disagreed but consented to wait. During Hus' absence, however, he began granting the cup to the laity.[58] Thereupon a conflict broke out among the members of the reforming party, some opposing Jakoubek bitterly, others enthusiastically agreeing with him. Among the former was Havlík, Hus' substitute at the Bethlehem Chapel. Before his arrest, Hus himself had written a treatise

[56] Quoted in Novotný, *Jan Hus, Život a dílo*, II, p. 392, n. 4.
[57] Novotný, *Korespondence*, No. 118.
[58] "Počátky kalicha v Čechách," in F. M. Bartoš, *Husitství a cizina* (Praha, 1931), p. 59.

dealing with the subject of communion in both kinds.[59] In it he agreed with Jakoubek, although with reservations. On January 4, John of Chlum wrote to Hus requesting him earnestly to give his "reasoned and final opinion concerning the communion of the cup, so that they might show it to friends at an appropriate time. For there is still some disagreement among the brethren and many are disquieted on that account, referring to you and your decision in accordance with some treatise of yours."[60] Hus replied the same day that he did not know what to add to what he had written in the treatise, "except that the Gospel and St. Paul's letter sound definite and that it had been practiced in the primitive Church."[61] He advised, nevertheless, that a papal bull be secured granting permission at least to those "who request it from devotion." This advice had the unexpected result that Hus' friends induced the royal Council, if indeed not the king himself, to send an emissary to Constance to find out what the chances of petitioning the Council to grant the communion in both kinds were. The man chosen for the task was Hus' old friend and benefactor, Christian of Prachatice.[62] He arrived in Constance as a member of the royal embassy about the middle of February. He visited Hus in prison unexpectedly. Hus was so deeply moved that he could not restrain tears from gushing from his eyes.[63] But at the instigation of Michael de Causis, Christian was arrested and subjected to a rigorous examination by the commissioners. However, he was released on condition

[59] "Utrum expediat laicis fidelibus sumere sanguinam Christi sub specie vini," in *Historia et monumenta*, I, pp. 52-55.

[60] Novotný, *Korespondence*, No. 105; my translation (see n. 5), Part II, No. 8.

[61] *Ibid.*, No. 9.

[62] This is Bartoš' interpretation of the purpose of Christian's embassy. Novotný does not mention it.

[63] Novotný, *Korespondence*, No. 114. It is dated March 5.

that he leave a representative in Constance until his case could be adjudicated. Then he was to return to receive his sentence. He left Constance on March 18 or 19 without ever returning. Surprisingly, he was accompanied, it appears, both on the journey and the escape, by John of Jesenice, who, contrary to Hus' earnest warning, dared to venture secretly into Constance.[64] Moreover, the commission lost its jurisdiction within a few days thereafter.

The same fate overtook another member of the Czech royal embassy, Bishop Nicholas of Nezero, the Prague inquisitor. He had granted Hus a testimony of his complete orthodoxy, witnessing that he had eaten and drunk with him and had heard him on many occasions but "had never found in him any error or heresy."[65] On that account he was nicknamed in Constance "Nicholas sup-with-the-devil." He was promptly arrested and questioned by Cardinal d'Ailly. In order to secure his release, he testified that King Wenceslas had forced Hus to attend the Council in order to clear the kingdom from the charge of heresy. This being welcome "evidence" that Hus did not come to Constance freely and of his own will, as he claimed, the unhappy bishop was released. He promptly left Constance for the more salubrious climate of Prague.

In considering the question of the *communio utraque panis et vini species*, the Council heard, among others, the testimony of that most formidable opponent of all reform, Bishop John "the Iron" of Litomyšl. He greatly prejudiced the case against it by his witness. He told the Council that "the most precious blood of Christ is being carried about Bohemia in flasks and that cobblers

[64] "Husův advokát," in F. M. Bartoš *Bojovníci a mučedníci* (Praha, Kalich, 1939), pp. 10-13; also Jiří Kejř, *Husitský právník, M. Jan z Jesenice* (Praha, Československa akademie věd, 1965), p. 92.

[65] Mladoňovic, *Relatio*, p. 58; my translation (see n. 5), Part I, p. 143.

are hearing confessions and administering the body of Christ to others." He expressly called these people Wyclifites: ". . . the followers of this sect in many cities, villages, and places of that kingdom, laymen of both sexes, commune in both kinds of bread and wine and persistently teach that this is the way communion must be administered."[66] Thereupon the Council, on June 15, forbade the granting of the cup to the laity under severe penalties. Should any priest disobey, he was to be declared a heretic unless he desisted, and would be punished as such, "invoking, if need be, the aid of the secular arm."[67] Hus denounced this decree as madness, for it condemned as error and heresy Christ's command and the institution St. Paul received, as he said, directly from Christ. He particularly castigated the effrontery of placing a custom of the Roman Church above the holy Scriptures.[68] He also wrote to his pupil and substitute at Bethlehem Chapel, Havlík, urging him not to oppose the granting of the cup to lay people. "I beseech you for God's sake to attack Master Jakoubek no longer, lest a schism occur among the faithful that would delight the devil." Thus at last Hus came out openly and frankly in support of the practice which initiated, among the Utraquists of Bohemia and later among all Protestants, the communion in both kinds.

Then an event took place which radically changed the conditions under which the Council was held. It also affected adversely Hus' situation. Pope John XXIII, who on March 1 and 2 had solemnly promised to resign, provided his rivals would likewise cede their claims to the papacy, on March 21 fled in disguise from Constance. He

[66] Mladoňovic, *Relatio*, pp. 47-48; my translation (see n. 5), Part I, pp. 127-128.

[67] The decree is published in Hefele–Leclercq (see n. 25), VII/I, pp. 284-287.

[68] Novotný, *Korespondence*, No. 139; my translation (see n. 5), Part II, No. 19.

intended to seek refuge in Burgundy. When he reached Schaffhausen, he peremptorily summoned the cardinals to join him. Had they obeyed, the Council would most likely have come to an end. Fortunately for the ending of the Schism, Sigismund declared his resolve to continue the Council. Jean Gerson was able, by his sermon delivered on behalf of the French nation, to persuade the whole Council to continue their work without the pope. In fact, that body soon rallied and on April 6 issued the famous decree *Sacrosancta*. This revolutionary document declared that the Council possessed its power directly from Christ and that "all persons of whatever rank or dignity, even a pope, are bound to obey it in matters pertaining to faith and the end of the Schism and the general reformation of the said Church of God in head and members." Only eight cardinals attended this session and acquiesced in the measure; four others, d'Ailly among them, absented themselves. It is on this ground that Hefele and Leclercq deny the binding character of the *Sacrosancta*, claiming that Pope Martin V approved only the acts of the Council *in materiis fidei conciliariter et non aliter nec alio modo*.[69] Pope John was seized as he was ready to cross the Rhine at Breisach. Cardinal de Viviers, dean of the sacred College, henceforth presided over all the sessions until the election of Martin V.

These events affected Hus as well, since his jailers followed the pope, having left the keys to Hus' prison in the hands of the Council. That body thereupon turned them over to Sigismund. Nothing stood in his way to free Hus from prison. But by this time he no longer regarded himself as bound by his safe-conduct, having already annulled it. Instead of releasing Hus, he turned him over to the bishop of Constance, Otto III of Hachberg. That dignitary had Hus transferred at night, under strong armed convoy, from the Dominican prison to his

69 Hefele–Leclercq (see n. 25), VII/I, pp. 209, 211.

own castle of Gottlieben. Here he was kept in strict isolation, having his feet in bonds during the day and being chained by one hand to the wall at night. During his imprisonment there (March 24 to June 3) he lost all contact with his friends. He could write no letters to them throughout that period. Furthermore, since the papal commission appointed to try him had lost its mandate with the flight of the pope, new judges were selected by the Council. After some changes in personnel, the three men who dominated the new commission were Cardinal d'Ailly, Jean Gerson, and Cardinal Zabarella. Since we know the deep-seated bias of Gerson against Hus, from whom the other two members did not differ materially, it is obvious that Hus could expect no just treatment from them.

The attitude of the new commission soon became apparent. Wyclif's condemnation at the Roman Council of 1412-13 was solemnly confirmed on May 4. The forty-five articles were expressly included in the condemnation, and two hundred and sixty others were added to them for good measure. Later, in 1427, Pope Martin V ordered Wyclif's body, already forty-three years in the grave, to be removed from consecrated ground. It was burned at Lutterworth the next year by order of Bishop Richard Fleming.[70]

Ten days later Pope John XXIII was charged with a whole catalogue of seventy-two assorted crimes and other transgressions. Many of them were of a shocking nature.[71] Later the number was reduced to fifty-four. This reduction was made not because the deleted charges had been disproved, but "in order to spare the honor of the supreme pontiff." How his honor could be spared even

[70] *Ibid.*, vii/i, pp. 224-226. The text of the forty-five articles is given in n. 2. Herbert B. Workman, *John Wyclif*, 2 vols. (Oxford, Clarendon Press, 1926), ii, p. 320.

[71] Hefele–Leclercq (see n. 25), pp. 230-232, 234f., and 244-245, where the seventy-two charges are fully stated.

when the most heinous charges were deleted is not clear!
John was then deposed on May 29 and reduced to the
status of a mere Baldassare Cossa.

Hus' case was taken up next. On May 18 Cardinal
d'Ailly, along with eight representatives of the four
nations of which the Council was composed, visited Hus
at Gottlieben. D'Ailly undoubtedly had hoped that the
cruel sufferings of the prisoner would have induced him
to recant. It was with considerable moderation and
assumed kindness of manner that Hus was asked to
abjure the errors the commission had found in his teaching and that the witnesses had testified to. Hus, however,
asked to be allowed to present his case before the whole
Council, as it had been promised him many times previously. He professed himself willing to submit to its
decisions. The commission thereupon returned home disappointed. One of the delegates, Dr. Theodore Kerkering of the University of Cologne, expressed his opinion
that Hus would be condemned to death at the next
session.[72]

Fortunately, the Czech and Polish nobles intervened.
They had protested to the Council on May 13, praying
for Hus' release, and repeated their request on May 31.
This latter appeal was also presented to Emperor Sigismund. They offered to give any guarantee which might
be demanded, if Hus were released and placed either in
their keeping or in the custody of some bishop.[73] The answer to this request was delivered to them by the president
of the French delegation, Dr. Jean Mauroux, titular
patriarch of Antioch. He declared that whether Hus
were innocent or guilty, the trial would show. He promised that the Council would hear Hus at a public meet-

[72] Novotný, *Jan Hus, Život a dílo*, II, p. 410, basing it on Kerkering's report in E. Martène and U. Durande, *Thesaurus novus anecdotorum*, 5 vols. (Paris, 1917), II, pp. 1634-1638.
[73] Mladoňovic, *Relatio*, pp. 54-57; my translation (see n. 5),
Part I, p. 140.

ing on June 5. As for releasing him into the custody of some bishop, he declared that "even if a thousand such guarantors were offered, it is against the conscience of the deputies to surrender such a man into the hands of the guarantors; for under no circumstances is he to be trusted."[74] Thus at last, five months after Sigismund had secured the Council's pledge to afford Hus a hearing, he was definitely promised it!

The long-desired, stoutly fought for, and hopefully awaited public hearing was at last at hand. Hus had been transferred from Gottlieben to the prison of the Franciscan monastery on June 3.[75] The vacancy thus created at the castle was filled two days later by the arrival of a new prisoner—Baldassare Cossa. On Wednesday, June 5, the session of the commission was held in the refectory of the Franciscan monastery. The business on hand was the reading of the articles and testimonies against Hus, but in his as well as his friends' absence.[76] Nevertheless, a servant of Lord John of Chlum, Ulrich, who for some reason happened to be present, thought that this was an attempt to condemn Hus in his absence. He ran to inform Mladoňovic, who in turn alarmed John of Chlum and Wenceslas of Dubá. The two nobles then hastened to the emperor, who dispatched two of his trusted servants, Duke Ludwig of the Palatinate and Friedrich of Nuremberg, with an order that nothing be done concerning Hus in his absence. The Czech nobles also sent the Council the three principal works

[74] Mladoňovic, *Relatio*, p. 57; my translation (see n. 5), p. 141. Hefele–Leclercq (p. 258, n. 2) express doubt that the patriarch would use such rude language, but offer no substantiation. In its absence, Mladoňovic's report must be accepted as reliable. Certainly from the beginning Hus was treated as one whose protestations were not to be believed.

[75] It was located on the main street of the city, not far from the cathedral. It was converted in modern times to other uses.

[76] Mladoňovic, *Relatio*, pp. 72-73; my translation (see n. 5), Part I, pp. 164-165.

of Hus on which the charges were based—*De ecclesia,
Contra Stanislaum,* and *Contra Paletz*—so that the alleged quotations from these treatises could be verified
by comparison with the text written by his own hand.
For Hus had complained that the distortions of his text
or its meaning had been persistently practiced from the
beginning. It was only then that Hus was brought into
the refectory by Archbishop John Wallenrode of Riga,
into whose keeping he had been committed. No one
of his friends, however, was admitted. They stood outside and heard him defend himself against the disorderly
shouts of his attackers, but could not report in detail
what took place. They, however, did hear that when
he tried to explain his own meaning of some distorted
charge, his attackers immediately shouted: "Leave off
your sophistry and say 'Yes' or 'No'!" When he quoted
the authority of the Fathers for his views, they rejected
it as inapplicable. When he remained silent, concluding that it was useless to argue, they shouted: "Look, since
you are silent, it is a sign that you consent to these
errors!" Finally, the leaders of the Council concluded
that the tumult and commotion were too great for any
useful proceeding with the examination and adjourned
the hearing to the next Friday, June 7.

Later in the month in a letter[77] "to all faithful Czechs,"
Hus wrote, ". . . when I stood before the Council the first
day, seeing that there was no order in it whatever, I
said aloud, when they were all quiet: 'I had supposed
that there would be greater honesty, goodness, and better order in this Council than there is!'" Cardinal
d'Ailly rebuked him that he had spoken more humbly
at Gottlieben. To which Hus replied that there nobody
shouted at him, while here all were shouting. Mladoňovic, however, records this incident as having occurred

---

[77] Novotný, *Korespondence,* No. 153; my translation (see n. 5),
Part II, No. 28. The letter is dated June 26.

during the second hearing on June 7. When Hus was taken back to prison, he shook hands with his friends, saying, "Do not fear for me!" to which they responded: "We do not fear." He then added, "I know well—I know well!" Thus ended the long-awaited first hearing.

Then on Friday, June 7, Hus was again brought into the refectory of the Franciscan monastery and the examination was continued. On this occasion Sigismund presided, but arrived late, while the hearing was already in progress. He brought along with him the two Czech knights, accompanied by Peter of Mladoňovice. The examination was again conducted under the chairmanship of Cardinal d'Ailly, and dealt with the testimonies of the Prague and Constance witnesses. Since Peter and the party in the entourage of Sigismund arrived late, he recorded only the part of the examination at which he was present. The testimony of witnesses[78] comprising unnamed doctors, prelates, and masters which was then read, asserted that in the month of June 1410, Hus had defended Wyclif's remanence. He denied it, professing his sincere adherence to the dogma of transubstantiation. Then Cardinal d'Ailly subjected Hus to a rigorous examination dealing with his philosophical realism. To the cardinal, a thoroughgoing nominalist, the realist principles necessarily led to remanence. He argued that in transubstantiation, when the substance of the material bread was changed into the body of Christ, it also ceased to exist as a universal entity. As realists insisted that universals cannot cease to exist, it must necessarily follow therefrom that the material bread in the sacrament did not cease to exist. This was correct enough as far as Wyclif's philosophical view was concerned. What the cardinal could not or would not admit, despite all Hus' declarations to the contrary, was that although Hus gladly profited by what he regarded as good and whole-

[78] The text is found in Sedlák, *Jan Hus*, supplement, pp. 338-343.

*360*

some in Wyclif's teaching, he did not accept such tenets as he knew to be doctrinally unsound. He had never agreed with Wyclif on the subject of remanence, as he had shown many times before. Therefore, he replied to the cardinal that the substance of the bread was transubstantiated, although the accidents, the outward appearance with all its characteristics, remained unchanged. This was, of course, the official dogma of the Church. Did d'Ailly believe Hus? No! He was so deeply convinced that Hus was a Wyclifite that all Hus' protestations were in vain. One may likewise remark that these nominalist-realist squabbles should not have been introduced into an investigation dealing with Hus' Christian faith. They had, nevertheless, a deleterious effect on it. Gerson wrote: "Damnata est inter errores Hus et Hieronymi positio ista de universalium et aeternorum positione."[79]

Two English masters entered the conversation with inconsequential remarks, while another Englishman, Master William Corfe,[80] warned that Hus dealt as craftily and evasively with the subject as Wyclif had done. Hus denied this. Thereupon, Master William tried to pin Hus down to an absolutely irrefutable statement by asking him whether the body of Christ is in the sacrament "totally, really, and manifoldly." Hus answered by affirming the formula and adding that it is "the same body of Christ which had been born of the Virgin, had suffered, died, and had been resurrected, and that was seated at the right hand of the Father." One would have thought that such an explicit statement would have left no room for any doubt. Indeed, one

[79] Quoted in Hefele–Leclercq (see n. 25), p. 261, n. 2.

[80] There exists a confusion about the name of this Englishman; in some references he is named "Corne" and in others "Corfe." The available evidence favors "Corfe." He died in Constance in 1417, Bishop Flemyng of Lincoln delivering on the occasion a highly eulogistic oration.

of the Englishmen who had spoken before, expressed himself satisfied. Master John Stokes, however, who had had an encounter with Hus during his stop in Prague in 1411,[81] and who had Wyclif on his brain so that he saw him under every bush, threw discredit on this declaration of Hus' by commenting that he had seen in Prague a treatise ascribed to Hus which expressly affirmed remanence. He could not have seen any such treatise, since Hus had never written one. Perhaps he had seen Stanislav's treatise of 1403! Or if he did see Hus' treatise *De corpore Christi*, written against the faulty decree of Archbishop Zbyněk, he completely subverted its plain argument. That treatise explained clearly the orthodox dogma of transubstantiation.

Then they brought against Hus the ridiculous accusation that he had called St. Gregory "a joker and a rimester." When he denied it, Cardinal Zabarella said, "Here are well-nigh twenty witnesses against you," although he admitted some of them "depose from common hearsay, others however from knowledge." Cardinal d'Ailly added, "We cannot judge according to your conscience, but according to what has been proven and deduced here against you and some things you had confessed. We must believe them." He further chided Hus that he suspected Stephen Páleč and even Jean Gerson, "than whom surely no more renowned doctor could be found in all Christendom," of unfair dealing.[82] To both cardinals apparently any word of any witness was the proven truth, and every word of Hus was a lie.

Once started on Hus' "Wyclifism," the members of the commission were loath to give up. They brought up the charge that Hus had "obstinately preached and defended the erroneous articles of Wyclif in schools

[81] "Replica contra Anglicum Joannem Stokes, Wicleffi calumniatorem," in *Historia et monumenta*, I, pp. 135ff.

[82] Mladoňovic, *Relatio*, p. 76; my translation (see n. 5), Part I, pp. 170-171.

and public sermons." Hus made short shrift of that old canard by declaring that he had defended neither the erroneous doctrine of Wyclif nor of anyone else. "And if Wyclif disseminated some errors, let the English see to it."

They further objected that he had resisted the condemnation of the forty-five articles of Wyclif. He replied, as he had always done, that he had objected to their indiscriminate condemnation without Scriptural proof to the contrary. He further pointed out that some articles he did defend, but had qualified them by the saving word "worthily," as indeed he had. Then they charged him with saying that when Wyclif was placed on trial at St. Paul's Cathedral, lightning struck the doors of the church so that the gathered masters and monks scarcely escaped into the city. Thereupon, he was said to have exclaimed: "Would that my soul were where the soul of Wyclif is!" Hus replied that the story went back twelve years, before Wyclif's theological works had been available to him. Having known nothing of him but what was good, he had said: "I know not where the soul of John Wyclif is. I hope that he is saved, but fear lest he be damned. Nevertheless, I desire in hope that my soul were where the soul of John Wyclif is!" At this, the gathered fathers laughed a great deal. They, of course, knew without the slightest doubt that Wyclif's soul was in hell!

However, the members of the commission were indefatigable in their charges of Wyclifism. They accused Hus further that he had opposed the condemnation of Wyclif's books. He defended himself by saying that he had personally brought his copies to Archbishop Zbyněk, asking him (somewhat ironically, to be sure) to "command them to be marked, for I am willing to declare it [your emendations] as such before the whole community." Further they charged him with supporting others who defended Wyclif's errors. He launched into a sharp rebuttal, saying that he knew of no Czech who had been or was now a heretic, although some could be. At first sight this might seem less than a candid and true statement. After all, he knew that Stanislav and Páleč had held Wyclifite views of remanence, since he himself had accused them of it in his polemical treatises. What a sensation it would have created had he pointed his finger at Páleč and said, "There is your man!" It must, however, be recalled that in 1411 Archbishop Zbyněk had been induced to admit that he had found no heretic in the land. This statement was too valuable not to be urged by Hus at the time of the trial.

The commission further objected to Hus' appeal to Christ. This must have been a particularly sore point with them, for it is included in the definitive sentence passed on Hus on July 6. There it is characterized as despising and contemning the due ecclesiastical process by resorting to an appeal to Jesus Christ as the Supreme Judge. At the hearing, the Council members only laughed at him when he reaffirmed that there is no more just and effective appeal than to Christ.

He also was made responsible for the "expelling" of the German masters from the University of Prague (1409). Hus defended himself by truthfully asserting that the Germans had left of their own free will, because they had refused to accept King Wenceslas' decree of Kutná Hora changing the constitution of the university in favor of the Czech nation. The royal emissary, Náz, and the ever-ready Páleč confirmed the accusation by reporting the events in a garbled and truncated fashion, thus in effect falsifying them. For Hus was not responsible for the retaliatory action of the Germans, intended to inflict an irreparable damage, if not destruction, on the university. Hus pointed to Archbishop Warrentrappe, who had been dean of the faculty of arts in

1409, and the leader among the German masters, as participating in the action.

Then Cardinal d'Ailly came back to Hus' assertion that he had come to Constance of his own free will, asserting that neither King Wenceslas nor Emperor Sigismund could have forced him to come. Was that true? Hus answered most positively that it was. Had he not wished to come, many Czech lords had been ready to afford him refuge in their castles and to protect him against both kings. This was, of course, in direct contradiction to the forced testimony of the Prague inquisitor, Bishop Nicholas, given in order to obtain his release from jail. Lord John of Chlum came to Hus' aid by confirming his statement. He went on to say that even he, a poor knight, would have been willing to protect him for a year "whether it would please or displease anyone."

At the end Cardinal d'Ailly counselled Hus to abjure his errors, promising that the Council would deal mercifully with him. Sigismund confirmed this. The emperor then publicly testified that he had given Hus his safe-conduct, adding mistakenly, "even before you had left Prague," guaranteeing him a free hearing before the Council. He further declared that the Council had given Hus "a public, peaceable, and honest hearing"; this was far from being true, and Sigismund should have known it. He also joined the cardinal in advising Hus to hold nothing obstinately, but to throw himself wholly on the mercy of the Council. Should he refuse, "then indeed they know well what they must do." He was not willing to protect a heretic and said that if Hus should remain obstinate, he himself "would kindle the fire and burn him."[83]

The next day, June 8, the examination was continued.

[83] Mladoňovic, *Relatio*, p. 81; my translation (see n. 5), Part I, pp. 179-180.

It consisted principally in comparing the new set of charges drawn from Hus' *De ecclesia, Contra Paletz,* and *Contra Stanislaum,* with the books themselves. (Peter of Mladoňovice made a similar comparison later to judge how accurately the charges had been drawn. In many instances he stated that they had distorted the sense either by inexact quoting or by perversion of the meaning.) Occasionally, Hus added an additional explanation, although sometimes he was forbidden to do so. D'Ailly also interjected the comment here and there that the original text rendered the statement under discussion worse than it read in the charges.[84] Since, however, it would be intolerably redundant to examine the charges in detail or to consider the quotations from the above-named books again, we may wait until the consideration of the final thirty articles to which the accusations were ultimately reduced. The commission had changed the articles several times, although some remained either the same or were retained in a slightly altered form. Thus of the original forty-two articles drawn up by Páleč in January from *De ecclesia,* only eleven were retained, although fifteen others were added, some from Gerson's twenty articles, but others newly extracted. Of the charges drawn from *Contra Paletz* and *Contra Stanislaum,* thirteen were retained. The total, then, examined on this third day of public hearings, amounted to thirty-nine in all.[85]

After the conclusion of the lengthy examination, Cardinal d'Ailly addressed Hus, endeavoring to elicit from him a recantation. He said:

Master John! behold, two ways are placed before you, of which choose one. Either you throw yourself entirely and totally on the grace and into the hands of

---

[84] Mladoňovic, *Relatio,* chap. IV passim; my translation (see n. 5), Part I, pp. 182ff.
[85] Sedlák, *Jan Hus,* supplement, pp. 319-331.

the Council, that whatever it shall dictate to you, therewith you shall be content. And the Council, out of reverence for the lord king of the Romans here and his brother, the king of Bohemia, and for your own good, will deal kindly and humanely with you. Or if you still wish to hold and defend some articles of the forementioned, and if you desire still another hearing, it shall be granted you. But consider that there are here great and enlightened men—doctors and masters—who have such strong reasons against your articles that it is to be feared lest you become involved in greater errors, if you wish to defend and hold these articles. I counsel you; I do not speak as judge.[86]

To this kindly spoken and apparently considerate speech Hus replied as he had always done: that he wished to hold nothing obstinately and was ready to submit to the instruction of the Council.

I pray, however, for God's sake, that a hearing be granted me for the explanation of my meaning of the articles brought against me and of the writings of the holy doctors. And if my reasons and Scripture will not suffice, I wish to submit humbly to the instruction of the Council.[87]

Here was the real rub! The Council was determined to judge Hus on the basis of the articles drawn up by his avowed enemies and demanded of him unconditional submission. On his part, he begged to be allowed to state his own views and to be shown from Scripture where he was wrong. So far, he had not been given such an opportunity, nor was there the slightest likelihood that the Council would grant it. This constituted an un-

[86] Mladoňovic, *Relatio*, p. 103; my translation (see n. 5), Part I, pp. 213-214.
[87] *Ibid.*, p. 214.

resolvable impasse. For conscience's sake, Hus could not submit unconditionally; the Council, on its part, could not yield its declared purpose to judge all Christians, including the popes, and so much more Hus. He begged pitifully:

> I pray for God's sake that you desire not to lay a snare of damnation for me, that I be not forced to lie and abjure those articles of which—God and conscience are my witnesses—I know nothing. . . . Those, however, of which I know and which are stated in my books, if I be instructed as to their opposite, I am willing humbly to revoke.[88]

He quoted the definition of the term "abjure" from the *Catholicon* as meaning to renounce a formerly held error. Accordingly, if he abjured what he had never held, he would lie and commit perjury. Many in the Council shouted that such was not the meaning of the word. Even Sigismund took part in the dispute and urged Hus to abjure, declaring that he should be willing to recant all and any errors, whether or not he had held them. One can easily understand that Sigismund would; but Hus would not! It is a proof of the real moral grandeur of Hus that he could not be swayed by this chorus of the highest representatives of the Roman Church, tumultuously urging him to an act of lying and perjury!

Thereupon, Cardinal Zabarella promised Hus a sufficiently qualified formula which, he said, Hus then could accept. The emperor again urged Hus to reconsider: "You are old enough, you could well understand if you wished." After the session was over, however, the emperor proved his barefaced insincerity. After almost all the members of the Council had departed and only the cardinals and perhaps a few others remained, Sigismund spoke to them in private. He failed to notice that

[88] *Ibid.*, pp. 214-215.

John of Chlum and Wenceslas of Dubá, with Peter of Mladoňovice, stood near the window. The emperor then urged the group of Council dignitaries to burn Hus if he would not recant. But even if Hus should abjure, he said, "do not believe him, nor would I believe him." He warned them not to let Hus return to Bohemia (did any such possibility exist?), for he would there continue to disseminate his heresies. Eradicate the heresies already existing in Bohemia and Poland, he insisted. Put to death Jerome as well, although at the moment he could not think of his name.[89] Here we have the real Sigismund! In the light of these sentiments, can one believe him when he wrote the next year to the Czech and Moravian nobles, "God knows that we were so very sorry as to what happened to him that we could not be more grieved"?[90] This speech overheard by the two Czech nobles, as Palacký remarks, nearly cost Sigismund the succession to the Bohemian throne. "The words spoken in a corner of the Minorite refectory were soon broadcast through the Czech land and nearly cost Sigismund the inheritance of the crown."[91] The nobles and the common people, particularly the Taborites, were so incensed against him that their refusal to acknowledge him as the successor of Wenceslas led to the fourteen years of the Hussite wars. Hus was also deeply wounded by what he regarded as a betrayal by Sigismund. "He condemned me sooner than did my enemies. If at least he had answered like the pagan Pilate, who, having heard the accusations, said: 'I find no fault in this man. . . . ' "[92]

The amended articles, promised by Cardinal Zabarella, were submitted to Hus on June 18. The commission had

[89] *Ibid.*, pp. 221-222.    [90] Palacký, *Documenta*, p. 610.
[91] F. Palacký, *Dějiny národu českého*, 4 vols. (Chicago, 1881), III, p. 99.
[92] Novotný, *Korespondence*, No. 131; my translation (see n. 5), Part II, No. 14.

reduced them from thirty-nine to thirty by deleting eleven and adding two new ones. The text of the articles was also modified.[93] Hus copied them so that he could inform his friends of the final terms. Moreover, he wrote rather short comments on them, inserting them inter-linearly. He had so often made responses to these charges, both in writing and orally, that an extended reply was hardly necessary. The final version of the articles made no essential change in the situation: they still accused him of errors he had not held, nor did he receive in-struction on Scriptural or patristic bases to prove that those he did hold were erroneous. He commented at the end of his copy of the articles that "nothing is left but either to recant or to die at the stake." He decided for the latter. Contrary to the promise made on June 8 by both Cardinal Zabarella and Emperor Sigismund, Hus was not granted another hearing. For that matter, it would have been as useless and inconclusive as the previous ones. These articles received the papal sanc-tion (in 1417) when they were incorporated essentially unchanged into Pope Martin's bull *Inter cunctas*.[94]

In analyzing these final articles on the basis of which Hus was condemned to death, we need concern our-selves but briefly with the testimonies of the witnesses, since they were not included in the pope's bull approv-ing the decisions of the Council. The thirty articles, without a single exception, were declared by Hus to be erroneously formulated. His brief comments (to which we ought to add his previous explanations made in Constance on the same points, as well as his voluminous treatment of these subjects during his entire prior min-istry) state plainly what he actually held contrary to

[93] Palacký, *Documenta*, pp. 225-234; Sedlák, *Jan Hus*, supple-ment, pp. 331-338; my translation (see n. 5), Appendix; also Ap-pendix II of this work.

[94] Hefele–Leclercq (see n. 25), VII/I, pp. 519-522; also C. Mirbt, *Quellen zur Geschichte des Papstum* (Tübingen, 1924), pp. 219ff.

the distorted charges. Of course, that does not prove that he was right in accordance with the doctrinal standards then current. It does prove, however, that what the Council condemned were not Hus' actual doctrinal views but a perverted version of them. Nevertheless, had the Council known them, it is probable that it would have condemned them just the same. Even so it is a remarkable fact that not one of the thirty articles dealt with Scripture or the patristic teaching, on the basis of which Hus was always ready to accept correction of his views.

Examining the charges (see Appendix II) in a summary fashion, it is difficult to see what is wrong with such articles as No. 2, "Paul was never a member of the devil," or No. 4, Jesus Christ is constituted of two natures, human and divine. After all this is exactly the dogmatic formula adopted at the Fourth General Council at Chalcedon (451) and remains the orthodox definition of the dogma to this day. De Vooght also had difficulty in understanding what wrong sense the Council could have seen in this article.[95] The commissioners further accepted the distorted meaning of Nos. 1, 3, 5, and 20. These articles stated that the Church universal consists *only* [*dumtaxat*] of the predestinate who never finally fall away from it. The judges read into this formula a denial of the Church militant. Hus' own meaning had been explained to them so many times that they could not reasonably plead ignorance or doubt of it. In fact, the Council deliberately falsified the formula by refusing, during the third hearing, to admit the other connotation of the word "Church," namely, the mixed Church. Be it further noted that the Council never explicitly acknowledged this tacit subversion; for how could it argue openly that the Church triumphant includes the foreknown? In the sense held by Hus, the Church is

[95] De Vooght, *L'hérésie*, p. 420.

indeed an article of faith (No. 6), as is proved by the clause in the Apostles' Creed asserting belief in the *una, sancta, catholica et apostolica ecclesia*. Even Páleč had so understood the clause.[96] In what sense, then, was Hus wrong in asserting that of *this* catholic Church neither Peter nor any of his successors was the head, but Christ alone? (No. 7). Article 5, asserting that the foreknown is never part of the Church catholic while the predestinate, despite a temporary fall, always remains a member, was declared by the Council to be an error when understood of *all* the predestinate. If any of the predestinate are not members in the sense specified, then indeed they are not members of the *ecclesia catholica propriissime dicta*. This is the well-known confusion, pointed out many times before, of the concepts of the Church catholic held by Hus and by his foes. Is it not obvious that the Church triumphant consists only of the *numerus praedestinatorum*? Did Gerson, who had originally inserted this article into the charges, doubt or deny this obvious truth? Article 16, asserting that Hus taught that a vicious man always commits vicious acts while a virtuous man always performs virtuous deeds, was interpreted by the Council as a denial that a wicked man could ever do a seeming good deed. Hus did not teach this.

Twelve of the articles deal with the papacy. It is remarkable that the Council, which had deposed two popes and secured the abdication of the third, was so morbidly sensitive on this subject. In article 9 it charged Hus with error or heresy because of his asserting that the papal dignity was granted by a number of emperors. This is no more than a historical fact. Surely the papal territories were acquired by imperial grants and, as we now know, by the aid of the forged decretals. Christ had no such possessions and therefore could not have

[96] Jan Sedlák, "Pálčův spis proti Husovu traktátu 'De ecclesia,'" *Hlídka* (Brno, 1912), p. 11, n. 1.

passed them on to the popes. What the article suppressed was Hus' free recognition of the papal spiritual powers as derived from Christ. Furthermore, since no one can be positively certain of his predestinatory status, neither can the pope (Nos. 10 and 11). Moreover, no one occupies the place of Christ or Peter worthily unless he proves it by emulating them in his life (Nos. 12, 13, 21, and 24). Did John XXIII occupy that place meritoriously? Even the legitimate election of the pope does not guarantee his moral qualities (No. 26). This most important distinction which Hus made between a *veritable* pope or prelate and one merely legitimately elected had ever been offensive to his foes. Hus did not, however, deny that even a wicked and foreknown pope exercises his powers legitimately, provided he does not order anything contrary to God's commands. He is a legitimate, but not a *veritable* shepherd of Christ's sheep. Moreover, why was it an error worthy of death to object to the title *sanctissimus* as applied to the pope? (No. 22). Was not the title *sanctus*, conceded by Hus, sufficient? Was John XXIII even a *sanctus*? Nor is a visible head ruling vicariously in Christ's stead absolutely necessary (No. 27), although Hus never advocated the abolition of the papacy as Wyclif did. On the contrary, he acknowledged it repeatedly by his own appeals to it. Christ could rule His Church better without the wicked popes (No. 28), through His faithful priests, as He had done prior to the establishment of the papacy (No. 29).

Priests living criminally pollute the priestly power (No. 8). Did not the Council admit that as true? A good priest ought to preach, an unlawful excommunication notwithstanding, even if the pope forbids it (Nos. 17 and 18). The stress here is on the *unlawful* excommunication. Hus did not deny the lawful exercise of ecclesiastical jurisdiction. Irregular and illegal exercise of ecclesiastical power proceeds from Antichrist (No. 19).

Surely, the Council did not mean to condone such *illegal* acts? After all it solemnly declared that its aim was the reformation of the Church in head and members. Furthermore, the assertion of the Prague doctors that whoever refuses to be subjected to ecclesiastical censure is to be turned over to secular judgment to be put to death (No. 14) is not in accordance with Christ's teaching. With a few exceptions, Hus denied that the death penalty should be imposed for religious opinions. In this he was ahead of his age. Even De Vooght comments sarcastically that it is a mystery where in the Gospels the doctors found the doctrine. No one is secular or ecclesiastical lord while in mortal sin (No. 30). How many times, however, did Hus explain that no one is such *worthily*, in the sight of God, although *de facto* he legitimately holds his office? Again, is that heresy? Surely, men in mortal sin do not hold their office as God intended that they should. Similarly about the condemnation of Wyclif's forty-five articles (No. 25) and about ecclesiastical obedience (No. 15); the correct explanation had been offered by Hus so many times previously that it need not be repeated.

As for the testimonies of the witnesses, Hus categorically denied seventeen of them with a flat "It is not true." Of three he says that they are partly true, but for the rest false. He acknowledges as true only Nos. 15 and 16, which assert that he refused to obey the papal order forbidding preaching in chapels.

From this point on, Hus' fate was sealed. He knew it, and several times he mentioned his foreboding of imminent death in his letters. He wrote on June 21: "This is my final intention in the name of Jesus Christ: that I refuse to confess as erroneous the articles which have been truthfully abstracted and, to abjure the articles ascribed to me by false witnesses. . . . For God knows that I have never preached those errors which they have concocted. . . ."[97]

Yet the Council did not act to pronounce the final judgment. It preferred to induce Hus to recant rather than to burn him at the stake. In fact, one of the members of the Council either took it upon himself voluntarily or was commissioned to attempt to change Hus' resolution. It was this Council dignitary who delivered to Hus a revised formula, which read:

I, ——, aside from my former declarations which I made and which I now repeat, declare again that despite all the charges with which I am charged and which I have never dreamed of, I submit humbly as to all the points of which I am accused to the decision and correction of the holy general Council, and accept all abjurations, retractions, penitence and other measures which the holy Council, to which I recommend myself, shall judge proper to determine for the salvation of my soul.[98]

In his replies, Hus addresses this person as "Father." Of course, any member of the Council could be so addressed. Bartoš, however, ventures a guess that this was Master John "Cardinal" of Rejnštejn, the delegate representing the University of Prague, although he advances no other substantiation of his theory than that he was known among Hus' intimate friends as "Father."[99] The three letters exchanged by the two men (the first

[97] Novotný, *Korespondence*, No. 140; my translation (see n. 5), Part II, No. 20.

[98] Hefele–Leclercq (see n. 25), VII/I, p. 299.

[99] Bartoš (see n. 1), p. 438. Lenfant, in his *Histoire de Concile de Constance*, had advanced the same idea. It does not seem probable to me. John "Cardinal" was Hus' pupil and intimate friend. He came to Constance in Hus' company and remained in close touch with his friends during his stay. The respectful and formal tone of Hus' letters gives no hint of an intimacy of this sort. Furthermore, it does not seem probable that John "Cardinal" would try to convince Hus that he should recant, even though it

one, written by the "Father," is not extant)[100] bear witness to the attitude of the most favorably inclined member of the Council and to the valiant and firm stand of Hus. In his reply to the first letter Hus writes that he dare not submit, for he would thereby condemn truths he had preached and so fall into perjury. He would thus scandalize the people who had heard him preach. To this the "Father" replied that it would not be he who would condemn the truth but those "who are at present your as well as our superiors." As to perjury, "it would not redound upon you, but upon those who exact it." This was pure sophistry and Hus treated it as such. He repeats in his reply the same reasons for non-compliance as before: "How could I, who have for so many years preached about patience and constancy, fall into many lies and perjury and give offense to many sons of God? Be it far, far from me!" In another letter Hus speaks of a great many other people who exhorted him to recant. Some asserted that the term "abjure" does not mean renouncing a professed heresy. Others that it is meritorious to submit to the Church out of humility even if one is not guilty of the crime charged. An Englishman cited to him the example of recantation made by some English masters suspected of Wyclif's opinions. A certain doctor argued that even if the Council declared that he had only one eye although he had two, he should consent to it.[101]

Páleč came to visit Hus at his request, for Hus had asked that he be assigned him as his confessor. This is

---

involved lying and perjury. Only four days later Hus wrote to Peter and John "Cardinal" and calls them angels having been sent to comfort and strengthen him in his trials. Had the latter attempted to shake his resolution, it is most improbable that he would have written him in that vein.

[100] Novotný, *Korespondence*, Nos. 136-138; my translation (see n. 5), Part II, Nos. 16-18.

[101] Novotný, No. 143; my translation, No. 21.

one of the most poignant and deeply touching scenes of Hus' last days. He had asked for Páleč "because he is my principal adversary." (Actually, some monk was given him as confessor.) When Páleč came and attempted to persuade Hus to recant, Hus asked him what he would do if he were requested to recant errors he was certain of never having held. To that he replied: "That is difficult," and began to weep.[102] Hus asked his former intimate friend to forgive him, particularly for having called him *Fictor*, a deceiver. Hus also recalled many denunciations Páleč had hurled against him, most of which he denied. They wept together.

After the Council condemned his books—later he found that only the treatises, presumably those submitted to it, had been condemned—Hus wrote to his friends in Bohemia exhorting them not to be terrified into giving up reading them. He told them of the deposition of Pope John (which had taken place about a month before) and challenged the papalist faction:

> Answer now, you preachers who preach that the pope is the earthly god, that he cannot sin and cannot commit simony! The jurists say that the pope . . . is the heart of the holy Church which he nourishes spiritually; that he is the fountain from which flows all power and goodness; that he is the sun of the holy Church; that he is the unfailing refuge to which every Christian must flee. Well! that head is already cut off, the god of this world is bound and his sins are already made manifest; the fountain has already dried up, the sun is darkened, the heart is torn out, and the refuge is fled from Constance and is imprisoned so that no one will flee to it.[103]

He reproves the members of the Council that before the condemnation of John they knelt before him and kissed

102 Novotný, Nos. 143, 145; my translation, Nos. 21, 23.
103 Novotný, No. 146; my translation, No. 24.

his feet, although they knew that "he was a heretic, a murderer, and a Sodomite," the sins they themselves later made public. In a letter to "all faithful Czechs" Hus wrote later:

O, had you seen that Council which calls itself most holy, that cannot err, you would surely have seen the greatest abomination! For I have heard it commonly said by the Swabians that Constance . . . would not for thirty years rid itself of the sins which that Council committed in their city.[104]

All attempts at inducing Hus to abjure having proved in vain, the Council at last decided to act. It must have given Hus an intimation of this, for he wrote on June 26, 27, and 29 beautiful letters of farewell to his friends in Bohemia, to his faithful protectors, John of Chlum and Wenceslas of Dubá, to the University of Prague, and to Peter of Mladoňovice.[105] To the last-named he wrote a particularly poignant letter full of gratitude. He was still deeply worried because of his inability to repay Lord John for the expenses incurred by him in connection with Hus' journey. To Peter he wrote: "Be assured that there is not enough money with which I should like to recompense you for your most fervent, most firm, and most faithful love which you have for the truth and for your services and consolations which you have shown me in my tribulations. May God be your great reward, for I have not whence to reward you!"[106] He signed himself as "standing on the shore of the present life, expecting tomorrow a terrible death. . . ."

Again he was mistaken. The Council still did not see fit to take the final step. It was not until July 5 that Hus knew for certain that the verdict would be pro-

[104] Novotný, No. 153; my translation, No. 28.
[105] Novotný, Nos. 152-153, 155-156, 160; my translation, Nos. 27-31.
[106] *Ibid.*, No. 31.

nounced the next day. Sigismund sent the two Czech nobles, John of Chlum and Wenceslas of Dubá, along with four bishops, to the Minorite monastery to hear Hus' final decision. When Hus was brought out of the prison to meet them, Lord John said to him that they, as laymen, did not know how to advise him. If he felt guilty, he should not fear to be instructed. But if he did not, let him remain steadfast to death. Hus then, weeping, assured Lord John that if he knew of any heresy of his own, he would humbly recant if he were shown his error. One of the bishops asked whether Hus regarded himself as wiser than the whole Council. Hus then once more begged to be given "the least one of the Council" to instruct him from Scripture as to his error and that he would then instantly recant. The bishops, exclaiming that Hus was obstinate in his heresy, went away.

Thereupon Hus wrote to his friends in Constance that tomorrow at the sixth hour he would have to say whether he was willing to acknowledge every one of the thirty articles as erroneous; to confess that he preached what the witnesses had testified against him; and to recant all these proven errors. To this he intended to reply in writing:

> I, John Hus, in hope a servant of Jesus Christ, am not willing to declare that every article drawn from my books is erroneous. . . . Secondly, concerning the articles ascribed to me by false witnesses, I am not willing to confess that I have asserted, preached, and held them. Thirdly, I am not willing to recant lest I commit perjury.[107]

Brave words of a courageous servant of God! His wish to remain steadfast and firm in the truth was fulfilled. Then the next day, July 6, Hus was led by the arch-

[107] Novotný, No. 163; my translation, No. 33.

bishop of Riga into the cathedral. Sigismund presided at this session. When Hus had been brought into the church, Jacob Balardi Arrigoni, bishop of Lodi, delivered a sermon on the text "that the body of sin might be destroyed."[108] Taken out of its context, it served his purpose well. He denounced heresies, although Paul had put a quite different meaning into the text. The bishop quoted Jerome as having written that "rotten limbs must be cut out of the body lest the whole body be infected by rottenness and perish."

> Who cares for the keys of the Church? Who is afraid of its punishments? Who defends its immunity? . . . The goods of the clergy, the alms of the poor and the pilgrims, bought with the blood of the Savior and the martyrs, are seized and scattered.[109]

Thereupon, Henry of Piro, procurator of the Council, proceeded with the formalities required on such occasions. He was followed by Bertold of Wildungen, the curial auditor, who read the final thirty articles and the testimonies of the witnesses. Hus tried to protest or correct certain statements, but Cardinal d'Ailly bade him be silent and to reply to all at the end. However, at the end he was not given a chance to reply. Cardinal Zabarella shouted at him, "Be silent now. We have already heard you enough." He also ordered the soldiers to carry out the order of silencing him. Thereupon, Bishop Anthony of Concordia read the definitive sentence.[110] There were two texts of it held in readiness: one for use in case Hus should recant at the last moment, another if he should not. Hus was declared an obstinate disciple of Wyclif, repeatedly disobedient to the eccle-

---

[108] Rom. 6:6.          [109] Bartoš (see n. 1), p. 446.

[110] The text is given in Novotný, *Fontes rerum Bohemicarum*, VIII, pp. 501ff. My translation (see n. 5), Part II, No. 35. Sedlák, *Studie a texty*, I, pp. 349ff., and in his *Jan Hus*, supplement, pp. 344-353, published the two preliminary drafts of the sentence.

siastical authorities, unlawfully appealing his case to Jesus Christ. As an incorrigible heretic he was declared sentenced to the deprivation of his priestly office and then to be turned over to the secular authorities. His books were to be publicly burned. Hus, falling on his knees, prayed: "Lord Jesus Christ, I implore Thee, forgive all my enemies for Thy great mercy's sake. . . ." It is interesting to note from the draft prepared for the eventuality that Hus might recant, that he would in that case have been "perpetually incarcerated."[111]

Thereupon, the seven bishops appointed for the task, proceeded with the ceremony of depriving Hus of the priestly office. He was ordered to mount a platform erected in the middle of the cathedral and to put on the vestments as for the celebration of the mass. Then the bishops took the cup from his hands, pronouncing a curse at the same time. Hus loudly exclaimed that he hoped to drink from it in the heavenly kingdom. Then they divested him of the vestments, pronouncing with each article an appropriate curse. Hus responded that he was willing to suffer it for the sake of Christ. They proceeded then to obliterate his tonsure. But a dispute arose among them whether it ought to be done with a razor or merely with scissors. In the end, the latter method was adopted. They cut his tonsure into four parts, pronouncing him deprived of all ecclesiastical rights. They placed a paper crown on his head on which were painted three devils, fighting for his soul. It bore the inscription, "This is a heresiarch." Therewith they committed his soul to the devil. Hus responded by committing himself to Jesus Christ. He was then turned over to the secular arm.

Sigismund, on whom Hus turned his eyes after the sentence, turned red. When Hus was committed to him, the emperor turned him over to Duke Ludwig of the

111 Sedlák, *Jan Hus*, supplement, p. 351.

Palatinate, the son of the one-time king of the Romans, Ruprecht, known as Clem (Clement). Ludwig then placed him in the hands of the executioners.

When the sad procession passed the cemetery of the church where his books were being burned, Hus smiled. They took him outside the city gate to a meadow. Almost the whole town accompanied him. He fell on his knees and prayed to God for His mercy. He was divested of his clothing down to his shirt and tied to the stake with ropes and an old rusty chain. Bundles of wood mixed with straw were stacked up to his chin. Before the pyre was kindled, the imperial marshal, Hoppe of Poppenheim, and Duke Ludwig, approached the stake, exhorting him for the last time to recant. Hus replied: "God is my witness that those things that are falsely ascribed to me and of which false witnesses accuse me, I have never taught nor preached. . . ." The executioners were then ordered to kindle the pyre. Hus sang in a loud voice, "Christ, Thou son of the living God, have mercy on me," and repeated it. When he began to sing it the third time, the wind blew the fire into his face. He continued to pray silently until he expired.

The executioners burned what was left of his body. Finding his heart, they impaled it on a sharpened stick and incinerated it. They were then ordered to burn his clothing. When all was consumed, they loaded the ashes into a cart and threw the whole load into the Rhine.

Thus died Master John Hus for the truth he had found and would never surrender. Mladoňovic concludes his epic with the words that he wrote the account "in order that the memory of the Master, the most steadfast champion of truth, might thus live in the future."

## CHAPTER XI

## CONCLUSION

I N judging Hus' personality and character, it behooves us to remember that in a real sense we thereby judge ourselves. Our judgments inevitably reflect our life-experiences and the convictions formed on this necessarily personal basis. Thus our judgment of Hus is a confession and revelation of our own personality. Proceeding then frankly on this basis, I find Hus' character revealed in the clearest light in his letters, although of course his entire academic and public career must be included as well. All these sources testify that he was essentially a reformer whose ideal was the pure Church. Against the tragic background of an era of general decline and even degradation of the Church, caused to a large extent by the shocking rivalry of two and later three popes fighting with each other for the high prize of the Apostolic See, Hus' reform efforts are conspicuously poignant. In his endeavor he followed in the footsteps not only of his own Czech predecessors, but also of the numerous advocates of reform throughout the fourteenth and the early fifteenth centuries. Not the least among them was John Wyclif, who afforded Hus an example of courageous striving for reform as well as its theoretical underpinning. Hus himself is revealed in this his life-work, as a zealous, straightforward, courageous realist. There is no trace of pretense, hypocrisy, or sham about him. His is an honest, plain-speaking, utterly committed, down-to-earth personality. There is no mystic exaltation in his composition, although he is capable of eloquent enthusiasm. He prefers sober, practical, concretely religious and ethical themes to abstract theoretical speculation or flights of fancy. He occupies a moderate theological position vis-à-vis both his foes and friends. There is no essential or radical change in his views throughout his public ministry. The violent polemics, beginning with his opposition to Pope John's "crusading bull," were called forth by the extreme papalism of his opponents, and by the charges of heresy they leveled at him, which he answered to a degree in kind. Despite his moderation, however, he was utterly uncompromising and unyielding where any *essential* truth was concerned. He himself summarized this attitude in the memorable passage:

> Therefore, faithful Christian, seek the truth, hear the truth, learn the truth, love the truth, speak the truth, adhere to the truth to death. . . .[1]

He practiced this devotion to truth consistently, even to his hurt and ultimate death. Thus he deserves the tribute paid him by Peter of Mladoňovice: "the most steadfast champion" of truth. Hus did not hesitate to denounce even the pope or to disobey the express command of the king in the crucial test of his spiritual integrity during the struggle over indulgences. Nor did he ultimately flinch the supreme test at the Council of Constance, when even Cardinal d'Ailly and Emperor Sigismund urged him to save his life by what Hus rightly regarded as lying and perjury. For him not to defend truth was to betray it.

His piety was genuine and even ascetical. He shared the medieval view that faith formed by love alone is the saving faith. He therefore not only exhorted his hearers to a life of emulation of Christ by virtuous works, but his own life of apostolic poverty and practice of piety preached the doctrine as eloquently as his words. He never arrogantly asserted his own "saved" status. In the *Sermones de sanctis* he penitently acknowl-

[1] "Výklad víry," p. 15 in F. Žilka, ed., *Mistra Jana Husi Vybrané spisy*, 2 vols. (Jilemnice, n.d.), p. 15.

edged his own failings by confessing that three things had kept him humble before God: (1) his excessive sins against God's commandments; (2) the desire to be esteemed by men, even to be held better than he was; and (3) his uncertainty whether he would be saved; for although he had a firm hope of salvation, yet he feared he might not persevere to the end and might thus be damned. "The first among these three I esteem the gravest, the second less grave, and the third the least. . . ." He was extremely sensitive about even the smallest of his former faults and to the very end regretted his youthful chess playing and love of fine clothes.

In his religious and theological views Hus, contrary to the prevailing popular opinion, was generally more conservative and "orthodox" than Wyclif and some of his friends of the "evangelical" party. Men like Jakoubek of Stříbro and Jerome of Prague were definitely more radical than he. Even Peter of Chelčice, who was not of his party, later criticized him severely for retaining the traditional division of society into the three estates of clergy, nobility, and the common people. Peter recognized no distinction of social status among the members of the Church of Christ. Nevertheless, Hus' forward-looking, creatively progressive ideas represented the initial stages of the Reformation. Its basic elements were already present in Hus' thought.

Hus' emphasis on Scripture was rigorous, although he admitted tradition as a source of doctrine, provided it was consonant with Scripture. Thus although for him the law of God was the norm and criterion of all Christian doctrine, he did not teach the *sola Scriptura* tenet of the later Reformers. Strictly speaking, they too did not teach it in the narrow sense which is sometimes ascribed to them. They interpreted it, just as Hus did, in accordance with the creeds and the patristic teaching of the first five centuries. For instance, Calvin's *Institutes of the Christian Religion* is actually an extended commentary on the Apostles' Creed. Hus did not say that nothing is to be tolerated in the Church which is not found in Scripture, but only nothing which is contrary to it. It was in accordance with this principle that he believed in the resurrection and ascension to heaven of the Virgin Mary, which was certainly an unscriptural doctrine preserved only in tradition. He held her in surprisingly high veneration as the intercessor for sinners, ranking above the angelic host. Nevertheless, she was still only a created being, although the highest among the human race. He likewise believed in the saints, but warned against superstitious reverence of them bordering on worship. Only God is to be worshipped. The purgatory and the customary aids for the relief of the souls therein were also among his traditional beliefs. His chief emphasis as preacher and theologian was the stress laid on good works as necessary for salvation. He heartily and unreservedly accepted the dogma of transubstantiation as well as the other sacraments, and objected only to their abuse, not their proper use. He acknowledged the distinctions inherent in the sacrament of orders and the legitimacy of the jurisdiction of the prelates. Even the wicked priest or the prelate in mortal sin performs his office validly, although not worthily.

If Hus shared with his age the many traditional doctrines, he was ahead of his age in professing and defending some genuinely forward-looking beliefs. These were basic to all his reformatory purposes and practices. Among them was, first of all, Hus' insistence on the right of private understanding and interpretation of Scripture, rather than the slavish acceptance of, and submission to, the exclusive magisterial authority of the Church in interpreting Scripture. The believer had the duty of scrutinizing whether the commands of his superior were not contrary to Scripture; if they were, he had to reject them. Such a position, regarded by the ecclesiastical authorities as the height of audacious disobedience and plain rebellion, necessarily implied the duty of judging all the commands of both ecclesiastical and secular authorities whether they conform to the commands of Christ and His apostles. In other words, he asserted the right and duty of the individual to hold and declare the truth of which he is convinced. Hus' age was not ready for such a revolutionary innovation. Nor was the Church or society ready to concede freedom of conscience for several centuries thereafter.

Among the new elements of Hus' outlook one of the most important was the concept of the Church universal consisting of the predestined alone. This differed radically from the concept of the Church as consisting of all baptized believers, the *communio fidelium*, which the Roman, the Eastern Orthodox, and some Protestant churches hold to this day. Predestination was in a sense the means of attaining the goal of a Church "without spot or wrinkle." Although Hus did not deny the existence of the Church militant—in our way of speaking the visible institution comprising all members irrespective of their spiritual condition—it is obvious from all his emphatic declarations on the subject that for him the real and true Church was the body of Christ, composed of Christ's elect, of which He alone is the Head. No person in whatever place of authority, even the pope, not a member of this true Church, is a *veritable* pastor of Christ's sheep. This distinction between the *veritable* and the technically valid, *de facto* office-holding is basic to Hus' thought. It may best be understood by recalling the figure of the good Bishop Bienvenue in Hugo's *Les Misérables*. He was a *veritable* bishop as against the many in the French Church who were merely canonically consecrated. Hus insisted on spiritual and ethical qual-

ities, in addition to ecclesiastical ordination or consecration, as necessary to all clerics. Such qualities are
then evidenced by a life emulating the virtues of Christ
and his apostles. Office alone does not make a priest or
prelate any more than the name of Christian makes a
man a member of the body of Christ. This inexorable
demand of Hus' was a necessary means of reforming the
Church "in head and members." It was also the chief
cause of his conflict with the Church authorities.

Of great importance is Hus' forward-looking concept
of the "federal" nature of the Church. The Church militant is divided into a number of particular churches—
the Roman, Eastern Orthodox, Monophysite, Nestorian,
and others. Later the Protestant particular churches were
to be added to the list. The Roman Church by itself is
not the whole Church militant, nor is the papacy divinely
instituted to rule it, even though Hus conceded a certain
preeminence to it. Of the Eastern Orthodox or the other
churches Hus had but a vague and fragmentary knowledge; yet he recognized the legitimacy of their ecclesiastical autonomy. He thus held in essence the ancient
theory that the five patriarchates—Rome, Constantinople, Alexandria, Antioch, and Jerusalem—together
constituted the supreme authority in Christendom; the
pope of Rome was acknowledged as *primus inter pares*
among the patriarchs, but by no means as their superior.
Although Hus' immediate milieu was Roman Catholic,
yet he fought its universalist pretensions without regard
for consequences.

Even more far-ranging was his ecumenical outlook.
Since the Church is one, composed of all who possess
the spirit of Christ (for that is the actual content and
significance of the theological term "predestination"),
all members of the Church militant having this spirit
form the one, true, invisible Church. No matter of
what particular church they are members, no matter in

what non-essential element of ecclesiastical custom or
doctrinal formulation they differ, they are one in Christ.
They alone constitute the body of Christ, the true
Church catholic. Theirs is a spiritual unity, not merely
an organizational union of particular churches, as many
present-day ecumenical leaders envisage it. This *una,
sancta, catholica, apostolica ecclesia,* in which the Roman
Church shares, but which it does not constitute, is the
essence of Hus' "heresy." His ecclesiology was universal:
the Church is the body of Christ, the invisible Church
comprising all Christ's elect within all visible churches.
No partial category fits him: from our own vantage point
of five hundred and fifty years, we may better understand
and appreciate more fully Hus' life-long endeavor to
affirm this ecumenical concept than any previous age,
not so conscious of ecumenical goals, could do. He continually stressed the *one* Church invisible. It mattered
not to which particular church—in our terminology
"denomination"—the elect belonged. If this be "heresy,"
as it is considered even today by those whose horizon
is limited by an inadequate and mistaken concept of the
Church, then many of the best Christian spirits before
us and among us share the obloquy.

Finally, among the new emphases in Hus' teaching is
his rejection of any but the "ministerial," declaratory
function of the priest in dispensing the sacraments, particularly that of penance. Only God forgives sins, the
priest merely declares the fact when the necessary conditions of forgiveness have been satisfied. It consequently
follows, therefore, that every believer has direct access
to God, without the priestly intermediation. This is the
tenet later known as "the priesthood of all believers."
Hus also joined Jakoubek of Stříbro in demanding communion in both species of bread and wine and denounced
its prohibition by the Council. This practice, inaugu-
rated in the church of St. Martin in the Wall in Prague

late in 1414, even prior to Hus' consent, has become the established norm in all Protestant churches. They are debtors to these two men for the reintroduction into the worship of the Church of the practice declared by the Apostle Paul as commanded by the Lord Himself. Furthermore, Hus declared the preaching of the Word as the prime duty of the Church and deprecated the multiplication of rites and ceremonies which crowded out preaching from the services of worship.

As for Hus' personality and character, he was genuinely devoted to his friends and forgiving toward his enemies. His letters from Constance bear eloquent testimony of his tender concern for even the humblest of his Bethlehem congregation—the shoemakers, tailors, and other poor artisans. He exhorted them:

> . . . obey the Lord God, extol His Word, and gladly hear and follow it. I pray that you hold that truth of God which I have drawn from the law of God and have preached and written from the teachings of the saints. I also beseech you that if anyone has heard in my preaching or in private anything against the truth of God, or if I have written anything anywhere —and I trust God there is nothing—that he does not hold it. I also beseech you that if anyone has seen in me any levity of morals in speaking or actions, that he does not hold them, but that he pray God for me that He may be pleased to forgive me.[2]

He concluded the letter with the appeal: "I beseech you, particularly the Praguers, to be kind toward Bethlehem as long as the Lord God will be pleased that the Word of God be preached there." He had among his congregation also members of the upper classes. Even Queen

[2] V. Novotný, ed., *M. Jana Husi Korespondence a dokumenty* (Praha, 1920), No. 129; my translation in *John Hus at the Council of Constance* (New York, Columbia University Press, 1965), Part II, No. 13.

Sophia occasionally visited the services. In the letter quoted above he asked his congregation to pray for the king and the queen, despite Wenceslas' abandonment of him to his enemies. Had the king continued his former support and defense of Hus, he probably would not have suffered death. One must remember that it was the protection of John, the Duke of Lancaster, that saved Wyclif; and that of the Elector Frederick of Saxony that did the same for Luther. Hus' solicitude for these different groups among his hearers moved him to write, in exile, most of his Czech treatises. His extraordinarily friendly interest in people of all stations in life is attested even by the short tracts he wrote for his jailers in the Dominican prison. Nor did he forget his colleagues among the university masters, for all of whom, students included, he expressed tender care. He admonished them to faithfulness in upholding the truth and concord among themselves. In the farewell letter written ten days before his death he wrote:

> I exhort you for the sake of the most kind Jesus Himself that you love one another, root out schisms, and promote the honor of God before all else. Remember that I have always sought the advancement of the university to the honor of God, that I grieved over your discords and excesses, and wished to unite our illustrious nation into one. . . . Moreover, dearly beloved in Christ Jesus, stand in the truth you have learned, for it conquers all and is mighty to eternity. . . . I said that I detest whatever false sense exists in any of the articles, and commit it to the correction of the Lord Jesus Christ, who knows my sincere intention and does not interpret it in a wrong sense which I do not intend. I exhort you also in the Lord that whatever wrong sense you may be able to discern in any of

those articles, that you relinquish it, but always preserve the truth that is intended.[3]

Hus also abounds in gratitude to his knightly protectors,
the lords John of Chlum and Wenceslas of Dubá, as
well as to his old benefactor, Christian of Prachatice.

He was forgiving to his enemies, even those who persistently worked for years for his condemnation and
death. He frequently prayed that God might forgive
them, particularly Stephen Páleč, Michael de Causis,
and Bishop John of Litomyšl. The deeply moving scene
when Páleč came to visit Hus in prison has already been
described.

His steadfast defense of Wyclif, which without a
doubt hurt him as much as his attack on Pope John's
"crusading bull," is another example of his faithful, even
recklessly daring devotion to his friends and to truth.
He admired Wyclif for his valiant struggle against corruption in high places and for his desire to reform the
Church on the evangelical pattern. Nor was he unaware
of Wyclif's "heresies." Thus, for instance, when he participated in the *Quodlibet* of July 1412, he plainly disagreed with those theses he defended and only argued
for their true, catholic sense. Even De Vooght declares
that Hus "corrected" Wyclif.[4] Thus the important thing
to observe is not only what Hus says about Wyclif but
what he leaves unsaid. What he omits in his direct quotations from Wyclif, both in acknowledged and unacknowl-
edged cases, is more important than what he adopts.
Moreover, it must ever be borne in mind that what Hus
really rejected was the distorted interpretation of Wyclif's teaching given it in the forty-five articles. The
"image" of Hus as a thoroughgoing Wyclifite, in the

[3] Novotný, *Korespondence*, No. 155; my translation (see n. 1),
Part II, No. 30.
[4] Paul de Vooght, *L'hérésie de Jean Huss* (Louvain, Publications
universitaire de Louvain, 1960), p. 214.

sense of the forty-five articles, which persists even to this day, was largely created by his enemies, both native and foreign. It was foisted on the Council "with malice afore-thought," because it was the easiest way to secure his condemnation and death. It is high time that historians stopped repeating this malicious falsehood and adopted a critical view of Hus based on a knowledge of his own views. Will this detract from his reputation as a reformer? Hus himself would not desire to enjoy a reputation based on less than strictly historical ground. He ever insisted that "Truth conquers all."

Since Hus really in many ways strove for the same goals as many earnest Conciliarists who dominated the Council did, why was he condemned by them? Ostensibly, as more than two-thirds of the final articles as well as the definitive verdict testify, for his Wyclifism and anti-papalism. The verdict, after damning the memory of Wyclif, states that "a certain John Hus in this sacred Council here personally present—a disciple not of Christ but of the heresiarch John Wyclif . . . ," dared to teach, assert and preach Wyclif's heresies. Hus' "anti-papalism" has been sufficiently dealt with in our analysis of the thirty articles. These, then, were the ostensible reasons for the verdict. What were the real, though un-acknowledged, motives for the condemnation? First of all—its declared aim—the Council had the tasks of terminating the Schism and eradicating heresies. It accomplished the first of these. The three outstanding cases of heresy to be dealt with were those of John Wyclif, John Hus, and Jerome of Prague. The first-named was easily disposed of, since Wyclif had been dead for more than thirty years. The cases of Hus and Jerome were then the only concrete instances to be considered. When we assess only Hus' case, it is abundantly evident that since the Council had accepted the false accusations and aspersions of heresy broadcast about him prior to his coming to

Constance, he had no chance of receiving a fair trial. His judges were deeply biased, determined to condemn him under any circumstances. In a way, they had to prove that they would not deal with heresy more leniently than with the popes. Even prior to Hus' arrest, the commissioners, as he wrote in a letter to John Chlum, "had issued a bull, which was read before me, in which I was called a heresiarch."[5] After his arrest, his judges made every effort to convict him of Wyclifism and, as the definitive sentence proves, never gave up their preconceived notion. The three "hearings" he was granted were but a forced concession to Sigismund and certainly failed to afford Hus the desired opportunity to state freely "the faith that was in him." His own denials of the charges were either ignored or disbelieved. As the Frenchman Jean Mauroux expressed it when denying the request of the Czech nobles that Hus be placed either in their or some bishop's custody, he was under no circumstances to be trusted. He was assumed to be a liar and, therefore, anything he said in his defense was regarded as essentially worthless. Since the Council never allowed him to state his own views or explain his own intended meaning of the charges against him, it actually condemned not Hus' own beliefs and teaching but the garbled charges of his enemies, in which his teachings were perverted from their proper meaning.

Moreover, Hus' concept of the Church was irreconcilable with that of the leading members of the Council. For Hus the Church was a spiritual entity, the fellowship of the saints, the body of Christ. Membership in it depended on God's election, not on man's choice. No one was a member *ex officio*, as the papalists held. Furthermore, his "federalist" theory of the Church, which in

[5] Novotný, *Korespondence*, No. 106; F. Palacký, ed., *Documenta Mag. Joannis Hus* (Praha, F. Tempský, 1869), No. 51; my translation (see n. 1), Part II, No. 9.

effect denied the primacy of the Roman Church and
logically implied the view of the primacy of the Church
invisible over all visible churches, was utterly repulsive
to the pretensions of the Roman Church. The Conciliarists, on the other hand, regarded the Church as a
juridical corporation, the *congregatio fidelium,* of which
the Council was the lawful and authoritative representative. The Roman Church was likewise a legal entity
composed principally of the pope, the cardinals, and the
hierarchy. It is this legalistic concept, formulated chiefly
by Cardinal Zabarella, that the Council identified with
the body of Christ. Brian Tierney defined it as "the
gradual assimilation into the canonistic theory of the
ancient doctrine of the Church as the Mystical Body of
Christ, with a consequent fusion between the theological
concept of mystical unity in the Church and the juristic
idea of legal incorporation. . . ."[6] These two concepts were
basically irreconcilable. The Council, instinctively sens-
ing and rightly recognizing the danger to their view in
Hus' concept, condemned him. From their own point of
view of the divinely instituted papal primacy and of the
Council's right to judge all members of the Church, they
were right. Hus' view was indeed destructive of all legalistic concepts, as was proved in the Lutheran and Calvinistic Reformation. They were damnedly wrong only
when the Church is regarded as a fellowship of those
possessing the spirit of Christ. This tragic conflict between the two concepts was the real cause of the charges
against Hus, even though it was never explicitly so
formulated.

The nominalistic opposition to the philosophical
realism of Hus, and the Germans' hatred of the man
whom they wrongly held responsible for the "expulsion"

[6] Brian Tierney, *Foundations of the Conciliar Theory* (Cambridge, Cambridge University Press, 1955), p. 246.

of the German masters from the university in 1409, served as additional reasons for the unfairness of Hus' trial.

In general, then, Hus, was a child of his age, sharing many elements of the theology and the world-view of the late medieval era, although he differed from it by his greater emphasis on Scriptural authority and on the patristic teaching of the first five centuries. On the other hand, he stood on the threshold of the new era which within a century of his death eventuated in the Reformation. That era repudiated much of his medieval heritage, but it also further developed and amplified the forward-looking elements of his thought. In the last analysis, judging from the perspective of our own times, Hus was not the victim of the Council; rather it was he who judged the Council. He judged the contemporaneous Church as well, as he judges ours today. In his moral stature, his unyielding devotion to truth as he knew it, in the purity and integrity of his character, and in his heroic and unswerving loyalty to the Church universal, the body of Christ, he is our judge as well as our inspiration. May he ever continue to give us courage of soul to share his conviction that "Truth conquers all"!

# WYCLIF'S FORTY-FIVE ARTICLES, CONDEMNED ON JULY 10, 1412[1]

1. Primo: Substantia panis materialis et similiter substantia vini manent in sacramento altaris. (*Haereticus est.*)

2. Item. Accidentia panis non manent sine subjecto in eodem sacramento. (*Haereticus est.*)

3. It. Christus non est in eodem sacramento identice et realiter, in propria praesentia corporali. (*Haereticus est.*)

4. It. Si episcopus vel sacerdos existat in peccato mortali non ordinat, non conficit, nec consecrat, nec baptisat. (*Haereticus est.*)

5. It. Non est fundatum in evangelio, quod Christus missam ordinaverit. (*Erroneus est.*)

6. It. Deus debet obedire diabolo. (*Erroneus.*)

7. It. Si homo fuerit debite contritus, omnis confessio exterior est sibi superflua et inutilis. (*Haereticus est.*)

8. It. Si papa sit praescitus et malus, et per consequens membrum diaboli, non habet potestatem super fideles ab aliquo sibi datam, nisi forte a Caesare. (*Falsus, erroneus et scandalosus.*)

9. It. Post Urbanum sextum non est aliquis recipiendus in papam, sed vivendum est more Graecorum sub legibus propriis. (*Falsus et erroneus.*)

10. It. Contra scripturam sacram est, quod viri ecclesiastici habeant possessiones. (*Temerarius.*)

11. It. Nullus praelatus debet aliquem excommunicare, nisi prius sciat ipsum excommunicatum a deo; et qui sic excommunicat, fit haereticus ex hoc vel excommunicatus. (*Falsus et male sonans.*)

[1] The first twenty-four articles had been condemned in London in 1382, although not always in the identical language or in the same order. Cf. H. B. Workman, *John Wyclif* (Oxford, at the Clarendon Press, 1926), II, pp. 416-417. The remaining twenty-one were selected by the German masters of the University of Prague, and all forty-five were condemned on May 28, 1403. The theological faculty condemned them again at the meeting at Žebrák on July 10, 1412, adding to them seven additional articles. F. Palacký, ed., *Documenta Mag. Johannis Hus* (Praha, F. Tempský, 1869), pp. 327-331 and 451-456. I am quoting the Žebrák version.

12. It. Praelatus excommunicans clericum, qui appellavit ad regem et ad consilium regni, eo ipso traditor est regis et regni. (*Temerarius et seditiosus.*)

13. It. Illi, qui dimittunt praedicare sive verbum dei audire propter excommunicationem hominum, sunt excommunicati, et in die judicii traditores Christi habebuntur. (*Temerarius et scandalosus.*)

14. It. Licet aliqui diacono vel presbytero praedicare verbum dei absque auctoritate sedis apostolicae et episcopi catholici. (*Falsus.*)

15. It. Nullus est dominus civilis, nullus est praelatus, nullus episcopus, dum est in peccato mortali. (*Falsus et erroneus.*)

16. It. Domini temporales possunt ad arbitrium suum auferre bona temporalia ab ecclesia et possessionatis habitualiter delinquentibus. (*Falsus, seditiosus.*)

17. It. Populares possunt ad arbitrium suum dominos delinquentes corrigere. (*Falsus, temerarius et seditiosus.*)

18. It. Decimae sunt purae elemosynae, et parochiani possunt propter peccata suorum praelatorum ad libitum suum auferre. (*Falsus et contra bonos mores.*)

19. It. Speciales orationes applicatae uni personae per praelatos vel religiosos non plus prosunt eidem, quam generales, ceteris paribus. (*Contra ecclesiam.*)

20. It. Conferens elemosynam fratribus est excommunicatus eo facto. (*Falsus et contra caritatem.*)

21. It. Si aliquis ingreditur religionem privatam qualemcunque tam possessionatorum quam mendicantium, redditur ineptior et inhabilior ad observantiam mandatorum dei. (*Falsus et erroneus.*)

22. It. Sancti instituentes religiones, sic instituendo peccaverunt. (*Falsus et erroneus.*)

23. It. Religiosi viventes in religionibus privatis non sunt de religione Christiana. (*Falsus et erroneus.*)

24. It. Fratres tenentur per labores manuum victum acquirere, non per mandicitatem. (*Falsus.*)

25. It. Omnes sunt simoniaci, qui se obligant orare pro aliis, eis in temporalibus subvenientibus. (*Falsus.*)

26. It. Oratio praesciti nulli valet. (*Falsus universaliter.*)

27. It. Omnia de necessitate absoluta eveniunt. (*Haereticus.*)

28. It. Confirmatio juvenum, clericorum ordinatio, locorum consecratio, reservata papae et episcopis propter cupiditatem lucri temporalis et honoris. (*Erroneus et scandalosus.*)

29. It. Universitates, studia, collegia, graduationes et

magisteria in eisdem sunt vana gentilitate introducta, et tantum prosunt ecclesiae sicut diabolus. (*Falsus et scandalosus.*)

30. It. Excommunicatio papae vel cujuscunque praelati non est curanda, quia est censura Antichristi. (*Falsus et contra bonos mores.*)

31. It. Peccant fundantes claustra, et ingredientes sunt viri diabolici. (*Falsus, seditiosus et scandalosus.*)

32. It. Ditare clerum est contra regulam Christi. (*Falsus, seditiosus et scandalosus.*)

33. It. Silvester papa et Constantinus imperator erraverunt ecclesiam dotando. (*Scandalosus et seditiosus.*)

34. It. Omnes de ordine mendicantium sunt heretici, et dantes eis elemosynam sunt excommunicati. (*Erroneus, scandalosus et contra bonos mores.*)

35. It. Ingrediens ordinem aut aliquam religionem eo ipso inhabilis est ad observandum divina praecepta, et per consequens perveniendi ad regnum coelorum, nisi apostataverit ad eisdem. (*Erroneus et scandalosus.*)

36. It. Papa cum omnibus clericis suis possessionem habentibus sunt haeretici, eo quo possessiones habent, et omnes consentientes eis, scil. domini seculares et laici ceteri. (*Temerarius, scandalosus, falsus et erroneus.*)

37. It. Ecclesia Romana est synagoga Satanae, nec papa est immediatus et proximus vicarius Christi et apostolorum. (*Haereticus.*)

38. It. Decretales epistolae sunt apocryphae et seducunt a fide Christi, et clerici sunt stulti, qui eas student. (*Temerarius, scandalosus et erroneus.*)

39. It. Imperator et domini seculares seducti sunt a diabolo, ut ecclesiam dotarent de bonis temporalibus. (*Seditiosus, temerarius et falsus.*)

40. It. Electio papae a cardinalibus per diabolum est introducta. (*Falsus, erroneus et contra determinationem ecclesiae.*)

41. It. Non est de necessitate salutis, credere, Romanam ecclesiam esse supremam inter alias ecclesias. (*Falsus, erroneus.*)

42. It. Fatuum est credere indulgentias papae et episcoporum. (*Temerarius et a salute retractivus.*)

43. It. Juramenta illicita sunt, quae fiunt ad roborandum humanos contractus et commercia civilia. (*Contra jura et bonos mores.*)

44. It. Augustinus, Benedictus et Bernhardus damnati sunt, nisi poenituerunt de hoc, quod habuerunt possessiones et instituerunt et intraverunt religiones; et sic a papa usque ad

infimum religiosum omnes sunt haeretici. (*Falsus, erroneus et contra approbationem ecclesiae.*)

45. It. Omnes religiones indifferenter introductae sunt a diabolo. (*Falsus, erroneus.*)

The following seven articles were added:

1. Primo: Qui aliter sentit de sacramentis et clavibus ecclesiae, quam sancta Romana ecclesia, *censetur haereticus.*

2. It. Quod his diebus sit ille magnus Antichristus et regnet, qui secundum fidem ecclesiae et secundum scripturam sacram et sanctos doctores in fine seculi est venturus, *est error evidens secundum experientiam.*

3. It. Dicere, quod constitutiones sanctorum patrum et consuetudines laudabiles in ecclesia non sit tenendae, quia in scriptura bibliae non continentur, *est error.*

4. It. Quod reliquiae et ossa sanctorum, et similiter vestes et habitus eorum, non sunt venerandae nec venerandi a Christi fidelibus, *error est.*

5. It. Quod sacerdotes non absolvunt a peccatis nec dimittunt peccata ministerialiter, conferendo et applicando sacramentum poenitentiae, sed quod solum denuntient confitentem absolutum, *est error.*

6. It. Quod papa non possit in necessitate evocare personas Christi fidelium, aut subsidia ab eis temporalia petere ad defendendum sedem apostolicam, statum sanctae Rom. ecclesiae et urbis, et ad compenscendum et revocandum adversarios et inimicos Christianos, largiendo Christi fidelibus fideliter subvenientibus, vere poenitentibus, confessis et contritis plenam remissionem omnium peccatorum, *est error.*

7. Item, quod mandatum domini nostri regis et dominorum civium de eo, quod nullus clamaret contra praedicatores, nec contra bullas papae, est et fuit justum, rationabile atque sanctum.

# THE THIRTY FINAL ARTICLES,
## WITH HUS' RESPONSES[1]

Articuli Joannis Hus, extracti ex libro de Ecclesia et quibusdam aliis tractatulis:

*propriissime dicta secundum Augustinum*
1. Unica est sancta universalis ecclesia, quae est praede-
*propriissime dicta*
stinatorum universitas. Et infra sequitur: Universalis sancta
*quae non est pars ad aliam proprie dictam*
ecclesia tantum est una, sicut tantum est unus numerus praedestinatorum.

*praescitum quo ad finalem adhaerentiam*
2. Paulus numquam fuit membrum diaboli, licet fecerit quosdam actus, actibus ecclesiae malignantium consimiles.

*catholicae propriissime dictae*
3. Praesciti non sunt partes ecclesiae, cum nulla pars ab ea finaliter excidit, eo quod praedestinationis caritas, quae ipsam ligat, non excidit.

*concretive*
*copulatim*
4. Duae naturae, divinitas et humanitas, sunt unus Christus.
*Ista saepe sententiantur a beato Augustino super Joanne*
Et infra ca⁰ 10⁰: Omnis homo est spiritus, cum sit duarum naturarum utraque.

5. Praescitus, etsi aliquando sit in gratia secundum prae-
*catholicae propriissime dictae*
sentem justitiam, tamen numquam est pars sanctae ecclesiae, et praedestinatus semper manet membrum ecclesiae, licet aliquando excidit a gratia adventitia, sed non a gratia praedestinationis.

*est sententia beati Augustini super Joann. It.*
*super Enchiridion. It. super psalterium. It.*
*de doctrina Christiana in libro de Ove*
6. Sumendo ecclesiam pro convocatione praedestinatorum,

[1] F. Palacký, ed., *Documenta Mag. Johannis Hus* (Praha, F. Tempský, 1869), pp. 225-234; C. J. Hefele and H. Leclercq, *Histoire des conciles*, 10 vols. in 20 (Paris, Letouzey et Ané, 1907-63), VII/I, pp. 316-323; cf. my translation in *John Hus at the Council of Constance* (New York, Columbia University Press, 1965), Part II, No. 15. Hus' comments are inserted interlinearly and italicized.

sive sint in gratia sive non secundum praesentem justitiam, isto modo ecclesia est articulus fidei.

*universalis propriissime*
7. Petrus non fuit nec est caput sanctae ecclesiae catho-
*dictae*
licae.

8. Sacerdotes quomodolibet criminose viventes sacerdotii
*et Deutero. 32: generatio perversa et infideles filii*
polluunt potestatem, et sicut filii infideles sentiunt infideliter de septem sacramentis ecclesiae, de clavibus, officiis et sacris rebus ecclesiae, cerimoniis, censuris, moribus, veneratione reliquiar- um, indulgentiis et ordinibus.

*Pro isto dicitur in psalmo 77º: Dilexerunt eam in ore suo, et in lingua sua mentiti sunt ei; cor autem eorum non erat rectum, nec fideles habiti sunt in testamento suo.*

9. Papalis dignitas a Caesare inolevit, et papae praefectio et institutio a Caesaris potentia emanavit.

*Quoad dominationem in temporalibus et ornatum impe- rialem et praefecturam super quatuor ecclesias. Patet dist.96 et 63.*

*speciali, quia Eccles. 9 dicitur: nemo scit, an gratia vel odio dignus sit.*
10. Nullus sine revelatione assereret rationabiliter de se vel de alio, quod esset caput ecclesiae particularis sanctae, nec Romanus pontifex caput Romanae ecclesiae.

11. Non oporteret credere, quod iste quicumque Romanus
*secundum vitae meritum perseverans*
pontifex sit caput cujuscumque particularis ecclesiae sanctae, nisi deus eum praedestinaverit.

*officio et merito*
12. Nemo gerit vicem Christi vel Petri, nisi sequatur eum
*sub alia*
in moribus, cum nulla alia sequela sit pertinentior nec aliter
*conditione*
recipiat a deo procuratoriam potestatem, quia ad illud officium
*de congruentia*
vicarium requiritur et morum conformitas, et instituentis aucto- ritas.

*officio et merito*
13. Papa non est manifestus et verus successor principis apostolorum Petri, si vivit moribus contrariis Petro. Et si quaerit avaritiam, tunc est vicarius Judae Scharioth secundum muta- tionem avaritiae. Et pari evidentia cardinales non sunt mani- festi et veri successores collegii aliorum apostolorum Christi, nisi vixerint more apostolorum, servantes mandata et consilia domini Jesu Christi.

*402*

14. Doctores ponentes, quod aliquis per censuram ecclesiasticam emendandus, si corrigi noluerit, seculari judicio est tradendus, pro certo sequuntur in hoc pontifices, scribas et Pharisaeos, qui Christum non volentem eis obedire in omnibus, dicentes: "Nobis non licet interficere quemquam," ipsum sec-

*ibi relatio est illorum, qui Christum Pilate tradiderunt, ut patet ibidem*

ulari judicio tradiderunt, et quod tales sunt graviores homicidae quam Pilatus.

*Ibi dixi de doctoribus Pragensibus octo, qui scripserunt, quod qui non obedierit eorum dictamini, quod brachio seculari est tradendus.*

15. Obedientia ecclesiastica est obedientia secundum adinventionem sacerdotum ecclesiae, praeter expressam auctoritatem scripturae.

*Ista descriptio est obedientiae, quae distinguitur contra obedientiam legis Christi explicitam, ut patet ibi, ubi iste articulus est receptus; sed absit, quod omnis obedientia legis dei sit hujusmodi, quae dicitur etiam uno modo obedientia ecclesiae.*

16. Divisio immediata humanorum operum est, quod sunt vel virtuosa vel vitiosa. Quia si homo est vitiosus et agit quidquam, tunc agit vitiose; et si est virtuosus et agit quidquam, tunc agit virtuose, quia sicut vitium, quod crimen dicitur sive mortale peccatum, inficit universaliter actus hominis, sic virtus vivificat omnes actus hominis virtuose.

17. Sacerdos Christi, vivens secundum legem ejus, habens scripturae notitiam et affectum ad aedificandum populum, debet

*injuriosa et illicita ex malitia fulminata*

praedicare non obstante praetensa excommunicatione; et infra: Quod si papa vel alius praepositus mandat sacerdoti sic disposito non praedicare, non debet subditus obedire.

*Istud dictum est multorum sanctorum, Augustini,*

18. Quilibet praedicantis officium de mandato accipit, qui *Gregorii, Isidori, etc.* ad sacerdotium accedit, et illud mandatum debet exsequi, prae-

*injuriosa et illicita, ex malitia fulminata*

tensa excommunicatione non obstante.

*heu saepe fit per abusum illarum censurarum, quae possunt fieri et fiunt saepe licite*

19. Per censuras ecclesiasticas excommunicationis, suspensionis, interdicti, ad sui exaltationem clerus populum laicalem sibi subpeditat, avaritiam multiplicat, per malitiam protegit et viam praeparat Antichristo. Signum autem evidens est, quod ab Antichristo procedunt tales censurae, quas vocant in suis processibus fulminationes, quibus clerus procedit principalissime

contra illos, qui denudant nequitiam Antichristi, qui clerum pro se maxime usurpavit.

20. Gratia praedestinationis est vinculum, quo corpus ecclesiae et quodlibet ejus membrum jungitur ipsi capiti insolubiliter.[2]

21. Si papa est malus, et praesertim si est praescitus, tunc ut Judas apostolus est diabolus, fur et filius perditionis, et non *secundum vitae meritum perseverans finaliter* est caput sanctae militantis ecclesiae, cum nec sit membrum ejus.

*quia non secundum officium et vitae meritum, sed solum secundum officium*

22. Papa vel praelatus malus et praescitus aequivoce (est) pastor et vere fur et latro.

*quia solus deus est sanctissimus*

23. Papa non debet dici sanctissimus etiam secundum officium, quia alias rex etiam deberet dici sanctissimus secundum officium, et tortores et praecones dicerentur sancti, imo etiam diabolus deberet vocari sanctus, cum sit officiarius dei.

24. Si papa vivit Christo contrarie, etiam si ascenderet per ritam et legitimam electionem secundum constitutionem *quia se per superbiam supra Christum elevaret* humanam vulgatam, tamen aliunde ascenderet, quam per Christum, dato etiam quod intraret per electionem a deo principaliter factam; nam Judas Scharioth rite et legitime est electus *quia non ambulat per humile ostium scil. Christum, qui dicit: Ego sum ostium, per me si quis intraverit, salvabitur.* a deo Christo Jesu ad episcopatum, et tamen ascendit aliunde in ovile ovium.

*Istud dixi disputative, exspectans majorem informationem.*

25. Condemnatio 45 articulorum Wiclef per doctores facta est irrationabilis et iniqua, et male ficta est causa per eos allegata, videlicet quod nullus ex eis est catholicus, sed quilibet eorum aut est haereticus, aut erroneus, aut scandalosus.

26. Non eo ipso, quod electores vel major pars eorum *patet instantia in Agnete, quae ab ecclesia aestimabatur esse legitimus papa* consenserit viva voce secundum ritus hominum in personam aliquam, eo ipso illa persona legitime est electa, vel quod eo ipso *officio et vitae merito* est verus et manifestus successor vel vicarius Petri apostoli, vel

---

[2] Palacký combines articles 20 and 21 into one, thus having a total of 29; I follow all other authorities, who divide these articles, so that they total 30 articles in all.

alterius apostoli in officio ecclesiastico; unde sive electores bene vel male elegerunt, operibus electi debemus credere, nam eo ipso, quo quis copiosius operatur meritorie ad profectum ecclesiae, habet a deo ad hoc copiosius potestatem.

27. Non est scintilla apparentiae, quod oportet esse unum caput in spiritualibus regens ecclesiam, quod semper cum ipsa militante ecclesia conversetur; patet, quia stat, ecclesiam pro magno tempore esse sine papa, ut jam stat post condemnationem Joannis XXIII.

*ut sine Agnete et Joan. XXIII et aliis, qui fuerunt haeretici vel aliter criminosi*

28. Christus sine talibus monstruosis capitibus per suos veraces discipulos sparsos per orbem terrarum melius suam ecclesiam regularet.

29. Apostoli et fideles sacerdotes domini strenue in necessariis ad salutem regularunt ecclesiam, antequam papae officium *quoad temporalem* foret introductum. Sic facerent deficiente per summe possibile *dominationem et praefecturam* papa usque in diem judicii.

30. Nullus est dominus civilis, nullus est praelatus, nullus est episcopus, dum est in peccato mortali.

*Secundum officium et vitae meritum, ut sancti sententiant, Ozeae 8: Ipsi regnaverunt, et non ex me principes exstiterunt, et ego non cognovi. Illud adducunt communiter Sancti Gregorius, Bernardus, etc.*

*Hic jam ponunt articulos extractos de processu causae; et ubi scriptura vel ratio in contrarium posita, sed potius falsa et injusta, sibi ascribunt testes, dicentes fore fide dignos, qui tamen fuerunt ejus inimici, vali (sic) et sibi suspecti.*

*Articuli extracti ex processu causae contra Joannem Hus sufficienter deducti et probati per testes fide dignos.*

Et primo articulus 4 et etiam 8, in quibus continetur, quod Joannes Hus pertinaciter articulos erroneos Wiclef in civitate Pragensi in scholis et praedicationibus publicis praedicavit et defendit.

*Non est verum, quod umquam talia procurassem, cum sub protestatione posui argumenta pro aliquibus articulis, qui videbantur mihi veri.*

Item articulus 9, in quo continetur, quod propter praemissa in civitate Pragensi secuta est seditio grandis, facta dolo et culpa Joannis Hus, in tantum, quod notabiles viri et catholici deum timentes coacti sunt exire et latere extra civitatem praedictam, stragesque, damnationes, sacrilegia aliaque horribilia exsecrabilia orta et secuta sunt, operam dante et procurante praefato Joanne Hus cum suis complicibus.

*Non est verum, quod umquam talia procurassem.*

Item articulus 10, in quo continetur, quod Joannes Hus continue in dicta civitate Pragensi fuit et erat sectator, fautor et eruditor ac defensor errorum quondam Joannis Wiclef haeresiarchae, et ut talis et pro tali tentus, nominatus et reputatus in dicta civitate et in partibus vicinis.

*Non est verum, quamvis aliqui inimici talem me reputarunt.*

Item articulus 15 et etiam 16, in quibus continetur, quod dominus archiepiscopus Pragensis exsequendo mandatum domini Alexandri, felicis recordationis papae quinti, quo sibi mandavit et commisit, ne ex tunc in antea aliquis auderet in locis privatis dictae civitatis, nisi in ecclesiis cathedralibus, collegiatis, parochialibus, monasteriis et eorum cimiteriis ad populum praedicare, quod praefatus dominus archiepiscopus continuando literarum apostolicarum executionem, hujusmodi inhibuit in generali synodo tunc Pragae congregata. Ipse vero Joannes Hus executioni dictarum literarum, nec non sententiae et prohibitioni hujusmodi de facto se opposuit, et post eandem prohibitionem de mense Junii, et praesertim XXII die illius mensis, et ex post pluribus et diversis vicibus, in quadam capella Bethleem nuncupata ad populum praedicavit, et ibidem populum copiosum convocavit et convocari procuravit, contra prohibitionem antedictam.

*Verum est, quia appellaveram ad ipsum Alexandrum pro meliori informatione, sicut patet in processu causae.*

Item articulus 17, in quo continetur, quod praefatus Joannes Hus tam de dicto mense Junii anni domini millesimi CCCCX, quam etiam ante et post in dicta capella praedicando ad populum ibidem collectum, et etiam in diversis aliis locis civitatis Pragensis, diversis vicibus multos errores et haereses, tam ex dictis libris dicti quondam Joannis Wiclef, quam ex sua protervitate et dolositate astruxit, docuit, disputavit et pro posse defendit, maxime infrascriptos, videlicet, quod post consecrationem hostiae in altari maneat panis materialis vel substantia panis.

*Non est verum.*

Item articulos 18, in quo continetur, quod sacerdos existens in peccato mortali non conficit corpus Christi, non ordinat, non baptisat.

*Non est verum; nam praedicavi oppositum.*

Item articulus 19, in quo continetur, quod indulgentiae papae seu episcoporum concessae nihil prosunt.

*Non est verum; pecuniarias autem indulgentias cum taxa, et erectionem crucis factam contra Christianos reprobavi, et scripsi de indulgentiis, quod sacerdotes Christi possunt ministerialiter dare remissionem peccatorum vere contritis et confessis a poena et a culpa.*

Item articulus 21, in quo continetur, quod Romana ecclesia sit synagoga Satanae.

*Non est verum; nam pono in libro "de Ecclesia," esse sanctam Romanam ecclesiam, quae est, secundum sanctos, omnes fideles Christiani ad obedientiam Romani pontificis juxta legem Christi pertinentes.*

Item articulus 24, in quo continetur, quod nulla haeresis debeat exterminari per potentiam, sed per disputationem in scholis.

*Non est verum; sed dixi, quod primo scriptura vel ratione debet convinci haereticus, sicut dicunt sancti Augustinus et Bernardus.*

Item articulus 26, in quo continetur, quod dictus Joannes Hus ad seducendum populum et simplices ausu temerario dixit, quod in Anglia multi monachi et alii magistri convenissent in quadam ecclesia sancti Pauli contra M. Joannem Wiclef, et non poterant eum convincere, sed statim tonitru et fulgur de coelo descendisset super eos, et rupisset ostium ecclesiae, ita quod magistri et monachi vix evasissent ad civitatem Londoniensem. Et hoc dixit ad auctorisandum dictum Joannem Wiclef, unde prorumpendo in verba dixit ad populum in haec verba: Utinam anima mea esset ibi, ubi est anima Joannis Wiclef! Et post literam quandam falsificatam sub sigillo falso universitatis studii Oxoniensis pluries publicavit, in qua continetur, licet false, Joannem Wiclef fuisse verum, catholicum et doctorem evangelicum, bonae famae et conversationis laudabilis, ab aevo suae juventutis usque in diem exitus sui.

*Non est verus iste articulus in multis punctis, et plenus est convolutis mendatiis.*

Item articulus 29, in quo continetur, quod seculares debeant auferre bona temporalia, quod hoc esset meritorium.

*Non est verum.*

Item 32 et etiam 37 articuli, in quibus continetur, quod Joannes Hus, existens in excommunicatione et aggravatione, divinis se immiscuit, populo praedicavit et publice dixit, quod non curaret excommunicationem, quia non potest excommunicari quis ab homine, nisi per prius sit excommunicatus a deo.

*Non est verum, sed dixi, quod sub appellatione possum praedicare, et quod injusta excommunicatione non nocet homini justo, dum ipsam humiliter tolerat propter deum.*

Item articulus 38, in quo continetur, quod Joannes Hus diversos errores praedicavit, ex quibus scandala exorta sunt inter praelatos et populum regni Bohemiae et magistros et scholares studii Pragensis.

*Non est verum.*

Item articulus VII, in partibus, in causa inquisitionis coram archiepiscopo Pragensi datus et oblatus contra Joan. Hus, in quo continetur, qualiter Joan. Hus ad populum dixit: Ecce papa nuper defunctus, videlicet Alexander papa quintus, nuper scripsit archiepiscopo Pragensi pro exstirpandis erroribus Joan. Wiclef in Bohemia et Moravia, et quod ibi sunt multi homines, opiniones et errores Wiclef contra fidem tenentes, quorum corda sunt haeresi infecta; et ego dico, et deo regratior, quod ego nullum Bohemum vidi haereticum; et quod ad verba praemissa populus clamabat: Mentitur, mentitur!

*Non est verum quoad finem, quod sic populus clamasset; nam clamaverunt dicentes: Mentiuntur, qui nos dicunt haereticos; et verus est articulus quoad principium.*

Item articulus IX, in quo continetur, quod idem Joannes Hus dixit in vulgari ad populum: Ecce impleta est prophetia quam praedixit Jacobus de Tharamo, quod anno domini MCCCCIX surget unus, qui evangelium et epistolas et fidem Christi persequetur, per hoc denotando D. Alexandrum, qui in suis bullis mandavit libros Wiclef cremari.

*Non est verum in forma, sed aliqua dixi, nec ipse Alexander mandavit in bulla Wiclef cremari.*

Item articulus XI, in quo continetur, quod Joan. Hus dixit, quod Alexander papa nuper defunctus, nescio tamen, si sit in coelo vel in inferno, scribit in cutibus suis asinisis, quod archiepiscopus cremare deberet libros Joannis Wiclef, in quibus multa bona continentur.

*Verum est quoad primum quod dixi, sed quod praeciperet cremare non dixi, quia non scripsit hoc in bulla.*

Item articulus alius de responsione sua, in qua continetur, quod dictus Joannes Hus literam post ejus recessum de Bohemia dimisit ad legendum populo, quae continet, ut pensantes laborem ejus sollicitum, quem cum eis habuit—

## THE THIRTY FINAL ARTICLES

*Ecce non plus scripserunt de isto articulo, ad quem aestimo habetis in responsione, in copia primorum articulorum in primo carcere copiatorum.*

*Ultimo stabat scriptum*: Articuli lecti contra doctrinam et personam Joannis Hus, die Martis i.e. feria 3rd post Viti, XVIII mensis Junii, in congregatione publica, et traditi notario.

*Et ego Joannes Hus, semper in spe servus Jesu Christi, scripsi responsiones ad articulos in eorum copia, sicut et in ista, juxta meam conscientiam, de qua omnipotenti domino debeo reddere rationem.*

*Ad articulos extractos de libellis meis non potui sententias scribere, et propter brevitatem temporis, et propter carentiam papyri, et propter periculum, etc. Et aestimo, quod in primis articulis sunt ad aliquos explanandos et probandos positae sanctorum auctoritates.*

*Jam restat vel revocare et abjurare et poenitentiam mirabilem suscipere, vel comburi. Pater et filius et spiritus sanctus, unus deus, in quem credo et confido, dabit, intercedentibus omnibus sanctis et hominibus justis, spiritum consilii et fortitudinis, ut possim laqueum Satanae effugere, et in ipsius gratia finaliter permanere. Amen.*

---

*Omnes articuli ex libellis et ex processu causae sic sunt glossati in responsione concilii, sicut hic sunt glossati breviter, oblati fer. III post Viti* (18 Jun.).

Datum feria quinta proxima post festum sancti Viti martyris (20 Jun.), de carcere apud fratres dictos Minores vel Bosáci.

# SELECTED BIBLIOGRAPHY

## PRIMARY SOURCES: WORKS OF JOHN HUS

Císařová-Kolářová, Anna, ed. and transl., *M. Jan Hus, Betlemské poselství* [The Bethlehem Message], 2 vols. (Praha, Jan Laichter, 1947).

Dobiáš, F. M., and Molnár, Amedeo, transl., *Mistr Jan Hus, O církvi* [On the Church] (Praha, Československá akademie věd, 1965).

Erben, K. J., ed., *Mistra Jana Husi Sebrané spisy české z nejstarších pramenů* [Czech Works Collected from the Oldest Sources], 3 vols. (Praha, 1865-68).

Flajšhans, V., ed., *Mag. Io. Hus Sermones in Bethlehem, 1410-1411*, 5 vols. (Praha, Královská česká společnost nauk, 1938-42).

Flajšhans, V., and Komínková, M., eds., *Spisy M. Jana Husi* [Works], 8 vols. (Praha, Jaroslav Bursík a J. R. Vilímek, 1903-1907), I, Expositio decalogi; II, De corpore Christi; III, De sanguine Christi; IV-VI, Super IV sententiarum; VII-VIII, Sermones de sanctis.

*Historia et monumenta Joannis Hus atque Hieronymi Pragensis, confessorum Christi*, 2 vols.; new edition of the work of 1558 (Norimberg, J. Montanus et U. Neuber, 1715).

Jeschke, J. B., ed., *Mistr Jan Hus, Postilla* [Postil] (Praha, Komenského ev. fakulta bohoslovecká, 1952).

Mareš, B., transl., *Listy Husovy* [Letters], 2nd edn. (Praha, "Samostatnost," 1901).

Novotný, Václav, ed., *M. Jana Husi Korespondence a dokumenty* (Praha, Komise pro vydávání pramenů náboženského hnutí českého, 1920).

——, *Fontes rerum Bohemicarum*, VIII (Praha, Nadání Františka Palackého, 1932). Contains "Petri de Mladoniowicz, Relatio de Magistro Johanne Hus" and many other pertinent documents.

Palacký, František, ed., *Documenta Mag. Johannis Hus* (Praha, F. Tempský, 1869).

Ryba, B., ed., *Magistri Johannis Hus Quodlibet* (Praha, Orbis, 1948).

——, ed. and transl., *Sto listů M. Jana Husi* [One Hundred Letters] (Praha, Jan Laichter, 1949).

——, *Betlemské texty* [The Bethlehem Texts] (Praha, Orbis, 1951).

Schaff, David S., transl., *John Hus, The Church* (New York, Charles Scribner's Sons, 1915).

Schmidtová, Anežka, ed., *Magistri Joannis Hus, Sermones de tempore qui Collecta dicuntur* (Praha, Československá akademie věd, 1959).

Sedlák, Jan, Articles from *Hlídka*, Vols. 28-30 (Brno, 1911-13). Contains treatises of Stanislav of Znojmo, "Sermo contra 5 art. Wiclef"; "Tractatus de Romana ecclesia"; and Stephen Páleč's "Sermo contra aliquos art. Wiclef"; "De equivocatione nominis ecclesia"; "Antihus"; and "Několik textů z doby husitské."

——,*M. Jan Hus* (Praha, Dědictví sv. Prokopa, 1915). The second part contains Páleč's, " 'Tractatus de ecclesia,' partes selectae."

Šimek, F., ed., *Mistr Jan Hus, Česká kázáni sváteční* [The Czech Holyday Sermons] (Praha, Blahoslav, n.d.).

Spinka, Matthew, ed. and transl., "Hus on Simony," in *Advocates of Reform*, Library of Christian Classics XIV (Philadelphia, The Westminster Press, 1953), pp. 199-278.

——, transl., *John Hus at the Council of Constance* (New York and London, Columbia University Press, 1965).

Stein, Evžen, ed. and transl., *M. Jan Hus jako universitní rektor a profesor* [M. Jan Hus as Rector and Professor of the University] (Praha, Jan Laichter, 1948).

Svoboda, M., and Flajšhans, V., transl. and eds., *Mistra Jana Husi Sebrané spisy* [Collected Works] (Praha, Jaroslav Bursík a J. R. Vilímek, 1904–n.d.).

Thomson, S. Harrison, ed., *Magistri Joannis Hus Tractatus de Ecclesia* (Boulder, Colorado, University of Colorado Press, 1956).

Workman, H. B., and Pope, R. M., transl., *The Letters of John Hus* (London, Hodder and Stoughton, 1904).

Žilka, F., ed., *Mistra Jana Husi Vybrané spisy* [Selected Works], 2 vols. (Jilemnice, n.d.).

## PRIMARY WORKS ON THE CONCILIAR LEADERS AND HUSSIANA

Cameron, James Kerr, "Conciliarism in Theory and Practice, 1378-1418," 2 vols. An unpublished doctoral dissertation at the Hartford Seminary Foundation, Hartford, Connecticut,

1953. Vol. II comprises translations of selected works of Henry of Langenstein, Jean Gerson, Pierre d'Ailly, and Dietrich of Niem. Selections of them were published in Matthew Spinka, *Advocates of Reform*.

Finke, Heinrich, et al., eds., *Acta Consilii Constantiensis*, 4 vols. (Münster, Regensburg, 1896-1928).

——, *Forschungen und Quellen zur Geschichte des Konstanzer Konzils* (Paderborn, Schöningh, 1889).

Friedberg, E., ed., *Corpus juris canonici*, 2 vols. (Leipzig, Tauchnitz, 1879). Vol. I comprises Gratian's *Decretum*.

Gerson, Jean, *Opera omnia*, edited by E. du Pin, 4 vols. (Antwerp, 1706).

——, "De auctoritate concilii," edited by Z. Rüger, *Revue d'Histoire Ecclesiastique* (Louvain, 1953), pp. 775-795.

Hardt, Hermann van der, ed., *Magni et universalis Constantiensis concilii tomi VI* (Frankfurt and Leipzig, Gensius, 1697-1700). Completed by a seventh volume of indices by C. Ch. Bohnstedt (Berlin, Henningius, 1742).

Hefele, C. J., and Leclercq, H., *Historie des conciles*, 10 vols. in 20 (Paris, Letouzey et Ané, 1907-38).

Lagarde, George de, *La naissance de l'esprit laïque*, IV, *Guillaume d'Ockham: Défense de l'Empire*; V, *Critique des structures ecclésiales* (Louvain and Paris, 1962-63).

Loomis, Louise, R., transl., *The Council of Constance: The Unification of the Church*, edited by John H. Mundy and Kennerly M. Moody (New York, Columbia University Press, 1961).

Migne, J.-P., *Patrologia latina*, 221 vols. (Paris, Garnier Fratres, 1878-90).

Ockham, W., *Dialogus de potestate papae et imperatoris* (Torino, Bottega d'Erasmo, 1959).

Pez, B., ed., *Thesaurus anecdotorum novissimus*, 6 vols. (Augsburg, 1721-29). Contains treatises of Stephen of Dolany, "Medulla tritici, seu Antiwickliffus"; "Antihussus"; "Dialogus volatilis inter Aucam et Passerem adversus Hussum"; and "Liber epistolaris ad Hussitas."

Richental, Ulrich von, *Chronik des Constanzer Conzils*, edited by Michael R. Buck (Hildesheim, 1962).

Sedlák, Jan. *Studie a texty k náboženským dějinám českým* [Studies and Texts in Czech Religious History], 2 vols. Olomouc, Matice Cyrilo-Methodějská, 1913-19).

Sikes, J. G., et al., eds., *Guillaume Occami Opera politica*, 3 vols. (Manchester, University of Manchester Press, 1940-56).

Šimek, F., ed., *Jakoubek ze Stříbra, Výklad na zjevenie sv. Jana* [Exposition of St. John's Revelation] (Praha, 1933).

## SECONDARY WORKS

Bartoš, F. M., *Husitství a cizina* [Hussitism and the Lands Abroad] (Praha, Čin, 1931).

——, *Bojovníci a mučednici* [Warriors and Martyrs] (Praha, Kalich, 1939).

——, *Co víme o Husovi nového* [Our New Knowledge about Hus] (Praha, Pokrok, 1946).

——, *Čechy v době Husově, 1378-1415* [Bohemia in the Time of Hus, 1378-1415] (Praha, Jan Laichter, 1947).

——, *Knihy a zápasy* [Books and Conflicts] (Praha, Husova ev. fakulta bohoslovecká, 1948).

——, *Ze zápasů české reformace* [The Conflicts of the Czech Reformation] (Praha, Kalich, 1959).

——, *Světci a kacíři* [Saints and Heretics] (Praha, Husova ev. fakulta bohoslovecká, 1949).

——, *Literární činnost M. Jana Husi* [Literary Activity of Hus] (Praha, Česká akademie věd a umění, 1948).

——, *Husitská revoluce* I, *Doba Žižkova, 1415-26* [Hussite Revolution, Žižka's Period] (Praha, Československá akademie věd, 1965).

Bliemetzrieder, F., *Das Generalkonzil im grossen abendländischen Schisma* (Paderborn, 1904).

Boehner, Philotheus, *Collected Articles on Ockham*, edited by E. M. Buytaert (Bonaventure, New York, The Franciscan Institute, 1958).

Combes, André, *Jean Gerson: commentateur dionysien* (Paris, 1940).

Dress, Walter, *Die Theologie Gersons* (Gütersloh, 1931).

Franzen, A., and Muller, W., *Das Konzil von Konstanz* (Freiburg, Basel, Wien, Herder, 1964).

Girgensohn, D., *Peter von Pulkau und die Wiedereinführung des Laienkelches; Leben und Wirken eines Wiener Theologen in der Zeit des grossen Schismas* (Göttingen, Vandenhoeck und Ruprecht, 1964).

Hauck, Albert, *Kirchengeschichte Deutschlands*, 5th edn. (Berlin, Akademie-Verlag, 1953), Vol. v/II.

——, *Studien zu Jan Hus* (Leipzig, 1916).

Havránek, B., et al., *Výbor z české literatury doby husitské* [Selections from the Czech Literature of the Hussite Period], 2 vols. (Praha, Československá akademie věd, 1963-64).

# BIBLIOGRAPHY

Heimpel, H., *Dietrich von Niem* (Münster, Regensberg, 1932).

Jacob, E. F., *Essays in the Conciliar Epoch*, 3rd edn. (Manchester, University of Manchester Press, 1963).

Kejř, Jiří, *Husitský právnik, M. Jan z Jesenice* [The Hussite Lawyer, M. John of Jesenice] (Praha, Československá akademie věd, 1965).

Krofta, K., *Listy z náboženských dějin českých* [Leaves from the Czech Religious History] (Praha, Historický klub, 1936).

Kybal, V., *Matěj z Janova, jeho život, spisy a učeni* [Matthew of Janov, his Life, Works, and Teaching] (Praha, Královská česká společnost nauk, 1905).

——, *M. Jan Hus, Učeni*, 3 vols. (Praha, Jan Laichter, 1923-31). See also under Novotný and Kybal.

Lenfant, Jacques, *Histoire du concile de Constance*, 2 vols. (Amsterdam, 1714).

Loomis, Louise R., "The Organization of Nations at Constance," *Church History*, Vol. I, pp. 191ff.

Lützow, F., *The Life and Times of Master John Hus* (New York, E. P. Dutton & Co., n.d.).

McGowan, John T., *Pierre d'Ailly and the Council of Constance* (Washington, Catholic University, 1936).

McNeill, John T., "The Emergence of Conciliarism," in *Medieval and Historical Essays in honor of James Westfall Thompson* (Chicago, University of Chicago Press, 1938), pp. 269ff.

Meller, B., *Studien zur Erkentnislehre des Peter von Ailly* (Freiburg, 1954).

Morall, John B., *Gerson and the Great Schism* (Manchester, University of Manchester Press, 1960).

Mourin, Louis, *Jean Gerson, predicateur français* (Bruges, 1952).

Neander, Augustus, *General History of the Christian Religion and Church*, translated by Joseph Torrey (Boston, Houghton, Mifflin & Co., 1871), Vol. v.

Novotný, V., *Náboženské hnuti české v 14. a 15. stoleti* [The Czech Religious Movement in the Fourteenth and Fifteenth Centuries] (Praha, J. Otto, n.d.).

Novotný, V., and Kybal, V., *M. Jan Hus, Život a učeni* [Life and Teaching], 5 vols. (Praha, Jan Laichter, 1919-31). I deal with the work separately: V. Novotný, *Jan Hus, Život a dilo* [Life and Work], 2 vols. (Praha, Jan Laichter, 1919-21); V. Kybal, *Jan Hus, Učeni*, 3 vols. (Praha, Jan Laichter, 1923-31).

*415*

Oakley, Francis, *The Political Thought of Pierre d'Ailly* (New Haven, Yale University Press, 1965).

Oberman, Heiko A., *The Harvest of Medieval Theology* (Cambridge, Mass., Harvard University Press, 1963).

Odložilík, Otakar, *Jan Milíč z Kroměříže* (Kroměříž, Kostnická Jednota, 1924).

——, *M. Štepán z Kolína* (Praha, Společnost Husova musea, 1924).

——, *Wyclif and Bohemia* (Praha, 1937).

——, *Jan Hus* (Chicago, Národní Jednota Československých Protestantů, 1953).

Roberts, Agnes E., "Peter d'Ailly and the Council of Constance," *Transactions of the Royal Historical Society*, 4th ser., XVIII (London, 1935).

Salembier, L., *Le grand Schisme d'occident*, 5th edn. (Paris, 1921).

Schaff, David S., *John Hus, His Life, Teachings and Death after Five Hundred Years* (New York, Charles Scribner's Sons, 1915).

Scholtz, R., *Unbekannte kirchenpolitische Streitschriften aus der Zeit Ludwigs des Bayern, 1327-1354*, 2 vols. (Rom, Loescher & Co., 1914).

Schwab, J. B., *Johannes Gerson, Professor der Theologie und Kanzler der Universität* (Würzburg, 1858).

Spinka, Matthew, *John Hus and the Czech Reform* (Chicago, University of Chicago Press, 1941).

Stacey, John, *John Wyclif and Reform* (Philadelphia, The Westminster Press, 1964).

Thomson, S. Harrison, "Philosophical Basis of Wyclif's Theology," *Journal of Religion*, 1931, pp. 86-116.

Tierney, Brian, "Ockham, the Conciliar Theory, and the Canonists," *Journal of the History of Ideas*, 1954, pp. 40-70.

——, *Foundations of the Conciliar Theory* (New York, Cambridge University Press, 1955).

Tschackert, P., *Peter von Ailly* (Gotha, Perthes, 1877).

Valois, Noel, *La France et le grand Schisme*, 4 vols. (Paris, Picard, 1900-02).

Vischer, Melchior, *Jan Hus, sein Leben und seine Zeit*, 2 vols. (Frankfurt, 1940).

Vooght, Paul de, *Les sources de la doctrine chrétienne* (Paris, Desclée de Brouwer, 1954).

——, *L'hérésie de Jean Huss* (Louvain, Publications universitaires de Louvain, 1960).

# BIBLIOGRAPHY

——, *Hussiana* (Louvain, Publications universitaires de Louvain, 1960).

Ullmann, W., *The Origins of the Great Schism* (London, Burns, Oates and Washbourne, 1948).

Workman, H. B., *John Wyclif*, 2 vols. (Oxford, Clarendon Press, 1926).

Wylie, J. H., *The Council of Constance to the Death of John Hus* (London, 1900).

# INDEX

Aachen, 337

Abel, 256

Act of Toleration, 132

Adam, 26; Adam and Eve, 187

*Adversus indulgentias papales* (Hus), 110

Africa, 240, 277

Agnes, known as Pope John, 185, 199, 201, 224, 265, 272, 273

Albert of Engelschalk, 12, 37

Albik of Uničov, archbishop of Prague, 107, 116, 117, 146, 159

Alexander V, pope, 92, 93, 94, 96, 105, 131, 186, 197, 212, 226, 227

Alexandria, patriarchate of, 265, 271

All Saints College, 37, 119, 146

*Alma et venerabilis . . .* (Stanislav of Znojmo), 177, 178

Amalek, 288

Ambrose, bishop, 33, 162, 174, 202, 208, 275

Anabaptists of Zurich, 132

Anacletus, bishop, 276

*An credi possit in papam* (Holešov), 152

Andrew of Brod, 177

Anne, wife of King Richard II, 35

Anonymous, 151, 248, 249, 250

Anselm, 22, 33, 162

Anthony of Concordia, bishop, 380

Antichrist, 15, 27, 28, 85, 161, 184, 199, 221, 229, 234, 261, 268, 272, 288, 303, 348, 373; church of, 19

*Antihus* (Páleč), 209, 228, 230, 236, 237, 241, 245

Antioch, 169, 182, 200, 203, 265; patriarchate of, 388

Apollos, 167

Apostles, 28, 162, 166, 173, 198, 202, 204, 205, 267, 302

Apostles' Creed, 162, 211, 215, 248, 372, 386

Apostolic poverty, 28, 88

Apostolic See, 124, 142, 143, 144, 155, 158, 161, 169, 187, 216, 280, 281, 282, 294, 383

appeal to Christ, 138, 381

Aquinas, Thomas, 22, 53, 65, 66, 127, 263

Aristotle, 100, 128, 301

Arius, 101, 224; Arian heresy, 155

"Armenian sect," the, 160, 163

Athanasian Creed, 162

attrition, 76

Augustin, St., 22, 24, 33, 53, 55, 62, 63, 65, 70, 73, 75, 85, 97, 100, 101, 127, 128, 152, 156, 160, 162, 174, 182, 191, 202, 210, 220, 222, 231, 233, 256, 275, 284, 289, 301, 307, 319, 324, 325; Augustinianism, 13, 26, 41

Averroism, 23

Avignon, 15, 182

Balaam, 299; Balaam's ass, 102, 113, 299

Baldassare Cossa, cardinal, 81, 357, 358

baptism, 46, 73, 320, 321

Barrow, Henry, 132

Bartholomew, St., 326

Bartoš, F. M., 7, 13, 329-334, 337, 375

Basil the Great, 162

Benedict XIII, pope, 87, 240, 349

Berdyaev, Nicholas, 6

Bernard, bishop of Castellamare, 341

Bernard of Clairvaux, 62, 162, 171, 174, 202, 231, 282, 291, 317

Beroun, 210

Bertold of Wildungen, curial auditor, 380

Bethlehem Chapel, 9, 37, 42, 43, 44, 54, 56, 96, 103, 120, 131, 138, 139, 140, 158, 227, 232, 252, 284, 288, 290, 291, 351, 354, 390

Bible, 41, 326; English, 34; Czech, 17, 290, 326

Bienvenue, bishop in Hugo's *Les Miserables*, 387

bishop (s), 28, 29, 77, 78, 123, 124, 127, 132, 166, 171, 210, 230, 277, 297, 301, 302, 311, 313; jurisdiction of, 130, 131, 183

Blackfriar Synod, 34, 50, 123

"Black Rose," 80, 238

blasphemy, 308

Bohemia, vii, 3, 7, 35, 56, 87, 93, 96, 99, 103, 110, 121, 125, 136, 147, 180, 186, 240, 279, 330, 331, 333, 335, 337, 349, 350, 354, 369, 377, 378; nation, 134; kingdom of, 141, 142, 143, 144, 149, 178, 200, 229, 238, 244, 369

Bologna, 81, 98, 172, 182; university of, 98

Bonaventura, 65, 162

Boniface VIII, pope, 217, 259, 263, 270, 271

Boniface IX, pope, 145, 192, 224, 243, 283

Bradwardine, Thomas, 22, 23

Bratislava, 106

Braybroke, 56

Breisach, 355

Břevnov, monastery of, 151

Britain, 240, 277

Brod, 210

Bruges, 27

Burgundy, 355

burning of Wyclif's books, 97, 98

Caim, orders of, 30

Cain, 26

Caesar (s), 30, 125, 225

Calvinistic Reformation, 395

Canon law, 124, 171, 181, 191, 311

cardinals, 87, 88, 107, 122, 142, 143, 144, 145, 166, 190, 195, 197, 199, 207, 216, 218, 297, 340, 347, 349; form the body of the Church, 5, 59, 143, 148, 172, 173, 174, 176, 179, 274

*Catholicon*, 368

Cestrensis (Ralph of Higden), 279

Charles IV, emperor, 11, 14, 247

Charles College, 37, 122

Chotek, Bernard, 138

Christ, 15, 30, 63, 75, 83, 95, 99, 110, 111, 123-27, 138, 148, 154, 156, 159, 161-63, 167, 172, 185, 187, 190, 200-203, 210, 220, 221, 233, 237, 241; the sole head of the Church, 5, 28, 179, 180, 204-06, 215, 216, 219, 224, 226, 241, 260, 270, 271-73, 281, 282, 298, 301-03, 305, 308, 328, 336, 354, 361, 364, 372, 373, 387; following of, 26, 27, 45, 221, 247, 303; secular rulers vicars of Christ, 31; granted Peter the keys of office, 64; Church His mystical body, *corpus mysticum*, 68, 176, 196; spirit of Christ, 124, 241; only Christ forgives sins, 165, 269; Christ on war, 171, 298, 374; His two natures, 340, 371

Christendom, 179, 180, 201, 205, 217, 237, 238, 240, 242, 243, 244, 296, 309, 332, 388

Christian life, 24, 72, 128, 129, 230, 317

Christian of Prachatice, 146, 148, 352, 392

*Chronicles* of Martinus Polonus, 279

Chrysostom, John, patriarch, 63, 65, 101, 111, 127, 162, 202, 231, 275, 301, 325

Church, concept of, vii, 3, 4, 17, 18, 25, 47, 58, 59, 60, 61, 62, 84, 99, 142, 148, 184, 204, 209, 210, 211, 214, 221, 255, 256, 261, 263, 289, 290, 294; *congregatio fidelium*, 5, 68, 264, 387, 396; a spiritual fellowship, 5, 198, 394, 395; a papal monarchy, 5, 248; a juridical corporation, 5, 173, 217, 395; church of Antichrist, 19, 58, 61, 69, 262; Church militant, 19, 20, 25, 26, 58, 59, 201, 214, 241, 248, 249, 257; *communio sanctorum*, the elect, 19, 58, 59, 61, 68, 69, 214, 244, 255, 256, 262, 387, 394; Wyclif's concept, 24ff; Church triumphant, 25, 59, 214, 257; Church dormient, 25, 59, 214, 257; reform of, 28, 30, 45, 126; Church catholic or universal is the totality of the predestinate, 68, 211, 213, 214, 255-57, 264, 265, 271, 292, 347, 389; infallible, 88; possesses only the spiritual sword, 111, 202; Church and state, 125, 126; consists of the clergy, 152, 156, 175, 176; founded not on Peter but on his confession, 153, 264, 266, 267; confusion between the Church catholic and the Church militant, 156, 214, 225, 249, 371, 372; is a mystico-ecclesiastical *compositum* of the pope and the cardinals, 172-74, 178, 179, 183, 191, 195, 207, 210-12, 216, 217, 235, 242, 261, 263, 265, 272, 278; mystical body of Christ, 196-98, 256, 258, 260, 261, 266, 274, 385, 387, 394, 395; *una, sancta, catholica et apostolica ecclesia*, 248, 372; is a federalist episcopal organization, 277, 388, 394; possesses two swords, 297

Church Fathers, 101, 128, 144, 160, 162, 179, 181, 359
*Cid* of Corneille, 292
Cistercian Order, 15
civil rule refused by Christ, 30, 31
*Civitas Dei et civitas terrena* (Augustine), 26, 70
Clement, pope, 271
Clement VII, pope, 13, 27, 224
Cologne, university of, 357
Colossians, epistle to the, 179
communion, 46, 47, 75, 76, 351, 353, 354, 389
*compositum*, 172-74, 195
Conciliarists, 5, 175, 212, 250, 393
*Conditiones concordiae* of the theological faculty, 146, 149, 177, 180, 189
confession, 76, 231, 321
confirmation, 73, 320
*congregatio fidelium*, 5, 24, 68, 152, 156, 178, 214, 253
*congregatio praedestinatorum*, 156, 214
Conrad of Gelnhausen, 14
Conrad of Vechta, bishop, later archbishop, 118, 121, 141, 329, 335, 349, 350
*Consilium* of the theological faculty, 142-47, 177, 192, 209, 213, 222, 225-28, 252, 269, 270, 284
Constance, 331-34, 337, 338, 341, 345-47, 349, 351-54, 370, 378, 379, 390, 394; burgomaster of, 339; witnesses of, 360
Constantine, emperor, 28, 194, 224, 272, 275; Constantinian endowment, 29, 223; Donation of, 224, 272, 275
Constantine II, pope, 272
Constantinopolitan patriarchate, 265, 277
*Contra occultum adversarium* (Hus), 247
*Contra octo doctores* (Hus), 157-61, 163-169, 170, 209

# INDEX

*Contra Paletz* (Hus), 209, 228, 348, 359, 366

*Contra Stanislaum* (Hus), 193, 198, 359, 366

contrition, 76, 171

Corfe, William, 361

Corinthians, 165, 166

Council of Carthage, 271

Council of Chalcedon, 162, 371

Council of Cividale, 93

Council of Constance, vii, 4, 5, 67, 68, 84, 92, 93, 131, 150, 161, 212, 215, 217, 233, 236, 246, 252, 258, 329-33, 335, 336, 338, 341, 343-46, 348, 352-59, 365, 367-71, 374-79, 384, 389, 393-96

Council of Constantinople, 162

Council of Ephesus, 162

Council of Nicaea, 162, 224, 272, 311

Council of Pisa, 12, 27, 88, 90, 92, 93, 110, 184, 186, 218, 243, 279, 349

Council of Rome, 135, 136, 330, 342, 356

Council of Trent, 222

Council of Tribur, 83

Councils, general, 27, 88, 162, 210, 218, 219, 226, 250

Courtenay, bishop, later archbishop of London, 34

Cracow, 213; university of, 53

*cujus regio, ejus religio*, 132

Cyprian, bishop of Carthage, 155, 200

Czech clergy, 228

Czech communists, 5, 280

Czech nation, 136, 178, 364

Czech native reform, 14, 15, 17, 35, 42, 49, 151, 172

Czech treatises, 290

Czech university masters, 50-52, 80, 88

D'Ailly, Pierre, cardinal, 16, 338, 353, 356, 357, 359-62, 365, 366, 380, 384

*Daughter, The* (Hus), 291

Day of Judgment, 58, 123, 164, 201, 204, 234, 242, 257, 258, 262, 294

*De aequivocatione nominis ecclesia* (Páleč), 209, 214, 255, 292, 293

*De arguendo clero pro concione* (Hus), 84

*De benedicta incarnatione* (Wyclif), 66

*De civili dominio* (Wyclif), 31, 126, 127

*De corpore Christi* (Hus), 55, 362

*De corpore Christi* (Stanislav of Znojmo), 190

*De ecclesia* (Hus), 193, 209, 212, 213, 221, 247, 251, 252, 254, 255, 263, 289, 329, 346-49, 359, 366

*De ecclesia* (Páleč), 209, 213

*De ecclesia* (Wyclif), 112, 253, 254, 262

*Decretum* of Gratian, 163, 231, 265, 285, 289

*De eucharistia* (Wyclif), 32, 40, 81

*De ideis* (Wyclif), 36

*De interiori domo* (Bernard), 317

*De libris haereticorum legendis* (Hus), 97

*De materia et forma* (Wyclif), 36

*De monarchia* (Dante), 297

*De pace* (Hus), 336

*De potestate papae* (Wyclif), 253

*De simonia* (Wyclif), 40, 292, 308

*De sufficientia legis Christi* (Hus), 335

*De trinitate* (Wyclif), 98

*De veritate sacrae Scripturae* (Wyclif), 23

Decalogue, 168

*Decalogue* (Wyclif), 98

Deuteronomy, book of, 181, 278

# INDEX

De Viviers, cardinal, 355
De Vooght, Paul, vii, 4, 6, 7, 23, 65, 66, 68, 78, 112, 113, 115, 130, 131, 144, 157, 248, 253, 254, 276, 292, 330-34, 347-49, 371, 373, 392
*Dialogus* (Wyclif), 40, 81
Didachus de Moxena, Franciscan friar, 339, 340
Dietrich of Niem, 103, 116
Dionysius the Areopagite, 275
Dobiáš, F. M., 254
Dominicans, 12; Dominican monastery in Constance, 341, 355, 391
Donatism, 232

East, the, 240; Eastern Orthodox Churches, 277, 387, 388; Eastern patriarchates, 180, 205
ecclesiology, 151, 172, 209
ecumenicity, 241, 388
Eli, prophet, 288
Elizabeth I, queen, 132
empire, 125
England (or the English), 116, 136, 159, 180, 350, 363
Ephesians, epistle to, 264
Epinge, Friedrich, 122, 195
Ernest of Pardubice, archbishop, 14
Erasmus, 4
eucharist, 33, 46, 47, 54, 55, 74, 221, 274, 320, 323, 324
Eugubia, 277
Eulogius, patriarch of Alexandria, 271
Evagrius, 277
evangelical clergy, 179, 181, 184, 206, 239, 277
excommunication, 78, 97, 99, 103, 104, 123, 135, 187, 189, 284, 288; major, 137, 144, 283, 286, 287, 300, 301, 343; unlawful, 373, 374
*Exposition of the Decalogue* (Hus), 114, 291, 292, 329

*Exposition of the Faith* (Hus), 291, 292, 329
*Exposition of the Lord's Prayer* (Hus), 291, 292, 329

faith, 23, 26, 58, 72, 73, 96, 152, 156, 218, 237, 266, 318, 319; faith formed by love, 73, 230, 260, 266, 319; article of the faith, 236, 264, 273; unformed faith, 260, 317; *sola fide*, 266
fall, doctrine of, 46
Fantuciis of Bologna, 110
"Father" a member of the Council, 375, 376
Faulfiš, Nicholas, 56, 327
Fida, widow, 338
Fitz-Ralph, Richard, archbishop, 13, 30, 31
Flajšhans, V., 65
Fleming, Richard, bishop, 356
foreknowledge, 26, 293; foreknown, 58
forgiveness of sins, 34, 76, 77, 113, 114, 115, 163, 164, 165, 167, 222; God alone forgives sins, 111, 112, 231, 269, 322, 389; granted on repentance, no money payment, 112, 269
forty-five articles of Wyclif, 50, 51, 52, 53, 81, 85, 96, 119, 121, 122, 134, 144, 145, 178, 181, 183, 194, 236, 341-43, 346, 356, 363, 374, 393
France (or French), 116, 159, 180, 184, 186, 243, 355
Francis of Assisi, 317
Francis, papal servant, 340
Franciscan or Minorite monastery in Constance, 359, 360, 369, 379
Frederick of Saxony, elector, 391
free will, 23, 25, 294, 318
Friedrich of Nuremberg, 359

Galatians, epistle to, 262
Gaul, 240, 277
Gehazi, 309

*423*

Gennesaret, lake of, 95
George of Kněhnice, 56
Germans, 11, 12, 138, 285, 398; university masters, 50, 89, 91, 92, 136, 364, 365, 396; "German mass," 228
Germany, 337
Gerson, Jean, 92, 130, 280, 349-51, 355, 356, 361, 362, 372
Glaber, Rudolf of Cluny, 279
God, 95, 103, 161, 235, 303, 386; alone to be believed in, 72, 73, 152, 167, 226, 256, 293, 301, 317, 319, 326; the Father, 75; He alone forgives sins, 76, 77, 222; confers all spiritual grace, 77; has ordered preaching, 101, 102
Gospel, 162, 187, 191, 355; gospels, 88, 95, 374
Gottlieben, castle of, 356-59
grace according to predestination, 259; prevenient, 72, 318; present, 260; sanctifying, 215
Greeks, 184, 263
Greenwood, John, 132
Gregory of Nazianzen, 162
Gregory the Great, pope, 65, 162, 167, 174, 202, 271, 275, 301, 311, 362
Gregory VI, pope, 272
Gregory XI, pope, 27, 136
Gregory XII, pope, 12, 81, 87, 88, 89, 91, 92, 93, 109, 110, 117, 186, 197, 240, 349
Grosseteste, Robert, bishop, 22, 281

Hagar, 58, 262
Havlik, preacher at Bethlehem, 351, 354
Hebrews, epistle to, 318
Hefele-Leclercq, *Histoire des Conciles*, 341, 355
Heidelberg, university of, 12, 79, 81
Henry of Bitterfeld, 13
Henry of Lacembok, 330

Henry of Langenstein, 14
Henry Lefl of Lažany, 329, 331-33, 337
Henry of Piro, 380
Henry of Segusia (Hostiensis), 148
heresy (or heretical), 24, 27, 51, 53, 66, 79, 80, 86, 87, 92, 93, 94, 96, 97, 100, 124, 135, 183, 205, 227, 232, 236, 246, 276, 308, 365, 369, 372, 378, 379, 393; Czechs accused of heresy, 102, 104, 136, 364; heresiarch, 381, 394
Hermann the Eremite, 177
Hilary, bishop, 155
Holy Spirit, Paraclete, 15, 18, 19, 23, 24, 72, 77, 152, 154, 176, 203, 204, 210, 219, 232, 263, 275, 296, 301, 305, 309, 320, 325
hope, 72
Hoppe of Poppenheim, 382
Hübner, John, 50, 51, 53
Hugo of Strasbourg, 65
Hungary, 283
Hus, John, vii, viii, 3-5, 21, 45, 57-59; his preparation, 3-41; date of birth, 7; attended school at Prachatice, 7; his parents, 8; entered Prague University, 8; B.A. in 1393, M.A. in 1396, 8; full membership in the faculty, 1398, 8; lectured on Lombard, 8; ordained 1400 and appointed preacher of the Bethlehem Chapel 1402, 9, 37, 42, 48, 56 his "conversion," 9-11, 41; accepted Wyclif's realism critically, 35, 36, 39, 40, 52; his ministry at Bethlehem, 42ff.; earliest sermons, 43-49; orthodoxy, 44; academic activity, 49, 50; condemnation of Wyclif's forty-five articles, 50-53; rejected remanence, 52; supported by Archbishop Zbyněk,

54; wrote *De corpore Christi*, 55

his sermons *Collecta*, 56-60; synodical sermons, 60, 61; sermon of 1407, 61, 62; *Sermones de sanctis*, 62-64; his lectures on Lombard's *Sentences*, 64-78

conflict with Zbyněk, 79-106; accused by the Prague clergy, 82-84; Decree of Kutná Hora, 87-90; *Quodlibet* of 1409, 90, 91; elected rector, 92; refused to stop preaching and appealed to John XXIII, 96, 97; excommunicated, 97, 98

*Sermones in Bethlehem, 1410-11*, 101, 102; charged with remanence by Michael de Causis, 102, 103; wrote to the pope and the cardinals, 105; opposed papal bulls of indulgences, 110f.; meeting at Žebrák castle, 118; defended Wyclif's five articles, 122-32; final break with the king, Stanislav of Znojmo, and Páleč, 132-35

excommunicated by Cardinal Peter degli Stephaneschi, 137, 138; appealed to God and Christ, 138; left Prague, 139; the royal council negotiations, 146-50

conflict with Páleč in *Contra octo doctores*, 157-71; with Stanislav of Znojmo, 172, 177, 185, 187-98, 200-08; *Contra Paletz*, 209, 212, 213, 217, 219-35, 237-46; attacked by the Anonymous, 247-50; *De ecclesia*, 252-55, 257-64, 266-89; Czech treatises, 290-328

trial at the Council of Constance, 329-82; his personality and significance, 383-96

Husinec, 7

Hussenstrasse in Constance, 338

Hussite wars, 369

impenitence, the cause of condemnation, 263

India, 240, 277

indulgences, 34, 37, 49, 59, 60, 114; bull of John XXIII, 109-11, 113, 120, 144, 157, 160, 163, 171, 234, 239, 271, 323

Innocent IV, pope, 281

Innocent VII, pope, 145, 192, 243, 284

*Institutes of the Christian Religion* (Calvin), 385, 386

*Inter cunctas*, bull of Martin V, 370

interdict, 104, 139, 286, 287, 288, 289

Israel, children of, 169, 225, 228, 233

Italy, 340

Jacob Balardi Arrigoni, bishop, 380

Jacques de Nouvion, of Paris university, 88

Jakoubek of Stříbro, 35, 54, 80, 88, 98, 118, 122, 144, 146, 223, 229, 351, 352, 354, 385, 389

James, brother of Jesus, 200

James, epistle of, 319

James of Dubá, 119, 146

James of Tharamo, 96

Jerome, St., 78, 101, 160, 162, 174, 182, 202, 231, 240, 275, 277, 301, 380

Jerome of Prague, 35, 40, 79, 90, 91, 116, 117, 331, 341, 369, 385, 393

Jerusalem, 182, 204, 286, 296, 297, 304; "Jerusalem" in Prague, 15, 43; Jerusalem Council, 200; patriarchate of, 265, 388

Jeschke, J. B., 291

Jews, 194, 202, 203, 265, 279, 324; in Prague, 161

John, gospel of, 231, 324, 326

## INDEX

John, St., 271
John XXII, pope, 310
John XXIII, the late pope, 5
John XXIII (Baldassare Cossa),
9, 94, 96, 98, 103, 105, 107, 131,
135, 144, 172, 196, 197, 199,
212, 218, 223, 234, 235, 236,
240, 248, 250, 281, 322, 329,
338, 340, 354-56, 373, 377,
378; his "crusading bull,"
8, 109, 115, 124, 139, 157, 159,
163, 166, 169, 170, 207, 226,
227, 323, 384
John the Baptist, 271
John of Bořenice, bishop of Lubus, 341
John of Chlum, 330, 332, 333,
334, 336, 339-41, 344, 345, 352,
358, 360, 365, 369, 378, 379,
392, 394
John of Chocenice, 118
John of Damascus, St., 275
John Eliášův, 146, 147, 177, 284
John Hildesen, 177
John of Holešov, 151-56
John of Gaunt, duke of Lan-
caster, 34, 391
John of Jenstein, archbishop, 13
John of Jesenice, 96, 103, 109,
136, 139, 140, 146, 177, 178,
179, 181-84, 186-89, 193, 239,
287, 335, 344, 353
John of Jičín, 120
John of Litomyšl, bishop, 89, 93,
106, 141, 329, 356, 395, 353,
392
John of Mýto, 35
John Oldcastle, lord Cobham, 99
John of Paris, 65
John of Pomuky (St. John of
Nepomuky), 17
John of Rakovník, 85, 86
John of Rejnštejn, "the Cardi-
nal," 103, 336, 375
John of Rupiscissa, patriarch,
341, 344
John Scotus, 65

John of Thomariis, papal auditor, 103
Judas Iscariot, apostle, 180, 198,
221, 259, 303

Karlstein, 104
Kbel, John, 80, 87
Kemerton, 56
Kerkering, Theodore, 360
*Kernel of Christian Doctrine,
The* (Hus), 292
Keys, power of the, 64, 77, 78,
168, 184, 202, 221, 222, 239,
269; to be exercised *minis-
terialiter*, 269
Kozí Hrádek, 252, 291, 329
Krakovec, 329, 330, 336
Králík, Wenceslas, patriarch,
121, 329
Kříž, Václav, merchant, 42
Kutná Hora, decree of, 91, 92,
367
Kybal, V., 65, 122, 123, 214, 217,
236, 262, 277

Ladislas, king of Naples, 109,
117, 139, 160, 170
Lateran Council, Fourth, 32
Lateran palace, 224
*Lectura super Yzaiam prophe-
tam* (Stephen of Kolín), 38,
39
Legates, apostolic, 116, 117
Leipzig, university of, 92
Leo, pope, 110, 155
Levitical priests, 121, 126, 169;
Leviticus, book of, 181
Lewis, emperor, 275
*Lex evangelica*, 24
Liberius, pope, 199, 224, 272
Lincoln cathedral, 281
Litomyšl, 59, 147, 210, 324
Locke, John, 132
Lollards, 34, 56, 99
Lombard, Peter, 8, 13, 50, 53, 66,
152, 321, 322; his *Sentences*,
13, 64-78, 101, 168, 222
London, 136

Loserth, Johann, 4, 7, 65, 112, 253
Love, 72, 75, 260
Ludwig, duke, 361, 384, 385
Luther, 4, 73, 315, 391; Lutheran, 395
Lutterworth, 34, 56

Mark, evangelist, 206, 326
Mark of Hradec, 90, 116, 122, 195
Martin V, pope, 161, 355, 356, 370
Martin, John, and Stašek (three young men), beheaded, 120
Martin in the Wall, St., church of, 389
Mary, Virgin, 29, 47, 63, 75, 156, 271, 302, 325, 326, 361, 386
Mary Magdalene, 71, 274
mass of the ass, 306
matrimony, 74, 320
Matthew, gospel of, 264, 305, 326
Matthew of Cracow, 12, 37, 38
Matthew of Janov, 16-21, 35, 38, 41, 88, 304, 324; his Regulae veteris et novi testamenti, 16, 17
Matthew of Knín, 80, 90
Matthew of Zbraslav, 177
Matthias, apostle, 200
Maurice Rvačka, 84, 91, 126, 145, 192, 243, 246
Mauroux, Jean, patriarch, 357, 394
medieval thought, 73
Meditatio de humana conditione (Bernard), 317
Meisterman, Ludolf, 81
merit, saving, 24; meritum de congruo, 24, 25, 71; meritum de condigno, 25, 71, 72, 73
Michael de Causis, 102, 109, 135, 329, 339, 341, 345, 352, 392
Mikeš Divoký of Jemniště, 331, 332, 333, 337
Milheim, John of, 42, 54
Milíč of Kroměříž, 14, 15, 38,

41, 42, 43, 304; his "Jerusalem," 15, 43
"miracles" of bleeding hosts, 59
Mirror of the Sinful Man, The (Hus), 292, 317
Mohammedans, 244
monastic orders, monks and nuns, 49, 61, 218, 312
Monophysite churches, 205, 388
Moravia, 93, 96, 147, 149; nobles of, 140, 369
Moses, 169, 185, 186; Moses' seat, 261, 281

Naaman, 309
Naples, Neapolitans, 107, 159, 161, 240, 329
Náz, John, royal official, 103
Nestorian church, 205, 388
Nicene Creed, 162
Nicholas, pope, 155
Nicholas, St., 325
Nicholas Biceps, 13
Nicholas of Litomyšl, 35
Nicholas of Lyra, 226
Nicholas of Nezero, bishop, 121, 122, 335, 353, 365
Nicodemus, 194
Nine Golden Theses, The (Hus), 292, 321
nominalism and nominalists, 12, 22, 50, 237, 360, 395
Novotný, Václav, 7, 8, 85, 86, 330, 331, 332
Nuremberg, 291, 337

obedience, 95, 97, 102, 103, 144, 145, 148, 226, 228, 229, 243, 279, 280, 299, 300, 374; "intermediate" commands, 185, 186, 279, 282, 283, 289; Roman Church must be obeyed in all things, 284, 285
Ockham, William of, 22
Odložilík, O., 38
Odo de Colonna, cardinal, 98, 103, 107
Old Town Hall, 120-23, 138, 141, 195, 229, 252

Olomouc, 210, 329

*Opus evangelicum* (Wyclif), 57, 101

orders, sacrament of, 74, 77, 124, 222, 301, 302, 311, 312, 313, 320

Orient, 277

Orleans, duke of, 343

Otto III of Hachberg, bishop, 355

Oxford, university of, 13, 14, 23, 34, 35, 56, 79, 90, 100, 136, 308, 327

Palacký, F., 369

Palatinate, The, 12, 88

papacy, 3, 27, 28, 30, 134, 135, 152, 154, 174, 204, 216, 218, 266, 276, 372, 395

Paris, 100

Paris, university of, 13, 14, 16, 79, 88, 340, 349, 351

Pascal, pope, 275

Patmos, island of, 271

Paul, apostle, 3, 45, 63, 83, 85, 97, 114, 125, 126, 159, 163-69, 171, 173, 182, 197, 198, 200, 202, 204, 206, 216, 240, 257-59, 267, 276, 280, 302, 313, 352, 354, 390

Pelagianism, 23

penance, 74, 76, 171, 320-23

Persia, 240, 277

Perugia, 182

Peter, apostle, 27, 28, 63, 64, 85, 89, 110, 145, 155, 159, 164, 166, 167-69, 182, 185, 190, 197-203, 206, 210, 219-22, 235, 236, 240, 241, 248, 259, 264, 267, 268, 271, 274-76, 282, 286, 372, 373

Peter, epistle of, 247

Peter of Chelčice, 280, 385

Peter of Mladoňovice, 336, 340, 358-60, 366, 369, 378, 382, 384

Peter degli Stephaneschi, cardinal, 108, 137, 139, 188, 189, 288

Peter of Stoupno, 82

Peter of Všeruby, 82, 83

Peter of Znojmo, 146, 147, 177, 228, 284

Pharisees, 95, 185, 203, 243, 247, 281, 284

Phocas, emperor, 223

physicists, 301

Pilate, 187, 279, 369

Pileo de Prata, cardinal, 35

Pilgrim Fathers, 132

Plzeň, 323

Poland, 369

Polish nobles, 333, 357

Pope, 59, 63, 64, 107, 117, 121, 124, 125, 135, 144, 165, 168, 170, 171, 187, 190, 192, 197, 199, 200, 206, 210, 211, 218, 219, 222, 226, 230, 232, 274, 276, 296, 309, 310, 326, 340, 348, 377; is the head, heart, river-bed, source and refuge of the Church, 5, 27, 166; is not infallible, but can sin and err, 27, 77, 110, 160; pope's power spiritual, not temporal, 27, 268, 375; moral qualifications necessary, 27, 154, 198, 231, 232, 235, 247, 282, 295; vicar of Christ, 28, 148, 152, 168, 247, 268; is not the head of the Church, 28, 144, 295; received temporal possessions and rank from Caesars, 125, 277, 372; *sanctissimus*, 152-54, 233, 274-76; should be worshipped, 154, 274, 296, 297; "universal pope," 174, 224, 271, 272; is the head *ministeriale*, 180, 199, 201; is the Antichrist, 184, 223, 229; legitimate election makes the pope, 235, 373; no absolute necessity for the pope, 275; is all-powerful, 277; exempt from all censure, 286; foreknown pope, 295; is *primus inter pares*, 388

Portugal, 136

*Postilla* or *Postil* (Hus), 44, 114, 291, 324, 329
poverty, voluntary, 48, 316; Lady Poverty, 317
Prachatice, 7, 8, 86
Prague, 7, 8, 43, 56, 82, 87, 97, 99, 100, 103, 104, 110, 117, 136, 137, 139, 147, 151, 172, 182, 210, 227, 255, 285, 304, 311, 327, 330, 334, 335, 342, 344, 353, 362, 365, 390; pastors and the higher clergy of, 79-82, 85, 96, 138, 187, 188, 192, 227, 286, 287; archbishopric of, 309-11, 314; Prague witnesses, 363
Prague, university of, 11, 12, 13, 35, 50-52, 80, 87-93, 97, 105, 121, 122, 125, 134, 138, 144, 149, 238, 301, 336, 364, 375, 378, 391, 392
preaching, 29, 60, 99, 124, 135, 166, 227; prohibited, 94, 95, 158; God-given duty, 101, 123, 124, 131, 132, 284, 302, 303, 390
predestinate, 23, 26, 179, 230, 249, 253, 273, 274, 294; sole members of the Church, 5; *universitas praedestinatorum*, 24, 68, 253, 274, 372
predestination, 59, 175, 196, 215, 259, 260, 261, 263, 318, 373, 388
prelates, 49, 79, 96, 102, 127, 132, 230, 288, 299; *worthy* of their office, 129
priests, priestly office, 29, 30, 48, 60, 64, 74, 77, 78, 134, 302-07, 312, 373; priests-fornicators, 61, 304, 305, 313; delinquent priests, 124, 125, 129; priests and deacons, 124; their functions ministerial, 222, 389; their power spiritual, not coercive, 268, 269; abuse of their power, 270, 306, 307; priests'

substitutes, 304, 313, 314; excommunicated priests, 305
Procopius of Plzeň, 122, 195
property rights, 128; consecrated property, 133; church property a trust, 296
Protestants, 5; churches, 390
Protestant Reformation, 73
Protiva, John, 84
Providence, divine, 154
Purgatory, 66, 271
Puritans, 132

Quintin Folkhyrde, Scotts Lollard, 100
*Quod libet*, 90, 91, 223, 392

Rainald de Brancacci, cardinal, 109
Ranke, Leopold von, 6, 7
realism, philosophical, 22, 32, 73, 242, 360, 395; at the University of Prague, 35, 36
Reformation, 222, 385, 395, 396
reformers, 3, 4
*regium*, 277
*regula fidei*, 162
remanence, 32, 52, 53, 80, 84, 102, 145, 172, 190, 229, 323, 339, 360; not consubstantiation, 33
*Replicatio contra Quidamistas* (Páleč), 209, 228
*Replicatio magistrorum Pragensium* (Jesenic and Hus), 145, 177, 178, 181, 194, 209
*Responsio finalis* (Hus), 148
Revelation, book of, 223, 348
Rhine valley, 240, 297; river, 355
Richental, Ulrich von, 341
Roman Church, vii, viii, 5, 85, 119, 142, 143, 144, 145, 147, 148, 172, 175, 178, 181, 183, 187, 190, 191, 194, 195, 202, 205, 208, 209, 210, 215, 217, 218, 219, 224, 225, 229, 232, 237, 238, 239, 241, 242-45, 249, 250, 59, 263, 264, 265, 271, 289, 354, 368, 387, 388, 395; Roman

hierarchy and curia, 25, 28, 53, 85, 144, 146, 150, 206, 207, 279, 281, 283; Roman primacy, 216; Roman patriarchate, 388

Roman empire, 283

Romans, epistle to, 126, 247, 297

Rome, 15, 16, 87, 100, 109, 145, 169, 173, 180, 182, 184, 203-05, 224, 229, 230, 265, 271, 277, 282, 285, 307, 323

Roudnice, 87, 97, 104

Ruprecht of the Palatinate, 12, 88, 91, 382

Russian metropolitanate, 205

Sabellius, 100

sacraments, 73, 74, 75, 134, 142, 218, 222, 268, 270, 320; of the altar or eucharist, 33, 46, 47, 54, 55, 74, 221, 274, 320, 324; *sacramentalia*, 218, 268

*Sacrosancta* decree, 355

safe-conduct, 330-32, 337, 346

St. Gall's church, 135

St. James church, 120

St. Lawrence, feast of, 114

St. Michael, church of, 43, 44, 146

St. Paul's Cathedral in London, 363

St. Paul Street in Constance, 338

St. Peter, church of, 224

St. Peter's basilica in Rome, 136

St. Wenceslas' day, 113, 114

St. Vitus' cathedral, 13, 16, 53, 120; canons of, 102

saints, 62, 63, 64, 325, 386

Sts. Philip and James, church of, 42, 43

Samaria and Samaritans, 111, 227

Sarah, 58, 262

Satan, 148, 286

Saul, king, 233, 234, 288

Schism, Great, 21, 27, 92, 186, 239, 279, 330, 355, 393; schisms caused by clerics, 61, 202; schismatics, 241

Scotland, 100, 353; Scottish Covenanters, 132

Scriptures, Holy, 15, 18, 22-24, 41, 62, 67, 68, 83, 84, 88, 97, 100, 110, 114, 119, 123, 124, 134, 144, 160, 161-64, 171, 175, 179, 181, 183, 184-86, 190, 191, 194, 195, 206, 207, 210, 217, 219, 225, 226, 232, 235-37, 242, 243, 245, 248, 254, 258, 266, 270, 272, 273, 275, 277, 278, 283, 288, 289, 297, 299, 300, 307, 308, 310, 319, 320, 326-28, 343, 347, 354, 363, 367, 370, 371, 379, 385-87, 396; versions in other languages, 326, 327

Sedlák, Jan, 36, 45, 65, 213, 224, 225, 226, 248, 253, 308, 350

Seitenstetten, monastery of, 248

*Sermones de sanctis* (Hus), 387

*Sermones in Bethlehem* (Hus), 299

Sezimovo Ústí, 329

Sigismund, king of Hungary, 100, 106, 145, 192, 243, 283, 330-33, 337, 338, 344-46, 355, 358, 360, 365, 367-70, 379-81, 384, 394

Simon Magus, 168

Simon of Tišnov, 146

simony, 21, 270, 307, 308, 309, 311-16

*Simony, On,* (Hus), 292, 307, 329

sin (s), 149, 171; venial and mortal, 76, 78, 127, 129, 132, 287, 294, 300, 308, 318, 321, 324, 343; satisfaction for, 77; its origin, 318; those in mortal sin, 156, 230

*Six Errors, The* (Hus), 292

Sodom, 282

Soltau, Conrad, 11

Sophie, queen, 98, 394

Sorbonne, The, 13

Spain, 240

Speyer, 340

Stacey, John, *John Wyclif and Reform*, 31
Stanislav of Znojmo, 35, 36, 37, 43, 51, 53, 54, 55, 79, 81, 82, 87, 108, 115, 130, 132, 145, 147, 149, 151, 158, 166, 171, 172, 174-80, 183-96, 198-206, 208, 210, 212, 213, 217, 218, 228, 229, 237, 238, 244, 248, 249, 252, 257, 284, 286, 339, 349, 362, 364; *De corpore Christi*, 52, 81
Štěkna, John, 53
Stephen of Kolín, 36-39, 43, 52, 82
Stephen Páleč, 35, 36, 43, 51, 52, 79, 81, 82, 107, 115, 116, 121, 130, 132, 133-35, 145, 146, 147, 149, 151, 157, 158, 172, 177, 201, 210, 211, 212, 213, 215-18, 220-43, 246, 248, 252, 257, 278, 292, 339, 341, 346-49, 362, 364, 372, 376, 377, 392; called *"Fictor,"* 234, 235, 236, 240, 242, 244, 245, 377; *Contra Paletz* (Hus), 209, 228, 235, 236, 239, 241
*Steps of Humility* (Bernard), 318
Stockholm, 36
Stokes, John, 100, 101, 362
Strahov MS., 45
*Super IV Sententiarum* (Hus), 263
suspension, 286, 287, 288
Swabians, 378
Sylvester, pope, 28, 194, 224, 272, 276

Taborites, 316, 372
temporal or secular lords, 124-29, 132
Tennyson's *Ulysses*, 6
Testaments, Old and New, 74, 125, 169, 182, 219, 288, 321
"testimonies of witnesses," 84, 374
Thamis, 277

theological faculty, 117, 118, 121, 134, 141, 145, 146, 147, 149, 150, 157, 158, 177, 208, 222, 284, 290
Thessalonians, epistle to, 179
thirty articles, final, 5, 370-73
Thomas of Štítné, 290, 291
Thomas of Strasbourg, 65
Thomism, 12, 13, 41
Thomson, S. Harrison, 22, 254
*Three-stranded Cord, The* (Hus), 291
Tiber, river, 250
Tiem, Wenceslas, dean of Passau, 111
Tierney, Brian, 398
tithes, 127, 133, 316
Totting of Oyta, Henry, 11
*Tractatus gloriosus* (Páleč), 118, 151, 157-60, 162-65, 167-69
*Tractatus de Romana ecclesia* (Stanislav of Znojmo), 172, 174, 185
tradition, 18, 19, 134, 162, 210, 219, 242
transubstantiation, 363; Hus' definition of, 55, 74, 75, 323, 324; Wyclif's rejection of, 32
treasury of merits, 34
*Treatise on Simony* (Hus), 291
*Trialogus* (Wyclif) 22, 40, 65, 81
truth, 6, 320, 387, 396, 399
Týn church, 120, 132, 238

Ulrich, servant, 358
*Unam sanctam*, bull of Boniface VIII, 217, 259, 263, 270
*Unitas Fratrum*, 280
*Unity of the Church* (Cyprian), 155; unity of the Church is spiritual, 240
*universitas praedestinatorum*, 24, 26
Urban VI, pope, 16, 27, 224
Utraquists, 354

Vatican Council I, 157; Vatican II, viii; Vatican MS., 350

# INDEX

Vienna, 116

Vltava, river, 181, 250

Vojtěch Rankův of Ježov (Adalbertus Ranconis de Ericinio), 13, 16

Voksa of Valdštejn, 99, 118

Vyšehrad, 119

Waldensian heresy, 160, 163, 164

Waldhauser, Conrad, 14, 304

Wallenrode, John, archbishop, 359, 380

war, 169, 170, 171, 299

Warrentrappe, Albert, archbishop, 367

Wenceslas IV, king of Bohemia, 12, 54, 84, 86, 88, 91, 92, 98, 99, 102, 104, 110, 118, 120, 121, 132, 136, 141, 145, 150, 192, 243, 283, 315, 329, 331, 332, 340, 353, 364, 369, 391

Wenceslas of Dubá, 330, 333, 336, 337, 358, 360, 369, 378, 379, 392

William of Paris, 222

Wilsnack, 59

Word of God, 15, 29, 123, 124, 159, 227, 303, 327, 328, 390

Worship, 306

Wyclif, John, or Wyclifites, 4, 9, 13, 14, 18, 21-36, 40, 51-54, 56, 65, 66, 78, 79, 80, 83, 85, 86, 90, 93, 94, 96, 100, 103, 121, 122, 126-30, 132, 134-36, 162, 178, 179, 190, 191, 194, 195, 215, 217-19, 221, 223, 227, 237-39, 244-46, 253-55, 263, 276,

294, 308, 327, 329, 331, 339-44, 347, 350, 354, 356, 360-64, 380, 383, 385, 391, 394; his *Trialogus*, 22, 40, 65, 81; *De veritate sacrae scripturae*, 23; *De dominio divino*, 31, 126, 127; *De civili dominio*, 31, 126, 127; *De eucharistia*, 32, 40, 81; *De individuone temporis*, 36; *De ideis*, 36; *De materia et forma*, 36; *De universalibus*, 36; *Dialogus*, 40, 81; *De simonia*, 40, 292, 308; *Opus evangelicum*, 57, 101; *De benedicta incarnatione*, 66; *De trinitate*, 98; *Decalogue*, 98; *De ecclesia*, 112, 253, 254, 262; *De potestate papae*, 253

Wyclifism, 54, 85, 90, 93, 96, 130, 134, 136, 172

Wyche, Richard, 99

Zabarella, Francesco, cardinal, 107, 108, 356, 362, 368, 369, 370, 380, 395

Žatec, 210

Záviš of Zapy, 86

Zbyněk Zajíc of Hasenburk, archbishop, 53-55, 62, 79-81, 83, 84, 87, 89, 90, 92-94, 96, 98, 99, 102-07, 109, 149, 191, 226, 234, 238, 314, 362-64

Zdeněk of Labouň, 118, 146

Žebrák, castle of, 118, 121, 123, 146, 158

Zeiselmeister, Nicholas, 43

Žižka, Jan, 316